WITHDRAWN

Introduction to Acting

FOURTH EDITION

Stanley Kahan

*California State University
Long Beach*

Kenneth W. Rugg

*Professor Emeritus
California State University
Long Beach*

Allyn and Bacon

Boston   London   Toronto   Sydney   Tokyo   Singapore

Dedicated to Charlene
whose help and encouragement have made these editions possible

Vice President: Paul Smith
Series editorial assistant: Kathy Rubino
Manufacturing buyer: David Suspanic

Copyright © 1998, 1991, 1985, 1962 by Allyn & Bacon
A Viacom Company
Needham Heights, MA 02194

Internet: www.abacon.com
America Online: keyword: College Online

Library of Congress Cataloging-in-Publication Data

Kahan, Stanley
    Introduction to acting / Stanley Kahan, Kenneth W. Rugg. — 4th ed.
        p.   cm.
    Includes bibliographical references and index.
    ISBN 0–205–27004–2
    1. Acting.   I. Rugg, Kenneth W.   II. Title.
PN2061.K3   1997
792'.028—dc21   97–33976
                                                                                  CIP

Printed in the United States of America
10 9 8 7 6 5 4 3 2 1   01 00 99 98 97

CREDITS

Chapter opening photos:

CHAPTER 1 *Hamlet,* by William Shakespeare. National Theatre, London. Directed by Peter Hall. Denis Quilley as Claudius, Angela Lansbury as Gertrude. Photograph by Britain on View Photographic Library.

CHAPTER 2 Jacques Callot, *Scaramucia and Fricasso.* Rudolf L. Baumfeld Collection, National Gallery of Art, Washington, D.C.

CHAPTER 3 *The Wild Duck* by Henrik Ibsen. Swedish National Theatre, directed by Ingmar Bergman. Max von Sydow as Gregers Werle. Photo by Beata Bertstrom. Reprinted by permission of the Drottingsholms Teatermuseum.

Credits continue on page 364

Contents

Preface   *vii*

List of Scenes   *ix*

Chapter 1   An Overview: Some Questions Answered   1

Why Act?   2
Is There an Ideal Actor?   3
Can Actors Be Classified?   9
What Should the Actor Know?   15
What Is the "Illusion of the First Time"?   17
Questions and Exercises   19

Chapter 2   Early Acting and Acting Theories   20

The First Actors   21
What the Ancients Tell Us   21
The Decline of the Theatre   24
The Commedia dell'Arte   25
Shakespeare and His Actors   29
The Seventeenth Century   33
David Garrick: An Actor Speaks   35
The Great Debate—Emotion vs. Reason   38
Short Notes on the Heritage of Some Notable Actors   42
More Actors and Actresses   46
Suggestions for Further Reading   47

Chapter 3   Stanislavski and Beyond   48

The "Method"   51
After Stanislavski   54
The Director and Freedom for the Actor   58
Short Notes on the Heritage of Some Notable Actors   60
More Actors and Actresses   62
Suggestions for Further Reading   64

Chapter 4 The Body and Stage Movement 65

by Holly Harbinger

How the Body Is Organized 67
Tension and Relaxation 73
The Body in Action 75
Warming Up 80
Suggestions for Further Reading 97

Chapter 5 Voice and the Actor 98

One Voice or Many? 99
Factors of a Good Stage Voice 101
Vocal Production 102
Projection 110
Getting the Most from the Dialogue 111
Vocal Exercises 118
Suggestions for Further Reading 122

Chapter 6 Getting Around on the Stage 124

The Stage and Stage Areas 125
Stage Positions and the Actor 127
Stage Movement and the Audience 127
Using Movement 137
Specialized Stage Problems 141
Listening 148
Exercises 150

Chapter 7 Using Improvisation 152

Improvisations for Larger Groups 153
Improvisations for One Actor 155
Improvisations for Two or More Actors 157
Last-Line Improvisations 161

Chapter 8 Combating Stage Fright 163

What Is Stage Fright? 164
Some Suggested Causes 164
Do Experienced Actors Have Stage Fright? 167

What Can Be Done about It?   169
Suggestions for Further Reading   172

Chapter 9   Auditioning and Preparing a Role   **173**

The Audition Process   173
Basic Steps in Developing a Role   178
Finding One's Own Approach   192
Exercises   195
Ambiguous Dialogue   195
Suggestions for Further Reading   204
Monologues   205
Scenes   216

Chapter 10   Putting the Role Onstage   **244**

Rehearsal Guidelines   245
The Three Vs of Good Acting   247
Concentration   251
Getting into the Role   253
Judging the Actor's Work   256
Scenes   260

Chapter 11   Style and Other Problems   **299**

Comedy and Farce   300
Tragedy   304
Period Plays in General   306
Shakespearean Plays   307
Sustained Speeches   312
Central Staging   315
Suggestions for Further Reading   321
Scenes   323

Chapter 12   Acting for the Camera   **339**

Shooting the Television Drama   340
Television and the Theatre   341
Television Acting   342
Subtlety and Intimacy   349

Contents

Action and Reaction   353
Reviewing the Rules   355
Exercises   355
Suggestion for Further Reading   356

A Glossary of Theatre Terms   *357*

Index   *367*

Preface

Since this textbook was first published in 1962, it has served multiple generations of students of acting, as well as students who do not intend to enter the profession in any capacity. It has been widely adopted in senior colleges, junior colleges, and senior high schools. In preparing this new edition, the authors have reorganized the structure of the text to suggest various approaches involved in the process and training of the actor. Also added are amusing and illuminating anecdotes touching upon the life of the actor. There are significant changes in the exercises and scenes to reflect the world of the late twentieth century, its multiculturalism and various lifestyles.

The teacher of acting is well aware that all students are not alike. They do not all come into the classroom with the same level of training or experience, nor do they all have the same psychological or mental makeup. They have different problems and different questions to be answered. Much of the responsibility of dealing with this diversity falls on the instructor: this book has been organized to serve as a practical tool to facilitate solutions to training students with various backgrounds. The book takes an *eclectic* approach for the beginning actor and general student, many of whom may never take another acting class. Therefore, there is no attempt in this book to require the actor to follow any rigid or dogmatic system for developing his or her ability. The book serves as a major adjunct to the teacher's work in the classroom or studio. It stresses the point that each student should find the approach most helpful in achieving his or her own expressiveness.

There have been several changes and additions to the fourth edition. The most obvious of these is the addition of a co-author, Professor Kenneth Rugg, for thirty years a colleague of Dr. Stanley Kahan and a noted teacher of acting and award-winning director. Another major change is the reorganization of the chapters to reflect a different causal approach to the acting process. Several chapters were retitled to better express the philosophy of the contents. In the process of reorganization, the one chapter on the history of acting has been divided into two chapters. The first of these discusses the history of acting through the nineteenth century. The second chapter begins with the contributions of Stanislavski and considers twentieth-century acting processes. Characters in the improvisation exercises have been made devoid of gender and age. Several new ambiguous dialogues for two characters have been added, and three-character ambiguous dialogues have been introduced. A number of new photographs have replaced older photographs in order to represent new trends in acting styles, such as post-modernism and Brechtian or Epic Theatre. The suggested readings have been updated to include newly published volumes, and a number of actors' superstitions, trivia, anecdotes, and quotes were compiled and disseminated throughout in an attempt to put the student more in touch with the psyche of the working actor.

A continuing feature of the book has been the inclusion of scenes for exercises in acting. These scenes have been significantly amended to include contemporary prize-winning playwrights, whose plays reflect the diversity of the manifold cultures and lifestyles of the present *fin de siècle*. Scenes from plays by Crowley, Durang, Miller, Mamet, Shepard, Shakespeare, Shaffer, Valdez, Lanford Wilson, August Wilson, O'Neill, Zindel, Molière, Sheridan, Wasserstein, Jane Wagner, Williams, Gershe, McCullers, Wilde, Hellman, and others are included.

We are indebted to the performance faculty of the California State University at Long Beach (CSULB), who helped to devise some of the material concerned with the development of character. Grateful acknowledgment is also made to those colleagues in the profession who have been kind enough to provide photographs of productions from their institutions' and theatres' productions for inclusion in the text. The photographs from California State University, Long Beach, were taken by Mr. William Coleman, Mr. Robert J. Freligh, and Dr. Keith Ian Polakoff. To my late brother, Professor Gerald Kahan, for his generosity in securing iconographic material of the *Commedia dell'arte,* a heartfelt thank you.

We must extend a note of appreciation to George Herman, Ms. Wilma Meli, Matthew Gourley, and most particularly the late Professor T. William Smith of CSULB for the renderings that appear throughout the book.

To George Z. Wilson, John Kerr, Wilson Lehr, and Ronald Mitchell, a perpetual thank you.

Appreciation goes to the following reviewers for their comments on this manuscript: Brenda Buckley-Hunter, Judson College, and Kenneth Gardner, California Lutheran University.

To the many inquiring and stimulating students who posed the questions and challenges that prompted consideration of the first edition, and to those students and teachers who have used later editions over the years and revealed their strengths and weaknesses, we owe the greatest obligation of all.

Stanley Kahan
Kenneth Rugg

P.S. I have acknowledged in previous editions the editorial assistance that my wife continually provided me. This edition is dedicated to her loving memory.

Stanley Kahan

List of Scenes

Chapter 9

The Glass Menagerie by Tennessee Williams
for 1 woman
205

Sweet Bird of Youth by Tennessee Williams
for 1 woman
205

The Sea Gull by Anton Chekhov
for 1 woman
207

Death of a Salesman by Arthur Miller
for 1 man
207

Death of a Salesman by Arthur Miller
for 1 woman
208

Long Day's Journey into Night by Eugene O'Neill
for 1 man
209

Long Day's Journey into Night by Eugene O'Neill
for 1 woman
210

Georgia Peach by Howard Burman
for 1 man
211

After the Fall by Arthur Miller
for 1 man
211

After the Fall by Arthur Miller
for 1 woman
212

The Search for Signs of Intelligent Life in the Universe by Jane Wagner
for 1 woman
212

The Great Nebula in Orion by Lanford Wilson
for 1 woman
213

Two Trains Running by August Wilson
for 1 man
214

Lettice and Lovage by Peter Shaffer
for 2 women
216

The Children's Hour by Lillian Hellman
for 2 women
218

Bad Seed by Maxwell Anderson   **220**
for 2 women

Uncommon Women and Others by Wendy Wasserstein   **223**
for 2 women

Vanities by Jack Heifner   **225**
for 3 women

Buried Child by Sam Shepard   **228**
for 1 man, 1 woman

Butterflies Are Free by Leonard Gershe   **230**
for 1 man, 1 woman

The Member of the Wedding by Carson McCullers   **234**
for 1 girl, 1 boy

√ *The Diary of Anne Frank* by Frances Goodrich and Albert Hackett   **236**
for 1 man, 1 woman

Zoot Suit by Luis Valdez   **239**
for 1 man, 1 woman

The Piano Lesson by August Wilson   **241**
for 1 man, 1 woman

Chapter 10

√ *The Effect of Gamma Rays on Man-in-the-Moon Marigolds*
by Paul Zindel   **260**
for 2 women

Lettice and Lovage by Peter Shaffer   **262**
for 2 women

Uncommon Women and Others by Wendy Wasserstein   **264**
for 2 women

And Miss Reardon Drinks a Little by Paul Zindel   **266**
for 3 women

√ *Boys in the Band* by Mart Crowley   **269**
for 2 men

Beyond Therapy by Christopher Durang   **270**
for 1 man, 1 woman

√ *The Little Foxes* by Lillian Hellman   **272**
for 2 women

✓ *A Streetcar Named Desire* by Tennessee Williams   **274**
for 1 man, 1 woman

Georgia Peach by Howard Burman   **278**
for 1 man, 1 woman

Oleanna by David Mamet   **280**
for 1 man, 1 woman

✓ *The Crucible* by Arthur Miller   **282**
for 1 man, 1 woman

I Don't Have to Show You No Stinking Badges by Luis Valdez   **285**
for 1 man, 1 woman

The Heidi Chronicles by Wendy Wasserstein   **286**
for 1 man, 1 woman

Beyond Therapy by Christopher Durang   **289**
for 1 man, 1 woman

True West by Sam Shepard   **292**
for 2 men, 1 woman

A Streetcar Named Desire by Tennessee Williams   **295**
for 1 man, 2 women

Chapter 11

The Hairy Ape by Eugene O'Neill   **323**
for 1 man

The Rivals by Richard Brinsley Sheridan   **324**
for 2 men

The Miser by Molière   **326**
for 2 men

The Importance of Being Earnest by Oscar Wilde   **329**
for 2 women

The Doctor in Spite of Himself by Molière   **332**
for 2 men, 1 woman

The Taming of the Shrew by William Shakespeare   **336**
for 1 man, 1 woman

CHAPTER
ONE

An Overview: Some Questions Answered

If the sight of the blue skies fills you with joy, if a blade of grass springing up in the fields has power to move you, if the simple things of nature have a message that you understand, rejoice, for your soul is alive; and then aspire to learn that other truth, that the least of what you receive can be divided. To help, to continually help and share, that is the sum of all knowledge; that is the meaning of art.

The artist-actor gives the best of himself; through his interpretations he unveils his inner soul. By these interpretations only should he be accepted and judged. When the final curtain falls between him and his audience, nothing can be said or done, add or detract from his performance. His work is done, his message is delivered.

Eleanora Duse

Why Act?

One need only watch a group of children in the midst of their games to discover the universality of acting. Ask a child, or even an adult, to compose a sonata, carve a statue, or paint a landscape and the response would almost certainly be, "But I don't know enough about music, or sculpture, or painting, to do what you ask." If one were then to inquire whether or not that person would like to act in a play, the adult might hesitate a moment, claim not to be a really *good* actor, but offer to give it a try if his or her fellow performers possessed the same level of ability. The great number of thriving community theatres in the country today testifies to the continued interest in the theatre among those whose livelihood and profession lie in different areas. Children, of course, would find no challenge in the suggestion. After all, they act all the time with their friends—at "cowboys and Indians," "playing house," and "cops and robbers."

All human beings possess, to some degree, what can be termed the *mimetic instinct*, a compulsion to imitate other human beings. It is this mimetic instinct that is directly responsible for the infant's and young child's developmental learning of language and social behavior. As children grow older, they project creative activities into games with fantasy and role playing. By late adolescence, such activities are usually subordinated to the requirements of adult society. Nevertheless, we never lose our impulse to dramatize situations, to alter in our imaginations unpleasant experiences, or to synthesize new ones. For example, how many of us have not personally fantasized ourselves into positions of authority, even inventing "dialogue" we might use in a given situation?

Yet acting is much more than this. At its best it is a creative force in our lives and in our culture, requiring as much competence as any creative or recreative art. Although the theatre is a collection of many arts—poetry; dance; music; scenic, costume, and lighting design; literary and philosophical thought—it is the actor who makes the theatre come to life. It is the actor who gives the written drama its vitality and its reason for existence. It is the actor who takes the ideas and dreams of the playwright and gives them shape, substance, and, above all, life.

The intangible rewards of acting may explain the irrepressible surge of young men and women to the theatre and their dedication to it despite the most overwhelming handicaps. Often we may come upon actors in the least likely locale—a street mime in front of a large hotel or restaurant, hand puppets in the underground Metro in Paris or Oslo, a couple performing a "scene" on the sidewalks of many large cities—performing not only for some hope of small financial reward, but practicing in order to achieve both financial and creative gain.

The odds against security and financial reward are high; yet this fact deters few. In our conservatories, in college, university, and community theatres, we find a large number of dedicated men and women whose interest in the theatre has produced work of very high caliber indeed. Local, state, regional, and national theatre festivals surely point to the undiminished vitality of the young artists who will make up the theatre of tomorrow. As long as theatre continues to provide an artistic opportunity for those whose creativity must find a meaningful means of expression, the question "Why act?" should not be difficult to answer. Acting provides rewards measurable by the satisfaction derived from all creative endeavors when the job is well done. In the long run, this may be the most meaningful reward of all.

Is There an Ideal Actor?

One of the most misleading comments heard about actors and acting is that certain physical and vocal attributes automatically ensure success. This belief is quite widespread, and its results are seen not only in the theatre but also in television and film, where attractive but otherwise unqualified youngsters hope for quick success. It is certainly true that physical attractiveness is an essential ingredient in the portrayal of *certain types* of roles. The belief that physical attractiveness alone provides a sure road to success, to the exclusion of other attributes, is damaging to the realization that there is no substitute for training and an understanding of the essentials of good acting.

Occasionally a particular type may be in demand and can find suitable employment—until the fashion changes. Many years ago the film industry was particularly on the lookout for attractive sex-symbols, regardless of the actor's or actress's ability to act. There followed, in the 1960s and 1970s,

> *After The Wizard of Oz I was type-cast as a lion, and there aren't all that many parts for lions.*
>
> Bert Lahr

the period of the antihero, where a certain insouciance and rebelliousness were deemed more important than simply looking pretty. Errol Flynn and Tyrone Power gave way to Dustin Hoffman, Woody Allen, and Jean-Paul Belmondo. During the 1980s the antiheroes of the 1970s had matured into major stars whose range now moved into middle-aged, street-wise survivors, from Hoffman to Al Pacino and Robert de Niro. Stars of the 1980s, such as Kevin Costner, Harrison Ford, Tom Cruise, Sigourney Weaver, Sean Young, and Debra Winger, suggested the sexual attractiveness of film performers of earlier generations combined with the new worldly cynicism of the previous decade. It will be interesting to assess the 1990s after the decade draws to a close. Taste and fashions clearly change, often in a short space of time. Who knows what tomorrow may bring?

**John Gielgud in *Julius Caesar* by William Shakespeare.
National Theatre, London. Photograph by Britain on
View Photographic Library.**

Physical Standards

There is no specific type of physique required for good acting. The belief that
one type of body is suited to acting in all roles is contradicted both by the evidence of history and by the variety of roles found in almost every play. Some
of the great roles in Shakespeare's plays provide an interesting array of character types. Let us consider just two such roles, Cassius in *Julius Caesar* and
the immortal comic creation Falstaff, found in three of Shakespeare's plays.
Cassius is very carefully described as having a "lean and hungry look." As
admirable an actor as Danny De Vito is, he would have difficulty in giving a
truly realistic portrait of this character. This in no way detracts from his ability as an actor. Consider also Falstaff, who throughout the plays in which he
appears is referred to as "fat Jack," "this huge hill of flesh," "that swollen par-

> *If you're my height and look the way I do and you can't have an abundance of ego and self-esteem, you become a basket case, one of life's prime losers, because height and looks and suave and all those qualities are worshipped.*
>
> Danny De Vito

cel of dropsies, that huge bombard of sack." One can think of any number of fine actors who, because of their physical makeup alone, would be unable to undertake the portrayal of this delightful character, even with the aid of padding!

Nor do seemingly restrictive physical characteristics always serve to limit the quality or range of the intelligent actor. In the long history of the English-speaking theatre, Thomas Betterton, David Garrick, Edmund Kean, Edwin Booth, and John Barrymore stand among the giants of the acting pro-

Timon of Athens by Shakespeare. Yale Repertory Theatre, directed by Lloyd Richards. James Earl Jones as Timon and James Greene as Flavius. Photo by Gerry Goodstein.

fession. Betterton was the unexcelled actor of the English Restoration in the seventeenth century; Garrick was the most notable actor of the eighteenth century; Kean was the finest of all nineteenth-century romantic actors; Booth is still generally regarded as the greatest of American actors; and John Barrymore's remarkable performances as Hamlet and Richard III are yet another proud part of the American theatre's heritage. All were versatile and exciting actors who overcame seemingly great physical limitations to rise to the pinnacle of their profession. Betterton was short and stout; he had a pair of beady eyes set in a huge face marked by the ravages of smallpox. Yet he was universally admired for his portrayals of the great heroes of Shakespeare's plays and the dignified gentlemen of Restoration comedy. In the commentary of biographers and observers of the other great actors, we find the constant reminder that such a possible limitation as short stature in no way affected the quality of their acting or their success in a wide range of leading and character roles.

> *I'm actually a thin serious person but I play fat and funny, but only for the movies.*
>
> Dom De Luise

It was said of David Garrick:

> His short stature (he was five feet four inches according to his measurements) proved an irritating handicap. Nevertheless, no other English actor of his standing has been better equipped for his calling. When he held the stage for a prologue or a soliloquy, his slight build gave the illusion of average height, and as soon as the action began, he moved about the stage rapidly and added so much new and ingenious byplay that the audience forgot to make comparisons. . . . Every muscle in his lithe young body was in perfect control. . . .[1]

And Playfair wrote of Edmund Kean:

> This is what impressed his admirers most—his ability to make them forget that he was really an undersized little man with an unmelodious voice. Perhaps he was particularly suited to Richard [III] or Shylock or Iago. . . . Yet as Hamlet . . . he revealed beauties before undreamed of. . . . "By God he is a Soul," said Byron.[2]

Otis Skinner wrote about Edwin Booth:

> Although a small, even a frail man, I could swear at times in *Othello* and in *Macbeth* he was seven feet tall.[3]

---

1. Margaret Barton, *Garrick* (New York: MacMillan, 1949), p. 41.
2. Giles Playfair, *Kean* (London: Reinhardt and Evans, 1950), p. 116.
3. Otis Skinner, *Footlights and Spotlights* (New York: Bobbs-Merrill, 1924), p. 93.

John Barrymore as Hamlet. Culver Pictures, Inc.

John Barrymore was barely five feet nine inches tall, and one might note that Al Pacino and Dustin Hoffman, who are among today's best actors, are remarkably short in height.

If there is any physical standard that should be used to evaluate either the ability or potentiality of an actor, it is the level of *control* that the actor maintains over his or her body. Actors must learn to use their physical apparatus expressively and with economy of motion. The great actors just referred to refused to permit any physical limitations to interfere with their careers; rather, they accepted the challenge to utilize existing elements to make their acting even more exciting and vital. The distinguished director Tyrone Guthrie made this point very clearly when he noted that "audiences look at actors who have some kind of magnetism. This is largely a matter of self-confidence on the actor's part, the belief that he is, in fact, worth looking at."[4] The only true physical limitation is an actor's inability or refusal to use physical equipment with intelligence and imagination.

> *I was a fourteen-year-old boy for thirty years.*
>
> Mickey Rooney

---

4. Tyrone Guthrie, *Tyrone Guthrie on Acting* (New York: Viking Press, 1971), p. 13.

Vocal Standards

The same qualifications discussed in relation to physical standards might just as easily be applied to the voice. There is no type of voice best suited to the theatre. We may hear the suggestion that a particularly beautiful or striking voice is a definite asset for an actor. It is true that an attractive voice may be useful in the portrayal of certain roles, and a voice that is well produced and free of annoying habits should be of great value to an actor. John Dolman, Jr. has clearly defined the requirements of the good stage voice.

> It need not be a supremely beautiful voice in the musical sense; it will, in fact, be more useful if not too beautiful, since an excessively beautiful voice may hypnotize an audience into admiring the tones rather than listening to the play. . . . What the actor needs to develop is a voice that is highly adaptable to a variety of uses, and so managed as to withstand fatigue, and even abuse.[5]

The first and most important function of the voice in the theatre is that it be heard and understood. This indicates a primary responsibility on the part of any actor to develop proper projection and articulation. No matter how expressive or how lively, the voice that cannot be heard and understood is a meaningless tool of communication for the actor. It is of course true that the voice must also be used in the projection of shades of meaning, nuances, and subtleties. This may be accomplished by the development of flexibility and variety in pitch, rate, and volume.

It is obvious that the voice can be an important asset to any actor. One of the famous legends of the theatre tells of the wonderful vocal expressiveness of the great Polish actress Helena Modjeska. Once at a dinner party, when asked to perform one of her famous scenes for the assembled guests, the actress complied by giving a very brief monologue. Many onlookers were moved to tears by the gripping effect of Modjeska's eloquence, despite the fact the she performed the "scene" in Polish! After she had finished she was asked which great and touching selection she had chosen to move her audience so deeply. It must have been with a sly wink that she confided that in fact she had recited the Polish alphabet. Such effectiveness was made possible not only by her sense of the dramatic but by a supple and expressive voice, delicately tuned with a great versatility to the needs of every occasion.

> *I am sure acting is a deeply neurotic thing to do. I veer away from trying to understand why I do it.*
>
> Ralph Fiennes

---

5. John Dolman, Jr., *The Art of Acting* (New York: Harper and Brothers, 1949), pp. 187–188.

Can Actors Be Classified?

There are many kinds of actors, just as there are many philosophies on how to act or how to train actors. Although many students of the theatre have tried to systematize acting into a set of rules applicable to all occasions, it is clear that such an approach is impractical when one deals with human beings. Theoretically, it should be possible to arrive at a universal set of rules, useful to all actors at all times. However, the diversity of acting styles and techniques in the theatre shows that fine acting may be, and is, achieved by more than one means.

Interviews with many actors have shown that there are several different roads leading to the final goal, to make the actor and actress as expressive and creative as possible. However the work is approached, there should be no mistaking the fact that it is hard work. No matter how an actor undertakes this work, it is worth bearing in mind the words of Charlton Heston. Talking about his preparation for a play under the direction of Laurence Olivier, Heston noted in his diary:

> I've never felt such an overwhelming sense of the *difficulty* of acting. . . . who said it was supposed to be easy?[6]

There are a number of ways by which one may classify actors—in reference to their styles, personal characteristics and idiosyncrasies, philosophy, temperament, technique or lack of it, successful repetition of one type of role, and so on. It may be useful to examine some of these distinctions that tend to suggest how actors differ and why. However, a word of warning is in order. We can no more pigeonhole all actors into definite classifications than we can indicate a universal formula for successful acting. Many performers do not fall neatly into any specific classification and on certain occasions may depart sharply from their usual style or technique. If we are prepared to accept these classifications as not too rigid, it is possible to point to three areas that help illustrate distinctive differences in acting.

> *I have always hated that James Bond.*
> Sean Connery
>
> *I would have liked to be James Bond.*
> Terence Stamp

Emotional vs. Technical Acting

If he does not really feel the anguish of the betrayed lover or the dishonored father, if he does not temporarily escape from the dullness of his existence in

---

6. Charlton Heston, *The Actor's Life: Journals 1956–1976*, ed. Hollis Alpert (New York: Pocket Books, 1979), p. 112.

order to throw himself wholeheartedly into the most acute crises, he will move nobody. How can he convince another of his emotion, of the sincerity of his passions, if he is unable to convince himself to the point of actually becoming the character that he has to impersonate?[7]

Sarah Bernhardt here summarizes very clearly the point of view of the actor who believes it is necessary to feel the role during the performance. All actors face the elemental problem of deciding whether or not they should feel emotion in the playing of a role, and to what degree they should feel it. We shall look carefully at this important problem in Chapter 2, but at this point let us consider how actors may be evaluated on the matter of emotion and technique in their acting.

Many performers give themselves over entirely to the character they are enacting. They literally *become* that individual, feeling his or her emotions and passions and often losing themselves entirely in the role. The emotional actor usually is not concerned with techniques of acting in relation to the voice or body. One interesting study of emotionalism in acting has suggested that "gesture, movement, and performance of stage business are likely to be impromptu, unstudied and haphazard."[8] The emotional actor relies on impulse and the springs of inspiration, to make a character's reactions and feelings meaningful. Such acting may often produce exciting and admirable performances, but its very nature suggests that it will lack consistency. Estelle Parsons, a multiple winner of acting awards, including two Off-Broadway Obies, two Tony nominations, and an Academy Award, has little respect for this kind of acting. She states quite clearly:

> An actress is someone who's able to use herself, not just lose control. That would be self-indulgence; that wouldn't be acting.[9]

It is not uncommon to encounter actors and actresses who are so overcome by a role they may be playing that the effect lingers upon them long after they have left the stage.

On the other hand, the actor who eliminates all feeling from acting relies completely on the principles of stage technique and internal honesty to make a character meaningful to an audience. The actor will have the details of a performance carefully planned, with nothing left to chance or to sudden whims for unplanned emotional outbursts onstage. Raymond Massey indicated that this was his fundamental philosophy of acting. He has written:

---

7. Sarah Bernhardt, *The Art of the Theatre* (London: G. Bles, 1924), p. 104.
8. Garff B. Wilson, "Emotionalism in Acting," *Quarterly Journal of Speech* 42 (February 1956), p. 44.
9. Estelle Parsons, quoted in Joanmarie Kalter, *Actors on Acting* (New York: Sterling, 1979), p. 226.

If he [the actor] allows his emotion to dominate the performance, he will lose all unity, all power of reproducing the character. . . . Personally, I have not "felt the part" before an audience in twenty years. Acting, to me, is always a case of "outside looking in." Without that detachment it is impossible for me to maintain the control necessary to keep the performance at proper pitch.[10]

There are, of course, many actors who seek the middle ground, combining elements of both emotionalism and technique. The brilliant character actor Donald Pleasance was this kind of actor, telling us that when he was onstage he was completely immersed in a role, but he was never lost in the part. Some lean more heavily toward one procedure than the other. It is evident, nevertheless, that an individual's approach to "feeling the part" is one legitimate way of differentiating among actors. Obviously it can be difficult to determine the level of emotionalism or technique used in any given performance. Very often the successful technical actor may so perfectly perform a role with all its emotional nuances that the audience will be certain they have witnessed emotional acting. A story is told in theatre circles about one of the most respected actors of our time. Another fine actor, watching him perform from the wings, was astonished to see him exit, after a deeply moving sequence (which had held even his fellow-actors in awe), and ask as he entered the wings, with tears streaming down his face, how the poker game was going backstage.

The American actor Alfred Lunt recalled an incident when his wife, Lynne Fontanne, invited a maid to the country for a weekend. When told that there was no church of her denomination near their home, excepting a Catholic church, the maid replied that it didn't bother her since "we're all heading for the same place." Lunt noted that "I often think of that in connection with acting. We're all just heading for the same place."[11]

The distinction between emotionalism and technique is a difference in the means rather than in the end, which in this case is a living performance.

Personality vs. Character Acting

It might seem on first consideration that personality and character acting are simply extensions of the two approaches discussed as emotional and technical acting. This is not true, however, in the sense in which these terms are used here. Nor, it must be added, does the term *character acting* carry the connotation that is usually attached to it. We often hear the term applied to an

---

10. Raymond Massey, "Acting," from *The New Theatre Handbook and Digest of Plays,* ed. Bernard Sobel. Copyright 1940, 1948, 1959 by Crown Publishers, Inc.

11. Quoted in Lewis Funke and John E. Booth, *Actors Talk about Acting* (New York: Random House, 1961).

actor who consistently plays a general character type in a large portion of the plays, films, or television series in which he or she appears. In the present practice of type casting, such actors continue successfully to portray the same basic character over and over again. This is not, however, character acting in the most meaningful sense.

In some ways this use of the term *type casting* is misleading. During the 1930s three of the most famous gangster actors in the Warner Brothers "stable" were Edward G. Robinson—"The Little Caesar"; James Cagney—"The Public Enemy"; and Humphrey Bogart—"A Gangster for All Seasons." Yet in real life these actors were quite different from their screen images. Robinson was a soft-spoken art collector and reflective pipe smoker, Bogart an excellent chess player and avid yachtsman, and Cagney (in his early days) an effective song-and-dance man.

> *I play John Wayne in every picture regardless of the character, and I've been doing all right, haven't I?*
>
> John Wayne

The true character actor alters his or her personality to fit the demands of any role. This type of actor eliminates those features of his or her own personality that audiences would recognize and seeks to emphasize the personality of the role being undertaken. There are many fine actors of this type, of whom Laurence Olivier, Peter Sellers, Helen Hayes, and Alec Guinness are among the best known. One splendid example of this type of acting was the work of Alec Guinness in the English film *Kind Hearts and Coronets*. In this droll comedy Guinness played *eight* roles, each with a specific and well-defined personality and character. He also played a Japanese widower in *A Majority of One*; Hitler in *Hitler, The Last Ten Days*; Obi-Wan Kenobe in *Star Wars*; and a blind butler in *Murder by Death*. Much of the career of Marlon Brando was built on his desire to "stretch" himself in this way, more successfully in certain roles than in others.

True character acting, then, requires great flexibility in the projection of age, social status, manners, and temperament. There are, however, two conclusions that should not be drawn from this appraisal of character acting. First, *the character actor does not necessarily feel the role*. Submergence of one's own personality in a character may be done either internally or externally. The distinction is this: How successfully does the actor eliminate his or her own personality in the playing of a role? It may be a very studied and carefully thought-out transition, or it may come almost entirely from the inner resources of the performer. Neither manner is directly related to character acting. The second conclusion often drawn is a qualitative evaluation of the two types of acting: *The character actor is not always a better actor than the noncharacter, or personality, actor.* We shall now see why this is so.

The personality actor creates a role within the framework of his or her own personality and mannerisms. In this type of acting the actor makes the

**Albert Finney as Hamlet. National Theatre, London.
Courtesy of British Tourist Authority.**

role over in his or her own image, using personal characteristics to illustrate facets of the role being played. This does not suggest that the personality actor distorts the role. It does mean, however, that the actor comments on the character through his or her own personality. Charlton Heston is an excellent example of an actor whose personality permeates all the roles in which he appears. This certainly does not lessen his ability to create exciting characterizations, but it should be clear that his approach is fundamentally different from that of Alec Guinness and Ms. Hayes. Nor should it be assumed that Mr. Heston or other personality actors, such as the late James Stewart, Henry Fonda, or Gary Cooper were less able than their colleagues whose approach to a role is somewhat different. We often hear this comment about a given actor: "He is the same in every role he plays." Such criticism implies indiffer-

> *I'm not an actress who can create a character. I play me.*
> Mary Tyler Moore

ent or inexperienced acting, but the comment may be somewhat misleading. John Mason Brown found this type of acting, in many respects, the more admirable.

> Then there are those precious few, standing at the top of their profession, whose high gift it is to act themselves, to adapt their spirits to the spirits of the parts they are playing, to possess and then to be possessed by the characters they project, and to give them the benefit of their beauty and their intelligence, their sympathy and their virtuosity, their poetry and their inner radiance, their imagination and their glamour.[12]

In agreement with this point of view is the reflection of Tyrone Guthrie, who noted that some of the greatest actors did not have very great range, but much was to be admired in their skill, imagination, and taste. He punctuated that idea with the comment that ". . . range is not the ultimate in theatrical accomplishment."[13]

It should be apparent here, as in the previous discussion of emotionalism, that there are likely to be performers who fall between these two poles, combining distinctive characterizations with the use of their own personality. There is a need for both types of acting in the theatre, both on the amateur and professional level.

Representational vs. Presentational Acting

On many occasions, the type of play in which the actor is performing will affect his or her approach to a role and the manner of presentation. Although a number of stylistic distinctions can be made among numerous plays, the most fundamental differences in acting styles relate specifically to those plays that may be characterized as either *representational* or *presentational*. The representational style derives its name from the fact that the actors give the illusion that the audience is watching a *representation* of life. The acting suggests that the audience does not exist, by proceeding on the assumption that the invisible "fourth wall" of the setting separates actor and audience. The audience is given the impression that they are peeking in on human beings who are unaware of the existence of observers sitting in the house. Acting in this style is required in realistic plays,[14] which constitute a large portion of contemporary drama, and may also be found as the fundamental approach in contemporary motion-picture and television drama.

---

12. John Mason Brown, *The Art of Playgoing* (New York: Norton, 1936), p. 194.
13. Guthrie, *Tyrone Guthrie on Acting*, p. 74.
14. This style will, on occasion, also be used in plays that are not realistic. A fantasy, for example, would not be classified as a realistic play, yet an attempt to suggest the illusion of a fourth wall may still be used. It is this factor that distinguishes the representational style of acting.

Representational acting should not be confused with the absence of any of the usual techniques of acting. The representational actor artfully conceals many of the important techniques in order to be seen and heard by the

> *People I meet really want me to be J. R., so it's hard to disappoint them.*
>
> Larry Hagman

audience and maintain the illusion that he or she is simulating life. However, this concealment of the actor's art does not eliminate the need for the basic techniques of acting.

Presentational acting, on the other hand, is frankly theatrical, with little attempt to disguise the fact that the actor is performing on a stage before an audience. Speeches are often spoken directly to the audience; movement and action will attempt not necessarily to suggest life but to heighten it and sharpen its salient features. The presentational style is to be found in most of the dramas of the past: the tragedies of the Greeks, the dramas of Shakespeare and his contemporaries, and the great seventeenth-century comedies of the English Restoration and Molière. Today musical comedy frequently uses this technique. The actor, in fact, is telling the audience, "Look, I know you are there, and I'm performing for you, so let us enjoy it together."

The clearest distinction between presentational and representational acting is in the focus of the actor's attention. In general, *representational acting is centered on the other actors in the play* and within the area of the stage setting itself. *Presentational acting tends to be audience-centered*, with a continual awareness of the existence of the audience as the focal point of the action. As we shall see later, there are other subtle distinctions relating to the projection of these concepts, but they all are directed toward the fundamental goals just suggested. Many actors are adept at both styles of playing; others seem to find one style more harmonious with their training and temperament. It should be obvious that factors of emotionalism–technique and personality–character are not directly related to the use of either the presentational or the representational style.

What Should the Actor Know?

The good actor is an *intelligent* human being. He or she knows the techniques and conventions of the theatre, is usually well read, knows the great books and plays, has studied historical manners and customs, and is a generally well-informed individual. American actor Edward Herrmann states flatly, "The best actors are inclusive of experience, not the ones who are overly specialized in the theatre."[15] It is perfectly clear that the wider the range of ex-

---

15. Edward Herrmann, quoted in Susan Shacter and Don Shewey, *Caught in the Act* (New York: New American Library, 1986), p. 76.

perience and knowledge upon which an actor can draw, the finer actor he or she is likely to be. The world's great novels and plays depict a panorama of human emotions, motives, and personalities. This alone would be reason enough to enrich the mind with the views of the most observant students of human nature. Serving as a storehouse of our heritage, great literature provides the sensitive actor with an elemental source to tap for his or her own enrichment as a human being, and therefore as an actor as well.

There are also more practical considerations. The drama encompasses the entire range of human history. Princes, thieves, vagabonds, philosophers, and adventurers are found among the characters of thousands of plays. The actor undertaking such roles as these will find it literally impossible to draw on first-hand information. Yet the actor must understand the motives of such individuals, the customs and habits of their times, and their ambitions and their conflicts, in order to realize meaningful characterizations. Dedicated actors have long realized the necessity to broaden their viewpoints and knowledge.

> *When I played drunks I had to remain sober because I didn't know how to play them when I was drunk.*
>
> Richard Burton

The experienced actor Barnard Hughes strongly reinforces this point. He tells us:

> I think actors should expose themselves to practically everything under the sun and have an interest in everything. I've always found actors to be the best company in the word, the most fascinating people because they're interested in absolutely everything—in the man across the street, the man across the globe, everyone.[16]

Hughes's comment represents by no means an isolated viewpoint. It stems from the very heart of the problem of intelligent and purposeful acting. Sarah Bernhardt expressed very much the same thing when, after a life spent in the theatre, she wrote:

> Consequently the actor must become familiar with the entire past of humanity . . . the manners, the customs, and the passions of different peoples and of different times. It is certain that love does not reveal itself in every age in the same forms, and that the expressions of hate vary from century to century, and from people to people. . . . Now how can these sentiments be embodied without dipping into books—for the past—and into the current of life—for the present. . . .[17]

---

16. Barnard Hughes, quoted in Kalter, *Actors on Acting*, p. 238.
17. Bernhardt, *Art of the Theater*, pp. 88–89.

The actor who strives to improve the range of experience upon which to draw in the preparation of a role needs to be aware that all that he or she chooses to read, or is able to observe, serves to strengthen and nourish his or her acting ability.

What Is the "Illusion of the First Time"?

One of the most difficult critical problems in the theatre is that of evaluating the work of actors and actresses from one performance to another. Why did one actor succeed in making a character come to life where another failed, and why may an actor at a given performance fall below the level of the night before? There are any number of standards relating to the technical competence of an actor by which we may evaluate a specific performance. There is one element, however, that serves as a basis for the study of acting as discussed in this book. This factor has been described by actors in countless ways, but the description by the American actor William Gillette (the theatre's first Sherlock Holmes) is perhaps the most precise. He spoke of the actor's duty to maintain for the audience the "illusion of the first time." By this he meant that the members of the audience must sense that the character in the play is experiencing and reacting to the varied situations not for the tenth or twentieth or hundredth time, as the actor is likely to do after numerous rehearsals and performances, but for the first time. Sidney Poitier calls this "refuelling." Specifically, he says, "With me—as with other actors, I believe—it's quite a job to prevent the work from becoming mechanical. You have to find ways to keep refuelling the impulse."[18]

Often audiences will be hard put to specify the exact nature of a weak performance, sensing, however, that they have witnessed a stale repetition of something that had been done many times before. The element of spontaneity is essential to all good performances. This spontaneity is as meaningful in plays of a poetic and presentational style as in the most realistic dramas. Gillette was insistent on this point.

> Each successive audience before which [the presentation] is given must feel—not think or reason about, but *feel*—that it is witnessing, not one of a thousand weary repetitions, but a life episode that is being lived just across the magic barrier of the footlights. That is to say, the whole must have that indescribable life-spirit or effect which produces the Illusion of the First Time.[19]

---

18. Sidney Poitier, quoted in Lillian Ross and Helen Ross, *The Player: A Profile of an Art* (New York: Simon and Schuster, 1962), p. 110.

19. William Hooker Gillette, "The Illusion of the First Time in Acting," in *Papers on Acting*, ed. Brander Matthews (New York: Hill and Wang, 1958), p. 133.

Gillette's essay is perhaps the most articulate expression of this important facet of good acting. John Barrymore said much the same thing during an interview: "Acting is the art . . . of doing and saying the thing as spontaneously as if you were confronted with the situation in which you were acting for the first time."[20]

David Belasco wrote eloquently of the last public performance of Edwin Booth:

> The last time that ever I heard Booth speak Hamlet's immortal soliloquy on life and death was the last time that ever he spoke it in public, at the old Academy of Music, in Brooklyn, April 4, 1891. In the preceding fifteen years I had heard him speak that speech probably forty times; he was then old, worn and frail, yet the familiar words seemed to come from his lips for the first time, to utter thoughts then first formulated.[21]

And yet again Henry Fonda has said almost the same thing as Gillette. In referring to his multiple-year run on Broadway as Mister Roberts, and to the film version as well, he observed that the major problem in long run productions was that the actor ceased to listen to the other characters. He continually reminded himself that for the audience ". . . it was happening for the first time. I never got tired of it."[22]

For many actors this is an unconscious part of their art, grasped intuitively and made meaningful by experience. Every effort devoted to the expansion of the actor's dramatic potential must incorporate this element. Whatever is likely to become artificial, stilted, or stale can only detract from the projection of the essence of life upon the stage. It must be rejected—from whatever source it may come. It is through the actor's own personality that these techniques and ideas can be molded to find proper expression on the stage. The goal is that moment on stage when the audience will feel the essence that means "I believe it"—not because it is necessarily realistic but because it is *true and right*.

> *All they said I was good for was playing Indians.*
> Anthony Quinn

---

20. Helen Ten Broeck, "From Comedy to Tragedy: An Interview with John Barrymore," *Theatre*, July 1916, p. 23.

21. David Belasco, "About Acting," *Saturday Evening Post*, September 24, 1921, pp. 11ff.

22. Henry Fonda, quoted in Ross and Ross, *The Player*, pp. 89–90.

QUESTIONS AND EXERCISES

Questions for Discussion

1. Is acting a creative art or is it an interpretive art? How much that is original does the actor contribute to the playing of a role?
2. How does the acting of the silent film differ from the acting in films today? How does the acting in the early talking films of the 1930s vary from film and television acting today? Why have there been such distinctive changes in acting styles within a period of just over half a century?
3. Classify the following actors and actresses as either "character" or "personality" performers: (a) Marlon Brando, (b) Jon Voight, (c) Shirley MacLaine, (d) Bette Davis, (e) Dustin Hoffman, (f) Cecily Tyson, (g) Debra Winger, (h) Burt Reynolds, (i) Val Kilmer, (j) Harrison Ford, (k) Al Pacino, (l) Meryl Streep, (m) Denzel Washington, (n) Tom Hulce, (o) William Hurt, (p) John Lithgow, (q) Christopher Walken, (r) Will Smith, (s) John Malkovich, (t) Paul Newman, (u) Whoopi Goldberg, (v) Angela Lansbury, (w) Tom Cruise, (x) Meg Ryan, (y) Bill Cosby, (z) Tommy Lee Jones. Compare your conclusions with the conclusions of other people in class and discuss your differences of opinion.
4. Is it possible to tell when an actor is "feeling" the role?
5. Is there any value in attempting to classify types of actors? Is anything to be learned in studying other actors' means of approaching a role?
6. (a) Which actor whom you have seen on the stage, in film, or on television has the most expressive and versatile voice? (b) Which actor whom you have seen on the stage, in film, or on television has made the most expressive use of his or her body?
7. What qualities should a human being possess before entering a study of acting? Can anyone become a competent actor?
8. Read a portion of the biography of any actor of the past or present. Try to uncover the reason that made that individual turn to the stage as a career. Compare notes with other people in the class.

CHAPTER TWO

Scaramucia.   Fricasso.

Early Acting and Acting Theories

Many of the questions commonly asked about acting have been the concern of actors from the earliest days of the theatre. If we look at the work of the great actors of the past and read what they have written about their craft, we find a continual concern about certain persistent questions, indeed, the same questions we still ask today: *Does the actor feel the part? Does the actor completely subordinate his or her personality in playing various roles? What form should the actor's training take?*

Perhaps the most difficult question pondered over the years is that of the essential nature of the actor: *Is he or she a creative artist with a singular creative responsibility or simply an adept interpreter of the intention of the playwright or even of the director?* Each actor will undoubtedly find individual answers to these problems, but it is reassuring to know that the same questions have long been discussed by the great actors and critics.

It will be of value to examine the past to see what if any light it sheds on these persistent questions. We shall find little uniformity of opinion, but we shall discover that serious attention has always been paid to the art of the theatre and acting. In this one regard most actors are similar. They are truly concerned about the nature of their medium. Although final answers to these questions will not be found here, the ideas raised by the following discussion should help each actor think more carefully about his or her own acting.

The First Actors

The first actor was very likely a hunter in prehistoric times who described to his fellow tribesmen his adventures of that day. He gesticulated, exaggerated his cunning and resourcefulness, and described how the animal had fought valiantly against the hunter's guile. He was impersonating, imitating, and recalling previous events. He may even have used the tusks, antlers, or skin of the animal to enliven his impersonation. Enhanced by firelight and performing before an audience that shared his concerns, he probably did not realize that, in one sense, he was starting a tradition that would persist to the present day. Unfortunately neither this prehistoric hunter nor any of his viewers and listeners left a record of how he went about his performance. However, contemporary evidence indicates that such impromptu accounts of hunting stories involved masks and costumes and grew into intricate performances of long-standing myths. Eventually speech, dance, makeup, costume, music, pantomime, and the audience all contributed to the "production." It was a means of fulfilling the primitive society's need to understand the essential considerations of their group, from the stability of their food supply to their concern about the supernatural. Remnants of these rituals still exist in certain societies today. A concern about humanity's place in the universe has been a part of all the great ages of the theatre, from the Greek tragic playwrights to the existential and absurdist playwrights of today.

What the Ancients Tell Us

Theatre in the western world had its origins in Greece around the sixth century B.C.E. Religious festivals in honor of the god Dionysus were held every year with choral chants called *dithyrambs* and probably animal sacrifices. Dionysus was a nature god, a god of wine, fertility, and spring, and he was reborn every year. These choral chants, held in large outdoor arenas (see the accompanying photo), were essentially undramatic until an individual by the name of Thespis had the inspiration to include in the rituals a "responder" to the head of the chorus of priests. With this idea Western drama was born.

Greek Theatre at Epidaurus.

Two individuals responding to each other permitted conflict, action, and perhaps even the germ of a plot. The first "responder" or *protagonist* became the first actor. Regular Dionysian festivals were held annually as a form of competition for the writing of dithyrambs and tragedies, and Thespis was the winner of the first contest, held in Athens in 534 B.C.E. The name Thespis has been linked with the art of acting ever since. Gradually the form of these contests permitted greater freedom in the writing and performance of the plays.

Viewing the Greek drama of the past in broad perspective, certain perceptions we have about Greek acting become clearer. The theatres were vast open areas, with a circle for dancing by the chorus and with seating in a semicircle on the hillside for the spectators. This *theatron*, as it was called, often seated up to seventeen thousand spectators. The stone remnants of these theatrons can still be found in and around Greece.[1] Clearly such huge outdoor arenas required *presentational* acting of a highly exaggerated style. The actors

---

1. Recent discoveries of Greek theatres or paratheatrical areas have revealed rectangular and trapezoidal orchestras, suggesting greater variation in theatre forms and performance techniques than formerly thought possible. Clifford Ashby, *Greek Theatre: Many Questions and a Few Answers* (Stockholm: International Federation for Theatre Research, 1989, Collected Papers).

Greek Theatre at Delphi.

wore boots (*cothurni*) to add to their height and used masks that served to identify their characters from great distances, and may have helped to amplify their voices. There were no more than three main actors on the stage at any one time, and the same actors could play many roles in a tragedy simply by changing masks and costumes. All roles were played by men, including the great female characters of Greek tragedy.

The information we have concerning the Greek actor's approach to his role is quite meager, but scattered clues suggest some interesting conclusions. The Greek word *drama* literally meant an action or more precisely the "imitation of an action or deed," and one of the Greek words for actor, *hypocrite*, suggests that the actor's responsibility was to deceive the audience into believing the character the actor was performing. The actor also needed to bring certain gifts to his profession.

Not only did the Greek actor need to be an able dancer and singer, but he had to possess a beautiful and well-managed speaking voice. Aristotle, in fact, defined acting as "the proper management of voice to express several emotions." Obviously a well-managed and well-placed voice was essential in the huge outdoor theatres in which the Greek actor was required to perform.

It is likely that the Greeks believed that great acting was a matter of inspiration rather than technique and that only through inspiration could the actor achieve his effects. Plato gives us a clue to this view in one of his dialogues. In it Socrates is questioning the actor Ion.

> SOCRATES: I wish you would frankly tell me, Ion, what I am going to ask of you: When you produce the greatest effect upon the audience in the recitation of some striking passage . . . are you in your right mind? Are you not carried out of yourself, and does not your soul in an ecstasy seem to be among the persons or the places of which you are speaking . . . ?
>
> ION: . . . I must frankly confess that at the tale of pity my eyes are filled with tears, and when I speak of horrors, my hair stands on end and my heart throbs.[2]

We have other clues to support the belief that the Greek actor identified himself emotionally with his role. One famous anecdote reinforces this point and illustrates the lengths to which an actor might go to produce an effect. The Greek tragedian Polus, who had achieved notable success in portraying many tragic roles, lost a son whom he loved dearly. After his son's death Polus was called on to play the role of Electra in the play by Sophocles. In one scene Electra was required to mourn the death of her brother while carrying an urn supposedly holding his ashes. Polus carried in an urn holding the ashes of his own son and played the grief-stricken Electra with a genuine grief that evidently was startling. We are told that Polus "filled the arena, not with the appearance and suggestion of misery, but with true sorrow and grief. Although it seemed to some that a play was being performed it was indeed a real enactment of grief."[3]

Although the contemporary actor may gain little from the general approach of the Greeks to acting, it is of value to note two important points. First, acting was a matter of emotion and inspiration, evidently little concerned with any systematic approach; second, great reliance was placed on the voice as a means of conveying those emotions.

The Decline of the Theatre

After Greece's decline as a major power in the ancient world, the vacuum in theatre was filled by the Romans. During the period of the Roman republic, in the second and third centuries B.C.E., the comedies of Plautus and Terence attained some prominence, as did some Roman tragedies, which are now generally forgotten.

---

2. Plato, "Ion," *Dialogues*, tr. Benjamin Jowett (New York: Oxford University Press, 1892), vol. 1, pp. 497–504.
3. Reported in *Attic Nights* by the Roman grammarian Aulus Gellius.

One possible bit of evidence about the means used by Roman actors to achieve "emotional reality" is related by Plutarch, who reported that the famous actor Aesop, while playing the role of the raving Orestes, killed a slave with his sword when the slave was on some errand and inadvertently crossed the stage. It may suggest the actor's identification with a role, but the more practical application would seem to tell us to avoid unscripted entrances.

Gradually Roman entertainments moved to massive spectacles that included gladiatorial combats, the massacre of hundreds of animals in a single day, and realistically staged sea battles in which criminals and captured enemies fought to the death. Indeed, the best gladiators and pseudo-sailors were those who could die well, with some dignity. Unfortunately, these performances did not lend themselves to repeat engagements. If one did not die "well," the state could take a number of unpleasant measures against the bad "actor." With the construction of the huge amphitheatre completed during the reign of Titus Flavius in 80 C.E., spectacles of this sort completely superceded interest in acted drama. This amphitheatre, popularly known as the Colosseum, celebrated its opening by having nine to ten thousand animals slaughtered for sport during its first one hundred days. Other events held there were equally staggering to the imagination. It was probably the most "interesting" grand opening in history. Clearly, an audience that became satiated seeing animals and humans slaughtered in a variety of ingenious ways found traditional theatre fare rather pale entertainment. Several factors were at work, which would ultimately bring an end to the last semblance of theatre in the Roman Empire. Internal decay, the attacks of barbarians from without, the acceptance of Christianity, and the church's opposition to the theatre all contributed to the decline and demise of theatre in Rome. For all intents and purposes, in fact, the theatre and drama all but vanished from the Western world for almost a thousand years.

The Commedia dell'Arte

Sometime in the late fifteenth or early sixteenth century, the *commedia dell'arte* (comedy of professional players) evolved in Italy. When the Roman Empire finally dissolved, in the sixth century, actors dispersed, or "took to the road." They moved from one locale to another, performing at festivals, in little towns or in castles, for whatever they could earn. The traditions of early Greek and Roman farces were preserved, but they also underwent changes. Nevertheless, the character of Capitano, for example, a *commedia* figure of the sixteenth century, is a direct descendant of the braggart warrior in a comedy by the Roman Plautus.

By the time Italy moved into its great humanistic period, which we now call the Renaissance, the actors were ready to return. The *commedia dell'arte* was a theatre of improvisation, using stock plots, stock characters, and stock

Jacques Callot, *The Masked Comedian*. Rosenwald Collection, National Gallery of Art, Washington, D.C.

Jacques Callot, *Razullo and Cucurucu*. Rosenwald Collection, National Gallery of Art, Washington, D.C.

Jacques Callot, *Pantalone.* **Rudolf L. Baumfeld Collection, National Gallery of Art, Washington, D.C.**

bits of business. It is in the *commedia* that we find the characters of Pantalone, Scaramouche, and Capitano, as well as Pierrot, Harlequin, and Columbine.

Each actor became an expert in playing a certain type of role and frequently played that one stock character all of his (or her) life. The plots were typical farces, dealing with deceived husbands, mistaken identity, romantic intrigue, old husbands and young wives, loud-mouthed pseudo-intelligent buffoons, and clever servants.

The characters were permanently established by tradition, and each actor knew his or her bits of business. Thus, when a simple outline of a play was posted for the actors, they could fall back on their favorite dialogue, business, and gags, which they had refined over a lifetime of playing the same characters. Often they indulged in extensive pantomime and acrobatic tricks. They were travelling players, playing on crude wooden stages, or in town squares and market places (see the accompanying illustration of Pantalone). Many etchings of the *commedia* players' work that have survived not only show them in their habitual costumes but also in their surroundings. Such acting was clearly broad, presentational, highly exaggerated, and little given to subtlety. The *commedia* actors took great pride in their improvisational ability, even though it tended to become standardized over the years. One writer of many *commedia* scenarios insisted that at the end of the seventeenth century:

> . . . when a comedy which is improvised is produced by good actors it is as successful as a completely written play. . . . Any actor who knows how to improvise, which is most difficult, will find it easy to act in a written play, which is not as difficult.[4]

We may not necessarily completely agree with Andrea Perrucci, who was evidently involved in a bit of self-conceit, but we would agree that the *commedia* actors brought a rich and meaningful tradition back to Europe. Another observer writing a few years later insisted that the *commedia* actors also worked from a sense of nature, at least as well as the term was understood at that time. Luigi Riccoboni, who also wrote *commedia* scenarios, gave this advice to *commedia* actors in 1728:

> The principal idea for the actor is to show that he does not evade the truth, for only in this manner can he convince an audience that what he is doing is not false, and in this manner he can truly please them. In order to produce a natural effect, the actor should use not just his four limbs, but a fifth as well, that is his head, for he must feel what he acts . . . passion, rage, jealousy . . . The actor must act in proper proportion and not overstep the truth.[5]

---

4. Andrea Perruci, *Dell'arte rappresentativa, premeditata ed all'improviso* (Naples, 1699).
5. Luigi Riccoboni, *Advice to Actors* (Florence, Italy, 1728).

Commedia dell'arte character Pantalone in *The Servant of Two Masters* by Goldoni. California State University, Long Beach, directed by W. David Sievers.

Although the *commedia dell'arte* has passed away, its tradition is still found in modern puppet shows, the Punch of Punch and Judy, and the yearly English Christmas pantomimes. Many of the best comics of American vaudeville, burlesque, and television were and are the spiritual heirs of the *commedia dell'arte.*

Shakespeare and His Actors

With the return of humanism in the Renaissance, following the so-called dark ages, the professional theatre also flourished, notably in England during the age of Queen Elizabeth I (1533–1603). The Elizabethan Age followed a two-hundred-year period of invigorating dramas performed by amateurs in the churches, streets, fields, and schools of England. In particular, the period between 1585 and 1620 brought forth one of the most concentrated bursts of energy in the history of the theatre. It included certainly the greatest playwright of the late Renaissance, and possibly of all time, William Shakespeare. Shakespeare was the finest of the many playwrights of this time, but he had able colleagues and competitors in such men as Christopher Marlowe, Ben Jonson, Thomas Kyd, John Ford, John Webster, John Marston, George Chapman, Robert Greene, William Rowley, Thomas Dekker, Francis Beaumont, John Fletcher, and many others. It's a safe guess that such an outpouring of new plays meant there were both audiences willing to view and actors able to perform them.

Without doubt William Shakespeare (1564–1616) was one of the greatest playwrights who ever lived and the most important influence on the theatre of his time. Although it is well over four hundred years since his birth, his plays are regularly performed by professional companies in every English-speaking country in the world and most of the other nations of the world as well. Surprisingly, Shakespeare may very well have begun his career as an *actor*, gradually developing his talents as playwright and poet and continuing to act for many years with his own company.

> *Playing Hamlet in a full-length [stage] production had an extraordinary effect on me. In my life, this was a time for taking stock, a time for meditation. Hamlet agonizes over "Why are we here? What do we do? What is the point of everything?" and it was fascinating to play that. John Gielgud described the play as defining the very process of living, and playing it has been something like that to me.*
>
> Kenneth Branagh

From what we can surmise about Shakespeare's career, we know he was a member of a permanent acting company called, during much of its existence, the Lord Chamberlain's Men, and which later became the King's Men, under the patronage of the King himself. The company consisted of many permanent members (as well as bit players called in on special occasions for large casts and apprentices), with only a moderate turnover of actors. These facts are important if we are to understand how Shakespeare wrote for actors and his intentions regarding their work.

It is interesting to note that women did not appear on the Elizabethan stage and that young boys played the roles of women. It is possible that older men may have played such roles as the Nurse in *Romeo and Juliet* and the Witches in *Macbeth*, but it is a matter of record that Shakespeare wrote many of his greatest female roles—Juliet, Desdemona, Rosalind, Ophelia, and even Cleopatra—for young boys whose voices had not yet changed and whose acting training was at best somewhat limited.

Most of the performances of his plays took place out of doors, in large wooden buildings of various sizes that were either leased or owned by the acting company. Inasmuch as Shakespeare was a shareholder in the company, it was important that the plays be performed as successfully as possible, even under the moderately difficult conditions of noise, inclement weather (London is not noted as a health resort), and the general restlessness among people standing in the pit of an outdoor theatre (the groundlings). At first Shakespeare's company performed in a theatre aptly called the Theatre, owned in large part by the Burbage family, but by 1599, the beginning of Shakespeare's most creative and inspired period, a new theatre was constructed on the south bank of the Thames (Bankside).[6] This theatre was called the Globe, and its name is forever linked with this most important playwright who wrote his plays to be performed in a large, thatched, outdoor theatre.

It seems to have been a moderately stable company. We might liken it to an ensemble troupe today, which may stay together over a period of years. In such a group one gets to know the strengths and weaknesses of one's fellow actors. We know that there were many fine actors in Shakespeare's company; in fact most of the roles in his plays were created for specific actors. One such actor, Richard Burbage, was the leading actor of his day. It is very likely that the roles of Richard III, Hamlet, King Lear, Romeo, Othello, Macbeth, and Coriolanus were written for him. If Shakespeare had not had an actor of this magnificent range, the legend of Shakespeare's plays might have been very different indeed. At the same time, as the kinds of comic actors changed in Shakespeare's company, so did the kind of comic characters who appeared in his plays. Despite the thirty-seven or thirty-eight plays certainly written by Shakespeare, however, those who have tried to uncover Shakespeare's private life and affairs have been either unsuccessful or at odds with each other. The reason is simple: Shakespeare rarely revealed himself as an individual, but rather spoke in the individual and unique voice of each of his characters, from the smallest to the largest roles.

When we attempt to evaluate Elizabethan acting, we are dealing with a difficult and controversial subject. It is debatable whether Elizabethan acting was *presentational* or *representational*. Current criticism tends to suggest that it was *presentational* and that unusual attention was paid to the voice. This is not surprising, for the great and vigorous poetry and prose of the Elizabethan playwrights required a sensitive and well-modulated speaking voice. It is interesting to note the similar dependence on the voice in the Greek theatre.

Unfortunately we have very little direct testimony on how actors approached their roles or on their manner of presentation during this period. Shakespeare left no *direct* comment or criticism about the production of his

---

6. In 1997, a new theatre opened on Bankside modeled as closely as possible after the original Globe Theatre. The new Globe Theatre, which opened with *Henry V*, now plays regular seasons to enthusiastic playgoers from all over the world.

plays. What little we know about Burbage's acting, for example, suggests that he moved gracefully and was "natural" in style. An anonymous playgoer who had seen Burbage suggested after his death that he was also a consummate character actor. In part this admirer of Burbage's acting wrote:

> . . . every thought and mood
> Might thoroughly from thy face be understood
> And his whole action he could change with ease
> From ancient Lear to youthful Pericles.

However, as we shall continue to see, what was "natural" in one age was considered artificial in the next. Interestingly enough, one scrap of evidence describes Shakespeare as an actor, probably as Adam in *As You Like It*. In his old age, an observer vaguely remembered seeing Shakespeare

> . . . act a part in one of his own comedies, wherein being to personate a decrepit old man, he wore a long beard, and appeared so weak and drooping and unable to walk, that he was forced to be supported and carried by another person to a table, at which he was then seated among some company who were eating, and one of them sung a song.[7]

This description, if completely accurate, would suggest that *Shakespeare himself* utilized a high degree of what we would today call "natural" acting.

Some clues to the nature of Elizabethan acting may be gathered from the direct evidence of the plays themselves. The most helpful material of this kind comes from Shakespeare's *Hamlet*. At one point in the play, Hamlet speaks to a group of actors on the proper means of playing their roles. It is almost a detailed manual, and it is undoubtedly Shakespeare himself speaking to all actors on the responsibilities of their profession. He was concerned with certain important techniques and goals of acting, and we can note in this speech the following important points:

1. Good articulation is an essential ingredient of acting.
2. Overacting is to be avoided.
3. The good actor finds the proper balance between overacting and underacting.
4. The good actor projects a reasonable suggestion of what we may call "truth" or "nature."
5. The good actor does not act simply for the approval of the majority of his audience. Honesty in acting will be clear to the more discriminating members of the audience.

---

7. Reported in Bernard Grebanier's *Then Came Each Actor* (New York: David McKay, 1975), p. 15.

	HAMLET: Speak the speech, I pray you, as I pronounced it to you,
Point 1	trippingly on the tongue. But if you mouth it, as many of your
	players do, I had as lief the town crier spoke my lines. Nor do not
Point 2	saw the air too much with your hand, thus, but use all gently.

HAMLET: Speak the speech, I pray you, as I pronounced it to you,
Point 1   trippingly on the tongue. But if you mouth it, as many of your
players do, I had as lief the town crier spoke my lines. Nor do not
Point 2   saw the air too much with your hand, thus, but use all gently.
For in the very torrent, tempest, and, as I may say, whirlwind of
your passion, you must acquire and beget a temperance that
may give it smoothness. Oh, it offends me to the soul to hear
a robustious periwig-pated fellow tear a passion to tatters, to
very rags, to split the ears of the groundlings, who for the most
part are capable of nothing but inexplicable dumb shows and
Point 3   noise. . . . Be not too tame neither but let your own discretion be
your tutor. Suit the action to the word, the word to the action,
with this special observance, that you o'erstep not the modesty
Point 4   of nature. For anything so overdone is from the purpose of playing, whose end, both at the first and now, was and is to hold as
t'were the mirror up to Nature—to show Virtue her own feature,
Point 5   scorn her own image, and the very age and body of the time his
form and pressure. Now this overdone or come tardy off,
though it make the unskillful laugh, cannot but make the judi-
cious grieve, the censure of the which one must in your al-
lowance o'erweigh a whole theater of others. . . .

                                    William Shakespeare, *Hamlet*, Act III Sc. 2

Certainly these are important suggestions—as meaningful today in their actual application as they were in the age of Elizabeth I. We must continue to remember that "nature" did not necessarily mean natural or realistic acting in the sense in which we use it today. Theatre conventions change as do acting styles. The comments, nevertheless, indicate a serious concern on Shakespeare's part for the proper performance of his plays. It is one of the first detailed discussions on the art of acting that has validity for our own time as well.

The Seventeenth Century

From the period 1642 to 1660, during the Puritan Commonwealth, the theatres in England were closed or torn down and stage performances were forbidden by order of Parliament. After 1660 when the monarchy was restored (hence the name the Restoration), Charles II was an avid theatre-goer. Partly following the tradition of the past, but breaking new ground as well, the Restoration theatre began a line of continuity that extends to the present British and American theatre. Several noteworthy changes took place during the period of Restoration drama, generally in the last portion of the seventeenth century.

1. Theatres were permanently established indoors.
2. Theatres were artificially lit, primarily by candlelight, though also by oil lamps.

3. A theatre remained lit during the entire performance. If a candle sputtered, either in the house or on stage, an attendant or candle snuffer, "invisible" to the audience by the convention of the day, walked to the appropriate place and attended to the sputtering candle.
4. Women appeared on the English stage.
5. Visiting professional companies (primarily French theatre companies and *commedia* troupes) visited England.
6. Extensive scenery was used in the professional theatre, with wings on either side of the stage and flats that could be moved along grooves in the back.

This type of theatre was one that would seem to lend itself to a *presentational* style of acting, keeping the attention of playgoers even as "orange girls" and sellers of wine and other foods plied their "trade" during performances. In newly enclosed indoor theatres, lit and heated for hours by candles; in an era when bathing was minimal; with constant eating and hawking of food; spectators coming in late for half price and wearing heavy clothing; fops who often poked the feet of actors with their rapiers for amusement—the delights of theatre attendance in the English Restoration can be imagined. Many of the plays written during the Restoration were either overblown tragedies or comedies of manners that portrayed a world of money, elegance, rakes, and dandies. The plots dealt with adultery, attempts at seduction, opportunistic marriage alliances, vanity, flirtation, backbiting, scandals, and general useless frivolity. In this theatre world, a new generation of actors rose to ply their craft.

The most famous, and the best, actor of the Restoration theatre was Thomas Betterton (1635–1710), who not only played most of the roles originally performed by Burbage but also acted in the new plays of the age. Betterton dominated the English theatre until the early eighteenth century and trained many actors and actresses in the craft of acting. Indeed, he is an early and important exponent of rigid actor training. He was known as an actor of great dignity and sincerity and gave his audiences the appearance of being "natural," as opposed to other actors of his day who had a tendency to shout, rant, and "tear a passion to tatters." Samuel Pepys, whose diary gives invaluable first-hand information on Restoration performances and productions, said of Betterton that he had

> . . . a great head, a short thick neck . . . fat short arms, . . . his actions very few, but just. . . . His voice was low and grumbling, yet he could tune it by an artful climax which enforc'd universal attention even from the fops and orange girls.[8]

---

8. Samuel Pepys, *Diary and Correspondence*, 4 vols. (New York: n.d.).

Betterton, himself, had strong ideas about acting, and in comments ascribed to him, spoke about the importance of characterization in acting.

> He [the actor] must adjust every action; he must perfectly express the quality and manners of the man, whose person he assumes . . . A patriot, a prince, a beggar, a clown, etc., must each have their propriety, and distinction in action as well as words and language. An actor therefore . . . must transform himself into every person he represents . . .[9]

Such comments about, and by, Betterton suggest that even in an age when highly rhetorical and bombastic acting was in vogue, used by most performers, an actor who still followed Shakespeare's ideal of holding the "mirror up to nature" was respected as using the ideal approach to the art of acting. However, there were all too few Bettertons in the seventeenth century.

David Garrick: An Actor Speaks

In the two hundred years that followed the Elizabethan age, two names led the honor roll of great actors. Besides Thomas Betterton, who carved for himself one of the most successful careers in the history of acting, the second was David Garrick (1717–1779), undoubtedly the greatest actor of the eighteenth century and one of the most famous in the long tradition of the English-speaking theatre.

The most consistent comment about Garrick was his "naturalness" as an actor. "Naturalism" in Garrick's day, of course, meant something quite different from what it means now. Today we would probably consider Garrick's acting too stylized for our tastes. In the mid-eighteenth century, however, Garrick ushered in a refreshingly new style, diametrically opposed to the older, formalistic school, which required actors and actresses to intone their speeches in a deliberate monotone and in statuesque poses. Garrick brought variety back to acting: his characters differed one from the other, and he actually responded to what was happening on the stage around him. Today we take this all for granted, but in Garrick's time it was a distinct break with tradition. The earlier style had persisted since the mid-seventeenth century in imitation of French declamatory acting. To the great roles Garrick brought a new vitality and energy; in some ways he seemed to create a tradition that has extended to our own day.

Those who had the opportunity to watch Garrick have left ample evidence of his effectiveness as an actor. Early in his career he chose to perform in a play with his great rival James Quin, the champion of the older, declam-

---

9. Charles Giddon, *The Life of Thomas Betterton* (London: Printed for Robert Gosling, 1710).

David Garrick.

atory style. Quin was first on stage: the fat and aging actor recited the dialogue in a sing-song oratorical manner punctuated by a few mechanical gestures and stilted poses. A schoolboy in the audience, later to become a noted playwright himself, watched the exciting duel of personalities. Richard Cumberland wrote of that evening: "I beheld little Garrick, young and light and alive in every muscle and every feature, come bounding on the stage—heavens, what a transition!—it seemed as if a whole century had been stepped over in the transition of a single scene!"[10]

One of the most penetrating appraisals of David Garrick's acting came from the novelist Henry Fielding in his novel *Tom Jones*. During a performance of Garrick in *Hamlet*, the actor's projected terror at seeing the ghost of Hamlet's father almost made the audience forget they were watching a stage performance. In the novel, the unsophisticated Partridge, however, saw little to commend in the performance. "Why," he said, "I could act as well as he myself. I am sure if I had seen a ghost, I should have looked in the very same

---

10. Richard Cumberland, *Memoirs*, 2 vols. (London: Lockington, Allen, 1807).

manner and done just as he did." To Henry Fielding and his contemporaries, Garrick was an outstanding "naturalistic" actor.

Garrick knew, however, that there was no short cut to acting. All the great moments so admired by others in his performances were the result of concentrated study and attention paid to the most exacting detail. Garrick often resorted to pranks and game-playing to add to his dimensions as an actor, as the following story attests. While walking with some friends, he came to the top of a hill and began to gaze at the sky, muttering aloud, "I have never seen two before." Passersby stopped to look at Garrick and then looked in the direction where he was gazing. Upon being asked what Garrick was looking at, the actor said nothing but, "I have never seen two before." Before long a crowd had gathered on the hill looking off in the direction of Garrick's stare and exchanging comments. One stranger told another that there were obviously two storks in the distance, while another claimed that he saw only one. As Garrick began to play the role of a madman, he studied the faces of those looking at him, and later reassured his friends that he had been studying the faces of the passersby and had gained quite a few hints that would be of use to him as an actor.[11]

Fortunately we have some of Garrick's own words concerning the art of acting; they remain highly instructive. He consistently returns to the idea that study, observation, and integrity are the paths that lead to a successful stage career.

> The only way to arrive at great excellence in characters of humor, is to be very conversant with human nature, that is the noblest and best study, by this way you will more accurately discover the workings of spirit (or what other physical term you please to call it) upon the different modifications of matter.[12]

To a fellow actor Garrick gave this advice:

> Study hard, my friend, for [several] years, and you may play the rest of your life. I would advise you to read at your leisure other books besides plays in which you are concerned . . .[13]

Garrick believed strongly in the integrity of the good actor, and we find a distinct echo of Hamlet's advice to the players when Garrick also wrote:

> Do not sacrifice your taste and feelings to the applause of the multitude; a true genius will convert an audience to his manner, rather than be converted by them to what is false and unnatural . . .[14]

---

11. Reported in Grebanier, *Then Came Each Actor*, p. 94.
12. David Garrick, *An Essay on Acting* (London: Printed for W. Beckerton, 1744), p. 2.
13. David Garrick, *The Private Correspondence of David Garrick with the Most Celebrated Persons of His Times*, ed. James Boaden (London: Henry Colburn and Richard Bentley, 1831), vol. 1, p. 178.
14. Ibid.

A comment by a member of the audience at a performance of Garrick as Macbeth would do justice to any modern-day actor: "Every sentence rose in his mind and showed itself in his countenance before he uttered a word." A dedicated actor and reformer of the stage and acting, David Garrick is surely one of the great figures in the long and colorful history of the theatre.

The Great Debate—Emotion vs. Reason

One of the most persistent questions debated by actors everywhere is: Should an actor actually feel the emotions of the character he or she is portraying? It would be simple to take a poll of any group of actors to discover just how diversified the views on this subject are. Perhaps the most controversial book ever written on the subject was Denis Diderot's *The Paradox of Acting*, which served as the major argument of the anti-emotionalists and the prime target of the emotionalists.

Diderot—The Paradox of Acting

Although Diderot never acted professionally, he was nevertheless deeply interested in the theatre. He brought to his examination of the problem the same meticulous care shown in his labors on the *Encyclopédie*, the most prodigious work of scholarship of the eighteenth century. His short book *The Paradox of Acting* was not published until 1830, forty-six years after his death. It made a profound impression on actors at the time, and its translation into English by Walter Herries Pollock in 1883 stirred considerable debate among American and English actors. It is still stimulating and vital reading for anyone seriously interested in the art of acting.

It was because of a meeting with Garrick when the great English actor visited France in 1773 that Diderot set about to develop his famous paradox. Even before this time Diderot believed that the French stage needed greater vitality and energy through the use of emotional acting.

Garrick's success and technique were especially interesting to Diderot's enquiring mind. Here was an actor who planned every movement and response carefully and seemed to leave nothing to chance. His most startling and moving effects were achieved entirely by technique. Indeed, Garrick's comment that a good actor could as easily make love to a wooden table as to a beautiful woman gave Diderot food for thought. It was clearly the triumph of technique over what at the time seemed lack of emotional truth. Today, of course, we know that the film actor might say exactly the same thing that Garrick said, only substituting the word *camera* for *table*. Diderot also was aware that many actors and actresses acted by impulse. A performance might be electrifying one day and lackluster the next.

Diderot's contention, in his *Paradox*, was that the actor should never "feel" the role. The actor must be an "unmoved and disinterested onlooker. He must have, consequently, penetration and no sensibility."[15] The reason for this, Diderot indicated, was the actor's responsibility to sustain a performance night after night. He wrote:

> If the actor were full, really full, of feeling, how could he play the same part twice running with the same spirit and success? Full of fire at the first performance, he would be worn out and cold as marble at the third . . . what confirms me in this view is the unequal acting of players who play from the heart. From them you must expect no unity. . . . On the other hand, the actor who plays from thought . . . will be one and the same at all performances, will be always at his best mark; he has considered, combined, learnt and arranged the whole thing in his head.[16]

To the objection that feeling the role often produces a moving experience for both actor and audience, Diderot responded with a pointed illustration that is also a plea for a well-developed technique for acting:

> You give a recitation in a drawing room; your feelings are stirred . . . you burst into tears . . . you were carried away, you surprised and touched your hearers, you made a great hit. All this is true enough. But now transfer your easy tone, your simple expression, your everyday bearing, to the stage, and I assure you, you will be paltry and weak. You may cry to your heart's content, and the audience will only laugh.[17]

To make sure that no one missed his point, Diderot summed up the case as concisely as possible. "I hold to my point, and I tell you this: Extreme sensibility makes middling actors; middling sensibility makes the ruck of bad actors; in complete absence of sensibility is the possibility of a sublime actor."[18]

Naturally, when Diderot's *Paradox* was published, actors supported or denounced its thesis vigorously. Some insisted that, because he himself had never been an actor, Diderot was unaware of the means by which many actors achieved great moments on the stage.

Constant Coquelin

The most celebrated defender of Diderot's *Paradox* was Constant Coquelin (1841–1909), the French actor for whom Edmond Rostand wrote *Cyrano de*

---

15. Denis Diderot, "The Paradox of Acting" (1830) from *The Paradox of Acting—Masks or Faces* (New York: Hill and Wang, 1957), p. 14.

16. Ibid., pp. 14–15.

17. Ibid., pp. 20–21.

18. Ibid., p. 20.

Ten Nights in a Barroom, **nineteenth-century melodrama. Directed by Stanley Kahan, California State University, Long Beach.**

Bergerac—the play in which Coquelin achieved his greatest success in a long and illustrious career. Coquelin was an actor of persevering attention to detail and intellectual control.[19] In his comments about the use of emotion on the stage, Coquelin suggested that the actor had a dual personality, one self being the player, the second self the instrument. The first self, or the one that sees, should be the master over the second self, or the one that executes. The more absolute the subjugation to the first self, the supreme ruler or ruling intellect, the greater is the artist. Coquelin clearly believed in Diderot's doctrine of the rule of the intellect over feeling, as his following comment indicates:

> The actor should remain master of himself. Even when the public, carried away by his action, conceives him to be abandoned to his passion, he should be able to see what he is doing, to judge of his effects, and to control himself—in short, he should never feel the shadow of the sentiments to which he is giving ex-

---

19. American drama critic George Jean Nathan noted that Coquelin was "the only actor who ever lived who proved that he had a critical mind in the appraisal of acting."

pression at the very instant that he is representing them with the utmost power and truth. . . . The actor ought never to let his part "run away" with him—if you have no more consciousness where you are and what you are doing—you have ceased to be an actor; you are a madman.[20]

Just as Diderot's *Paradox* had created a stir among actors, so too did Coquelin's views when they were published. Sir Henry Irving, the celebrated English contemporary of Coquelin, and an "emotionalist," answered Coquelin in print with withering sarcasm, and the argument continued in the leading journals of the day.

Tommaso Salvini

The most eloquent rebuttal, however, came from the greatest of Italian actors, Tommaso Salvini (1829–1915). Salvini projected such vitality and energy in his performances that fellow actors as well as audiences were deeply moved. Salvini's acting was an important factor in stimulating Constantin Stanislavski to develop his well-known system of acting, of which we shall say more in the next chapter. Salvini firmly believed that the actor must *feel* a role in order to move the audience. Without this feeling, the actor could not expect to recreate the same sentiments in the audience. On this point Salvini wrote:

> I believe, then, that every great actor ought to be and is, moved by the emotion he portrays; that not only must he feel this emotion once or twice, or when he is studying the part, but that he must feel it in a greater or less degree—and to just that degree will he move the hearts of his audiences—whenever he plays the part, be it once or a thousand times.[21]

Salvini was well aware of Coquelin's philosophy of emotion on stage, and, although he admired the French actor, he believed that his great weakness was his refusal or inability to feel his role. Salvini attacked Coquelin directly on this issue:

> Accomplished and versatile an artist as he is [Coquelin], I have been struck more than once, as I enjoyed the pleasure of his performance, with the thought that something amid all the brilliancy of execution was lacking. . . . The actor who does not feel the emotion he portrays is but a skillful mechanician, setting in motion certain wheels and springs which may give his lay figure such an appearance of life that the observer is tempted to exclaim, "How marvelous! Were it only alive it would make me laugh or weep."[22]

---

20. Benoit Constant Coquelin, "Acting and Actors," *Harper's New Monthly Magazine*, May 1887, pp. 891–909.

21. Tommaso Salvini, "Some Views on Acting," *Theatre Workshop*, October 1936, pp. 73–78.

22. Ibid.

Salvini, however, did not believe that actors should lose themselves in the role. He believed that the actor must feel the emotions of the character but that there must always be the element of *restraint* to help the actor keep the ultimate objective in mind—not only to feel but to make the audience feel as well.

This great debate is not ended. It continues in the green room, in newspapers and magazines, and, of course, in the classroom. One conclusion we may reach is that actors have been able to express themselves successfully despite differing views on this point. Each actor synthesizes some technique in a manner that suits his or her personality and emotional makeup. Some actors feel a great deal, some feel only a little, and some do not feel at all. For those who believe that somewhere there must be a compromise, a middle ground between the "emotionalists" and the "rationalists" in acting, there are the reassuring words of Joseph Jefferson. His famous comment was brief but to the point—and he meant to refer only to himself, without attempting to indoctrinate anyone. It is the perfect compromise and a good starting point for any actor: *"For myself, I know that I act best when the heart is warm and the head is cool."*

Short Notes on the Heritage of Some Notable Actors

Thespis (fl. sixth century B.C.E.) Greek.　A Greek poet who is generally credited with adding the first actor into choral chants or *dithyrambs* during the Dionysian Theatre Festival held in Athens. He won the prize at the first tragic contest in 534 B.C.E. The term *Thespian* recalls his talents and evolved from nineteenth-century journalistic references to acting and actors.

Roscius (d. 62 B.C.E.) Roman.　The most famous actor of antiquity, particularly reknowned in comedy. Cicero praised his technical prowess as an actor, as one who thought out all his effects "in a manner befitting the occasion, and so done as to move and enchant all who saw and heard him." He was awarded a gold ring, the symbol of a rank equivalent to a knighthood, by the Roman dictator Sulla. Shakespeare makes reference to him in *Hamlet*, and many actors have since been praised by being called the "New Roscius," the "Young Roscius," the "African Roscius," and the like.

Will Kemp(e) (d. 1603) English.　Noted Elizabethan comic actor who performed many of the low-life or clown characters in the plays of the late sixteenth century. Many of Shakespeare's broad comic roles in his early plays were likely written specifically for Kempe.

Richard Burbage (c. 1567–1619) English.　A shareholder in the Lord Chamberlain's Company and later the King's Men, the same companies in which

Shakespeare held shares. Accounted the greatest actor of his era, it is very probable that Shakespeare wrote many of his greatest roles for this actor, of obviously prodigious range, including Hamlet, King Lear, Richard III, Othello, Macbeth, and perhaps even Falstaff. He also appeared in the first performances of plays by Thomas Kyd, Ben Jonson, John Webster, and others.

Edward Alleyn (1566–1626) English. A member of a competing theatrical company during the period of Shakespeare's early creative output, he nevertheless performed in plays by Shakespeare. He is considered the only rival to the preeminence of Burbage. Best roles were in Marlowe's *Dr. Faustus* and *Tamburlaine*.

Thomas Betterton (1635?–1710) English. Best actor of the English "Restoration Theatre" (c. 1660–1700), equally adept at playing both tragedy and comedy. He was married to Mary Sanderson (?–1712), one of the first women to appear professionally on the English stage. Betterton was admired particularly as Hamlet and as Sir Toby Belch in *Twelfth Night*.

Molière (1622–1673) French (also playwright). The greatest figure in the history of the French theatre, Molière began as a travelling actor in the provinces before coming to the notice and then under the protection of King Louis XIV. He excelled in comedy, particularly in roles of his own creation in such plays as *Tartuffe*, *The Misanthrope*, and *The Doctor in Spite of Himself*. The national theatre of France, the *Comédie-Française*, dates its existence back to Molière's troupe of actors. Ironically Molière suffered a fatal tubercular hemorrhage on stage during a performance in the title role of *The Imaginary Invalid*. He was carried home to die in the chair in which he was sitting during the performance he insisted on finishing.

Anne Bracegirdle (1673–1748) English. One of the earliest of English actresses, she was a pupil of Betterton. She was most adept in the playing of comedy, particularly in the plays of Congreve, such as *Love for Love* and *The Way of the World*.

Charles Macklin (1697?–1797) Irish-English. Long-lived Irish actor who, with Garrick, helped to infuse a higher degree of realism into English acting of the eighteenth century. Best remembered for converting the role of Shylock in *The Merchant of Venice* from that of low comedian to that of a tragic villain. His last performance on stage occurred in 1789 when he was at least almost ninety years of age. He was unable to finish due to failing memory and left the stage after a moving plea to the audience for forgiveness.

David Garrick (1717–1779) English. Greatest English actor of the eighteenth century and generally regarded as one of the finest actors in the history of performance. His ebullient style and energetic, detailed characterizations modelled on the concept of "observation of nature" were landmark innovations for his age. His work was also much admired on the European continent, where serious studies were made attempting to define his art. He was a superior actor in both tragedy and comedy and despite shortness of stature triumphed as Hamlet, Richard III, and most particularly as King Lear. He also was a theatre manager at London's Drury Lane and instituted changes in acting and production styles not only for this company but ultimately for the profession as well. He was buried in Westminster Abbey.

Peg Woffington (c. 1718–1760) Irish-English. Celebrated eighteenth-century actress who excelled in English comedies and in performances of "breeches" roles, or roles in which she played male parts. An intimate friend of both Garrick and Macklin, she did not follow their new style of acting but remained during her comparatively short lifetime a superior performer in high comedy. She was reputed to be the most beautiful woman of her time.

Mrs. Sarah Siddons [nee Sarah Kemble] (1755–1831) English. The greatest of English tragediennes and still celebrated as one of the most important performers ever to appear on the English stage. Sister of distinguished actors John Philip Kemble and Charles Kemble, she was acclaimed by writer Samuel Johnson, and Joshua Reynolds painted her as "The Tragic Muse," one of the most famous paintings of the eighteenth century. She was praised for her great nobility of bearing, beauty, and tender qualities. According to contemporary reports she was unexcelled as Lady Macbeth. Critic Leigh Hunt described her acting as a type of "natural carelessness." Her carefully planned performances seemed to be "the result of the impassioned moment; one can hardly imagine that there has been any such thing as a rehearsal."

John Philip Kemble (1757–1823) English. Younger brother of Mrs. Siddons, Kemble's performances were more concerned with external effects, classical poses, and "nobility of style." An important actor-manager, he excelled in roles calling for aristocratic bearing and elocution. His most celebrated roles were those of Hamlet and Coriolanus, whom he portrayed in a sustained intensity of emotion rather than a variety of feeling or mood.

François-Joseph Talma (1763–1826) French. Major French actor of the eighteenth century. He was educated in England and returned to France shortly before the French Revolution. His impassioned performances of revolutionary speeches in the theatre aroused audiences to fever pitch. He instituted many changes on the French stage, particularly in costuming under the influence of the painter David and in a more "natural" speaking of French metered verse. He assisted Napoleon in drawing up a new code for the

Comédie-Française, where his acting greatly influenced all his contemporaries. He appeared many times in London despite the tumult of the Napoleonic Wars and was a guest of honor at John Philip Kemble's farewell in 1817. He particularly excelled in the performance of both English and French tragedy.

Edmund Kean (1787–1833) English. The epitome of the nineteenth-century Romantic actor, Kean was by all accounts an electrifying performer, revitalizing the English stage from the elocutionary style of John Philip Kemble. Although he was frequently drunk and barely able to set foot on stage, his magnetic personality charmed a generation of theatre goers. Samuel Taylor Coleridge said that to see this little man with an unattractive voice perform was to see a role revealed by "flashes of lightning"; the comment suggests uneven but inspired moments in his performances. Others feared he would reduce his characters to what "he calls the level of real life." His greatest roles were Macbeth, Iago, Shylock, and Richard III. He collapsed on stage in 1833 during a performance of *Othello*, with his son Charles in the role of Iago, and died a few weeks later.

Edwin Forrest (1806–1872) American. First native-born American actor to achieve international status as an actor of the first rank. Powerfully built, he evidently performed in an elocutionary manner that emulated the style of early nineteenth-century English actors. His best roles were in the classic tragedies, but he also played for years the title role in a play about a native American, *Metamora*, which he brought to the prairie towns of America.

Joseph Jefferson (1829–1905) American. The third actor of this name (earlier actors being his father and his grandfather), he was one of the most beloved of American actors. He is best remembered as the portrayer of a distinct American character type, Rip Van Winkle. He played the role consistently for over forty years, representing a tradition of a star identified with a single role that is not dissimilar to traditions in television today.

Tommaso Salvini (1829–1915) Italian. Salvini possessed an "eminently expressive face, graceful and noble bearing," and great power in his performances of the major tragedies, particularly in the role of Othello. He achieved an international reputation, performing in his native Italian throughout Europe and North and South America. His passionate performances strongly influenced Stanislavski, who regarded him as the most "truthful" actor of his generation.

Edwin Booth (1833–1893) American. The finest American actor of the nineteenth century and certainly one of the most distinguished figures in the history of acting. His father, English actor Junius Brutus Booth, had emigrated to Maryland early in the century when he realized he could not compete with the preeminence of Edmund Kean. Three of the senior Booth children became actors, one of whom, John Wilkes Booth, is remembered as the assassin of Abraham Lincoln. Edwin Booth excelled in a wide repertory of roles, became an important theatre manager, and raised the level of American acting to a standard equal to the greatest European actors. He also presaged a new, more natural, less rhetorical type of acting that was unique among his contemporaries. After his death his house in Gramercy Park, New York City, became the home of the Player's Club, which still occupies the site. He was the most famous of all interpreters of Hamlet, having given one hundred performances of it in 1864, a record that stood until the 1920s when it was eclipsed by John Barrymore.

Henry Irving (1838–1905) English.   The dominant English actor of the second half of the nineteenth century, who with Ellen Terry as his professional partner scored triumphs in many classic roles and melodramas of the period. His management of and performances at the Lyceum Theatre, London, maintained the highest standards of the English theatre. He was the first actor to be knighted, an honor bestowed upon him and the profession by Queen Victoria in 1895.

Constant Coquelin (1841–1905) French.   Major actor of the *Comédie-Française* during the last portion of the nineteenth century. A large man with a large voice, he made his reputation in Molière's comic masterpieces, but he is best remembered as the actor for whom Rostand wrote *Cyrano de Bergerac*, one of the most flamboyant and romantic plays and parts in the theatre repertoire.

More Actors and Actresses

James Quin
  English (1693–1766)
George Frederick Cooke
  English (1745–1812)
William Charles Macready
  English (1793–1873)
Ira Aldridge
  American (1804–1867)
Adelaide Ristori
  Italian (1822–1906)

Charles Fechter
  German (1824–1879)
Helena Modjeska
  Polish (1844–1909)
Ellen Terry
  English (1847–1928)
Richard Mansfield
  American (1857–1907)

SUGGESTIONS FOR FURTHER READING

Barkworth, Peter. *About Acting.* North Pomfret, VT: David and Charles, 1980.

Callow, Simon. *Acting in Restoration Comedy*, ed. Maria Aitken. New York: Applause Theatre Book Publishers, 1988.

———. *Being an Actor.* New York: St. Martin, 1986.

Cole, Toby, & Helen Krich Chinoy, eds. *Actors on Acting.* New York: Crown Publishers, 1954.

Duerr, Edwin. *The Length and Depth of Acting.* New York: Holt, Rinehart and Winston, 1962.

Eynat-Confino, Irene. *Beyond the Mask: Edward Gordon Craig, Movement and the Actor.* Carbondale, IL: Southern Illinois University Press, 1987.

Harris, Julie. *Julie Harris Talks with Young Actors.* New York: Lothrop, Lee & Shepard, 1971.

Joseph, Bertram L. *Acting Shakespeare.* London: Routledge and Kegan Paul, 1960.

———. *Elizabethan Acting*, 2nd ed. London: Oxford University Press, 1964.

Olivier, Laurence. *On Acting.* New York: Simon and Schuster, 1987.

Redgrave, Michael. *The Actor's Ways and Means.* New York: Theatre Arts Books, 1979.

Roach, Joseph R. *The Player's Passion: Studies in the Science of Acting.* Cranbury, NJ: University of Delaware Press, Associated University Presses, 1985.

Seyler, Athene. *The Craft of Comedy* (correspondence between Athene Seyler and Stephen Haggard). New York: Theatre Arts, 1946.

Worthen, William. *The Idea of the Actor.* Princeton, NJ: Princeton University Press, 1984.

CHAPTER
THREE

Stanislavski and Beyond

> *Salvini approached the platform of the doges, thought a little while, concentrated himself and, unnoticed by any of us, took the entire audience of the Great Theatre into his hands. It seemed he did this with a single gesture—that he stretched his hand without looking into the public, grasped all of us in his palm, and held us there as if we were ants or flies. He closed his fist, and we felt the breath of death; he opened it, and we knew the warmth of bliss.*
>
> Stanislavski's observations on Salvini in the role of Othello

Constantin Stanislavski (1863–1938) was one of the most important theorists as well as one of the most practical men of the theatre. His work has profoundly influenced acting in the twentieth century. His name is known to those both in and out of the theatre, not only for his important contributions but as the focal point of the continuing debate about the actor and the question of emotional identification with a role.

Unfortunately, the work of Stanislavski is misunderstood by many who believe that he advocated feeling the role to the point of ignoring conventional stage training and technique. Because the work of Stanislavski should be understood by all actors, whether they subscribe to his theories or not, some consideration of it will be undertaken here. It is dangerous to attempt to synthesize all of Stanislavski's work in a few pages; this will not be attempted here. His work should be placed in proper perspective, however, and such a discussion may serve to stimulate further investigation.

Stanislavski was a moderately successful actor on the Russian stage during the late nineteenth and early twentieth centuries. In 1898 he established, with his Russian colleagues, the Moscow Art Theatre. Here he acted in and produced dramas of international origin, although special attention was given to his fellow countrymen Anton Chekhov and Maxim Gorki. (Much of Stanislavski's early career and the development of the Moscow Art Theatre can be traced in his autobiography, *My Life in Art*.) It was at this point in his career that he began to put into practice many of the theories that had stimulated him for years.

The fact that Stanislavski was a producer and director as well as an actor gave him a broader view of the problem of creating successful theatrical characterizations. For years he had been dissatisfied with his own acting; he had fallen more and more into the habit of using artificial tricks and devices rather than finding the basic truth in his characterizations. He felt this failing as a director as well, for too often he simply had imposed his will on other actors without permitting them the freedom of their own imagination and creative impulses. He was convinced that there must be a means by which the actor could avoid the tyranny of stage habits and conventionalized external devices. Above all he knew that it was necessary to refine ideas that would help actors work in the new realistic and naturalistic theatre forms that were emerging in the ferment of the late nineteenth century. New techniques were vital for the Ibsen and post-Ibsen period of European theatre.

As an actor Stanislavski was aware that some performances were better than others: that on a certain night he would give a truly memorable performance, only to follow it the next evening with an uneven or a poor one. Merely feeling the part was not enough, for there would be some evenings when he might feel physically better than others, and some evenings when that "magic spark" would come and some evenings when it might not. We can see how his thinking in one way parallels that of Diderot—who insisted, however, that emotion should be ruled out of the actor's performances entirely. Stanislavski's approach to the problem was quite different. Certainly, he believed, the actor must feel, but how can the actor be sure of feeling just the right thing at the right time on any given night, and would that feeling be truthful?

His solution was to develop a course of study, or a "system," that required more mental and physical discipline than most actors had ever experienced before. Although this system was originally designed for actors who already knew all the basic techniques of stage movement, composition, and the essential controls of body and voice, it has since developed into a complete method for actors on all levels of proficiency. The important fact that has been so often overlooked in Stanislavski's system is that the entire method should be studied, with proper attention devoted to all the important elements.

The Stanislavski system can be divided into two equal parts. The first concerns the *external,* or the development of proper stage technique and correct management of body and voice. This area includes ballet, acrobatics, stage movement, voice placement, diction, relaxation, and other related elements. The second part concerns the *internal,* or such areas as concentration, observation, imagination, and the use of emotional memory to help create a character from the inside as well as from the outside.

Stanislavski expounded his system in three books, *An Actor Prepares* (1936), *Building a Character* (1949), and *Creating a Role* (1961). The first deals with the internal aspects of his method and the second with the external, whereas the more recent publication, posthumously edited from his notes, is

Saturday, Sunday, Monday, by Eduardo De Filippo, directed by Franco Zefirelli, National Theatre. L to R: Joan Plowright, Laurence Olivier, Frank Finlay. Photograph by Britain on View Photographic Library.

a working manual helpful in the actual creation of a role on the stage. It serves to put his basic principles to the test of the living performance. Unfortunately the books were not published together, and until *Building a Character* was published the Stanislavski system was represented only by the book that dealt with internal acting. It is no wonder that confusion over Stanislavski's system developed and continues even to this day. The two parts of the system should be used together, with equal

> *I came to understand that creativeness begins from that moment when in the soul and imagination of the actor there appears the magical, creative if.*
>
> Stanislavski

emphasis on internal and external elements during the early stages. The system, in order to be used properly, requires many years of work and concentration, and even then it may not prove successful for all actors. Stanislavski said, "If it works for you, fine; if not—throw it away."

There is little that is really new in the Stanislavski system. It is an orderly compilation of the ideas and techniques that actors have always used, consciously or unconsciously. It was the sifting and organizing of these ideas that made Stanislavski's contribution so important. Stanislavski has written:

> You would be as justified to call a system any method of study that provides the ways and means to real creative work if only they are dealt with in a consistent manner. In my system we apply ourselves to the study of the powers and feelings which are inherited in man.[1]

The "Method"

Much has been written about the Method and Method actors, much of it very good and much that is distorted and confusing.

Associated with Method acting are such well-known and successful performers as Marlon Brando, Shelley Winters, Anthony Franciosa, Karl Malden, Ben Gazzara, Al Pacino, and Robert DeNiro. The term *Method* as used in this context is synonymous with *system*,

> *There is a mixture of anarchy and discipline in the way I work.*
>
> Robert De Niro

or more specifically the Stanislavski system. A Method actor, therefore, is one who has studied and is utilizing the Stanislavski system. There are many advocates of the Stanislavski training system in the United States, but

---

1. Quoted in David Margarshack, *Stanislavsky on the Art of the Stage* (London: Faber and Faber, 1950).

perhaps the best-known American training school devoted to teaching this system has been the Actor's Studio. In addition to the Actor's Studio, the late Lee Strasberg, Stella Adler, and Sanford Meisner worked effectively in utilizing aspects of the system in their teaching.

In the 1930s the Group Theatre in New York became the first American

One Flew over the Cuckoo's Nest by Dale Wasserman. **California State University Theatre, Long Beach. Directed by Ken Rugg. Photograph by Keith Ian Polakoff.**

professional theatre organization to use the Stanislavski system in producing its plays. Born of the depression, the Group Theatre disbanded in the 1940s, but its actors carried its spirit to other parts of the theatrical world. Luther Adler, Franchot Tone, John Garfield, Lee J. Cobb, Morris Carnovksy, Elia Kazan, Harold Clurman, and others continued to be vital influences in our theatre and encouraged those interested in learning more about the system they had used so successfully.

In 1947 Elia Kazan, Robert Lewis, and Cheryl Crawford started the Actor's Studio in order to provide a training ground for actors incorporating the principles that had guided the acting of the Group Theatre. Among those who attended classes the first year at the Actor's Studio were Marlon Brando, Montgomery Clift, Tom Ewell, John Forsythe, Mildred Dunnock, Karl Malden, and Maureen Stapleton.

There have even been major differences of opinion as to what the true Stanislavski system entailed, with Lee Strasberg strongly emphasizing the importance of emotional memory, Stella Adler stressing imagination, and Sanford Meisner emphasizing the necessity of keeping the performance moving from moment to moment. Harold Clurman, one of the founders of the Group Theatre, stated the case most clearly, when he wrote in 1980 that "... the so-called Stanislavski system ... has been and will continue to be an approach to acting in continuous evolution and never quite the same with any particular teacher or director. There is NO RIGHT WAY."[2]

Unfortunately there are those who have made of the Method something of a fetish. There are those who, misunderstanding the basic dogma of Stanislavski's teachings, complain, "I can't do it this way—I don't feel it," and there are those who have justly been classified as mumblers. This has

> *Acting is a question of absorbing other people's personalities and some of your own experience.*
>
> Paul Newman

produced a humorous picture in the public mind of some Method performers that is unfortunate, if not wholly undeserved. However, we must not lose sight of the fact that serious and exhaustive work on the Stanislavski system *as a whole* has given the theatre some of its finest actors. The Stanislavski Method is really one technique of acting. As Estelle Parsons, another student of the Actor's Studio, has commented:

> For a person like me—and I suspect for anyone who is any good—the material itself is inspiring enough to create its own emotions.[3]

---

2. Harold Clurman in Robert Lewis, *Advice to the Players* (New York: Harper and Row, 1980), p. xv.

3. Estelle Parsons in Joanmarie Kalter, *Actors on Acting* (New York: Sterling, 1979), p. 212.

Clearly Miss Parsons has her own way of working, as do all fine performers. There are many approaches to making the actor aware of his or her potential, and none is an end; each is only a means toward developing effective expression on the stage.

After Stanislavski

Although even Stanislavski himself would have agreed that his system was not the only means of training an actor, his impact on American acting has been very significant, perhaps more so here than in any country outside of Russia. However, there have been a number of major alternative approaches to the question of how the actor should best work in the theatre, and it would be useful to look at some of these twentieth-century concepts that have had profound repercussions in the study of acting.

Bertolt Brecht and Alienation

One of the major playwrights of the twentieth century was Bertolt Brecht (1898–1956), who made major conceptual leaps beyond the prevailing realistic theatre of his day. Brecht believed that the primary function of the theatre was to instruct, to convey the playwright's message to his audience. Unfortunately Brecht felt that audiences became so emotionally identified with the actor within his role that they ceased to think and instead were overcome by feeling or empathy for the performer. In his plays Brecht sought to separate the subject of the dramatic piece from the illusion of reality, by breaking the sequence of the action, raising and lowering tension, and introducing placards and songs to continually remind the audience that they were in a theatre and *not* watching real life. His basic theory, *Verfremdungseffekt*, usually translated as *alienation effect* or, perhaps better yet, *strangeness*, sought to keep the audience critically detached from the action on stage. The actor, consequently, needed to stand outside the character he was portraying, reminding the audience that he is an actor who is part of a theatrical event, rather than a "slice of real life." The Brechtian actor sets out to establish a relationship with the audience in frankly theatrical terms and consciously utilizes theatrical devices to sustain both the immediacy of the performance and contact with the audience.

Running counter to the Stanislavski system, Brecht's ideas have gradually transformed much of world theatre in the last half of the twentieth century. The Stanislavski system, which is particularly well suited to the needs of the realistic theatre and modern film technique, has given the actor and his or her character a psychological and social history to work from but often leaves the actor in difficulty in nonrealistic theatre forms. Many modern plays

Good Woman of Setzuan by Bertolt Brecht. Department of Drama, College of Fine Arts, Carnegie Mellon University. Directed by Anthony McKay.

deal with fragmented experience, the multiplicity of human nature, and utilize a nonlinear narrative style. This new narrative style started as early as the first years of the twentieth century with August Strindberg's *A Dream Play* (1902) and has been carried on through the absurd drama of the 1960s and 1970s. The work of Genet, Pinter, and others reinforces many of Brecht's ideas. Laurence Olivier fused both approaches superbly, and he has been called both an ideal Stanislavski and/or Brecht actor. English theatre critic Michael Billington described Olivier's power to affect an audience in a performance of *Coriolanus* by Shakespeare in these words: "[It] was a classic example of a Brechtian performance in that he indicated to us through myriad detail that the martial hero was emotionally flawed by his attachment to his mother's apron strings." What Billington points out is that Olivier was also commenting on his character as an actor—that "much of one's pleasure lies in the fact one *is* so conscious of Olivier's sharp ironic presence."[4]

The memorable Royal Shakespeare Company's eight-hour production of Dickens' *Nicholas Nickleby*, which played in London and throughout the

---

4. Michael Billington, *The Modern Actor* (London: Hamish Hamilton, 1973), p. 199.

United States, and was televised in a marathon number of evenings, was superbly conceived in Brechtian terms. Not only did a small company play 150 roles in the long production, but the actors told the audience at the outset that it too should join in the fun, they bombarded the audience with fresh buns from the stage, and cast members often wandered into the house to chat with those fortunate enough to be sitting on the aisles.

Artaud, Grotowski, and Others

Many actors and directors have made stimulating and exciting attempts to bring actors back to the most fundamental and primitive qualities of their being and to tap their inner resources, buried in the subconscious. Antonin Artaud (1896–1948), director and actor, envisaged a Theatre of Cruelty, where, by the reduction of language to a minimum and reliance on symbolic gesture, pantomime, sound, and rhythm the actor could find common roots to communicate to the audience on the most primal level. When mankind is most violent and cruel, he argued, mankind is closest to its true self, which it seldom wants to confront honestly, particularly in the theatre. Using many of these

Marat/Sade by Peter Weiss. California State University, Long Beach, directed by Michael Lyman.

Variations on Measure for Measure. **Freely adapted by
Charles Marowitz after William Shakespeare.
California Repertory Theatre, California State
University, Long Beach, directed by Charles Marowitz.
Photo by Keith Ian Polakoff.**

ideas, stage director Peter Brook developed his memorable production of
Peter Weiss's *Marat/Sade,* which contained a reenactment of actual paratheatrical events that took place in the early nineteenth century in the
Charenton Insane Asylum under the
direction of the notorious Marquis de
Sade. Before the cast ever saw the
script of the play they studied the
paintings and etchings of Breughel,
Hogarth, and Goya and studied films
and books on madness. Glenda Jackson, a member of the original cast,
said: "We were all convinced that we
were going loony." The basic idea, however, to strip away the artifice and
pretense that often serves as our armour against the world, was fundamental to getting to the core of the actor. Taking their cue from Artaud, modern

> *I am able to play monsters well. I under-
> stand monsters. I understand madmen. I
> can understand what makes people tick
> in these darker levels.*
>
> Sir Anthony Hopkins

directors Peter Brook and Charles Marowitz have experimented widely with the important theoretical question of what precisely is theatre language.

In a related though somewhat different vein the Polish theatre director Jerzy Grotowski envisages a theatre in which the actor is paramount—actors possessed of every mental and physical attribute available, through group-ings, mime, intonation, harmony, chanting, and absolute total commitment and discipline. Grotowski's "Poor Theatre," as he calls it, is the stripping away of every nonessential in the theatre, leaving only those elements that arouse and disturb the spectator, forcing the audience into a process of self-analysis. The recent work of director Peter Brook has been strongly influ-enced by Grotowski and Artaud, as has that of Broadway choreographer and director Jerome Robbins. Charles Marowitz and his college productions of Shakespeare have continued this exploration of both the theoretical and prac-tical boundaries of theatrical experience.

The Director and Freedom for the Actor

The actor must ultimately work with a director, who will assume responsi-bility for the fundamental approach to any production. Some directors con-trol the production to the extent that they feel it necessary to dictate every movement and gesture of the actor; they will insist that lines be read in ex-actly the manner that they indicate. The most articulate defender of this point of view is Gordon Craig, who has gone so far as to suggest that the human actor could give way to the "super-marionette," which would be able to exe-cute a role perfectly without any of the failings of a human competitor: under no circumstances would the actor be permitted to create for him- or herself. Such directors feel that only one individual should be responsible for the total design and execution of the play. This type of director-actor relationship, they believe, should exist not only for the beginning actor but for the most ex-perienced actor as well. "The finer the actor," said Craig, "the finer his intel-ligence and taste, and therefore the more easily controlled."

Opposed to this point of view are many directors who believe that the actor must collaborate in the creative process with the director. Such a view is certain to be shared by actors who feel confident in their ability to utilize their training and imagination. Representing this school of thought was the eminent American director Arthur Hopkins. We are all creative, Hopkins believed, and the director who continually stifles the actor and shuts off the actor's creative impulse is guilty of wiring false fruit to a tree that has never flowered. "The highest function of the stage director," he wrote, "is to help the seeker open the door to his own riches."[5]

---

5. Arthur Hopkins, *Reference Point* (New York: Samuel French, 1948), p. 50.

Come Back, Little Sheba, by William Inge. California State University, Long Beach. Directed by Stanley Kahan.

Every actor will work with directors of varying viewpoints and philosophies. They may belong to different schools of thought and have diametrically opposed plans of directing the actor. Whatever relationship develops between the actor and director, and whatever approach to acting the actor takes, there is one goal upon which many of them agree: "We must always realize that the chief mission of the theatre is to reveal to ourselves, and to others, the inner riches that are the only surviving essence of all of us."[6]

> *I don't act, I react.*
>
> James Stewart

---

6. Ibid., p. 53.

Short Notes on the Heritage of Some Notable Actors

Sarah Bernhardt (1845–1923) French.   Given the name "The Divine Sarah" by her many admirers, Bernhardt had a voice described as a "golden bell" and a "silver stream of water." She was intermittently associated with the *Comédie-Française* but in her later years undertook a series of tours, including so many farewell tours that they became the subject of amusement. Her repertoire of roles included Phèdre, Camille, Fedora, and Tosca. Her few film appearances, left as a legacy of her stage roles, reveal an actress in the grand manner of the nineteenth century.

Eleonora Duse (1858–1924) Italian.   Emerging from a troupe of struggling touring players, Duse first appeared on the stage at the age of four. Gradually developing into the major rival of Bernhardt on the European stage, she developed a warmth and charm in her acting that presaged the greater naturalism of twentieth-century acting. Her Camille was admired worldwide, and George Bernard Shaw was moved to note that without qualification "it is the best modern acting I have ever seen." One comparison of the two great rivals, Bernhardt and Duse, suggests that Bernhardt moved you by her personal charm and Duse by the charm of the character.

William Gillette (1855–1937) American.   Both an actor and playwright, Gillette excelled in the movement in acting at the end of the nineteenth century variously termed *realism* and/or *naturalism.* His "natural" delivery of dialogue and stage movement that for the time was unique (such as turning his back to his audiences during dialogue) was a major break with the traditions of the American theatre. He also strongly advocated the concept of the "illusion of the first time" as the aim of good acting. He was the first major actor to star as Conan Doyle's *Sherlock Holmes,* in an adaptation Gillette himself had written.

Constantin Stanislavski (1863–1938) Russian.   Actor, teacher, and director, Stanislavski (born Alexeyev) had a profound effect on the teaching of acting, particularly in Russia and the United States. A moderately successful actor in the Russian theatre, his pioneering work, together with that of his colleague Vladimir Nemirovich-Danchenko, led to the formation of the Moscow Art Theatre and the salvaging of the playwriting career of Anton Chekhov. (See the section on Stanislavski earlier in this chapter for a fuller overview of his contribution to the art of acting.)

John Barrymore (1882–1942) American.   Brilliant but erratic leading man whose brother Lionel (1878–1954) and sister Ethel (1879–1959) also carved illustrious careers for themselves in the theatre and film. Inspired portrayals of Richard III and Hamlet on the Broadway and London stages earned him the reputation as America's greatest classical actor. Laurence Olivier recalls Barrymore's Hamlet being one of the freshest and most illuminating he had ever seen. In the 1930s Barrymore devoted his time almost exclusively to Hollywood, where his acute alcoholism gradually reduced this once great actor to a shadow of his former brilliance. His magnetism and range as an actor are partially preserved on film in such works as *Grand Hotel, A Bill of Divorcement, Topaze,* and *Counsellor-at Law.*

Ralph Richardson (1902–1982) English.   With Laurence Olivier and John Gielgud, one of the remarkable actors who created during half a century of performances what has been called the "golden age of English acting." A brilliant character actor, he spent several years with Olivier as director of the Old Vic, in which he gave remarkable performances as Ibsen's Peer Gynt and Shakespeare's Falstaff. In the 1970s he appeared with John Gielgud in two highly acclaimed productions, David Storey's *Home* and Harold Pinter's *No Man's Land.* He was knighted for his services to the theatre in 1947, the same year in which Olivier received his knighthood.

John Gielgud (1904–   ) English.   A descendant of a distinguished acting family, Gielgud has enjoyed one of the most prolific theatre careers of the twentieth century, beginning with his first appearance at the Old Vic in 1921. Considered the finest speaker of English verse on the world's stages, his Hamlet, given in the 1930s, is generally regarded as the most poetic interpretation of the role in this century. At first his film appearances were few and relatively undistinguished, but by his seventy-fifth year he became one of the busiest and most successful of film actors. He has continued to give moving and carefully delineated performances well into his nineties. He was knighted in 1953 for his services to the stage.

Laurence Olivier (1907–1989) English.   English actor of prodigous range, in tragedy, comedy, classical, and modern drama. Many of his roles became yardsticks by which other actors have been measured, particularly his performances in *Macbeth, Richard III,* and *Othello,* which one critic called a summary statement on all that we have learned about acting in the past three centuries. His undertaking in the role of *Oedipus Rex* (1946) was voted by a panel of American theatre artists as the greatest performance of the first half of the twentieth century. Turning to film he modified his stage technique, after some initial difficulty, to the greater subtlety needed for film and has left a legacy of memorable performances in such films as *Wuthering Heights, Hamlet, Henry V, Carrie, The Entertainer, The Merchant of Venice,* and the documentary film of his stage performance of *Othello.* He received several Academy Awards for his film work, and he was also the recipient of innumerable international stage, film, and television awards. He was knighted in 1947, the youngest actor to be so honored, and in 1971 became Baron (Lord) Olivier for his services to the theatre. Olivier announced his retirement on the eve of his eightieth birthday in 1987, two years before his death, after over sixty years as a professional actor. He has frequently been called the greatest theatre artist of the twentieth century.

Marlon Brando (1924–   ) American.   Stage actor, who after triumphing on Broadway in *A Streetcar Named Desire*, centered his career in Hollywood, bringing the Method with him and revolutionizing the way we look at film acting. Early film performances in *Streetcar, Viva Zapata, The Wild One*, and *On the Waterfront* seemed to create the image of a shambling mumbler whose passion lay behind the mask of an inarticulate misfit. He extended his range, almost deliberately following these early film successes to play Napoleon in *Desirée*, Mark Antony in *Julius Caesar*, and a German officer in *The Young Lions.* His charismatic authority communicated itself to an entire generation of film-goers and culminated in two splendid performances in the early 1970s, *The Godfather* and *Last Tango in Paris.*

> *A lotta cats copy the Mona Lisa, but people still line up to see the original.*
> Louis Armstrong

More Actors and Actresses

Otis Skinner
American (1858–1942)

Vassili Kachalov
Russian (1875–1948)

Lynne Fontanne
American (1887–1983)

Louis Jouvet
French (1887–1951)

Edith Evans
English (1888–1976)

Charles Chaplin
English (1889–1977)

Alfred Lunt
American (1892–1977)

Paul Muni
American (1895–1967)

Frederic March
American (1897–1975)

Irene Dunne
American (1898–1990)

Judith Anderson
Australian (1898–1992)

Paul Robeson
American (1898–1976)

Katherine Cornell
American (1898–1974)

Charles Laughton
English/American (1899–1962)

Spencer Tracy
American (1900–1967)

Helen Hayes
American (1900–1993)

Maurice Evans
English/American (1901–1989)

Donald Wolfit
English (1902–1969)

Henry Fonda
American (1905–1982)

Greta Garbo
Swedish (1905–1990)

Peggy Ashcroft
  English (1907–1991)
Bette Davis
  American (1908–1989)
Michael Redgrave
  English (1908–1985)
Greer Garson
  Irish/American (1908–1996)
Katharine Hepburn
  American (1909–   )
E. G. Marshall
  American (1910–   )
Alec Guinness
  English (1914–   )
Orson Welles
  American (1915–1985)
Ingrid Bergman
  Swedish/American
  (1915–1982)
Gregory Peck
  American (1916–   )
Paul Scofield
  English (1922–   )
Jack Lemmon
  American (1923–   )
Marcello Mastroianni
  Italian (1923–1996)
Richard Burton
  English (1925–1984)
Angela Lansbury
  English/American
  (1925–   )
Peter Sellers
  English (1925–1982)
Max Von Sydow
  Swedish (1929–   )
Robert Duvall
  American (1930–   )
James Earl Jones
  American (1931–   )
Gene Hackman
  American (1931–   )
Peter O'Toole
  Irish (1933–   )

Michael Caine
  English (1933–   )
Judi Dench
  English (1934–   )
Maggie Smith
  English (1934–   )
Albert Finney
  English (1936–   )
Anthony Hopkins
  English (1937–   )
Glenda Jackson
  English (1937–   )
Dustin Hoffman
  American (1937–   )
Jack Nicholson
  American (1937–   )
Morgan Freeman
  American (1937–   )
Nicol Williamson
  Scottish/English (1938–   )
Diana Rigg
  English (1938–   )
Ian McKellan
  English (1939–   )
Michael Gambon
  English (1940–   )
Al Pacino
  American (1940–   )
Raul Julia
  American (1940–1994)
Giancarlo Giannini
  Italian (1942–   )
Christopher Walken
  American (1943–   )
Robert De Niro
  American (1943–   )
David Suchet
  English (1946–   )
Glenn Close
  American (1947–   )
Gérard Depardieu
  French (1948–   )
Meryl Streep
  American (1949–   )

Denzel Washington	Kenneth Branagh
American (1954–)	English (1960–)
Emma Thompson	Matthew Broderick
English (1959–)	American (1962–)

Are there any other actors you believe should be on this list?

SUGGESTIONS FOR FURTHER READING

Adler, Stella. *The Technique of Acting.* New York: Bantam Books, 1988.

Blum, Richard A. *American Film Acting: The Stanislaviski Heritage* (Studies in Cinema No. 28). Ann Arbor, MI: UMI Research Press, 1984.

Brook, Peter. *The Open Door.* New York: Theatre Communications Group, 1995.

Chaikin, Joseph. *The Presence of the Actor.* New York: Theatre Communications Group, 1972/1991.

Checkhov, Michael. *To the Actor.* New York: Harper and Brothers, 1953.

Grotowski, Jerzy. *Towards a Poor Theatre.* New York: Simon and Schuster, 1968.

Hagen, Uta. *A Challenge for the Actor.* New York: Charles Scribner's Sons, 1991.

Hull, S. Lorraine. *Strasberg's Method.* Woodbridge, CT: Ox Bow Publishers, 1985.

Law, Alma, and Mel Gordon. *Meyerhold, Eisenstein and Biomechanics.* Jefferson, NC: McFarland and Company, 1996.

Lewis, Robert. *Advice to the Players.* New York: Harper & Row, 1980.

Meisner, Sanford, and Dennis Longwell. *Sanford Meisner on Acting.* New York: Vintage Books, 1987.

Morris, Eric. *Acting from the Ultimate Consciousness.* Los Angeles: Ermor Enterprises, 1988.

Moskowitz, Florence. *The Case against the Stanislaviski "System" of Acting.* New York: Vantage Press, 1966.

Munk, Erika, ed. *Stanislavski and America.* New York: Hill and Wang, 1966.

Parke, Lawrence. *Acting Truth and Fictions.* Hollywood: Acting World Books, 1995.

Silverberg, Larry. *The Sandford Meisner Approach: An Actor's Workbook.* Lyme, NH: Smith and Kraus, 1994.

Stanislavski, Constantin. *An Actor Prepares.* tr. E. R. Hapgood. New York: Theatre Arts Books, 1936.

———. *Building a Character,* tr. E. R. Hapgood. New York: Theatre Arts Books, 1949.

———. *Creating a Role.* tr. E. R. Hapgood. New York: Theatre Arts Books, 1961.

Strasberg, Lee. *A Dream of Passion: The Development of the Method.* New York: Penguin USA, 1988.

CHAPTER FOUR

The Body and Stage Movement

by Holly Harbinger

In the art of the theatre, the body is the actor's instrument. It is the tangible vehicle through which all creativity, imagination, intelligence, and vitality must pass. It is what the audience sees and responds to on a visceral level. Just as the violinist uses the violin to make music, so the actor uses the body to create physical characterization. The more we understand the body, the more effectively we can use it. The more control we have over it, the more choices we can make.

We need to be as articulate with our bodies as we are with our speech. Just as every role makes specific demands on the voice, so too it makes specific demands on the body. These demands are different from those of everyday life and require that we understand and respect how the body works. When we disregard our bodies, we literally disregard ourselves.

Acting is as much physical as it is verbal. From the most basic sitting, standing, walking, and running to working with all kinds of stage props and costumes, to the rigors of tumbling, dancing, fighting, and handling stage weapons, we use our bodies. The best actors have the skills to perform all these activities and the stamina to repeat them night after night—ideally without injury. Consider a typical farce, with its broadly drawn characters and plots and exaggerated physicality. It may require that the actors repeatedly run up and down stairs, crawl in and out of windows, climb over furniture, roll out of hiding places, give and receive punches, kicks, and slaps, all the while dealing with props, costumes, and, of course, text. If we are ignorant of how the body works, our only choice is to "play ourselves," with all

A Midsummer Night's Dream, **by William Shakespeare. Royal Shakespeare Company, Stratford. Patrick Stewart as Oberon. Photograph by Britain on View Photographic Library.**

our idiosyncratic movement mannerisms. In addition, if we neglect body training and maintenance, we may develop new areas of tension, muscle fatigue, strain, or even injury. Obviously we cannot afford this. As actors, we all need a body that is richly expressive and healthy.

In this chapter we shall look at the instrument itself, the actor's body, to understand it and learn to use it effectively.

How the Body Is Organized

The human body is beautifully designed to perform a great variety of actions. They range from the delicate to the strong, the quick to the sustained, the controlled to the free-flowing. They range from the intricate, high-speed footwork of the ballerina to the powerful, running attacks of the football player, to the soaring, twisting routines of the gymnast. Certainly there are particular body types more suited to one activity than another, but we all share the same basic design. Let us examine that design.

The Skeleton

It is useful to think of the skeleton as our bony architecture, our inner framework (see Figures 4.1a and 4.1b). Everything else in the body either sits on it, braces against it, or attaches to it. For protection, the delicate inner organs—such as heart, lungs, and diaphragm—are located inside it. Ligaments connect bone to bone and tendons connect bone to muscle. Together, they bind us in an interlacing network that also provides considerable range of motion. The spinal cord runs along the spine of the skeleton. Spinal nerves branch out from it to send information to the brain from sources both inside and outside the body. This information allows us to perform all our bodily functions and actions, both voluntary (like walking) and involuntary (like breathing). It is also important to understand that our skeleton is alive, that bones contain living tissue, oxygen, blood, and nerves. The skeleton as symbol of darkness and death may be appropriate for Halloween trick-or-treaters but not for actors. Inside each one of us, the skeleton (all 206 bones) is very much alive.

The Spine

The spine is our major skeletal support. Contrary to a common perception that the spine is near our back, on the exterior surface of the body, it is actually set internally into the center of the body. It is a round column that has two particularly important features. First, it is composed of thirty-three small

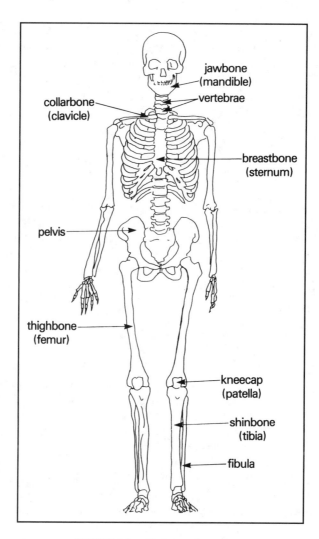

FIGURE 4.1a   Skeleton, front view.

bones, called vertebrae, with cushions made out of cartilage in between them. This design allows us to be flexible—to bend, twist, arch, spiral—and to absorb body shocks. Second, it has four curves: forward at the neck (the cervical curve), backward at the ribcage (the thoracic curve), forward at the waist (the lumbar curve), and backward at the back of the pelvis (the sacral curve). An extension of the sacral curve is the small vertebrae of the tailbone, or coccyx. These curves allow the spine to support the tremendous weight of the head, ribcage, and pelvis and to absorb and integrate movement from the rest of the body. But how often have we been told to "stand up straight" and then

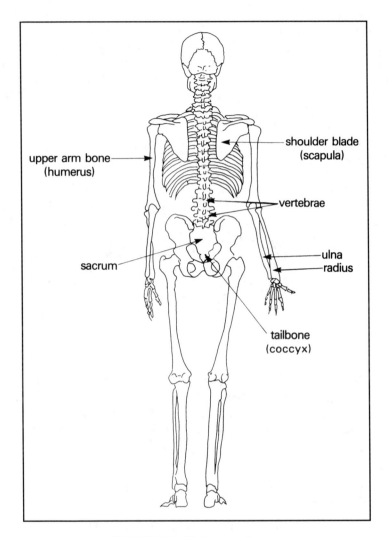

FIGURE 4.1b   Skeleton, back view.

jumped "to attention" with the image of a long, inflexible rod up the back? This image denies us the greatest assets of the spine, its curvature and cushioning, and literally locks us into our misconceptions.

The Head

The head (along with the ribcage and pelvis) is one of the heaviest weights in the body. How remarkable that it weighs about fifteen to twenty pounds yet sits so delicately on one small bone, the top vertebra of the spine, the atlas. Where the head and spine meet is a joint. There the center of the head can rock easily and in perfect balance on the cervical vertebrae. (To find the center of the head, place an index finger behind each earlobe and imagine a rod going from fingertip to fingertip. The middle of that imaginary rod is where the head sits on the atlas.)

The Shoulders

The shoulder girdle consists of the shoulder blades (scapula) in back and the collar bones (clavicle) in front. It rests on top of the torso. It has a fibrous connection to the top of the breastbone (sternum). It has only a muscular connection to the head and neck. With so little attachment to the rest of the skeleton, the shoulder blades and collar bones can move freely. The upper arm (humerus) fits into the shoulder joint cavity. In conjunction, the shoulder girdle and the shoulder joint allow the arms to move easily, without straining the neck and torso.

The Ribcage

The ribs attach at the spine. Twenty-four ribs—twelve pairs—are curved and attach with cartilage to the thoracic spine in back and (except for the two lowest "floating ribs") to the breastbone in front. This combination of curves and spongy attachment allows great flexibility to rise and sink, expand and contract.

The Pelvis

The pelvis, shaped like a deep, hollow bowl, is the largest bony structure in the body. It supports the weight of the head, shoulders, and torso above it. Their accumulated weight travels down to the back of the pelvis, the sacrum, which is also the lowest part of the spine. The sacrum is braced in place by the two sides of the pelvis, the ilia (where we rest our hands on our hips). This meeting place of ilia and sacrum is a joint (the sacroiliac joint), but it moves very little. Held together with strong ligaments, it is designed for strength and not mobility.

When you stand, the accumulated weight passes around the pelvic bowl to the front, where it transfers through the thigh sockets to the legs and feet and to the ground. When you sit, the weight passes around the pelvic bowl and then down to its base, the triangular-shaped ischium under each buttock. We call them the "sit-bones" because we literally sit right on top of them.

The pelvis is the center of weight and gravity in the body. It is like the hub of a wheel, with the spine and arms and legs being the spokes. The weight of the upper body does not collapse into the pelvis because of muscular support from the abdominals, the buttocks, and the legs.

Arms and Legs

Although the legs support weight and the arms do not, they are similar because both are appendages that attach to the body at a ball-and-socket joint. Such a joint is one in which a spherical knob fits into a socket so that motion is possible in almost every direction: inward and outward, up and down, forward and back. The knob at the top of the upper leg bone, the femur, fits into the thigh socket of the pelvis. The knob of the upper arm bone, the humerus, fits into the socket of the shoulder. The freedom of the arms and legs to move and expand the body into space depends, however, upon a strong muscular connection to the spine and pelvis. Support allows for movement. For example, an actor in a stage fight might prepare to throw a punch by "planting" himself, thus gathering support in his pelvis and legs, so he can swing his arms and fists freely, without losing balance.

What Is Good Alignment?

Now that we have examined basic body organization, how do we use that information to achieve good alignment—and why is that important? Consider the actor with an aching lower back who has to wear an elaborate period costume, including heels that thrust the body forward. Or consider the actor who locks the knees and thrusts weight onto one hip but has to be standing or walking onstage for much of the performance. The fatigue of performance will put a strain on almost any actor, even without the demands of unusual costumes, extended scenes, fighting, and dancing. Good alignment is achieved when the body parts are allowed the placement and function they were designed for. Here is a quick checklist from head to toe:

1. The head should sit easily on the neck and be able to rotate without strain.
2. The neck should feel long, relaxed, and the same length both front and back.
3. The shoulders should hang freely—not pressed up, down, forward, or back—and feel broad from side to side.
4. The arms should hang easily in the shoulder joints and be able to move freely without raising the shoulders or shortening the neck.
5. The ribcage should hang freely, not push forward or cave inward.

6. The lower back should lengthen, supported by the muscles in front, and not tuck under or hyperextend forward.
7. The pelvis should be balanced so that the "bowl" does not spill out its "contents" by tilting either forward or backward.
8. The legs should move easily in the thigh sockets and be balanced directly over the feet.
9. The feet should be parallel, with heels and toes spread fully and the weight centered over the balls of the feet.

The image of a plumb line (a long string with a weight attached to the bottom) is useful for quick and easy reference. Imagine that plumb line to start at the top and center of the head, falling through the center of the pelvis in front of the sacrum, and down between the legs to the floor. We distort that line when we pull the units of the body out of place. Imagine placing a finger on the plumb line and pulling it to one side. Immediately there is tension on the string and the weight at the bottom cannot come to rest. That is what we are doing when we push the shoulders forward and round the upper back; when we habitually stand over one leg with the hip stuck out; when we stand with our weight back on our heels; when we press the ribs forward, lock the knees, tuck the pelvis, and so on. We are then forcing the muscles to work extra hard, straining to hold the body together, attempting to regain balance. Chronic misalignment problems can result in muscle strains, sprains, or more serious injury.

Many of these problems are habitual—we have developed them over a long period of time and they feel "natural." They have become part of our personal physical signature that helps define us—for better or for worse. The actor, however, needs an instrument that can be neutral, without the misalignments that he or she is locked into. Then the actor can purposefully and specifically take on the physicality and idiosyncrasies of a particular character. Just as a particular dialect is not the appropriate vocal choice for every character, so too the same physical characteristics are not appropriate for every character.

Most important to understand is that good alignment is not static. It is not something that we "get" and then hold onto for fear of losing it. Once we freeze with it we have already lost it! It is a process of managing constant change from mobility to stability as we move through the activities of the day. The most simple series of actions requires tremendous physical reorganization. Try this sequence: Walk into a room; then reach to a high shelf to get a book; then cross the room to a chair and sit down; then start to read as you shift to a more comfortable position; then get up quickly to answer the phone on the other side of the room; then return the book to its shelf; then hurriedly leave the room. Imagine trying to perform that sequence without changing your alignment! Our task is to maintain harmony and balance in a body that is always in motion.

Tension and Relaxation

Good and Bad Tension

Tension is something we all have. Not all of it is bad. We all need "good tension," appropriate muscle support, for our bodies to move. When we bend an arm to pick up a book or bend a leg to perform a dance step, we are using muscular support—contracting one set of muscles and extending another set. A body without any tension would be utterly limp and unable to perform any kind of action. "Bad tension," excessive muscular activity, is different. It is the result of a body out of balance because of stress—physical, mental, or emotional. It gets in the way of effective movement, makes us prone to injury, and inhibits creativity.

Common Tension Areas

Many of us share the same tension areas and problems. We rub our shoulders when they are tight from being raised or squeezed together. We press our hands into our lumbar curve when our back aches from slumping. We rotate the head and rub the neck for relief from the pressure of holding the head and neck tightly together. We also have our own idiosyncratic tensions. One person may have a tight jaw from clenching the face—which impedes easy and efficient speech. Another may have a tight hip from carrying weight consistently off to one side—which impedes fluid walking, running, or jumping. Another may have sore knee joints from constantly locking the knees when standing—which impedes smooth rising, lowering, and shifting weight. Our tensions are part of our physical signature and are impossible to hide.

The same is true of the characters we are playing. It is difficult to play a "laid back" or "mellow" character if we cannot minimize some of our own residual tensions. On the other hand, if we want to play a character with one tension idiosyncrasy—such as nervous wringing of the hands—while the actor's signature habit is to rock back and forth from heels to toes, we need to displace our tension from one area to another.

Relaxation

Relaxation is not a complete letting go of tension and energy. Relaxation is achieved when the body is in balance—when the mind is clear and focused and when the bones are easily in place so that the muscles can move them efficiently. Relaxation for the actor is achieved when the body is prepared to respond quickly and easily, without awkward adjustments, to inner and outer stimuli—mental images, a character's intentions, verbal and physical cues from fellow actors, the response of the audience. Relaxation for the actor is readiness to act.

EXERCISES

Contract and Release

This exercise is a variation on the relaxation exercise in Chapter 5 for achieving good vocal tone.

Lie on your back on the floor. Make sure that your back, neck, arms, and legs are fully extended but not locked. Close your eyes and breathe easily. (1) Contract (tense) your whole body all at once, hold for several seconds, then release fully. (2) Now contract just the upper half of your body (from the waist up), hold for several seconds, then release fully. Repeat with the lower half of your body. (3) Starting with your face, isolate one part of your body at a time to contract, hold for several seconds, and then release fully. Involve only one part of your body at a time. Work down the body: face (eyes, nose, mouth, chin), neck, shoulders, right arm, right hand, left arm, left hand, ribcage, abdominals, buttocks, right leg, right foot, left leg, left foot.

Constructive Rest

This (see Figure 4.2) exercise is based on the recuperative power of yielding to gravity to relieve tension.[1] It is an excellent exercise to use when you are tired and have only a short time to rest before continuing to work, such as between a late rehearsal and a performance.

Lie on your back on the floor. Bend your legs and place your feet flat on the floor, hips' width apart. Let your knees drop toward each other so that they touch. Your legs should be able to stay in this position without tension anywhere. If your legs fall open, separate your feet a little more to make a wider base of support or tie a belt or long pieces of fabric around your knees. Fold your arms and drape them easily across your chest, letting your fingers dangle. For additional comfort, put a small pillow, sweater, or towel under your head. Close your eyes and breathe easily. Stay in this position for ten or fifteen minutes. Your goal is to yield all muscular control to gravity so that the body can truly rest (unlike sleeping, when we toss, turn, clench, and physically respond to our dreams). As you rest, focus all your attention into your body. Do not think about activities of the day. Mentally check your body for any tension spots and try to relax them by breathing into them.

----

1. This exercise is drawn from the work of Mabel Elsworth Todd, a seminal movement analyst of the twentieth century. Her book *The Thinking Body* is an important study of body mechanics and applied kinesiology.

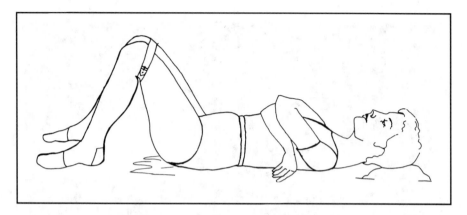

FIGURE 4.2   Constructive rest position.

The Body in Action

We have discussed how we must find a neutral starting place before building a physical characterization for a role. Let us consider now how to get ourselves into action. After all, a character is not defined by posture alone but by
how he or she moves and speaks. Choices in the use of space, weight, time,
and energy can provide the core of a character's movement.[2]

Moving through Space

When you move, you affect the space around you. That can be the space between you and another actor, between you and any point on the stage, between you and the audience. We do not work in a vacuum but in the world
of the theatre. We can define our relationship to space in two ways: directly
and expansively.

Directly.   Moving directly in space means approaching someone or something—another actor or a piece of stage furniture or a section of the audience—as a single, specific target. It means pinpointing that target and honing
in on it with total physical and visual focus. For example, a mugger facing
and pointing a gun at a victim is using space directly.

---

2. The concepts of weight, space, and time were originally conceived by Rudolf Laban,
Hungarian-born actor/choreographer and an important movement analyst of the twentieth century. This author has adapted his concepts to make them more readily accessible to the actor. For
further information about the work of Rudolf Laban, see *Mastery of Movement* and *A Primer for
Movement Description* listed at the end of this chapter.

Cyrano de Bergerac, by Edmund Rostand. California Repertory Theatre Company, Long Beach. Directed by Joanne Gordon. Fight choreography by Holly Harbinger. Photograph by Keith Ian Polakoff.

Expansively. Moving expansively means enlarging your focus so that you can take in a wide range of things all at once.[3] It means spreading out your field of attention and extending your body so that you can scan a landscape or contemplate a multitude of possibilities. For example, a politician addressing a large crowd and trying to hold everyone's attention is using space expansively.

EXERCISES

1. Move about the stage space to look at all the furniture and props in one continuous motion (expansively). Then focus on one item that interests you (directly).

---

3. Instead of the word *expansive,* Laban uses the word *indirect,* which can be confusing, implying "evasive" or "roundabout."

Walk to it and pick it up. *Example:* A jewel thief at a party "cases" the room. He or she then spots a necklace that has fallen on the floor and takes it.

2. Try to address all your fellow actors at once, without losing anyone's attention (expansively). Then select one person to speak to, ignoring the others (directly). *Example:* A gang member is surrounded by members of a rival gang and attempts to protect himself or herself on all sides. He or she then appeals directly to the gang leader for help.

3. Go to Chapter 7, "Using Improvisation," and select a character. Then imagine a situation for that character. Alternate back and forth between moving and speaking directly and expansively. *Example:* You are a lawyer in a courtroom trying a case. (1) Scan the entire courtroom audience to command its attention; (2) focus on the victim to win sympathy; (3) address the jury as a whole; (4) approach one person in that jury to convince him or her of your argument; (5) speak to the whole room to demand justice; (6) focus intently on the guilty party to make your accusation.

4. Go to Chapter 7 and try any of the "Actions" improvisations with clear use of space, alternating directly and expansively.

Using Weight

You are using weight whether you are moving through space or remaining in one place with shifts forward and back or side to side or up and down. When you move around the stage, you can either use your weight strongly for extra effect—like the proverbial bull in the china shop—or exert it as little as possible—as in walking on eggshells. However, do not confuse using weight with how much you weigh, with whether you are heavy or light. The concept refers to how you use your physical and emotional force to affect someone or something, lightly or strongly. Ask yourself if you want to have strong impact or light impact on the other character(s) in your scene. Either one can be highly effective. For example, a friend giving another who is grieving gentle pats or strokes on the back for comfort and reassurance is using weight lightly. Imagine trying to comfort someone with hearty slaps on the back! In contrast, an irate employee who has just been fired, who stomps into his employer's office, leans forcefully on the desk, and shakes a fist at him, is using weight strongly. A gentle knock on the door and a whispered complaint would not get the same result.

EXERCISES

1. Move around the stage space exerting as much weight as you can. *Example:* A child is having a tantrum.

2. Move around the stage space exerting as little weight as possible. *Example:* A burglar is cautiously prowling around to examine the contents in a house where people are sleeping.

3. Stand or sit in one place and try to convince someone of something. *Example:* You were caught at the scene of a murder but insist that you are innocent. First use strong weight: Stand your ground, look your accuser in the eye, and forcefully put the blame on that person for daring to accuse you. Then repeat the same argument using light weight: Shift weight forward onto the balls of your feet, delicately rub your hands together as you speak, and flirtatiously tease your accuser for having considered you as a suspect. Consider how these changes affect your argument and help define your character.

Using Time

We all move in time whether we choose to or not. We may move slowly and leisurely to mingle at a party. We may move quickly and frantically to chase a bus. We may walk with steady, measured steps to proceed up the aisle at a wedding. We may also combine time variations. For example, two lovers may rush to each other eagerly (quickly) and then leave each other reluctantly (slowly).

EXERCISES

1. Make an entrance quickly to bring good news. Repeat that entrance slowly. Make an entrance quickly to bring bad news. Repeat that entrance slowly.
2. Set up the stage space quickly and anxiously with furniture and props to prepare for a date who is to arrive at any moment. Remove all the furniture and props slowly and leisurely as you reminisce about the evening that has just ended.

Moving with Energy

Energy means both power in action and vitality of expression. Whether we release our energy fully or hold it in check can significantly affect how a character behaves. When we release energy our bodies expand and our muscles stretch. When we hold back energy our bodies narrow and our muscles tense. Both actions are full of dramatic possibilities. A parent scolding a child may release energy in a torrent of anger. The child, on the other hand, may hold back energy out of either respect or fear. A boxer in a fight may release energy fully to deliver a punch. The opponent, on the other hand, may narrow, tense, and tighten as a frightened defense.

As we shall see in the discussion of vitality in Chapter 10, there are also levels of energy, from high to low. Different people may be characterized as high-energy or low-energy people. The actor must determine the energy level of the character he or she is playing and decide how that level is affected

Rashomon, by Fay and Michael Kanin. Directed by Al Madalena. California State University, Long Beach.

by the circumstances of the play. Note that it rarely works to play passively, without any energy. Lack of energy tends to make a character "disappear" on stage.

EXERCISES

1. Accuse a fellow actor of a crime. Begin with as much controlled energy as you can and then complete your accusation with a burst of wild energy. *Example:* You accuse your spouse of having an affair. You begin with control to mask your jealousy but then explode with anger. Repeat the exercise but reverse your use of energy: Begin with a burst of energy and end by controlling it.
2. Set the stage space with furniture and props. Handle some with extreme care and caution, as if they were valuable and fragile. Handle others carelessly, toss-

ing, shoving, and pulling. Notice how your muscles work by tensing and re-leasing and how your body responds to accommodate the variety of actions.

3. Pick a "low-energy" character and find a situation in which that character would be pushed to act with high energy. *Example:* A timid school girl defends her best friend who is being threatened or teased by other students. Then do the reverse: a "high-energy" character behaving with low energy. *Example:* A vivacious host or hostess is very tired after a big party and is struggling to clean up and get to bed.

What Does Your Body Communicate?

You constantly communicate with your body whether you choose to or not. As an actor you need to make specific and purposeful choices about the characters you play. When you do not, your body still continues to speak for you. You may get only a few minutes to perform at an audition, but your body begins to communicate from the moment you walk in the door. Besides physical appearance, what is "speaking" is a combination of how you use space, weight, time, and energy as well as your posture.

Consider the two characters from *The Beaux' Stratagem* in the photo on the following page. You know simply from the way that they stand so close to each other that their conversation is of a seductive nature. The woman's body is in an open, inviting position. Her arms are spread out and asymmetrical, and their energy seems to flow lightly from her fingertips. She looks directly at the man but tilts her head coyly to the side. The man, in contrast, has firmly planted his weight in one spot. He focuses directly on the woman. His body is alert, energetic, and ready to respond to her. His legs are turned out and his arms hang gracefully, positions typical of a seventeenth- or eighteenth-century gentleman.

Warming Up

Is warming up really necessary? The answer is an emphatic yes. The actor who walks into a rehearsal or performance "cold" is unprepared to work effectively and is asking for trouble. Let us consider three important reasons why.

1. *Energizing the Body for Rehearsal and Performance.* Rehearsals can be many hours long, day after day, for weeks or even months. The demand on the actor is to be fully alert and energetic but relaxed and centered—in touch with his or her creativity, intelligence, and imagination. The actor must be ready to try new things—new blocking, complicated business with a prop, a fight, a dance—sometimes worked over and over until it is finally right or

The Beaux' Stratagem, by George Farquhar. National Theatre, London.
Directed by William Gaskill, with Maggie Smith and Robert Stephens.
Photograph by Britain on View Photographic Library.

discarded for something else. Repetition and rehearsals go together. Also, the actor who is mentally and physically prepared is better able to contribute to the rehearsal process, to make discoveries about how his or her character behaves and moves. After all, if the actor's instrument is inert, the character will be, too.

The body also needs to be prepared for performance. To expect the excitement of working in front of an audience to "inspire" us, to unleash that magic "something" that will give a performance energy and power, is both lazy and unreliable. We have already discussed how the actor behaves and moves differently onstage than in real life. He or she uses variations in weight, space, time, and energy that are not habitual, not "natural," to the performer. In addition, the actor must be able to project physically to reach every member of the audience, whether in a small, intimate studio or a large, multilevel theatre. That requires having "presence," that electric physicality that invigorates our fellow actors and compels the audience to watch us.

2. *Avoiding Injury.* A proper warm-up protects the actor from injury by preparing the muscles for the job they are about to do. The actor must be a kind of athlete, in shape and ready to commit his or her body on cue to whatever the role demands.

The actor may have areas of great tension, chronic strains, childhood injuries, or misalignment problems that will be aggravated during rehearsal and performance. Or the actor may simply have slept badly the night before and be full of odd aches and pains. A warm-up should carefully work all the areas of the body that are vulnerable or under stress. An injured instrument is not fully usable.

3. *Preparing for the Heightened Physicality of a Particular Role.* Some roles make extraordinary physical demands on the actor: to fall down a flight of stairs, get kicked in the stomach, punched in the face, die, faint, or otherwise carry on. There are stage techniques for performing all these feats that make them exciting and believable to the audience but safe for the performer. All require a thorough warm-up so that the body can stretch, absorb shock, respond quickly, and avoid injury. Actors enjoy making lots of noise during stage fights—moans, groans, grunts, shrieks, and so on—but it should not be for real!

For an example of heightened physicality we can look to Laurence Olivier, famous for his physical courage and daring exploits as an actor. In a 1960 production of Shakespeare's *Coriolanus*, he performed one of his most memorable physical feats. In the death scene, he fell forward from a promontory high above the stage and was caught by the ankles and left dangling upside-down. What a heroic, stunning, and physically demanding end!

Care in warming up is also needed for actors who have to dance in musicals. Turning, kicking, jumping, and quick changes of direction can cause strains, sprains, and tears if performed "cold." The instrument that is properly cared for will last.

Preparing for the World of the Play

Making the transition from our everyday world with its activities, distractions, and problems to the world of the play and its characters can be difficult. After all, we use the same instrument—ourselves—in both worlds. Simply trying to shut out the one to concentrate on the other is too negative an approach. A more positive approach is to actively engage the mind and body in activities that will relax, cleanse, and energize the actor. A warm-up can be an effective ritual for enabling the actor to be open and focused. The instrument that is prepared is in the best position to act.

Elements of a Basic Warm-up

A basic warm-up should work all the major muscle groups, energize the body, and reduce tension. The purpose of the warm-up is to prepare you for the rehearsal or performance, not to keep you in shape. It is definitely not a substitute for sports, dancing, aerobics, or other forms of exercise.

For rehearsals, wear any loose, comfortable clothing that does not restrict movement or constrict circulation. For performances, you may want to do the majority of the warm-up before putting on your costume. Once in costume, you may want to do additional exercises that apply specifically to the character you are playing. Being in costume can help you bring a character's movement mannerisms to life.

The Four S's

Shaking, swinging, sustaining, and stretching should each be included in your warm-up. There are variations suggested after each basic exercise, but you can discover countless others for yourself. Experiment.

1. Shaking

Shaking movements increase circulation, reduce tension, and generally help you to wake up. They are short, quick, quivering, and repetitive. To do them requires relaxation in the whole body and ease in the joints.

Arms and Legs. Start with your arms at your sides. Shake one hand as you slowly raise your arm until it is above your head. Then let the arm collapse softly at all the joints (shoulder, elbow, wrist) and drop to your side. Repeat with the other arm. Repeat with both arms at the same time. Monitor yourself: Be sure to keep the shoulder joints easy, the shoulders down, and the neck long as your arms rise.

Stand on one leg (the supporting leg) and place the other leg (the moving leg) in front of you, a few inches off the floor. Shake the moving leg in front of you, then at the side, and then directly behind you. Return to standing on two feet. Repeat with the other leg. For balance, work the moving leg a little higher, without lifting or tilting the hips. Monitor yourself: Be sure to keep your weight stable on the supporting leg and your upper body relaxed.

Torso and Pelvis. Start with legs parallel, feet hips' width apart, knees bent, and hands clasped together in front of you at chest level. Press your hands together as you shake your hips and buttocks so that they feel loose and jelly-like (see Figure 4.3). Stop, let your arms drop to your sides, and carefully straighten your legs. Then smoothly rise onto your toes and shake your shoulders and torso in a shimmying action. Lower yourself to stand flat. Repeat the entire sequence of lowering and rising until it is smooth and continuous and the shaking is fast and loose. Monitor yourself: Keep everything that is not shaking relaxed and keep your breathing unconstricted.

Change intensity and speed from gentle and slow to vigorous and fast. Shake body parts in different combinations (two arms and one leg at the same time, for example) until you can shake the whole body at once without tension (see Figure 4.4).

Variations

1. Work on different levels: up on your toes, standing on flat feet, sitting on the floor, or lying on the floor. For example, lie on your back on the floor and shake out your arms and legs.

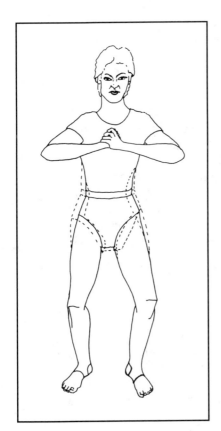

FIGURE 4.3 Shaking the pelvis.

FIGURE 4.4   Shaking arms and leg.

2. Work on balance and coordination by switching quickly from shaking one body part to another in any order. Practice the sequence until you can do it at various speeds without losing balance.
3. Vary movement quality by using images: Shake from the cold; shake with fear; shake like a dog who is all wet; shake as if you have ants all over your shirt, pants, shoes, and hair; shake with the quivering quality of the old and infirm.

2. Swinging

Swinging movements have a feeling of freedom, release, and ease. They are relaxed and flowing with an arc-like path through space. Each swing has a beginning, middle, and end: energy and push at the beginning to get started (top of the arc); release of weight and going with momentum in the middle (bottom of the arc); and suspension and lightness at the end (top of the arc). Imagine an enormous bell hanging in a church tower: The pull of the rope gets the bell moving; the weight of the bell as it drops and hits the gong inside creates sound; the tilt of the bell as it lifts to the other side is light and the sound fades. Or imagine the arc of a jump rope: the tug on the rope to start, the slap of the rope as it hits the ground, the light recovery as it lifts to one side or floats over the top before the whole cycle begins again.

Whole Body Swing Forward.   Stand on two feet with the legs parallel, feet hips' width apart, and arms fully extended over your head (see Figure 4.5). Trying to make a smooth arc, reach forward, then down, then behind you with your arms as you bend your legs, fold at the waist, then drop your head.

FIGURE 4.5   Whole body swing forward.

Then reverse that swing to come up and finish at your original starting position. Allow a pause, a stillness with breathing, at the end of each full swing. Do not freeze your position or lock your joints. Monitor yourself: Be sure to release any neck tension and let the head drop completely when you go with the momentum.

Whole Body Swing Side to Side.   Stand in a wide stance with your legs slightly turned out (about forty-five degrees) (see Figure 4.6). To prepare, reach high with both arms to one side as you shift your weight mostly over to one leg. To swing, bend your legs, fold at the waist, and drop your head as you swing the arms and upper body down in front of you; then recover over to the other side, finishing with legs straight, arms stretched overhead, and weight having shifted over to the other leg. Use the image of a jump rope (the schoolyard kind with a child holding on at each end) going from side to side. Then try combining side-to-side swings with full-circle swings: The jump rope goes

FIGURE 4.6   Whole body swing side to side.

side to side and then continues in a full circle, passing overhead. Monitor yourself: It is essential that you keep your knees directly over your feet at all times to avoid strain on the knees. Also, be sure to let your head drop down completely at the bottom of the arc to reduce neck tension. Finally, bending and straightening of the legs should be smooth and knees should never lock.

Variations

1. Let gentle swings of the upper body in any direction carry you through space with a soaring, free-wheeling sensation in the upper body that you support with balance in the lower body.
2. Return to full body swings forward, letting the beginning and end of each swing carry you up onto your toes. For balance, be sure to stand fully on all ten toes and to sense your connection with the floor, even as you resist it to rise. Then let your whole-body swings extend into small jumps. Be sure to cushion your landings. If your landings are noisy and your legs feel jarred, then you need to be more pliable and less brittle. Toes should land first and then heels should land fully as both knees bend.
3. Use images: Swing with a steady rhythm and heavy weight to hypnotize someone; swing freely and delicately through space like leaves blowing in the wind; swing in odd, irregular rhythms like someone who is wracked with pain.

3. Sustaining

Sustaining movements lengthen muscles as they combine balance and strength, control and fluidity. They are steady and continuous. Unlike shaking, which has a quick, repetitive rhythm, or swinging, which has a three-part rhythm, sustaining has a steady, uninterrupted rhythm that changes only when a movement is completed and another begins. Sustaining an impulse without variation requires control of the muscles and generates a feeling of restraint and calm.

Plié. An example of a sustaining movement is a *plié* or bend (pronounced "plee-ay"; this is a dance term that means "to bend" and is useful for our purposes because it is found in the warm-up for almost every kind of physical activity) (see Figure 4.7). Stand with your legs in a wide stance, about one or two feet apart, turned out about forty-five degrees, with your spine upright and long. Slowly bend your legs and lower toward the floor as far as you can without letting your heels come off the floor. To come up, straighten your legs in one smooth action by lengthening them down as your torso goes up. A good image for the *plié* is an elevator, but not one that jerks and drops from

FIGURE 4.7   Plié.

floor to floor and collapses at the bottom. Imagine one that takes you from the top floor to the bottom and back up again in one smooth ride. Monitor yourself: Protect your knees by keeping them directly over your feet. The stability of the foot provides support for the mobility of the knee joint. Also, keep your head and torso fully upright, with your shoulders aligned over your hips.

Repeat *pliés* in the following positions: (1) heels together, feet turned out about forty-five degrees and (2) legs in parallel position, about hips' width apart, knees and toes facing straight forward. In all positions the heels should remain on the floor.

Whole Body Forward or Side.   Another sustaining movement for the whole body uses the image of slow-motion basketball: straight shots forward or hook shots to the side, with an exaggerated recovery. For the straight shot, stand in parallel position, with the feet hips' width apart. Reach up and then forward with your arms, head, and torso as far as you can. Then lower the head and arms and drop over as you let everything bend (ankles, knees, hips). Roll up to standing: Let the spine uncurl one vertebra at a time, starting at the base, the tailbone, and ending with the neck and head. For the hook shot, take the same progression to the side: Reach with one arm overhead and then to the opposite side as far as you can without losing your balance. Then bend at the waist and release your arm down as you round your torso to the front. Roll up to finish upright with both legs straight (see Figure 4.8). Repeat on the other side. Monitor yourself: There should not be any sudden drops but a continuous flow of controlled energy.

Variations

1. Try sustaining movements for isolated body parts, being sure to identify where your balance and support are. Lead in any direction (forward, backward, right, left, up, or down) with one part of the body and

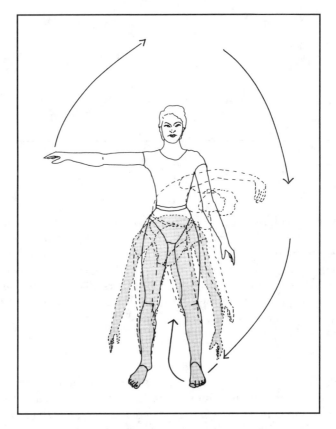

FIGURE 4.8 Sustaining movement to the side.

let the rest of the body respond and follow. Then switch to lead with another part of the body in another direction, and so on. As you move through this lead and follow sequence, keep it smooth and continuous and allow your weight to shift as necessary and even move about the room. For example, lead with your right arm toward the ceiling as the whole body rises to follow; then lead with the left hip down and to the left as the whole body lowers and pulls to the left; then lead with your chest forward as the whole body moves several steps forward, and so on.

2. Use actions that "dig" or "carve" into space, actions like reaching, expanding, offering, scooping. Fulfill them as sustaining movements. Try them low to the ground and then try them standing on your toes to test your balance and control.

3. Use images: thick molasses pouring from a spoon or a boat gliding smoothly across the water.

4. Stretching

Stretching movements lengthen the muscles and expand range of motion in the joints. They increase flexibility as they release constricted areas where we hold habitual tension. They also improve circulation as they work out stiffness and soreness from other activities of the day. All stretching requires relaxed, deep breathing. Muscles require oxygen in order to lengthen. Inhale as you prepare and then exhale as you stretch. The exhalation always goes with the stretch. Breathing in place as you stretch, rather than pulling or bouncing, is important. It will allow joints to open as muscles extend and will help avoid muscle tearing. How far should you stretch? Stretch only as far as you can without pain. Respect pain. "No pain, no gain" is nonsense!

Let us work down the body, from head to toes:

Face. From a standing position: Inhale and open your eyes and mouth and raise your eyebrows as fully as possible to stretch your whole face in what may look like an exaggerated scream. Exhale and reverse that stretch by contracting your entire face into what may look like an exaggerated squint.

Neck. From a standing position: Gently drop your head forward, then circle it to the side, then to the front again, then to the other side. Pause in each position and breathe fully several times.

Torso. First, from a standing position, with legs parallel and hips' width apart, bend your legs and clasp hands in front of you. Round your back, pull forward with your arms, and resist that pull by reaching backward with your waist (see Figure 4.9a). Do not simply "cave in," but let your spine be like an

FIGURE 4.9a   Torso stretch (rounding).

archer's bow that curves from tip to tip—that is, from head to tail, or coccyx. Return to an upright position. Next, clasp your hands behind your back, keeping your arms and legs straight. Gently pull down with your arms at about a forty-five degree angle from your buttocks and let your chest expand slightly forward (see Figure 4.9b). Be sure to keep your buttocks down to avoid arching your lower back and putting strain on your spine. Breathing follows this pattern: Inhale to prepare; exhale to round; inhale to return to upright position; exhale to stretch in back; inhale to return to starting position.

Pelvis.   From a standing position with legs parallel, hips' width apart, and knees bent: Gently rock your pelvis side to side and then forward and back. Then rotate your pelvis in complete circles in both directions. Keep your breathing even.

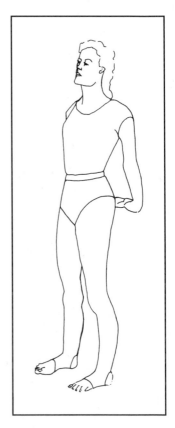

FIGURE 4.9b   Torso stretch (expanding).

Groin.   From a sitting position: Place the soles of your feet together and bring them as close to your body as possible without discomfort. Hold onto your ankles with both hands, inhale, and use your elbows to gently press your knees down as you exhale. Release the knees up.

Legs.   (1) From a standing position with heels together and feet turned out about forty-five degrees: Extend one leg (the stretching leg) to the side into a lunge position, with the leg bent and the foot fully arched (only the toes on the floor). Keep the opposite leg (the supporting leg) straight, the heel on the floor, and the hips even. Press and release gently several times to the side with the leg (see Figure 4.10). Return to standing on both legs. Repeat the stretch with the other leg. This stretch can also be done in parallel position, with the stretching leg in the front pressing forward and the supporting leg in the back remaining straight, with the heel on the floor.

FIGURE 4.10   **Leg stretch in lunge position.**

(2) From a lying-down-on-your-back position: Bend both legs in front of you and place both feet on the floor. Lift one leg (still bent) toward your chest and flex the foot. Then gently extend that leg toward the ceiling, leading with the heel of that flexed foot. Be sure that you do not lock your knees, and always keep the opposite hip down. If your hips move about, stabilize yourself by placing your hands at your waist. Bend the leg and lower it toward your chest; then replace the foot onto the floor to the parallel starting position. Repeat with the other leg.

Verb Phrases

Verbs are action words. Put several of them together (a verb phrase) and you immediately have a movement "script" that requires you to be physically involved. Including verb phrases at the end of a warm-up is an excellent way for the body to make a transition from the warm-up to the acting work of the day. When you warm up, your attention is primarily on yourself, on how your body feels, on your aches and pains. When you rehearse and perform, you need to be able to direct your attention outside of yourself, to focus on your fellow actors, to communicate through words and actions.

"Punch-kick-turn-jump-extend-collapse" is a simple verb phrase that tells you what to do. As in all acting, however, how you do it depends on the choices you make. For example, in the preceding verb phrase, the actor might consider the following:

1. *Energy*—Do you punch fiercely or timidly?
2. *Sequence*—Do you make one big punch or a series of small ones?
3. *Target*—Do you kick someone or something?
4. *Space*—Do you kick in front of you or in back?
5. *Timing*—Do you turn slowly or quickly?
6. *Weight*—Do you jump lightly or heavily?
7. *Size*—Do you extend partially or fully?
8. *Levels*—Do you collapse and remain standing or collapse fully onto the floor?

Another example of a simple verb phrase is "hide-pull-run-crouch-stretch-catch" (see Figure 4.11). What are some of the choices that you can make about each of the verbs? Almost any choice sets in motion an action sequence that is to some degree inherently "dramatic." That kind of physical drama can, in turn, spark your imagination and creativity to help connect mind and body.

The dictionary is full of verbs. For warm-up purposes, the ones that work best are those that are highly physical in nature: *run, roll, push, pull, search, hide, throw, catch, strike, punch,* and so on.

EXERCISES

1. Make up a simple verb phrase. Try doing the entire phrase dealing with timing (very fast or very slow), with weight (with delicacy or with strength), with levels (all on your toes, all down on the floor), and so on.
2. Make up another verb phrase and then list all the possible choices for each verb. Try doing the phrase with many different combinations of choices.
3. Choose a character from the list in Chapter 7 "Using Improvisation" or choose a character that you are working on in a play. Now consider how that character might perform one of your verb phrases. Allow yourself to be surprised. Do not make all the choices in advance.

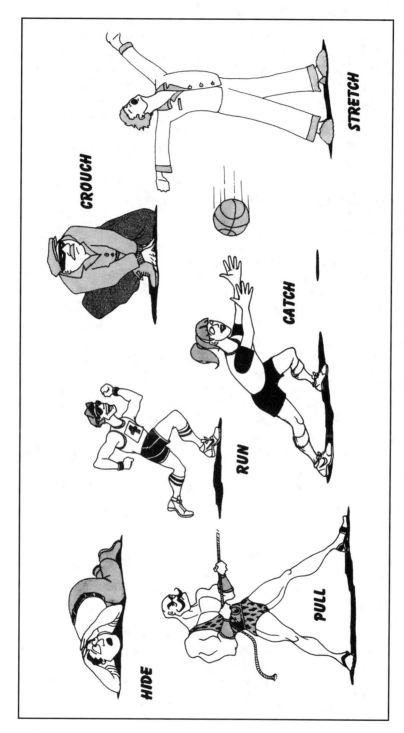

FIGURE 4.11   Verb phrase. 1 Hide; 2 Pull; 3 Run; 4 Crouch; 5 Stretch; 6 Catch.

SUGGESTIONS FOR FURTHER READING

Alter, Judy. *Stretch and Strengthen.* Boston: Houghton Mifflin, 1986.

Anderson, Bob. *Stretching.* Bolinas, CA: Shelter Publications, 1980.

Dell, Cecily. *A Primer for Movement Description.* New York: Dance Notation Bureau Press, 1979.

Kapit, Wynn, and Lawrence M. Elson. *The Anatomy Coloring Book.* New York: Harper and Row, 1977.

King, Nancy. *A Movement Approach to Acting.* Englewood Cliffs, NJ: Prentice-Hall, 1981.

Laban, Rudolf. *The Mastery of Movement.* Boston: MacDonald and Evans, 1971.

Rubin, Lucille S., ed. *Movement for the Actor.* New York: Drama Book Specialists, 1980.

Sweigard, Lulu E. *Human Movement Potential.* New York: Harper and Row, 1974.

Todd, Mabel Elsworth. *The Thinking Body.* Brooklyn, NY: Dance Horizons, 1959.

CHAPTER
FIVE

Voice and the Actor

In our examination of the fundamentals of stage movement, we have seen that firmly established rules govern many basic situations of the theatre. Within the framework of these rules the actor learns to be creative and imaginative. In the same manner, vocal technique must also be learned and used properly in order to achieve maximum effectiveness on stage.

When moving on stage the actor does not move, stand, or sit the way he or she does in everyday life. So too when using the voice certain modifications are necessary, due to the heightened sense of life that is necessary in the theatre before an audience.

This chapter will look at some of the most important considerations of vocal technique for the stage. A detailed study of the voice is not our purpose at this time; such an examination more properly belongs in a book surveying all the elements of voice training. (For making a thorough study of voice training, the reader may consult any of the excellent texts on the subject listed at the end of this chapter.) Here we shall be concerned specifically with two factors of speech in the theatre:

> *And to one of our home-grown tragedians, who had lost his voice by drinking, and who asked Salvini what was necessary in order to become a tragedian, Salvini answered:*
>   *"You need only three things: voice, voice and more voice!"*
>
> From *My Life in Art*—Stanislavski

1. *The voice for stage purposes:* Achieving maximum effectiveness of the voice as an instrument for communicating the character to an audience
2. *Getting the most from the dialogue:* Interpreting the dialogue so as to make it as expressive and meaningful as possible.

Learning to use the voice effectively on stage should be the goal of every actor, and it is the purpose of this chapter to help in achieving this end.

Although we often overlook voice training in our concentration on stage movement, character analysis, emotional representation, and other facets of the actor's work, the importance of a well-trained voice cannot be too strongly emphasized. Voice, body, and thought *all* contribute toward the realization of an effective characterization.

One Voice or Many?

A question that continually reasserts itself during the actor's development concerns versatility and flexibility of the voice. Is it better to have a voice that can project a wide variety of characters of different temperaments and ages or one that is consistent and easily identifiable with the personality of the actor? We recognize immediately that this question is related to the distinctions separating personality and character acting. We have seen that both types of acting are valid and in fact practiced with equal success by various actors. But let us not forget that the voice of uniform quality that conforms to consistent patterns of expression and phrasing will usually consign the actor to a succession of similar roles, a practice often termed *type casting*. The good personality actor possesses a voice that is diversified in quality and phrasing and so variable that it may project many emotional states, moods, and temperaments.

The beginning actor would do well to consider that it is useful to make the voice capable not only of communicating the subtleties of mood, temperament, and emotion, but of suggesting various characters as well. Flexibility of voice rather than a striking vocal attractiveness should be the actor's goal. There are many beautiful voices in the theatre that immediately attract us by their quality or distinctiveness. Let us agree that the attractive voice can be a desirable asset in the theatre, *but when we begin to listen to the voice rather than to what it is saying we are not necessarily hearing good acting.* The same frequently holds true for a voice that is unusual or possessed of a peculiar quality. The actor should aim for a well-modulated voice, capable of a variety of uses, serving many characters in varying situations.

Very often we are surprised to discover an unsuspected potential in an actor's voice that has been long buried in a succession of similar roles. Many years ago the noted director Arthur Hopkins was searching for an actor to play the role of a hardened killer in his production of *The Petrified Forest.* He was in the lobby of a theatre one day, out of sight of the stage, when he heard a dry, keen voice that suggested to him exactly the quality he wanted for the role of Duke Mantee. Thus the director was evaluating a potential performer on vocal quality alone, even before he knew who the actor was. Hopkins was surprised to learn that the voice belonged to an actor who had long played a series of light-comedy and stereotyped juvenile roles in which he strolled about countless drawing rooms with a tennis racket in one hand and a drink in the other. Hopkins followed his instinct and cast the actor in the role of the vicious gangster. The actor repeated his role in a film version of the play and eventually established a reputation as one of the finest "badmen" in films. Hopkins's hunch helped to establish the successful second phase of the career of Humphrey Bogart. It is interesting to note that although again he was type-cast in a series of roles as the "heavy," it was Bogart's amusing performance in *The African*

Judi Dench in *The Way of the World* by William Congreve. Aldwych Theatre, London. Photograph by Britain on View Photographic Library.

Queen as a weather-beaten, drunken captain of a small boat in Equatorial Africa that won for this distinguished actor his only Academy Award.

Stark Young has pointed out the importance of a flexible stage voice:

> In a comedy of manners like the *School for Scandal* the voice should be clear, finished, the lips expert, the tongue striking well on the teeth; the tone would go up and down but always be sure of its place in the throat, be crisp, shining, in hand, like the satin and gold of the furniture and costumes, the rapier at the wrist, the lace over it, the worldliness and the wit. In Chekhov it would have the last naturalness, every closeness to feeling and impulse that the moment reveals. In Shakespeare a range of elaborate music, suited to the style, clearness, with warmth of poetic emotion. In D'Annunzio's drama the voice would have to be rich and sensuous, metallic, shading infinitely, the voice of a degenerate god. And so on through the styles and moods of all drama.[1]

Factors of a Good Stage Voice

Good acting requires the effective use of the vocal mechanism to express the intellectual and emotional content of the dialogue. When the actor has succeeded in doing this we can say that he or she is using the voice properly. The following questions may help the actor gauge his or her effectiveness in meeting the demands of voice for the theatre.

- *Does the voice call attention to itself?* Do we listen to the voice rather than the matter it should be communicating? Listening to recordings of actors who were prominent in the early part of this century, such as E. H. Sothern, Rose Coghlan, Julia Marlowe, and others, one is struck by the emphasis on intonation and other discarded elocutionary tricks. Speeches took on the aspect of an operatic aria, designed to display the vocal resources of the actor rather than to communicate meaning. In the present day we have departed from this formal style of reading and choose to have the voice serve the dialogue rather than the actor. The voice should be completely appropriate to the requirements of the role.
- *Is the voice difficult to hear?* The voice should be heard easily by all members of the audience and projected with adequate volume and clarity in every situation. Volume may have to be increased or decreased by the demands of the action, but at no time should it fall below a level that is audible in every part of the auditorium.
- *Can the actor be understood?* Good articulation plays an important role in projection and in making dialogue meaningful. Slovenly articulation is never desirable, either in realistic or in presentational productions. In-

---

1. Stark Young, *Theatre Practice* (New York: Scribner, 1926), pp. 159–160.

deed, many of the great plays from the past require an extremely high degree of competence in stage diction and clarity of expression.

- *Is the voice monotonous?*   Variety in pitch, rate, and loudness is essential if the voice is to prove interesting. It is best if the actor does not use variety simply for the sake of avoiding monotony but permits the substance of the lines to indicate where variety will be most expressive of the meaning. Usually a comprehension of the character will induce such variety, but even well-produced and carefully articulated speech may fall short of effectiveness on the stage. As we may remember from our discussion of the physical aspect of acting, the actor should assimilate the techniques of voice for the stage into his or her work so that little thought is devoted to the technique itself. This requires a thorough knowledge of the proper use of voice and articulation. Often rehearsals produce excessive fatigue, especially during a trial-and-error period when many different qualities and inflectional patterns are tried. Understanding the potentials of the voice will make this period less difficult and not only provide the means of achieving the proper vocal characterization but also lessen the strain that often accompanies an attempt to alter the normal voice.

Vocal Production

Because our speaking mechanism consists of organs primarily designed for other purposes, we refer to speech as an *overlaid function.* Speech is secondary to other vital functions that the speech organs perform. The speech process consists of four parts: (1) breathing, (2) phonation, or the initial creation of sound, (3) resonation, or the amplifying of the sound, and (4) articulation, or the shaping of intelligible syllables.

The primary function of breathing is to sustain life, not to provide the power needed for vocalization. Although we tend to think that the larynx was designed specifically for the initiation of sound, it is in fact a type of valve designed to keep unwanted foreign matter from our lungs. Our tongue and teeth were designed for eating rather than articulation. When we undergo moments of great stress we often find that the organs are unable to perform their secondary functions.

Breathing

The lungs provide the power for the vocal mechanism. It is through the control of breathing that we can increase or decrease volume, regulate phrasing, and provide the necessary support for vocal tone. To better understand the function of breathing and vocal production, it might be helpful to compare the total mechanism with a wind instrument such as a clarinet (see Figure 5.1).

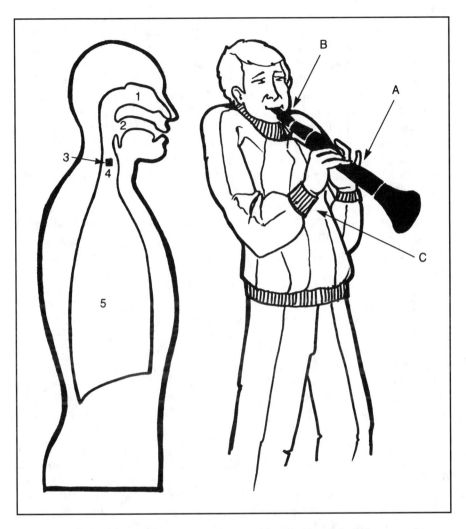

FIGURE 5.1 Vocal production. *Resonators:* **(1) nose, (2) mouth, (3) larynx, and (A) tube of clarinet.** *Vibrator:* **(4) vocal cords and (B) reed.** *Source of air pressure:* **(5) lungs and (C) lungs.**

In the clarinet, sound is produced when the reed is set in vibration by air blown into the tube. Comparing the diagram of the vocal mechanism with that of the clarinet, we may note that the vocal mechanism produces sound by means of an air stream passing through the larynx, with the vocal folds performing much the same function as the reed in the wind instrument. The resonating areas in the throat and head serve to reinforce the sound in the same manner as the tube of the wind instrument.

Unless one is afflicted with a disease of the respiratory system, inhalation poses no difficulty. Although in some cases the supply of air *inhaled* may be insufficient for sustained speech in the theatre, the difficulty more often lies in establishing good habits for controlled *exhalation*. As in our analogy with the wind instrument, we know that if we can exhale air in proper quantities and in a controlled manner, we can produce a loud, clear, and sustained tone. The question, in relation to the actor's needs, is this: *How can I get more air into my lungs and control its exhalation?*

Many beginning actors are surprised to learn that they are breathing improperly for stage purposes. Proper breathing involves the muscles of the thorax, the diaphragm, and the abdominal area.

The correct sequence of inhalation is as follows: (1) The muscles of the thorax elevate the ribs. (2) The diaphragm moves downward, expanding the area of the thorax. (3) The resulting differential of air pressures causes air to rush into the lungs. (4) The lungs fill the enlarged area of the thoracic cavity (see Figure 5.2).

Exhalation reverses this process. The muscles of the abdomen push the diaphragm up into the thoracic cavity, decreasing its size and forcing air from the lungs. It is not uncommon to expel a greater amount of air than is necessary during vocalization, causing shortness of breath or gasping and limiting the ability to phrase properly when reading dialogue. The steady stream of air needed for proper volume and sustained phrasing in acting can be achieved only if the muscles of the abdomen contract gradually to provide air continually rather than all at once.

One of the more common causes of a weak voice and poor tone quality is *chest breathing*. Chest breathing hinders the effective use of the voice on the speaker's platform or on the stage. This type of breathing utilizes only the upper chest for inhalation. The shoulders tense into a strained position and the collar bones rise during each inhalation. The consequences are an unsteady voice, lack of volume, and a jerkiness in exhalation during vocalization.

The following exercises should help the actor to determine whether the manner of breathing is hindering vocal effectiveness. The exercises will also provide ways to develop good breathing habits and make volume control more effective for stage purposes.

1. Lie down and place your hands on the abdominal area. Breathe as usual. Note whether the abdomen rises and falls during inhalation and exhalation. If the abdomen does not rise during inhalation, it is likely that breathing habits are poor. Relax and continue until you feel the abdomen rise and fall with each breath. Try this exercise first in a lying down position and then in a standing position. Inhale slowly and make an effort to push out the abdominal muscles as you inhale.

2. In a standing, relaxed position, inhale as deeply as possible. Hold the abdominal muscles as firm as possible. Count out loud in a clear, firm

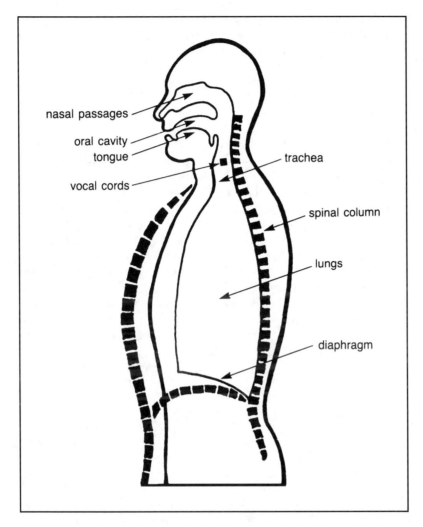

FIGURE 5.2   The speech organs. Dotted line shows effect of deep inhalation within the thoracic cavity.

voice. Make a definite effort not to contract or to release the abdominal muscles immediately. You should be able to count to twenty without too much difficulty. Continue this exercise until you can count to thirty. Now try to inhale in the upper chest area only. As you exhale, count out loud in a clear, firm voice. How does your count compare to your count when you used the abdominal area?

3. In a standing position inhale as deeply as possible, and then emit a stream of air with a hissing sound. Continue this exercise until you can continue this hissing sound without a break for thirty seconds.

4. In a standing position inhale as deeply as possible. In one breath repeat the following phrase. Make each repetition louder than the preceding one: *Cowards die many times before their death, the valiant never taste of death but once.*

Vocal Tone

Phonation, or the production of the vocal tone, is initiated by the vocal folds, which are located in the larynx, and amplified by the resonating chambers in the head and neck. The larynx consists of masses of cartilage and muscle that support and operate the vocal folds. These thick folds, which are variously called the vocal cords, vocal bands, or vocal lips, produce the vocal tone when their outer edges are set in vibration by the air stream exhaled from the lungs.

Tautness and constriction may be the most serious impediments to using the voice with maximal effectiveness. Constriction in the throat and laryngeal area may be brought on by nervousness, fatigue, or emotional stress and can become a serious problem, for it will affect both phonation and the resonation of vocal tone. Frequently the result is harshness and stridency. Projecting extensive dialogue from a constricted throat during successive performances may give rise to longer lasting consequences: The voice may eventually become hoarse and laryngitis may result.

Lynn Redgrave recalls problems with her voice during her years of training. She said:

> It used to go up from nerves a lot; it was fairly thin and didn't have much body to it . . . What I hadn't realized was how badly I had used it for a long time: I started to lose it even when I wasn't pushing it very hard . . . If you're using it wrong, it can be thrown out so early; a bit of nerves, you tighten and that's it.[2]

In more serious cases permanent damage may be done to the vocal folds.

The vocal tone initiated by the vibrating of the vocal folds is quite meager, and if it were not for the amplification of the sound by several resonating chambers, human speech would be almost inaudible. The major resonators are the pharynx, the mouth, and the nasal passages. Differences in the size and shape of these resonators from one person to another account for the distinctive quality of each person's voice. Any factor that influences the functioning of these resonating chambers will produce a marked change in vocal quality. The change in tone brought about by slight modifications of nasal resonance is known to every victim of hay fever and the common head cold.

The nasal passages have little function in resonation; the pharynx and

---

2. Lynn Redgrave, quoted in Joanmarie Kalter, *Actors on Acting* (New York: Sterling, 1979), p. 84.

mouth are more important. Like phonation, resonation is also hampered by tenseness and constriction. An "open" throat and mouth are essential for achieving proper resonance. Any partial closure of the resonating chambers may seriously hamper the production of good vocal tone. One such problem frequently encountered is a tendency to arch the back of the tongue during phonation. This simple habit narrows the oral opening, resulting in a considerable loss of volume and fullness of the tone.

Because acting may impose greater emotional stress and tension than a person's normal activities, projecting good vocal tone is often a serious problem. The importance of relaxation as the proper means of eliminating these difficulties cannot be stressed too strongly. Relaxation helps to produce good vocal quality, with fullness of tone and freedom from hoarseness, stridency, and strain. The following exercises are designed to help develop relaxation for the production of good vocal tone.

1. In order to clarify the difference between tension and relaxation, follow this procedure. (a) Stand at attention. Tense every muscle. Pull in the chin and the abdomen, keeping the back straight. Hold this position for ten seconds. Note how uncomfortable it is to retain this position. (b) Begin to relax *slowly*. Let the head and shoulders droop, the arms and hands hang loosely. Try to eliminate every semblance of tension. Try to feel the tension leave through the fingers. Wiggle them if it helps. Note the difference between the tensed and relaxed positions. (c) Sit down and tense yourself as you did in the standing position. After maintaining the tension for ten seconds, slowly relax. Again note the difference between the tensed and relaxed positions.

2. Work on Exercise 1 until you have little difficulty in making the transition from tension to relaxation. Try to make the change from an extremely tensed to an extremely relaxed position as rapidly as possible. Continue to do this so that you can make an immediate and complete change.

3. Tense your neck and throat until they become rigid. If possible make the cords stand out in the neck. Relax the throat by yawning several times. Read the following passages, first with a tense neck and throat and then after you have yawned and relaxed the throat. Compare your readings. After comparing the two readings, work for as full and rich a vocal tone as possible.

GHOST: I am thy father's spirit,
Doomed for a certain term to walk the night
And for the day confined to fast in fires
Till the foul crimes done in my days of nature
Are burnt and purged away.
William Shakespeare, *Hamlet*

ANTONY: This was the noblest Roman of them all.
All the conspirators, save only he,
Did that they did in envy of great Caesar;
He only, in a general honest thought
And common good to all, made one of them.
His life was gentle, and the elements
So mixed in him that Nature might stand up
And say to all the world, "This was a man."
William Shakespeare, *Julius Caesar*

Out upon the angry wind! how from sighing, it began to bluster round the merry forge, banging at the wicket, and grumbling in the chimney, as if it bullied the jolly bellows from doing anything to order.
Charles Dickens, *Martin Chuzzlewit*

4. Observe the back of your tongue and your soft palate in a mirror. Inhale as if to begin a yawn, and note the height of the soft palate and the lowered position of the tongue. Practice until you are able to develop this "open-throat" position without inhaling prior to the yawn.
5. Practice the open-throat position until you feel it to be relaxed. Remember that the tongue should be depressed and the soft palate raised. With the throat open, read the following short passages:

Oh, how I long for good oral tone.

Tomorrow, and tomorrow, and tomorrow,
Creeps in this petty pace from day to day,
To the last syllable of recorded time.
William Shakespeare, *Macbeth*

O you that are so strong and cold,
O blower, are you young or old?
Are you a beast of field and tree,
Or just a stronger child than me?
  O wind, a-blowing all day long,
  O wind, that sings so loud a song!
Robert Louis Stevenson

The voice of the west wind is wooing my footsteps,
The clouds scamper onward to show me the way:
The grasses are mocking the high, swaying treetops;
I'm off at their bidding—
  Away!
Author Unknown

Distinctness

Audiences have great difficulty in understanding speech that is poorly enunciated and slovenly. The stage situation focuses attention upon carelessness in speech that is generally overlooked in normal conversation.

Any number of factors can create improper articulation—among them substitution of improper speech sounds, incorrect use of the articulators, and foreign-language influences. Such functional speech problems, however, constitute only a small fraction of the difficulties that beset the actor when reading. *The most common articulation fault results from carelessness.* Poor enunciation may usually be traced to lazy or slovenly movement of the lips and tongue. The carry-over of habits from everyday conversation and the added tensions of stage activities simply amplify the problem.

Good articulation does not mean an overly precise or exaggerated pronunciation of every word. Exaggeration of this kind will only draw attention to itself and may be as detrimental as careless articulation. In striving to overcome poor enunciation, some actors overarticulate to the extent that their speech is obviously forced and false. Excessively precise articulation of syllables in unstressed positions may serve only to highlight the actor's problem. One young actor with careless speech learned this lesson when he was cast in the role of a gangster. Acutely aware of his diction problem, he attempted to correct it by consciously and carefully overarticulating every word he spoke on stage. The result was speech that had the tempo and rhythm of a hardened hoodlum but suggested that the character had spent a few months at an English finishing school for gentlemen. The audience's reaction to his performance can be imagined. Distinct speech on stage calls for the proper and clear articulation of sounds in the context of *correct pronunciation* and *stress.*

Distinctness can be improved by simply opening the mouth more than is habitual in nonstage speech and increasing the activity of the articulators, without adding any undue stress to the words themselves. No matter how well the actor has mastered control of volume, projection is seriously limited when speech is not crisp and clear.

An excellent exercise to help make the actor aware of the importance of the articulators involves the use of a pencil and some dialogue from any well-written play.

Read at usual stage projection level a passage such as those found at the end of this chapter. After finishing, take a pencil and place it lengthwise between the front teeth. Clamp down on the pencil with the teeth and reread the monologue for a period of two minutes. You will notice that proper articulation is difficult because of the impediment between the teeth. You will need to work harder than usual to make the passage meaningful. It is also very likely that the muscles around the jaw will hurt when you are doing this exercise. This sensation indicates that muscles that have not been used extensively are getting a good workout.

Nicholas Nickleby, by Charles Dickens. Adapted by David Edgar, Royal
Shakespeare Company. Directed by Trevor Nunn and John Caird. Photograph
by Britain on View Photographic Library.

Remove the pencil and read the speech a third time. You should be
aware immediately that this reading is more distinct than the first attempt.
You have been forced to use the articulators more than is customary, and it
has produced surprisingly crisp speech. Eventually the old habits will return, but continued practice with the pencil should help to eliminate the
habits causing indistinctiveness in speech.

Projection

Projection seems to have become an increasing problem during the past several years. A number of factors have contributed to this difficulty, especially
the frequency with which we watch television drama, and the increasing
"naturalism" of the motion picture. The close-up techniques of these media,

which produce an effect of intimacy, make projection above a conversational level inappropriate. New actors whose early exposure to acting technique has come primarily from these media may find particular difficulty with stage projection.

Undoubtedly the introspective nature of many contemporary plays has also served to amplify the problem. Also, the trend toward a quieter and less exuberant style of theatre produces in many young actors a natural reticence about really "letting go" on stage. Often the tensions of stage performance interfere with good speech habits and hence limit the ability of the actor to project the dialogue so that it is *heard and understood by every member of the audience.*

Projection is not synonymous with adequate volume level. Proper projection of dialogue includes effective use of the entire speech mechanism. The following three factors are directly related to good projection on stage:

1. *Controlled exhalation for adequate volume level.* This does not mean shouting or yelling, but the use of good breathing habits to produce a reasonably loud, firm voice.
2. *Proper phonation and resonation* so that the voice is not pinched and small. The throat should be relaxed and open.
3. *Crisp articulation* so that dialogue is spoken distinctly.

A breakdown in any of these three closely related elements will result in faulty projection, and with it failure to communicate to part of the audience.

Getting the Most from the Dialogue

> *I ain't paid to make good lines sound good. I'm paid to make bad lines sound good.*
>
> Walter Huston

Making the voice an instrument of the actor's intention requires both sensitivity and understanding. The sensitivity will grow as the actor's perception of the role increases. Although dialogue must never be read in accordance with inflexible and mechanical rules, knowledge of the basic factors of vocal expressiveness is essential.

Rate

The term *rate* refers to the *number of words spoken during a given period of time.* The rate of speech, therefore, will be affected both by the actual speed of speech and by the number and length of the pauses inserted. The average rate of speech varies considerably from one actor to another, and indeed during any given play it will differ for the same individual from one scene to the next. Usually the rate of stage speech is about 130 to 150 words per minute, but there will be occasions when a faster or slower rate is required. One point worth remembering is that *stage speech requires a much slower rate than that used in everyday conversation.* If one were to use the normal rate of everyday speech on stage, it might well be unintelligible. Certain considerations help to determine the appropriate rate of speech:

1. *The role.* The rate of speech used on stage often suggests certain character traits or temperament. A young, excitable, or dynamic individual might well use a faster rate than one who is aged, reflective, or of a quiet disposition.
2. *The type of play.* The tempo of a play may well determine the rate to be used by the entire cast. A comedy or farce, for example, will usually require a faster tempo than a melodrama or tragedy.
3. *The purpose of the dialogue.* The actual content of the dialogue often will suggest to the actor when rate should be increased or decreased. Material of a trivial or inconsequential nature will require a relatively faster rate. When the content is important or when important exposition is to be communicated, a decrease in rate will often help to make the dialogue more meaningful.

In plays that require a particularly rapid tempo, often it is wise to decrease the rate of the more important words or ideas. Significant phrases may be made relatively important by prolonging selected words or inserting pauses in the most meaningful places. It is well to remember that no matter what rate is dictated by the character or tempo of the play, *variety of rate* is essential to avoid monotony during the playing of any protracted scene. The best rule to follow when determining the rate to use is this: *Proper rate will vary with the demands of the action and the character.*

Pitch

Pitch refers to the position of the spoken sound on the musical scale. Voices are classified on both the basis of quality and pitch range. Thus, the tenor voice has a higher pitch range than that of the bass; the soprano voice is higher than the contralto. Pitch is also a major factor in the actor's technique of expression. There are normally three recurrent pitch difficulties that inhibit the actor's effectiveness:

1. *Pitch may be too high or too low.* The habitual pitch of the actor may be above or below the *optimum* or ideal pitch, limiting the actor in the range of pitch changes that are possible in one direction.
2. *There may be a lack of variety in pitch.* When there is failure to make pitch changes during speech, the result is *monopitch,* sometimes mistakenly called *monotone.* Such speech is dull, uninteresting, and unlikely to retain audience attention for long.
3. *The voice may fall into a pitch pattern.* There may be a number of pitch changes while speaking, but such changes may be repetitious and used without any regard for the exact nature of the material.

The actor will have occasion to depict a great range of emotions in various plays. Many of our basic emotional responses are normally associated with certain pitch levels, and it is imperative that the actor be able to call upon a pitch range adequate to project these emotions. Pitch levels have the following associated values for the listener:

Low pitch is generally associated with deep-keyed emotional states, such as religious awe and sorrow, and is also suggestive of sincerity.

High pitch is often associated with a heightened emotional state such as fear and terror, uncontrollable anger or rage, great excitement, and even hysteria.

As we have just noted in our discussion of rate, variety is important if the actor is to maintain the interest of the audience. Pitch, too, must be varied, not only to avoid monotony but to aid in the communication of meaning. The voice can be varied in pitch by the use of *step* and *inflection.* It is well to make a distinction between these two terms, because they are easily confused.

Step is a pitch change from word to word in a phrase or sentence. Pitch changes of this type are frequently used as a means of emphasizing a key word or idea. In a *step* pitch change, then, there is no change within a word but there is a change in pitch as the speaker moves from one word to another.

Inflection refers to pitch change or slide *within* one word or sound, in either an upward or downward direction. The word *really* serves as a simple example to illustrate how a change in inflection produces a change in meaning. If the word is read with an upward inflection (reálly) a question is clearly implied; read with a downward inflection (reàlly) it may connote boredom or an affirmative statement of understanding. A change in inflectional pitch often conveys a completely different meaning for the same word.

Changing pitch by step or inflection is a fundamental technique in stage speech and must be mastered by all competent actors. Variety in pitch will grow from the needs of the characterization and the drama. *Mechanical pitch changes made simply to avoid monotony in speech must not be used.*

Getting Meaning from the Line

In analyzing dialogue and attempting to extract meaning, the actor should be careful not to put too much value on the first reading given to any line. There is rarely only one right way to read a line.

Dialogue in any competently written play cannot be divorced from the play without suffering a fundamental loss of meaning. Because dialogue is written to advance action and illustrate character, to set mood or establish locale, a line may have several meanings suggestive of each of these factors. During the preliminary examination and early rehearsals we often tend to give dialogue a somewhat mechanical and stereotyped interpretation. As we proceed through the rehearsal period, we discover new and subtle relationships among several portions of the dialogue. As our understanding of the essence of the play and the purpose of each line of dialogue increases, we add nuances that make for an interpretation quite different from that which we gave to the dialogue during our first reading.

The actor should try to avoid imparting meaning simply by mechanical means during the early rehearsal period. Too often such readings become permanently fixed in the playing of the role. A mechanical and studied reading becomes all too evident to the audience, who will reject such a performance as lifeless and dull. The meaning and emotional color of a line or phrase will grow as perception of the character and the character's motivations grow. As an understanding of the play and character develops, the actor should be able to make the dialogue meaningful by the use of shading, organization, and emphasis.

Shading

The simplest word or vocal response may have a number of contrasting meanings. Seizing on the more obvious meaning may prevent a deeper understanding of its value in the scene or the play. This point can be easily illustrated by choosing as an example the simple exclamation "Oh." Let us assume that it is spoken in the following brief sequence of dialogue:

> JANE: Tom fell down and injured his leg.
> MARY: Oh.

How is one to interpret the exclamation "Oh"? The meaning "What a terrible thing to happen to Tom" may be absolutely correct. Further consideration, however, may suggest many different ways of replying to the statement about the unfortunate and clumsy young man. The short dialogue should be examined again to see how many of the following nine meanings it can be given.

Try to read the word "Oh" in a manner that will suggest each of the following possible reactions:

An Attitude	*That Intends to Convey the Meaning:*
1. Indifference	"It makes no difference to me. I couldn't care less!"
2. Comprehension	"So he did go through with his plan to climb the tree after all."
3. Noncomprehension	"I don't follow you. Who's Tom?"
4. Inattention	"I'm sorry, what did you say? I was thinking of something else."
5. Disbelief	"It couldn't possibly be Tom."
6. Disgust	"He did it again, the young fool."
7. Pity	"What a shame, he's such a nice young man."
8. Shock	"But Tom is due to play running back tomorrow in the football game."
9. Pleasure	"Good, I never liked him anyway. Serves him right."

It is clear that the response in itself has no inherent meaning until we relate it to the context of the play. Other words or exclamations easily provide the same type of exercise. They are helpful in sharpening our perception of the values that we might wish to attach to any word or short phrase. This list might include: "Really!" "So!" "Yes!" "No!" "Of course!" "You!" As an exercise, these words should be read with an attempt to give at least five different meanings to each.

Organization and Emphasis

We easily recognize that simple words and phrases may suggest various meanings and emotional colors. The extended phrase or complete sentence may call for more complex techniques. The way to decide on the organization and emphasis of words is to understand the *ideas* they convey. Mental laziness is often the cause of our failure to perceive the correct relationship between words and the ideas they are intended to convey.

Many individuals are unable to transmit the real meaning of what they intend to say. Confusion, misinterpretations, and misunderstandings frequently arise from our inability to state clearly what we mean. We develop a type of "mental laziness" that gives rise to a half-idea, a half-conception, a half-truth. This occurs not only in the theatre but in everyday life as well.

The following sentence serves as an illustration of how disaster will occur when we misplace a pause and fail to scrutinize the value of the *organization* of ideas in reading.

Victory unlikely for army to fail again.

Read the sentence with the pause after *victory* and we have:

Victory—unlikely for army to fail again.

Insert the pause after *unlikely* and the phrase reads:

Victory unlikely—for army to fail again.

Emphasis is the meaningful stress we give to any word in a phrase or sentence. Just as we may stress certain syllables in a word and leave others unstressed, so too we may stress key words in a phrase and give to others a subsidiary emphasis. Words may be emphasized by (1) force, (2) pause (before or after), (3) prolongation of the word, and (4) inflection. A phrase such as "John won the race today" may seem a simple statement of fact, but the shifting of emphasis from one key word to another may completely alter the significance of the sentence. All of the four devices for emphasis may be used in this phrase to connote the intended meaning.

1. "*John* won the race today." The phrase indicates clearly that John won against all competition. The others (our friends, perhaps?) lost.
2. "John won the *race* today." John may have lost in some other competition but he did win the race. Perhaps he failed his math exam.
3. "John *won* the race today." Despite the doubt raised in some quarters, John really did win. Those sore losers!
4. "John won the race *today*." John may not have won yesterday, but he was certainly victorious today. It's about time, too!

Clearly the implications are quite dissimilar, differentiated by the shift of emphasis from one key word to another. The importance of organization and emphasis may be illustrated by choosing any number of phrases or sentences taken at random from the dialogue of a play and searching for the key words.

The following straightforward sentence will serve to illustrate how it is possible, by means of organization and emphasis, to suggest numerous and almost unexpected meanings from one line of dialogue.

I want to go to the party with Jim Saturday night.

Try reading the sentence without any emotional overtones, attempting only to communicate a simple piece of information. How did you read it? What does it really mean? Might not any of the following implications be correct?

Read the line to mean:

1. I want to go not on Friday but on Saturday.
2. I want to go in the evening, not in the afternoon.
3. I don't want to go to the movies; I prefer the party.
4. I don't want to go with Harry, but with Jim.
5. I don't want to meet Jim there; I want him to take me.
6. Only one of us can go to the party, and I have decided to go.
7. What you may have heard is wrong; I really do want to go.
8. I don't want to go to the small party, but to the big formal.

Each of these meanings may be suggested directly by emphasis and organization *without* any emotional coloring. If we were to give to these various meanings the character's emotional viewpoint, the number of readings that might be given to the line would increase greatly. The character might be very happy and still intend to impart any of the eight suggested meanings relative to state of mind.

Now read the line with each of the meanings already suggested and any others you care to add, but include the following *emotional colorings: sadness, gaiety, anger, love, timidity, indifference.*

We now have forty-eight combinations that may correctly convey the meaning of the line. Many more are certainly possible. If we were to ask, "which meaning is correct?" the answer, of course, would be that we don't know. We do not have enough information about the character, the action, or the mood of the play. Such information comes as we delve into the play, analyze the character, and rehearse with our fellow actors. What we do know, however, is that it is possible to give even the simplest line of dialogue a multiplicity of meanings, deriving primarily from our comprehension of its purpose in the play. At any rate, let us hope the speaker gets to the party.

Vocal technique, then, is only a means to an end. When we understand and utilize its great potential, however, we take a great step forward on the road to the successful fulfillment of the actor's goal—a believable and *meaningful* portrayal of character.

Vocal Exercises

As important as it is to develop the physical mechanism in order to make it flexible and able to project the greatest possible range of physical expressiveness, so too must the actor make the voice adequate to the demands placed on it in any given role. The purpose of the following selections is to provide practical exercises that will help develop a wide range of vocal expressiveness. The first group of exercises contains articulation problems frequently found in certain types of plays. The second group makes demands on a greater range of vocal resources, including variety, phrasing, emphasis, and dramatic pointing. Although many of the selections are not from dramatic literature, all of them require the fullest competence in stage speech, if the actor is to realize their dramatic potential.

Articulation

Each of the following selections contains pitfalls for the actor with sloppy speech. Most of them are patter songs from the operettas of Gilbert and Sullivan. These passages require not only precise articulation but facility in delivery and careful pointing. Merely getting through the selection without error should not be the goal of the actor here: *Scintillating and seemingly effortless delivery* is necessary for the successful presentation of these exercises.

> Oh! my name is John Wellington Wells,
> I'm a dealer in magic and spells,
> > In blessings and curses
> > And ever-filled purses,
> In prophecies, witches, and knells.
>
> If you want a proud foe to "make tracks"—
> If you'd melt a rich uncle in wax—
> > You've but to look in
> > On our resident Djinn,
> Number seventy, Simmery Axe!
>
> We've a first-class assortment of magic;
> > And for raising a posthumous shade
> With effects that are comic or tragic,
> > There's no cheaper house in the trade.
> Love-philtre—we've quantities of it;
> > And for knowledge if any one burns,
> We keep an extremely small prophet, a prophet
> > Who brings us unbounded returns:

For he can prophesy
With a wink of his eye,
Peep with security
Into futurity,
Sum up your history,
Clear up a mystery,
Humour proclivity
For a nativity—for a nativity;
With mirrors so magical,
Tetrapods tragical,
Bogies spectacular,
Answers oracular,
Facts astronomical,
Solemn or comical,
And, if you want it, he
Makes a reduction on taking a quantity!

Oh! If any one anything lacks,
He'll find it all ready in stacks,
 If he'll only look in
 On the resident Djinn,
Number seventy, Simmery Axe!

"The Sorcerer's Song,"
W. S. Gilbert, *The Sorcerer*

I am the very model of a modern Major-General,
I've information vegetable, animal, and mineral,
I know the kings of England, and I quote the fights historical,
From Marathon to Waterloo, in order categorical;
I'm very well acquainted too with matters mathematical,
I understand equations, both the simple and quadratical,
About binomial theorem I'm teeming with a lot o' news—
With many cheerful facts about the square of the hypotenuse.
I'm very good at integral and differential calculus,
I know the scientific names of beings animalculous;
In short, in matters vegetable, animal, and mineral,
I am the very model of a modern Major-General.

"The Major-General's Song,"
W. S. Gilbert, *The Pirates of Penzance*

You're a regular wreck, with a crick in your neck; and no wonder you snore
 for your head's on the floor, and you're needles and pins from your soles
 to your shins; and your flesh is a-creep, and your left leg's asleep; and
 you've cramps in your toes, and a fly on your nose, and some fluff in your
 lung, and a feverish tongue, and a thirst that's intense, and a general sense
 that you haven't been sleeping in clover;

"The Lord Chancellor's Nightmare,"
W. S. Gilbert, *Iolanthe*

Vocal Variety

Many of the following selections test the actor's ability to work with material of a highly descriptive nature. All of the vocal resources of emphasis, phrasing, pause, and dramatic pointing should be called into play. Actual monologues from plays have not been widely used here because characterization is not a basic concern in this section; the actor's attention should be devoted primarily to the development of vocal flexibility. Extensive work in making these isolated examples of prose and poetry exciting and dramatically effective will serve to extend the range of the actor's vocal expressiveness. Such exercises provide a means of preparing the actor to cope with the full vocal demands of a play.

That is the issue that will continue in this country when these poor tongues of Judge Douglas and myself shall be silent. It is the eternal struggle between these two principles—right and wrong—throughout the world. They are the two principles that have stood face to face from the beginning of time; and will ever continue to struggle. The one is the common right of humanity, and the other the divine right of kings. It is the same principle in whatever shape it develops itself. It is the same spirit that says, "You toil and work and earn bread, and I'll eat it." No matter in what shape it comes, whether from the mouth of a king who seeks to bestride the people of his own nation and live by the fruit of their labor, or from one race of men as an apology for enslaving another race, it is the same tyrannical principle.

"On the Enslavement of Men," Abraham Lincoln,
Debate with Stephen Douglas, Alton, Illinois, October 15, 1858

It is said an Eastern monarch once charged his wise men to invent him a sentence to be ever in view, and which should be true and appropriate in all times and situations. They presented him the words: "And this, too, shall pass away." How much it expresses! How chastening in the hour of pride! How consoling in the depths of affliction! . . . And yet, let us hope, it is not quite true. Let us hope, rather, that by the best cultivation of the physical world beneath and around us, and the best intellectual and moral world within us, we shall secure an individual, social, and political prosperity and happiness, whose course shall be onward and upward, and which, while the earth endures, shall not pass away.

"A True Sentence?" Abraham Lincoln,
Address, September 30, 1859

But whatever may be our fate, be assured that this Declaration will stand. It may cost treasure and it may cost blood; but it will stand, and it will richly compensate for both. Through the thick gloom of the present, I see the brightness of the future as the sun in heaven. We shall make this a glorious, an immortal day. When we are in our graves, our children will honor it. They will celebrate it with thanksgiving, with festivity, with bonfires, and illuminations. On its annual return, they will shed tears, copious, gushing tears, not of subjection and slavery, not of agony and distress, but of exultation, of gratitude, and of joy.

Sir, before God, I believe the hour is come. My judgment approves this measure, and my whole heart is in it. All that I have, and all that I am, and all that I hope in this life, I am now ready here to stake upon it; and I leave off as I began, that, live or die, survive or perish, I am for the Declaration. It is my living sentiment, and by the blessing of God it shall be my dying sentiment—independence now, and INDEPENDENCE FOREVER!

"On the Declaration of Independence," Daniel Webster,
Supposed Speech of John Adams

It was the best of times, it was the worst of times, it was the age of wisdom, it was the age of foolishness, it was the epoch of belief, it was the epoch of incredulity, it was the season of Light, it was the season of Darkness, it was the string of hope, it was the winter of despair, we had everything before us, we had nothing before us, we were all going direct to Heaven, we were all going direct the other way—in short, the period was so far like the present period, that some of its noisiest authorities insisted on its being received, for good or for evil, in the superlative degree of comparison only.

There were a king with a large jaw and a queen with a plain face, on the throne of England; there were a king with a large jaw and a queen with a fair face, on the throne of France. In both countries it was clearer than crystal to the lords of the State preserves of loaves and fishes, that things in general were settled for ever.

"The Best of Times," Charles Dickens,
A Tale of Two Cities

Out upon the angry wind! how from sighing, it began to bluster round the merry forge, banging at the wicket, and grumbling in the chimney, as if it bullied the jolly bellows from doing anything to order. And what an impotent swaggerer it was, too, for all its poise; for if it had any influence on that hoarse companion, it was but to make him roar his cheerful song the louder, and by consequence to make the fire burn the brighter, and the sparks to dance more gayly yet; at length, they whizzed so madly round and round, that it was too much for such a surly wind to bear; so off it flew with a howl, giving the old sign before the alehouse door such a cuff as it went, that the Blue Dragon was more rampant than usual ever afterwards, and, indeed, before Christmas, reared clear out of his crazy frame.

"The Wind," Charles Dickens, *Martin Chuzzlewit*

When the eyes of Prince Prospero fell upon this spectral image (which with a slow and solemn movement, as if more fully to sustain its role, stalked to and fro among the waltzers) he was seen to be convulsed in the first moment with a strong shudder either of terror or distaste; but in the next his brow reddened with rage.

"Who dares?" he demanded hoarsely of the courtiers who stood near him—"who dares insult us with this blasphemous mockery? Seize him and unmask him, that we may know whom we have to hang at sunrise from the battlements!"

It was the eastern or blue chamber in which stood the Prince Prospero as he uttered these words. They rang throughout the seven rooms loudly and clearly—for the prince was a bold and robust man, and the music had become hushed at the waving of his hand.

It was in the blue room where stood the prince, with a group of pale courtiers by his side. At first, as he spoke, there was a slight rushing movement of this group in the direction of the intruder, who at the moment was also near at hand, and now, with deliberate and stately step, made closer approach to the speaker. But, from a certain nameless awe with which the mad assumptions of the mummer had inspired the whole party, there were found none who put forth hand to seize him; so that unimpeded he passed within a yard of the prince's person; and while the vast assembly, as if with one impulse, shrank from the centres of the rooms to the walls, he made his way uninterruptedly, but with the same solemn and measured step which had distinguished him from the first, through the blue chamber to the purple—through the purple to the green—through the green to the orange—through this again to the white—and even thence to the violet, ere a decided movement had been made to arrest him. It was then, however, that the Prince Prospero, maddening with rage and shame of his own momentary cowardice, rushed hurriedly through the six chambers, while none followed him on account of a deadly terror that had seized upon all. He bore aloft a drawn dagger, and had approached in rapid impetuosity, to within three or four feet of the retreating figure, when the latter, having attained the extremity of the velvet apartment, turned suddenly and confronted his pursuer. There was a sharp cry—and the dagger dropped gleaming upon the sable carpet, upon which, instantly afterwards, fell prostrate in death the Prince Prospero. Then, summoning the wild courage of despair, a throng of the revellers at once threw themselves into the black apartment, and, seizing the mummer, whose tall figure stood erect and motionless within the shadow of the ebony clock, gasped in unutterable horror at finding the grave cerements and corpse-like mask which they handled with so violent a rudeness, untenanted by any tangible form.

And now was acknowledged the presence of the Red Death. He had come like a thief in the night. And one by one dropped the revellers in the blood-bedewed halls of their revel, and died each in the despairing posture of his fall. And the life of the ebony clock went out with that of the last of the gay. And the flames of the tripods expired. And Darkness and Decay and the Red Death held illimitable dominion over all.

"The Uninvited Guest," Edgar Allan Poe,
The Masque of the Red Death

SUGGESTIONS FOR FURTHER READING

Akin, Johnnye. *And So We Speak: Voice and Articulation.* New York: Prentice-Hall, 1958.

Berry, Cecily. *Voice and the Actor.* New York: Macmillan, 1974.

———. *The Actor and His Text.* New York: Scribner, 1988.

Blu, Susan, and Molly A. Mullin. *Word of Mouth: A Guide to Commercial Voice-Over Excellence.* Los Angeles: Pomegranate Press, 1987.

Blunt, Jerry. *Stage Dialects.* San Francisco: Chandler, 1967.

Eisenson, Jon. *Voice and Diction,* 3rd ed. New York: Macmillan, 1974.

Hahn, Elise, et al. *Basic Voice Training for Speech.* New York: McGraw-Hill, 1957.

Kenyon, John S., and Thomas A. Knott. *A Pronouncing Dictionary of American English.* Springfield, MA: Merriam, 1944.

Lessac, Arthur, ed. *The Use and Training of the Human Voice.* New York: Drama Book Specialists, 1967.

Linklater, Kristin. *Freeing the Natural Voice.* New York: Drama Book Specialists, 1976.

Machlin, Evangeline. *Speech for the Stage.* New York: Theatre Arts Books, 1970.

Turner, J. Clifford. *Voice and Speech for the Theatre,* 3rd ed., rev. by Malcolm Morrison. New York: Drama Book Specialists, 1977.

CHAPTER
SIX

*Getting Around
on the Stage*

The purpose of this chapter is to examine the fundamentals on which the study of acting must build. It is as necessary for the actor to know the tools of the acting trade as for the painter to know the different kinds of brushes and paints and for the composer or pianist to know the notes of the scale. Sooner or later, it is imperative that an artist master the fundamentals, and all successful systems of acting require that the actor learn basic stage techniques. Moreover, a beginning actor is much more likely to be selected for roles in university, community, and other amateur productions after having studied these techniques. Directors are loath to drill actors or explain the fundamentals during rehearsal time when other important business needs to be conducted. Sound preparation in acting techniques will leave the actor free to concentrate on other requirements of a role. Charlton Heston recalls the value of this training. He has written:

[Laurence] Olivier uses a model of the set, moving little dolls while he reads the text with the actors watching. It goes much faster than standing around for hours bumping into each other.[1]

Clearly, from that point forward Mr. Heston and his fellow actors can rely on their basic stage technique and work on their roles.

The Stage and Stage Areas

The stage is divided into specific areas that are identified in theatre terminology by their relative positions.[2] When giving directions regarding stage movement, directors use the following terms to indicate the areas to be used.

Upstage and Downstage

The area nearest the audience and footlights is called *downstage*. The area in the back of the stage, near the back wall of the stage or setting, is called *upstage*. Both the upstage and downstage areas extend across the width of the stage.

Stage Left and Stage Right

Stage areas left and right are determined by the *actor's left and right* as he or she faces the audience. If the actor stands directly in the center of the stage, the area to the actor's right is *stage right* and the area to the actor's left is *stage left*. The director, therefore, sitting in the auditorium and watching the stage, reverses the areas when viewing them and relates them to the actor's position on stage. The area in the middle of the stage is called *stage center*.

The Stage Areas

Combining these classifications, the following basic stage areas provide the framework within which the actor must work (see Figure 6.1).

---

1. Charlton Heston, *The Actor's Life: Journals 1956–1976*, ed. Hollis Alpert (New York: Pocket Books, 1976), p. 109.
2. The following examinations of stage areas, movement, and body positions are directly related to the needs of the proscenium, or picture-frame, theatre. Although this is the design of the great majority of professional and educational theatres, there has been a substantial growth in recent years in the number of theatres using thrust, central, or arena staging. Under such conditions the customary stage-area and body-position designations are clearly inoperative or will need significant modification. Other rules are applicable, however, under all circumstances. The specific demands that central staging makes on the actor are discussed in Chapter 11.

1. Down left	4. Down center	7. Down right
2. Center left	5. Center	8. Center right
3. Up left	6. Up center	9. Up right

As a general rule certain areas of the stage are stronger than others. We might call this the "all-other-things-being-equal" factor. For example, the stage setting, furniture, lighting, color of the actor's costume, and so on will have a tendency to alter the relative strength of playing areas. However, as a general rule we should note that:

1. Down center is the "strongest" area, or the area that commands most attention.
2. The down left and down right areas are stronger than up left and up right.

Assuming that the actor holds to the same relative position in each area, it should be clear that the downstage areas are more emphatic and generally maintain a higher degree of audience attention than do the upstage areas.

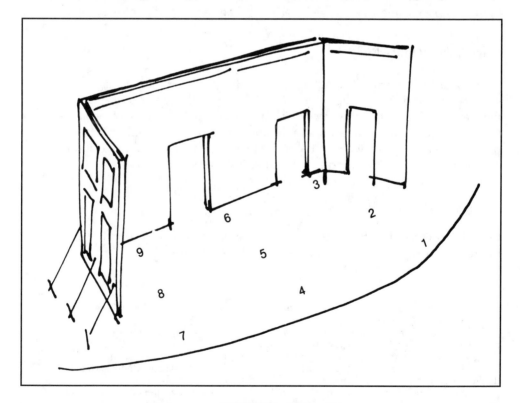

FIGURE 6.1 Stage areas.

Stage Positions and the Actor

There are five basic body positions that may be assumed *in relation to the audience*. There is also a great variety in the combinations of body positions and stage areas. We are concerned here only with the normal standing position.

1. Full front—The actor is facing the audience with both feet facing downstage and head also facing the audience. *This is the strongest and most "open" of all body positions.*
2. Full back—The actor faces the back wall of the stage, both feet facing upstage so that the audience sees only the actor's back.
3. Profile positions—The actor is in a position exactly between full front and full back so that the audience sees the side of the body. This position may be further divided:
   (a) Profile left—The actor is in profile position facing stage left.
   (b) Profile right—The actor is in profile position facing stage right.
4. One-quarter position—The actor stands halfway between the full front and the profile position. This position may be further divided:
   (a) One-quarter position left—The actor is in the one-quarter position facing the down left area.
   (b) One-quarter position right—The actor is in the one-quarter position facing the down right area.
5. Three-quarter position—The actor is in a position halfway between the full back and the profile position. Again, this position may be subdivided:
   (a) Three-quarter position left—The actor is in the three-quarter position facing the up left area.
   (b) Three-quarter position right—The actor is in the three-quarter position facing the up right area.

The terms for stage areas and body positions are obviously rather mechanical; they are intended to help the actor understand the most basic elements of working on a proscenium stage. These should become automatic, without the actor having to think consciously about them. Their real purpose is to help bring the actor a true theatrical sense of his or her working environment.

Stage Movement and the Audience

The general aspects of stage movement for the actor have been covered in full detail in Chapter 4, "The Body and Stage Movement." Nevertheless, it may be useful to discuss some general points now, particularly with regard to the more traditional rules of the actor's adjustment to the physical space in which he or she works. Remember, the following points are made according to the proscenium, or picture-frame, stage relationship of actor and audience.

Approaches

When an actor moves from one stage area to another it is usually for the purpose of coming closer to another actor, a piece of furniture or property, or a window or door. Two general types of approaches are possible: crossing in a straight line or making the approach in a curve.

The straight cross is most often used when approaching another actor or object *parallel* with your starting point. This should invariably place the actor in a profile position. Figures 6.2, 6.3, and 6.4 show correct and incorrect ways of making a straight cross to various stage areas.

It is possible to avoid such problems by the use of the curved stage cross (see Figure 6.5 and Figure 6.6). This permits the actor to approach another actor or object *without being forced to make an awkward adjustment in order to compensate for a difficult body position.*

FIGURE 6.2   The straight cross used correctly.

FIGURE 6.3   The straight cross used incorrectly. The approaching actress is upstaging herself.

The curved approach keeps the actor open to the audience during the movement and generally suggests a softer quality in the movement. This type of movement is especially desirable in costume plays and often helps to give the play a gentle and formal style.

How to Sit

Sitting may seem on first consideration to present no specific problems. Yet rules exist for sitting as they do for standing and walking. These simple rules can be outlined as follows:

1. When changing from the standing to the sitting position, the actor should try to avoid turning and looking at the chair. If at all possible the actor

FIGURE 6.4 **The straight cross used incorrectly. The actress being approached is forced to turn upstage.**

should be in a position to sit down with seemingly little effort. Feeling with the back of the leg for the chair edge may be helpful.

2. Men should generally sit with their feet on the same plane.

3. Women should generally sit with one foot in front of the other or one foot slightly under the chair and one slightly extended.

4. When sitting in a chair that is in profile, one should open up the body to a one-quarter position if a number of lines are to be spoken while remaining seated.

5. In rising, the back foot should push the body up to a standing position. *The first step is taken with the back foot.* (Try taking the first step with the front foot after rising and note how awkward it is.) If possible the rear

FIGURE 6.5   The curved cross.

foot, which pushes the body up to the standing position, should be the upstage foot.

The actor works with other actors. To achieve maximum effectiveness in a scene and to permit the greatest interaction with fellow actors, it is necessary to realize that stage and body positions are relative to those of other actors on stage. In addition, the element of basic stage courtesy is often neglected by beginning actors. This is usually not the result of bad manners but comes about because of a misunderstanding of some of the accepted stage conventions that should be conformed to by two or more actors in a scene. There are two common errors into which beginning actors fall; these should be understood before we proceed further.

FIGURE 6.6   The curved cross.

Upstaging a Fellow Actor

Upstaging can be most disturbing because it tends to place one actor in an extremely dominant position while relegating the other to an unnecessarily subordinate position. There may be times when a director may deliberately want such an imbalance between two actors, but the actor should never deliberately take such a position. Upstaging usually occurs when two actors are sharing a scene and speaking to each other. At this time they are on the same plane so that the audience can watch the actions and reactions of both. If one actor, however, moves *upstage* a few steps, the other is forced to turn away from the audience to look upstage. At the same time the upstage actor is able to open naturally to the audience. In Figure 6.7 Actor *A* is in a much stronger position than Actor *B*, who, to retain the suggestion of naturalness in the conversation, is forced to turn upstage toward *A*. Remember that the more "open" an actor is, the stronger is his or her stage position.

It has already been suggested that, in a scene in which Actor *A* must control the attention of the audience, upstaging may be necessary. All too often, however, upstaging is caused by a misunderstanding of basic technique.

FIGURE 6.7 Upstaging.

Upstaging Oneself

Not infrequently the actor may take a position that actually upstages him- or herself. In such a situation, the positions indicated above are reversed: Instead of standing upstage of a fellow performer, the actor stands downstage of another, causing the same relative imbalance as indicated in Figure 6.3, although the position of the "guilty party" is obviously reversed. No one could suggest that the actor is selfish in assuming this position, but the actor will look most uncomfortable if he or she has a number of lines to speak.

The Shared Position

The most usual position assumed by two actors during a brief scene can be classified as a "shared position." This position can take many forms. Essentially both actors are in the same relative body position and therefore are able to participate in a scene (from the physical standpoint) with equal emphasis.

Each of the following positions is considered shared because equal emphasis falls on each actor (see Figures 6.8 through 6.12).

1. Shared one-quarter position—the most common position, generally used for conversation.
2. Shared position in profile—also rather common, but indicating a situation of greater intensity, even conflict.

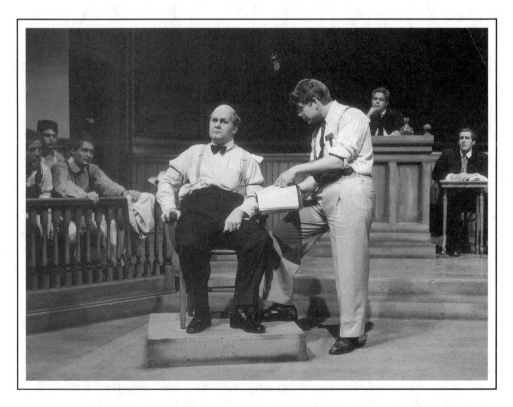

Inherit the Wind, **by Lawrence and Lee. California State University, Long Beach. Directed by Stanley Kahan.**

FIGURE 6.8   Shared one-quarter position.

3. Shared full front—much less common; likely to be found in musical comedy and in period plays of a presentational nature.
4. Shared three-quarter position—somewhat rare; may be used to suggest an element of secrecy. This position is usually held only briefly.
5. Shared full back—again a position not often used, although it serves to offer some pictorial variety. It is difficult to communicate audibly in this position unless the head is played in profile. In addition the audience is unable to follow facial reactions. Nonetheless this position may be used briefly to give the stage a suggestion of added dimension, and it can then easily blend into the shared three-quarter or shared profile positions.

The Given Position

The given position is not unlike "upstaging," although here the position is assumed deliberately. The given position should be used when one actor is clearly the dominant character in the scene—that is, when one character has

FIGURE 6.9   Shared profile position.

a great amount of narration or expositional material to deliver and the other character is generally passive. As shown in Figure 6.13, one actor will take a dominant, or "focused," position, usually the one-quarter position, or open up to almost the full front. The other actor may take a three-quarter back position or stay in profile. When there are three or more characters on stage, they may give the scene to a "focused" individual simply by turning toward that actor. This type of adjustment makes it relatively simple to adjust the focus and give a scene to the properly dominant character.

It is essential to remember, then, that *these positions are not static.* They can be easily changed as a scene shifts in intensity and emphasis. Most directors will tell actors when to share a scene and when to give or take it. The actor should know the basic body positions and be able to adjust as the situ-

FIGURE 6.10   Shared full front position.

ation requires. The mastery of such techniques will give the actor greater confidence in his or her own powers as well as the respect of fellow workers.

Using Movement

Up to this point we have examined the basic stage positions and the playing of scenes with other actors. It may have been noted that the patterns for movement and stage positions are somewhat mechanical and tend to suggest set pieces rather than living actors. The actor should understand that within the context of these fundamental rules he or she must be creative and interesting. The actual movement patterns, physical reactions, and exact relations to other actors will be determined by a number of factors. Let us look at those factors that affect how and why actors move on stage.

Movement as a Factor of Character.   Movement patterns will be affected by a character's age, social status, and education, as well as by any physical im-

FIGURE 6.11   Shared three-quarter position.

pairments he or she may have. A gangster's movement from one part of the stage to another should be quite different from that of a European nobleman; an aged charwoman obviously would not move as quickly or in the same manner as a society matron. Such factors of character will also affect smaller movements and positions assumed in relation to other characters. A fuller and more detailed examination of this factor is dealt with in Chapter 4, which explores this critical aspect of the actor's and character's physical behavior.

Movement as a Part of the Plot.   Movement patterns will be affected by the specific situations of the play, the relation of one character to another, and the content or the action of any given moment. An actor would make a very different full stage cross in Act I in order casually to mix a cocktail, than a full stage cross in Act III to prevent someone from taking poison.

Movement and Locale.   Movement patterns will be affected by the general locale and specific setting of a play. If the scene is set in a character's home, movements should be quite different from the character's movements in strange surroundings. Movement in a cold climate will differ from movement in an extremely hot and humid locale. A skilled actor is often able to suggest the nature of the setting by movement and elements of "business." The conscientious actor does not rely entirely on the designers to indicate the locale to the audience.

Movement and Furniture Properties. Movement patterns will be affected by the stage pieces in the playing area. Movement around these pieces should be planned carefully so that it seems natural. Set pieces also may have an additional specific use: Furniture may be gripped, leaned upon, or played around in scenes that otherwise require little movement.

Movement as an Indication of State of Mind. Movement patterns will be affected by a character's state of mind—health, anxiety, happiness, nervousness, or resoluteness. Movement can be an excellent device for suggesting these mental states to an audience even before specific lines indicate the fact.

FIGURE 6.12 **Shared full back position.**

FIGURE 6.13   The given position.

Movement to Sustain Mood.   Movement patterns will be affected by the general mood of a scene or play. Scenes requiring a particularly somber effect call for slow and deliberate movement, whereas a scene of sustained joy and hilarity will require greater vigor and energy. The projection of such moods demands a cooperative approach by all the actors.

Movement to Maintain the Style and Period of the Play.   Movement patterns will be affected by the basic style of the play. Each style will impose a definite design, to which the actor must adjust his or her movement. In order to maintain consistency, movement in a presentational production will differ from movement in one that is fundamentally representational. Comedy, tragedy, and melodrama will each require a different emphasis. The historical period of the play will also influence movement. The tempo of life, social conditions, class consciousness, and particularly costumes all contribute to particular historical attitudes and mores that are significantly different from the way we experience life today. Human beings in the past did not move in the same manner as we move today.

Such details of movement must be understood by actors working in plays of this kind. Style is an intricate problem, one that will be examined in somewhat greater detail in a later chapter. It is sufficient to say here that the actor's viewpoint must be not only that of an individual performer but also that of someone who is part of an entire production. It is the function of the director to provide the cohesive element necessary to unite the contributions of the individual actors.

Specialized Stage Problems

Acting was defined by Shakespeare, we may remember, as "holding . . . the mirror up to nature." We have seen, however, that one cannot take this suggestion *too* literally. Much that we must do on stage is guided by certain fundamental rules dealing with being seen, being heard, and focusing attention.

We now come to a number of problems that require highly specialized techniques. Such techniques *suggest to the audience* realistic action but actually are the adjustments and alterations of reality we must make for stage purposes. One of the most common of such techniques is called *covering*. Covering occurs when the audience is permitted to see only part of the actual business and is required to supply the remainder of the action with its own imagination. A useful formula to indicate the relation of covering to the completion of important but difficult stage business might be:

COVERING + SUGGESTION + REACTION = COMPLETED ACTION.

Let us look into this technique of covering in an examination of the special problems that follow.

Eating on Stage

Eating on stage is usually a matter of camouflage and substitution. For some unexplained reason, playwrights delight in writing plays in which eating and drinking are important pieces of business. In *The Petrified Forest* by Robert E. Sherwood, the central character is seated at a table down stage center where he must consume an entire meal including soup, coffee, and a bottle of beer! Throughout this scene, which lasts almost half the act, he is speaking constantly, describing his past and philosophizing about the fate of man. He also happens to be quite hungry.

He rarely is silent, yet during this time he must make the audience believe that he has eaten a good deal of the food put before him. Much of the eating and drinking in such a scene would be faked, although it must also be made believable for the audience.

There are three major reasons why the business of eating and drinking should be covered and substitutions made for the food and drink indicated

Tales from the Vienna Woods, **by Odon von Horvath.
National Theatre, London. Directed by Maximilian
Schell. Photograph by Britain on View Photographic
Library.**

in the script: (1) The mouth should remain relatively clear for proper articulation. Speaking with the mouth full is unpleasant for both actor and audience. (2) A combination of stage enunciation, the necessity for responding to specific cues, and hard and stringy foods can produce choking and severe difficulties in swallowing. (3) Eating or drinking large quantities of stage food and beverages is often unpleasant for the actor, especially during successive performances.

The foods actually used on stage are rarely the foods indicated in the script but are usually quite palatable. Hard foods are almost always avoided; softer foods such as eggs, bananas, bread, and rice make good substitutes.

Cold tea, ginger ale, cider, and water with vegetable color are excellent substitutes for whiskey, wine, champagne, and so on.

The actor should eat very little of the food itself. A good deal of time should be devoted to the cutting and arranging of the food with utensils. The actor should put only a small portion of food in the mouth at any one time but can indicate through the pantomiming of chewing and swallowing that a greater amount of food is being consumed. Because coffee and tea are usually served in opaque cups, it is difficult for an audience to tell how much liquid is actually in the cup. Usually the cup should be poured only half full; even then, little of the liquid should be drunk. When a glass is used, the actor's hand can cover part of the glass. Here also little of the liquid should actually be drunk, unless the plot absolutely demands otherwise.

The most important thing to remember is that eating and drinking, as important stage business, should be as carefully planned as any speaking cue. Nothing is more embarrassing than being forced to speak while in the process of swallowing a morsel of food or a drink.

In Edward Albee's *Who's Afraid of Virginia Woolf*, the four characters are engaged in a drinking bout that lasts almost the entire play. Somehow they must consume enormous amounts of alcohol, retain some semblance of consciousness, and still be brilliantly articulate over a wide range of subjects. Timing in this play is critical, and the continual drinking must be carefully planned.

Kissing and Love Scenes

Love scenes may sometimes prove embarrassing for the beginning actor. This is a perfectly natural reaction. To compensate, it is best to begin playing love scenes early in the rehearsal period, certainly by the time the actors become free of the script. At first there need be no more than a superficial embrace, but this will serve to make the more detailed and elaborate embraces easier. Audiences enjoy these scenes if they are handled with taste, but if the embrace and kiss are excessive and overdone, unless specifically required by the script, an audience will be as uncomfortable as they would be watching such a sequence handled with obvious timidity.

The standing embrace and kiss is the most difficult type of all, as it usually is performed in a very standard way, with only little variation. The most common fault to be discerned in inexperienced actors during such a sequence is in posture and body relationship (see Figure 6.14).

Very often the actors' positions tend to suggest a triangle, with their heads together and feet far apart, and the man and woman *leaning* toward each other. This stance suggests timidity on the part of the actors, and, unless this is the specific relationship required in the text of the play, the embrace

FIGURE 6.14 The standing embrace: (*left*) correct and (*right*) incorrect—unless awkwardness by the pair is intended.

can become amusing rather than affectionate. Therefore this kind of embrace should normally be avoided.

The man and woman should come close together, the man putting his downstage arm around the woman's waist and the other on her arm. His downstage foot should be extended slightly with the weight on this foot to help support the woman. The woman should have her downstage arm around the neck of the man or even on his shoulder, perhaps smoothing his coat. The upstage arm should usually be above the man's shoulder. In most cases their heads should tilt, an element of covering being provided by having the man's head downstage of the woman's during the actual kiss. The traditional dancing position frequently serves as a good starting point for the embrace and kiss.

Much greater variety in kissing can be developed when the couple is seated. The kiss may vary from a passionate embrace to a gentle caress. When seated, the person on the downstage part of the sofa should provide the covering. The script will usually suggest to the actors just what type of embrace is required. Garlic should be avoided before performances.

Stabbing

Accidents have occurred during stage stabbings and will continue to occur even when the greatest care is taken to blunt the weapons. Involved sequences in which sword or knife fights are an important part of the play need to be planned very carefully, often requiring the use of a stage-combat choreographer. In such plays as *Romeo and Juliet, Cyrano de Bergerac, West Side Story, Hamlet,* and *Othello,* perfectly timed movement and rhythm are carefully planned on paper, taking into account the historical period of the play, the number of combatants, their weapons, theatre size, costumes, and design. In many plays, however, the actor and director do not have the services of a choreographer trained in stage combat and must work within accepted techniques of handling weapons. We can begin by looking at stage stabbing, which may only involve a few individuals rather than a large battle or combat scene. The basis of successful stabbing on stage is covering. This makes stabbing from upstage the easiest and least dangerous method. Stabbing from downstage requires a definite technique. The downstage hand should hold the dagger and the person being stabbed should be a step or two upstage of the person with the dagger. The arm should swing around and the body should turn toward the person to be stabbed. The actor doing the stabbing should complete the slight turn so that he or she is covering the victim. The arm should start the supposed blow with great force but hold back the dagger at the last minute and *pass* it in front of the body. The victim should simulate the impact of the blow, usually by clutching the "wound" and turning his or her body in toward the supposed injury. The attacker also must react. In withdrawing the dagger, some visible effort should be suggested, or else it will be clear that the stabbing was faked.

The murder of Julius Caesar in Shakespeare's tragedy is a specific and important example of a scene that requires great ingenuity in the development of such details. Caesar receives innumerable wounds, all from different angles; all of them must be covered and made to seem realistic. In such a case the actors must find means of concealing the blows, while maintaining the element of variety. Killing on stage requires imagination!

It is useful to restate the important principle involved here:

COVERING + SUGGESTION + REACTION = COMPLETED ACTION.

Shooting

When a gun is fired on stage, the first rule to remember is never to point the gun at the audience. Guns should be fired upstage and never pointed directly at another actor. This point cannot be stressed too strongly. Guns loaded with blanks can still cause injury by discharging the wad. The gun should be aimed and fired in a position a few inches upstage of the intended victim. Audiences will not be aware of this bit of "stealing."

The actor who is shot can, of course, die in a variety of ways. Normally the actor grabs the part of the body that has been struck, staggers, and executes a safe "stage fall." The stage fall in a simulated shooting must be planned properly if it is not to look comic, and should suggest, where required, a semblance of reality.

Falling

A fall on stage can occur for a number of reasons. It may be due to violent action, such as a stabbing, shooting, or poisoning, or it may be the result of fainting, tripping, or other natural causes. Certain primary rules apply to all such cases. If the body has received a blow or wound, the actor should reach for the injury just before the actual fall begins. If the actor is close to a piece of furniture, this may be used to help break the fall. The fall should not be instantaneous and rigid, unless the effect intended is one of comedy. The *relaxed* body should sink (1) to one knee, (2) to the hip, (3) to the shoulder, and then (4) to the final position.

Even if a blow or wound has not been inflicted, falls induced by poison, by a heart attack, or by faintness should suggest to the actor some means of indicating the part of the body afflicted. Care must be taken, however, not to overplay such a scene. A good death scene on stage can be a moving moment, but if played to excess, with overdone grimaces and a prolonged fall, it can suggest only inept amateurism. It is no wonder that such moments are often chosen for parody, satire, and farce.

There are also some basic principles involved in completing the fall: (1) The feet should not bounce at the end of the fall (except for a highly comic effect). (2) The feet should not point downstage. Usually the body should approximate the one-quarter body position with the *head* toward the downstage area. (Again, an intended comic effect might reverse this rule.) (3) The arms should not be extended from the body either above the head or at right angles from the body.

Fights

The staging of a good fight sequence is necessarily a cooperative venture, in which covering and faking are essential. The action should usually take place so quickly that audiences will find it impossible to distinguish a well-planned stage fight from the real thing.

Of course, in film, special stunt men double for the leading actors, and the speed of the action and carefully planned camera angles permit a kind of pseudorealism that is simply not easily accomplished in the theatre. Nevertheless, if carefully planned onstage, a fight can look so realistic that audiences may react in a manner that will cross any barrier of aesthetic distance.

The most difficult aspect of the stage fight is the striking of blows. Three separate elements should be considered in making the punch, slap, or other type of blow realistic: (1) the blow, (2) the reaction, and (3) the sound. These occur at almost the same moment but can be examined in sequence.

The primary factor in suggesting a real fight and real blows is *proper covering*. If the audience is permitted to see only *part* of the action they will supply the additional elements that have only been suggested and in consequence will imagine they are witnessing an actual fight.

The actor striking *the blow* should be downstage, covering the person to be struck. The arm should be brought back, with the fist clenched, and then brought forward quickly. If the blow is to land on the chin, the fist should move past the face quickly. If it is to be a body blow, the fist should stop just short of the body as it is about to strike. The actor being struck will *react* to the blow immediately. The head will quickly snap back as the fist moves past the chin, or the actor will double up as a body blow is struck.

When someone is struck, the first reaction is to try to ward off the blow with his or her hands. In a stage fight the hands may also suggest this phase of the action, but in addition they should provide *the sound* by being slapped together quickly either in front of the face or near the body area being struck. If this is done correctly, the audience will not see it. What they will perceive is: (1) a fist moving quickly toward an actor partially covered by the aggressor, (2) a reaction as the "blow" lands, and (3) the sound of a blow as the fist approaches that portion of the body being struck.

The audience will combine in their minds the action they actually see and that which was only suggested; thus the impression of a realistic fight will be created. This technique, of course, saves a good deal of wear and tear on actors. The same procedure may be used if a particularly hard slap is indicated. Otherwise a normal slap need not be entirely covered; the fingers, rather than the entire hand, should execute the slap. In those cases where a prolonged fight is required, body positions should change rapidly and many blows may be struck. The basic principles still apply here, the most important being the proper covering of the action. With this in mind, an actor can employ an infinite variety of movement, blows, and reactions.

Listening

Certainly the actor's proper reading of lines requires intense preparation and concentration. The same may also be said for the development of movement, gestures, and essential business in the creation of a consistent character. Another of the essential elements of good acting, however, is often overlooked by beginning actors, yet it gets to the very heart of good acting. This is proper *listening* when other actors on stage are speaking. It might almost be called *re-acting* rather than acting, except that so simple a distinction would be highly misleading. Many otherwise successful performances have been ruined when an actor who had been speaking lines with intelligence and vitality became wooden and lifeless while others were speaking.

The actor cannot perform in a vacuum, oblivious of the work of his or her colleagues. Only the closest kind of rapport between actors can bring forward decent or memorable performances. The most experienced of twentieth-century actors, Laurence Olivier, speaks from a lifetime of experience when he tells us:

> Actors must understand each other, know each other, help each other, absolutely love each other: must, absolutely must.[3]

Proper listening and reacting will vary according to the situation, but it is important that the actor convey the idea that he or she hears what is being said and is *thinking* of his or her relationship to that situation. The actor should not stand woodenly on stage simply waiting for a cue and thinking of his or her next line. It is instructive for all actors today to remember that one of the most persuasive attributes of the truly great actors of the past and present was their ability to listen and react in a manner thoroughly consistent with their roles. Critics and playgoers of their times constantly referred to this admirable quality.

---

3. Laurence Olivier, in *Great Acting*, ed. Hal Burton (New York: Bonanza Books, 1967), p. 29.

Of Richard Burbage it was said that:

His auditors [were] never more delighted than when he spoke, nor more sorry than when he held his peace; yet even then he was an excellent actor still, never failing in his part when he had done speaking, but with his looks and gestures maintaining it still unto the height.[4]

Much the same quality was admired in David Garrick:

His voice [is] natural in its cadence and beautiful in its elocution. . . . When three or four are on the stage with him, he is attentive to whatever is spoken, and never drops his character when he has finished a speech.[5]

The noted American actress Julia Marlowe gave us an incisive description of Edwin Booth, made all the more meaningful because it was written after the first time she had seen him act. It is interesting to note the element that made the most profound impression on her.

I recall, when a young girl , the first time I saw Edwin Booth. He and Lawrence Barrett were appearing in *Othello*. Barrett impersonated Othello, and Booth, Iago. As I had never seen Booth, I did not know when he appeared on the scene. Suddenly I discovered a figure at the back of the stage intently watching the Moor. You could see plainly that he contemplated some demoniac act. His eye and manner at once caught the attention of the house long before he had said a word. The look on his face was crafty and devil-like. The one incident proved to me that there was very much more in acting than the polished delivery of lines.[6]

The great English actor Henry Irving has left us his impression of this important facet of good acting. He said simply: "One of the greatest tests of an actor is his capacity for listening."[7]

And we should not forget Henry Fonda's comment, quoted in Chapter 1, that no matter how many years an actor may play a role, he must avoid "the pitfall you get into in most long runs . . . you stop listening."[8]

There is obviously a close relationship between listening and William Gillette's concept of the "illusion of the first time." This illusion will be de-

---

4. Richard Flecknoe, *The Art of Richard Burbage* (1664), quoted by E. K. Chambers in *The Elizabethan Stage* (Oxford: Clarendon Press, 1923), vol. 4, p. 370.

5. Quoted in Percy H. Fitzgerald, *Life of David Garrick* (London: Tinsley Brothers, 1868).

6. Julia Marlowe, "The Eloquence of Silence," *Green Book* 9, no. 3 (March 1913), pp. 393–401.

7. Henry Irving, "The Art of Acting" (1893), reprinted in *Actors on Acting*, 2nd ed., eds. Toby Cole and Helen Krich Chinoy (New York: Crown Publishers, 1954), p. 333.

8. Henry Fonda in Lillian Ross and Helen Ross, *The Player: A Profile of an Art* (New York: Simon and Schuster, 1962), p. 89.

stroyed if the actor is unable to communicate the belief that he or she is hearing and reacting to the lines for the first time. Such listening and reacting also serve to sharpen the reading of the actor's own speeches, because they help the actor to see the total perspective of the scene.

The good actor *listens to what is said on stage—reacts—then speaks the lines.* In other words, the good actor acts all the time he or she is on the stage.

EXERCISES

The following exercises should help you develop a practical working knowledge of the fundamentals discussed in the chapter. You should be able to devise many more and practice these exercises until movement and body positions become almost an automatic part of your stage behavior.

Stage areas   Maintaining the full front position:

1. Move from D. L. to U. R.	5. Move from D. R. to U. C.
2. Move from U. R. to D. C.	6. Move from D. L. to U. L.
3. Move from U. C. to D. R.	7. Move from Stage Center to U. R.
4. Move from U. L. to D. C.	8. Move from Stage Center to D. R.

How many of the above stage crosses would you make in a straight line and how many in a curve? Why?

Stage areas and body positions   Simple crosses:

Body Position	Area		Body Position	Area
Profile left	D. R.	cross to	Full back	U. L.
Full front	D. C.	cross to	One-quarter right	U. L.
Three-quarter left	U. R.	cross to	One-quarter left	D. L.
One-quarter right	D. L.	cross to	Three-quarter left	U. L.
Full back	U. C.	cross to	One-quarter right	D. R.

Try making some of these crosses in a straight line and some with a curved line. Is there any difference? Are certain crosses better than others when made in a curved line?

Crosses that may cause some difficulty:

Body Position	Area		Body Position	Area
Profile left	D. L.	cross to	Profile right	U. R.
Full back	D. C.	cross to	Full front	U. L.
Three-quarter left	U. L.	cross to	Three-quarter right	D. R.
Full back	U. C.	cross to	One-quarter left	D. R.
Three-quarter right	U. L.	cross to	One-quarter right	D. R.

Working with another actor

1. Share a scene equally so that you are both open to the audience.
2. Make the scene above more intense pictorially but still share the scene equally.
3. One actor has a long speech. The other will listen. What adjustment will you make now?
4. The other actor will now be emphasized for part of the scene. Adjust again.
5. A secret is being confided. Share the scene. Would the one-quarter shared position be better than the three-quarter shared position?
6. "Give" the scene to one actor.
7. "Take" the scene.

Working with two other actors

Let three actors designated A, B, and C take stage center in a full front position. Then follow the indicated sequence.

1. A and B give the scene to C.
2. C and A give the scene to B.
3. C and B give the scene to A.
4. C focuses on A and B, who are sharing a scene.
5. A focuses on B and C, who are sharing a scene.

CHAPTER
SEVEN

Using Improvisation

Improvisatory work can be very useful either in preparing for a specific role or as process work in actor training. The value of improvisatory work is quite specific, and the following are some of the benefits to be derived from working with improvisations. These benefits are worth keeping in mind when working on the improvisations, either in groups or individually.

1. Improvisations aid the actor in developing self-awareness of mental, physical, and emotional powers that may be dormant.
2. Improvisations aid the actor in making decisions, both mental and physical, and require the utilization of stage space.
3. Improvisations with other actors create circumstances that require communication with other actors and force the actor to learn how to *listen*.
4. Improvisations introduce the actor to movement problems on stage.
5. Improvisations can be useful in freeing the actor from physical inhibitions.
6. Improvisations help a group or pairs to develop a shared relationship

and permit actors to communicate within a sphere of common experience and problem solving.

7. Improvisations force the actor to concentrate on intentions, objectives, environment, and interpersonal relationships of characters within a play or scene.

The improvisations in this chapter each suggest different means of making the actor sensitive to the objective of a character so that it can be translated into an actual role. When confronting any role, the actor must understand *why* he or she is in a scene from the content of the play itself. For the sake of clarity let us call the following our **W** checklist. This checklist should be applied to simple improvisations as well as to fully scripted plays. The questions the actor should ask can be enumerated as follows:

1. *Who* am I? (occupation, age, temperament, family history, social status, etc.)
2. *Where* am I? (location, size of area, climate, familiarity of locale)
3. *What* do I want in this scene or play?
4. *Why* do I want it?
5. *What* is preventing me from getting it? (Are there barriers in the way?)
6. *What* am I willing to do to get what I want? (How badly do I really want it?)
7. *Whom* do I want it from? (What is my relation to others?)
8. *When* do I want it? (How urgent is it that I get what I want?)

> *Having to confront policemen and judges is an excellent way to train your imagination. In a few seconds you have to improvise a role with talent and emotion.*
>
> Gérard Depardieu

Improvisations for Larger Groups

The following are improvisations intended for a large group of actors, perhaps somewhere between ten and twelve. The first step is to establish the basic locale and action; then determine what each actor would need to do in order to operate within that action and that locale. After the actors have determined their reason for being in a scene, and having established the locale and the action, it is not absolutely necessary to find an "ending" to the scene, which might distort the intentions or objectives of any given character. Do not force the scenes. It is useful to try these group improvisations in two different ways:

1. Each individual actor knows only his or her character's intention, motivation, and so on and must play the moment as it occurs depending on what discoveries are made about the other characters in the scene.
2. The actors know one another's character and objectives, and so on, and work "off" the other characters with some planning involved.

Group Improvisation 1. A large number of people are at a major American airport (select one) when the public address system announcer states that all incoming and outgoing flights have been cancelled until further notice. Each character reacts accordingly. One of the actors assumes the role of the public relations person at the airport.

Every actor in the improvisation will need to answer a number of questions before proceeding. Here are just a few:

- Do I work at the airport?
- Am I at the airport to meet someone?
- If so, *why* am I at the airport to meet someone?
- Am I scheduled for an outgoing flight?
- If so, how urgent is it that I get to where I am going on time?
- How frequently do I fly?
- Do I enjoy flying?
- Am I at the airport for a reason other than meeting someone or leaving?
- Am I alone or with someone?
- What do I do while I am waiting?

These are just a few of the questions the actor must be able to answer, in addition to such a fundamental question as "Who am I?" Certainly you can think of many other questions for the airport improvisation suggested above.

Here are some other group improvisations that will test imagination and creativity. Do not be concerned if the improvisation does not have a "neat" ending; doing it is the important thing.

Group Improvisation 2. A group of people are in the waiting room of a doctor's office. A nurse and health officer enter to inform the group that the office has been quarantined because the doctor has found a rare infectious disease in the previous patient.

Group Improvisation 3. A group of people are waiting in line to be part of the live audience for a top-rated television quiz program. A public relations person comes out to the group and tells them that the contestant who was to go on the show to try for $50,000 cannot attend that evening. The broadcasting company is looking for someone to go on the show, "Pot Luck," and try for the grand prize. Only the public relations person knows what kind of contestant they want, and he or she is not telling.

Group Improvisation 4.   A group of people are in line at a bus stop waiting for a bus that arrives every five minutes. One person in the group suddenly discovers that his or her wallet or purse has no money in it. The person must get across town in the next half hour and needs two dollars for fare. Will any stranger help the person in distress?

Improvisations for One Actor

The following improvisations will help the actor provide three of the critical **W**s from the checklist. In these exercises, the actor is given the *what* (the action), the *where* (the location), and the *who* (the character). It is imperative that the actor also know *why*, as well as many of the other **W**s from the list.

These improvisations contain all the necessary elements for a complete dramatic situation.

For each improvisation the actor should choose one action, one character, and one location from the lists that are provided. The actor may take the description of the action quite literally and add nothing of his or her own. Or the description may be used as a basic scenario, containing only the bare bones of the action, with the actor adding his or her own creative gifts and imagination to the scene, much as the *commedia dell'arte* performer of the past improvised richly on a few traditional formulas.

Several thousand improvisations would be possible from combinations of the items in these lists. In choosing an action, the actor must realize that within the context of that action many variables are present. It should be clear that different characters will react differently to the same stimulus. In addition, the environment in which a character operates and in which the action takes place may profoundly alter not only specific details, but the texture and execution of the entire improvisation.

At first the actor may find the three elements of the improvisation too generalized. They may even seem to follow certain stereotypes. This result, however, is to be expected from this type of improvisation. Yet, after some reflection, the actor will realize that not all bankers are the same, nor does every librarian resemble every other librarian. Within the context of the limited descriptions, the actor must add those elements of individuality that begin to bring a character and a scene to life. Taking this point of view, the actor will find that the number of improvisations is infinite.

Actions

1. You are determined to get evidence against a person who you believe has murdered your brother. You enter the premises to plant a tape

recorder in an appropriate place. You examine the location carefully and then test the machine. As you are installing the device, you hear someone entering the premises. You hide, and after a short time the person leaves without seeing you. After the device has been properly planted, you leave.

2. You enter the premises to keep an appointment. After waiting briefly, you detect smoke and note that a short circuit (or similar mishap) has caused a fire to break out. Unable to get any help and faced with the rapid spread of the fire, you are forced to put out the substantial blaze alone. After resting for a short time, you leave.

3. You enter the premises on a business call and find a one-year-old child alone, unhappy, and wet. The child has specific ideas about what he or she wants to do. You try to quiet the child and keep the child happy, as there is no one else in the vicinity. After a few minutes a telephone (or radio) call informs you that the child's parents are nearby and you are asked to take the child to them. You react to the request as you see fit.

4. You enter the premises intending to keep an appointment and sit in a chair. After starting to read a magazine or newspaper, you hear a strange sound and look up. Between you and the door is a large poisonous snake. You then react as your chosen character would under the circumstances.

5. You enter the premises to keep an appointment. You notice that the room is well stocked with fine old liqueurs and brandies. After some internal debating (the amount depends on the character you have chosen), you begin to sample the products and become progressively drunker. You finally react to your delayed appointment as dictated by your character and the number of samples tasted.

6. You enter the premises to keep an appointment with a friend you have not seen in several years. On a table you find a collection of materials, such as letters and photographs, that remind you of your old friendship. You examine the mementoes. After a while, a phone rings (telephone or radio). On answering it, you learn that your friend has been accidentally killed on the way to meet you. You react in character.

7. You enter the premises to keep an appointment. You look at your watch and realize you are an hour early. You decide to wait. While waiting, you notice a pile of papers and photographs on a table. You examine them and discover that they are documents and letters purporting to prove you guilty of murder. You react, taking whatever action is suitable to the character.

8. You enter the premises in order to prepare carefully the murder of someone who is due to arrive in five minutes. After giving your attention to planning how you will commit the murder, you lose your nerve and have to leave.

9. You enter the premises in order to keep an appointment. While waiting,

you decide to sample some food that has been left on the premises. After tasting it, you realize that you have been poisoned.

10. You enter the premises in order to plant a time bomb. You carefully place the bomb and discover that you cannot leave. You attempt to stop the time mechanism on the bomb but cannot. The bomb was set to explode three to five minutes after you placed it in position. React in character.

Characters. May be either male or female. You choose the age for the character.

Roadie	Groupie	Rock star
Mechanic	College student	Grad student
Personal trainer	Bank clerk	Postal worker
Used car salesman	Lawyer	Escaped felon
Nurse	Doctor	Bar dancer
Librarian	Teacher	Drug addict
U.S. sailor	Cheerleader	Bar tender
Lab scientist	Psychologist	Police officer
Airline pilot	Drug dealer	Politician
Construction worker	Movie star	Pro athlete

Locations

1. The small cabin of a ship at sea during a heavy storm
2. A business office late at night
3. A farmhouse
4. A dirty shack near an old mine in the mountains
5. A small grocery store in a New England village
6. A decrepit thatched hut in the tropics
7. The deserted stage of an old theatre
8. The kitchen of a famous restaurant
9. The living room of a palatial mansion
10. A stable
11. A penthouse
12. A deserted tomb
13. An igloo in the Arctic

Improvisations for Two or More Actors

The following improvisations make more complicated demands on the actor than did those for one character. The actor must now take into account the elements of reaction and interplay and must also be prepared to maintain the character and intentions as actions unfold that are not completely under his or her control. These exercises are intended to make the actor know precisely the *why* of the character in the scene, as well as to know the other **W**s from the list. How does the actor wish to see his or her problem resolved?

Each of the improvisations is a springboard for a large number of different actions. Let us examine the first improvisation. "A has come in response to an ad, placed in the newspaper by B, advertising a dog for sale." On the surface there seems to be little dramatic conflict suggested. However, on closer study we find that there are several possible purposes each character might have for participating in this situation.

It is possible that:

- A wants a dog as a pet for a small child.
- A wants a good watchdog.
- A wants to make the acquaintance of the person selling the dog.
- A wants a dog to give to someone else as a gift.
- A wants a dog for medical experiments.

It is also possible that:

- B wants to get rid of the dog at any price because it is vicious.
- B loves the dog but is now impoverished and cannot afford to keep it.
- B does not love the dog and needs a good deal of money.
- B hopes to find a good home for the dog because B is leaving the country.
- B is lonely and interested in making the acquaintance of anyone who might answer the ad.

Several other possibilities should also come to mind.

As each actor in turn chooses a central purpose and settles on specific character traits, the improvisation will take on a meaningful dramatic potential. It is also worth noting that one character in the improvisation need *not* know the purpose or the *why* of the other character(s).

The possible purposes and motivations of the characters in each improvisation should be analyzed and chosen before the improvisation is played. Possible questions that the actor might ask that are included after the improvisations are by no means complete. The improvisations have deliberately been made flexible enough to permit choices to be made by the actor.

1. A has come in response to an ad, placed in the newspaper by B, advertising a dog for sale.

2. A and B arrive at a bargain counter at the same moment. Each wants to buy the last remaining item on sale. C, the shop manager, is behind the counter at the time.

Possible questions: What is the article that is on sale? How important is the item for A and/or B? Do A and B know each other? What is the financial status of A and/or B? How important is it for C to sell this item? Is the item a genuine sale item or a special, brought in for a Christmas or summer sale? Is C's position secure? . . .

3. A and B are walking in opposite directions along the sidewalk. In the middle of the street is a twenty-dollar bill.

Possible questions: What is the financial status of A and/or B? Does money mean more than dignity? Do A and B know each other? Might they be attracted to each other? Is this a large street or a side street? . . .

4. B is answering an advertisement by A requesting an experienced tutor for a sweet child.

Possible questions: Is A's child really a sweet child? Is A the parent of the child? Can A afford a special tutor for the child? In what subject(s) does A want the child tutored? Is B a competent teacher? How badly does B need a position? How many interviews has A had recently? How many interview situations has B been in before? Does either have a hidden agenda? . . .

5. A is applying for a position in a theatre repertory company managed by B.

Possible questions: Is this A's first interview? Has A been in the profession a long time? How badly does A want and/or need the position? How many interviews has B had today? How experienced is B? How good a company is B managing? In what kind of financial situation is the theatre company? Does B have any motive other than interviewing for the best possible actor or actress? . . .

6. A and B are dining at the same table in a restaurant. When C, the waiter, comes with the bill(s), A looks in a pocket or purse and states that his or her wallet is missing.

Possible questions: What type and quality of restaurant are A and B dining in? What is the financial situation of A and B? Why are they dining in this particular restaurant at this particular time? Is A's wallet really missing? What else might be in the wallet? Does B know anything about the missing wallet before A notices that it is missing? Is C an experienced waiter? Has C ever encountered this type of situation before? Does C know anything about the missing wallet? . . .

7. A and B are soldiers in a wartime army. They report to C, their commanding officer, who must send one soldier on a mission that C knows will probably cause the soldier's death.

Possible questions: What is the relationship between A and B? Are they recruits or experienced soldiers? Does C know A and/or B well? What military reasons might dictate choosing either A or B? What personal reasons might enter into the choice? . . .

8. A and B arrive at the home of C at the same time in response to an ad stating that C wishes to sell a two-year-old Toyota automobile.

Possible questions: Work out the possibilities yourself. Look to improvisations 1, 2, and 4 for an approach to the circumstances, backgrounds, and motivations of these characters. Suppose that the automobile being sold is a top-of-the-line Mercedes. Does this change the circumstances and possibly the types of characters involved in this action? . . .

9. Student A is called into the office of teacher B, who announces that A's term paper is identical to another paper turned in that semester.

Possible questions: Has A plagiarized the paper from someone else? Was a copy of A's paper taken without A knowing about it? Did A write a copy of the paper for someone in another section of the same course? Has this happened to A before? Did A buy the paper from a term paper "mill"? What is A's academic standing? How important is it for A to pass this class? Does the teacher have two copies of the same paper in his or her possession? Does the teacher only suspect that there is another copy of the paper somewhere? Does the teacher believe that the paper simply was not written by the student? Does the teacher have some other reason for calling the student into the office? . . .

10. A and B are former school acquaintances. Now A is impoverished, B successful and wealthy. A calls on B in B's office to request a loan.

Possible questions: What was the relationship between A and B when they went to school together? Did A or B like the other equally? Is A impoverished because of unforeseen circumstances? Has A gone to other acquaintances for a loan? Has B had similar requests from other schoolmates before? How did B become successful and wealthy—inheritance, hard work, or luck? What will A do for money? . . .

11. A has just been hired for a clerical position and has arrived at the work station. B comes up to A and offers advice and help.

Possible questions: Is this A's first position? Is A an experienced office worker? Has B been working in this office for a long period? Does B have any supervisory responsibility for A? How badly does A need this position? What is the motive or motives for B offering to help A? . . .

12. A and B have been married for five years. A tells B that he or she wants a divorce. C, who is the next-door neighbor and who is closely "attached" either to A or B, enters through the back door during the discussion.

Possible questions: Does A really want a divorce? If so, why? Is this a surprise for B? How has the marriage progressed so far? How many material assets have been accumulated during the marriage? Why does C enter at this time? Does C have anything to do with the request for a divorce? Is C married? Does C want A to get a divorce? . . .

13. A and B have known each other for an extended period of time. A, however, dislikes one important thing about B and decides to tell B about it.

Possible questions: How close are A and B? Does B have a long-standing problem? Is A genuinely concerned about B's problem? Is the problem a habit, a matter of hygiene, or an attitude toward life? Does B take criticism well? Does B trust A? Does A have any reason other than wanting to help B for bringing up this matter? . . .

14. A is at home waiting for a very important phone call. B arrives to disconnect the phone and take it away because A is three months overdue in payment. C, the landlord or landlady, is also owed three months rent but is the only source of money for A. C enters during the "scene."

Possible questions: What information is A waiting for from the phone call? How important is it? Does B have any leeway insofar as disconnecting the phone service? How long has B been working for the phone company? What is A willing to do to keep the phone in service? What is C's relationship with A? How badly does C need the back rent? In what type of apartment building, rooming house, or private home does the action take place? . . .

15. A is watching a television program in the waiting room of a professional person. B comes into the room and changes the channel without asking permission.

Possible questions: What type of professional office is this? Why is A waiting for professional help? How important is the television program A is watching? How engrossed in the program is A? Why does B enter the room? What is B's relationship to the office? Does B know that A is watching the program? Do A and B know each other? . . .

Last-Line Improvisations

The following list of "last lines" gives the final line of dialogue of two-character improvisations. The two actors must supply all the necessary ingredients for playing the improvisation, including character, locale, intentions, and so on. The only requirement is that the improvisation *end* with one of the following lines. This is a useful improvisatory exercise requiring full use of the actor's imagination and inventiveness. It also requires integration of all the elements the actor needs to consider, before developing into a logical sequence leading to the last line.

1. We'll have to start all over again.
2. Someone help me, please help me.
3. This is the very last time!
4. That's it—you're fired.
5. I'm so glad you've come home.
6. I absolutely won't do it.
7. Don't let anyone else know.
8. Why did this have to happen to me?
9. What a terrible thing to do.
10. I can't believe it happened.
11. I knew it all the time.
12. I didn't mean to do it.
13. Thank heaven for that.
14. There's no way out of here.
15. Very well, I'll do it.
16. I'm sorry.
17. Let's do this again tomorrow.
18. Never again!
19. Idiot!
20. I don't know how to thank you.
21. Why don't we get something to eat.
22. You look very lovely tonight.
23. Can I put it on my credit card?
24. The whole truth, and nothing but the truth!
25. I'm not the same person I was yesterday.
26. Oh, just the secret police.
27. You won't have to leave again, will you?
28. Am I my brother's keeper?
29. I'm the one who's in a nightmare.
30. And that's the end of that, I hope.

CHAPTER
EIGHT

Combating Stage Fright

All acting is praiseworthy if for no other reason than that the actor has the courage to walk from the wings to the center of the stage.

William Ball

Stage fright has been examined by psychologists, as well as by teachers and students of acting and public speaking, from almost every conceivable viewpoint. It remains, however, one of the most common afflictions of those who work before the public. Stage fright besets actors at all levels of theatre work.

Supporting the all too observable fact that stage fright is a not uncommon circumstance in acting is the very interesting survey conducted among a large group of American adults that found that speaking in public was feared more than any other foreseeable event or object. The survey showed that 40.6 percent listed it as their greatest fear, with death registering 18.7 percent, serious illness 18.8 percent, dogs 11.2 percent, and escalators 4.8 percent. That stage fright is several times more frightening than escalators is understandable, but that it far outranks the fear of serious illness and death is a fascinating and *revealing* conclusion.[1] Although experience with audiences gradually reduces the problem, one of the most helpful means of easing the discomfort of stage fright is to understand it. Even if it cannot be entirely eliminated, the actor should try to turn it to advantage. It is with this ultimate goal in mind that we should read the following pages.

What Is Stage Fright?

Stage fright is not difficult to describe. Almost everybody at some time or another in life experiences the symptoms, although not everyone reacts to the tensions of a given situation in the same way. The athlete about to compete in an important contest would probably describe the same symptoms as the actor waiting in the wings for his or her first entrance. The student waiting to see the dean of the college on academic or disciplinary matters might describe the tensions of the situation in the same way as would the prospective employee waiting for an interview for an important job or the salesperson planning the approach to an important client. Each will undergo many of the symptoms that the actor may feel belong to acting alone.

Although the symptoms will vary from one person to another, it is usually not difficult to recognize the more common manifestations of stage fright. Some people find that they have suddenly hatched a horde of cocoons in their stomachs and that butterflies are beating wings within; some people's legs may become uncomfortably weak and shaky, and indeed would be capable of a continual rhythmic dance if given the chance; the muscles may become tense and refuse to obey; and the mouth may seem uncommonly dry, if not suddenly filled with cotton. Some people wonder if they have been suddenly stricken by some rare disease that causes heavy perspiration even though the hands seem cold and clammy. Stage fright, like seasickness, may be unpleasant for the victim, but it is hardly fatal.

Some Suggested Causes

As we learn more about what motivates us as human beings, we have discovered a good deal about our psychological motivations and "hang-ups." As we continue to learn more, we may be able to speak with greater certainty about the probable factors that induce stage fright.

---

1. "What Are Americans Afraid of?" *The Bruskin Report.* New Brunswick, NJ: R. H. Bruskin Associates, July 1973, p. 1.

The first and most important thing to remember is that stage fright is not pathological. It does not indicate in itself any personality deficiency, mental ineptitude, or neurotic tendencies. The great number of successful actors and public speakers who suffer from stage fright presents convincing evidence that such conclusions are nonsense. We might clarify the problem by reminding ourselves that stage fright is not simply a mental state. In our account of the symptoms of stage fright a variety of disorganized physical activities were noted. This disorganized behavior is caused by the overactivity of the endocrine system, set into high gear by a tension-laden situation. Adrenalin and glycogen are secreted into the blood stream to help cope with demanding emergencies. These secretions produce recognizable results: The heart beats faster; the respiratory system may become affected and cause gasping for breath; blood is drawn away from the organs and sent to the muscles in the arms and legs; a sinking feeling in the pit of the stomach may be experienced. *Unless the excess energy is used,* the symptoms may linger for a considerable period of time.

There are three explanations for the triggering of these physiological reactions in the acting situation. One is that *stage fright* is learned behavior. It has been suggested that stage fright is an individual's reaction to a set of circumstances that produced unpleasant effects earlier in that person's life. The origin may be as obvious as having once been embarrassed before a large group of people or having watched *someone else* in a relatively poor performance before an assembly or audience.

> *Many actors believe it is a sign of good luck to fall flat on one's face when making a first entrance, since nothing worse can then happen.*
> Theatrical Superstition

Any unpleasant experience related to a large group may transfer itself as a fear of audiences in general. Well-meaning parents or friends may have caused apprehension by commenting: "Now, Mary, don't be afraid. You won't forget to say and do everything properly," at one's first social engagement or contact with an audience. Or a parent may have chided an active youngster who is possibly too prone to "performing" before company: "Behave yourself, Andrew. No one is paying any attention to you." Such events may no longer be a conscious memory, but when a new situation with any circumstances similar to that of the original experience is faced, some psychologists hold that the past experience may reassert itself and bring on stage fright.

Another explanation is that *stage fright is caused by inadequacy in meeting a new situation.*[2] Within the limits of our environment and range of experiences we are able to deal with our daily problems successfully and with few difficulties. As a result of past experiences under certain conditions, we have

---

2. See C. W. Lomas, "The Psychology of Stage Fright," *Quarterly Journal of Speech* 23 (February 1937), pp. 35–44.

developed *patterns of response* (or behavior) that we adapt to situations of a similar nature. However, when new situations arise for which we have no experience, we have no patterned response that can be adapted to this new situation. Therefore, a response of uncertainty and fear may result. For example, we have a number of experiences in meeting people every day, particularly in informal situations, and we have set up a response pattern for such situations. But one day we may be presented to a high government official. Having had no past experience of this kind, we have no pattern of behavior to call on, and we become nervous and afraid of doing the wrong thing.

The actor about to go on the stage for the first time is likely to experience this reaction; the salesperson meeting a *new client* undergoes some emotional stress, and the experienced actor, facing a *new audience,* or appearing in a *new show,* may very well fall victim to the same fears that relatively inexperienced actors seem to think they alone suffer.

Recent research and studies in performance theory and analysis propose still another reason for stage fright.[3] There is the suggestion that *the actor fears to reveal his or her true self to an audience,* that somehow even the character being performed is not sufficient to hide the performer's real self from close scrutiny by the audience. Clinical psychologist Stephen Aaron has made the following observation:

> Actors experience the peak of their anxiety during the agonizing wait between "Places!" and "Curtain!" They have lost a sense of time; what may, in fact, take no more than five minutes, can seem like an eternity. . . . "Places!" orders him to remain still and silent, while "Curtain!" suggests that hidden thoughts and actions are about to be revealed to thousands of public eyes.[4]

Few professions have more taboos and superstitions than the theatre. Lucky items include three-leaved clovers, horseshoes, and anything made of ivory, while unlucky ones include peacock feathers, green clothes, and real flowers on stage.
Theatrical Superstition

The recent work of many psychologists implies that although stage fright is a perfectly normal component of stage acting it may differ from the type of anxiety associated with other fields and that studies of stage fright in the theatre belong in the area of psychoanalysis. The question is still open but, more

---

3. See Stephen Aaron, *Stage Fright: Its Role in Acting* (Chicago and London: University of Chicago Press, 1986).
4. Ibid., pp. 77–78.

pertinently, very serious studies are now underway in attempts to under-stand this important aspect of theatre acting, which has long been a neglected area of study.

Do Experienced Actors Have Stage Fright?

The answer to the question of whether or not experienced actors suffer stage fright has already been suggested earlier in this chapter. Not only do suc-cessful actors experience stage fright, but they are not hesitant about admit-ting it. It may be of some comfort to the student actor to realize that many of the most experienced actors, both in our time and in the past, have faced stage performances with less than equanimity. Edmund Kean, on the eve of his debut in London at Drury Lane, told his wife, "I wish I was going to be shot." After his successful debut as Shylock in *The Merchant of Venice*, he was sched-uled to appear again as Richard III. He was aware of what was expected of him and felt "so frightened, that my acting will be almost dumb-show tonight." Of course, he was magnificent on both occasions.

Laurence Olivier went through a prolonged bout of stage fright midway through his career, lasting for five and a half years from 1964 to 1970. Despite this difficulty, he gave some of his greatest performances, including those of Othello and Shylock. American actress Maureen Stapleton has been a fre-quent prey of stage fright, particularly on opening nights. She described her stage fright in detailed terms:

> When I work, it starts about six-thirty at night. I start to burp. I belch—almost non-stop. . . . I get so nervous that I can't remember what happened . . . I'm ner-vous every night, but opening night is more of a nightmare. . . . There's so much at stake that it just overpowers you.[5]

> *It is considered poor form to wish an actor good luck on open-ing night. The phrase "Break a leg" is preferred. In the German theatre they do it one better by cheerfully bidding actors to "Break your neck and your leg." ("Hals und Bein bruch!")*
> Theatrical Superstition

There is also a story of the great tenor Enrico Caruso, who was waiting in the wings one night before his performance in *A Masked Ball*. A young so-

---

5. Quoted in Aaron, *Stage Fright*, p. 62.

prano, Edith Mason, was nervous at the prospect of going on stage and observed Caruso shaking like a leaf in the wind. "You, Caruso, are afraid?" asked the soprano in disbelief. "When you sing, Mason," he replied, "the audience expects 100 percent. But when Caruso sings they expect 150 percent." He continued to tremble until the moment of his entrance, after which the glorious voice filled the Metropolitan Opera House with unforgettable sound.

Noel Coward was one of the most successful actors, composers, and playwrights of our time. As an exponent of debonair wit and relaxed drawingroom comedy, he would seem an unlikely candidate for stage fright. Yet his autobiography describes an encounter with stage fright during the New York premiere of his own play, *The Vortex*.

> I paced up and down on a strip of coconut matting at the side of the stage and was told by the theatre fireman to put out my cigarette. At last it was near my time to go on, and I stood holding the door knob with a clammy hand, frowning in an effort to keep my face from twitching. My cue came and I made my entrance. There was a second's silence, and then a terrific burst of applause which seemed to me to last for ever. Fortunately the first thing I had to do was embrace Lilian [Braithwaite], which I did with such fervor that her bones cracked. The applause continued, and there we stood locked in each other's arms until I felt her give me a little reassuring pat on the back, and I broke out of the clinch and managed, in a strangulated voice, to speak my first line.[6]

Lauren Bacall has candidly commented about her stage fright in her delightful biography. Recalling the first day of shooting in *To Have and Have Not* with Humphrey Bogart, she remembered that:

> My hand was shaking—my head was shaking—the cigarette was shaking. The harder I tried to stop, the more I shook. . . . What must Bogart be thinking. . . . I was in such pain.[7]

Even some time later Ms. Bacall remembers that an overseas radio broadcast with Bing Crosby and Bob Hope brought on the same trembling.

> There was a large audience, and I remember Bing standing next to me with his arm lightly around my waist, knowing my nerves and letting me know he was there helping—and Bob Hope doing handstands in front of us.[8]

Other actors tell essentially the same tale. Eva Le Gallienne, upon being asked after her thousandth performance in repertory whether she had stage fright, replied, "Yes. And it gets worse every year." Yet audiences usually are

---

6. Noel Coward, *Present Indicative* (New York: Doubleday, Doran and Co., 1937), p. 223.
7. Lauren Bacall, *Lauren Bacall by Myself* (New York: Ballantine Books, 1980), p. 123.
8. Ibid., p. 185.

not able to discern stage fright in the experienced actor. When all the excess energy is directed to the business at hand, the stage fright invariably disappears after the entrance on stage. *Most stage fright occurs in the anticipation rather than in the execution of the performance.* The very inexperienced actor, however, who is lacking in training or rehearsal time, may, on occasion, find that it will carry over to the performance. Lionel Barrymore has left us an amusing description of his first adventure on stage, in a minor role in Sheridan's comedy *The Rivals.*

> The horrible afternoon of my debut finally arrived and I was a wretched and frightened boy. . . . I crept on stage in an apathy of embarrassment and muttered my words like an automaton that needed the oil can. The scene was too much for me, as indeed, any scene would have been too much for me at that time.[9]

We find an interesting clue in Barrymore's remarks that "any scene would have been too much for me at that time." Certainly Barrymore's later performances belied the feebleness of his first efforts. The knowledge that he knew what he was doing kept his performances free of the chaos that marred his maiden effort. Although pre-performance jitters may not have disappeared entirely, once he stepped before an audience or camera his excess emotional energy was channeled in the proper direction. It is interesting to note that after two performances as Thomas in *The Rivals*, his scene was dropped from the production. Barrymore commented: "Since my debut, most performances of *The Rivals* have gone on without the front scene. I seem to have killed it for good, or perhaps directors have been worried lest I come back and play the part again."

> *Many actors believe it is bad luck to rehearse the last line of the play.*
> Theatrical Superstition

What Can Be Done about It?

Must we accept stage fright as an inevitable outcome of public performance, or can we begin to do something about it? Many of the difficulties already described can be lessened to a considerable degree by five means: understanding, progression and experience, concentration, refocusing, and making use of stage fright.

Understanding.   In the preceding pages we have discussed the causes of stage fright as well as its extent. Understanding it is the first important step in deal-

---

9. Lionel Barrymore, *We Barrymores* (New York: Appleton-Century-Crofts, 1951), p. 38.

ing with stage fright. As long as it remains a baffling mystery and the actor believes that he or she is afflicted with it to a unique degree, there is little likelihood that progress can be made. But by understanding it the actor has already taken a great step forward; stage fright is no longer seen simply as a terrifying accompaniment to one's own performances but as a not unnatural reaction experienced by many who are truly accomplished actors.

Progression and Experience.   Lionel Barrymore's early stage fright was due to inexperience and an inability to deal with a situation that at that time was overwhelming. Subsequent exposures to acting did not produce a repetition of this early difficulty. As he grew in experience and accustomed himself to difficult assignments, he was able to cope with the problem during performances. His great difficulty, in that first venture, was being asked to perform with a highly competent, professional company before a critical audience.

If the actor's experience can grow by degrees from relatively simple to complex stage assignments, the difficulty is usually eased. With this in mind, it should be easy to see that the exercises performed in acting class are an excellent means of exposing the problem in a relatively low-powered situation. As experience grows and the variety of roles increases, the actor discovers that stage fright during the performance often becomes less and less of a problem.

> *Whistling in the dressing room is frowned on as actors believe it will lead to a short run.*
> Theatrical Superstition

Concentration.   "If you are doing a good job of acting, you'll be too busy to worry about stage fright." This is one of the soundest maxims for the actor to learn. When the actor concentrates on the character and what he or she is doing, and on the projection of vitality and validity in the role, the engulfing emotion will not be the petty disturbances of fear and worry but a desire to do the best job possible. This does not necessarily mean that the actor must completely "live the role," but it does suggest that attention to the details of performance will leave no room for the entering wedge of stage fright.

In the discussion of concentration in Chapter 10, we note that attention can be focused either on the details of the performance or on objects and other actors. The proper focusing of attention will serve to combat, if not entirely eliminate, stage fright during the stage performance. The busy actor simply will not have time for it.

Refocusing.   Refocusing is a very interesting concept in the battle against stage fright, one that may seem somewhat contradictory to the use of concentration on the role. Actually, the two techniques are closely related, for refocusing means the adjustment of concentration on some other action or activity before going on stage, when stage fright is usually at its most awesome. Many experienced actors have developed a variety of routines, warm-ups, and exercises to direct their attention away from thinking about the imminent stage appearance. These activities force them to focus on something other than the coming performance. Some of these approaches are included here, although what works for one actor may not necessarily work for another. Frederic March would do up to ten minutes of vocal exercises, humming and articulating before going on stage. Laurence Olivier would stand in the wings and mutter insults under his breath to the audience, focusing his anger and fear at the object of his tension. Anthony Hopkins, before going on as Dysart in Shaffer's *Equus,* on opening night did imitations of how Marlon Brando, Richard Burton, John Gielgud, or Humphrey Bogart might play the role. Often actors find ways to direct their tensions and anxiety at audiences, and it is probably not coincidental that such phrases as "Lay them in the aisles" and "Knock them dead" are frequently heard comments that actors make to each other before going on.

Making Use of Stage Fright. If we remember that the tensions and excitement that grip the actor are in part the body's means of preparing for a challenging situation, then it is clear that the person under tension is actually better equipped to handle the exacting demands of acting. One psychiatrist who has made a special study of stage fright and its relationship to performance has asserted that all fine acting is, in fact, accompanied by stage fright.[10]

Acting requires a tremendous output of energy. In helping the actor to meet the stringent requirements of public performance, the endocrine system is performing an important function. The excess energy is not wasted in the disorganized activity of stage fright, however, if it is applied by the actor to the demands of the performance. Without it, most performances would be lifeless and rather dull. With it, a merely competent performance can turn into an exciting and memorable one.

Actor Frank Converse feels that a bit of stage fright is helpful before walking on stage. He has said, "I have a little flash of panic. . . . It's nice to panic. A lot of energy and spontaneity come from panic. I'm always worried if I don't feel a little trickle between my arm and my shirt."[11]

The "case of nerves" that many great actors experience *before* each performance is turned to their advantage when they make their entrance and the extra energy is needed. Helen Hayes underwent such nervousness before each performance. Yet in spite of it, or perhaps *because of it,* her acting was considered by many to be truly inspired, with a high level of consistency night after night.

Laurence Olivier, recalling his performance of Shylock in *The Merchant of Venice* during which he suffered badly from stage fright, mused, "I wonder

10. See Donald Kaplan, "On Stage Fright," *Drama Review* T45, pp. 60–83.

11. Frank Converse interview in Susan Shacter and Don Shewey, *Caught in the Act* (New York: New American Library, 1986), p. 247.

if that had anything to do with my performance's becoming fresh, open and naked again."[12]

The late American actor Richard Mansfield was acutely afflicted by stage fright, and opening nights particularly were hard on him. In his explanation, however, of why he refused to let it hamper him, we can see something of that unspoken determination that motivates all fine actors.

> The excitement of a first night is actual suffering; the nervousness actual torture. Yet as I walk . . . to the theatre . . . and note the impassive, imperturbable faces of the passersby, I must confess to myself that I would not change places with them—no, not for worlds. I have something that is filling my life brimful of interest. . . . It's like a battle. I shall win or die. . . .[13]

In rehearsal, if a Russian actor drops a script, he or she must immediately sit on it for a time or bad luck will ensue.

Theatrical Superstition

No matter how nervous the actor may be before or during the performance, the worst fears are seldom realized. This thought often sustains the actor in his or her worst moments. Yet sometimes more drastic measures than we have discussed are used to eliminate stage fright. On this point, we shall close with an anecdote often told about Alfred Hitchcock, the film director. During the filming of a sequence, a nervous actor kept muffing his lines. "Calm down," Hitchcock advised him. "Only your whole career depends on this scene."

SUGGESTIONS FOR FURTHER READING

Aaron, Stephen. *Stage Fright: Its Role in Acting.* Chicago: University of Chicago Press, 1986.

Fischer, W. F. *Theories of Anxiety.* New York: Harper and Row, 1970.

Goffman, E. *The Presentation of Self in Everyday Life.* Garden City, NY: Doubleday Anchor Books, 1959.

Kaplan, D. "On Stage Fright." *Drama Review* T45, pp. 105–116.

Moramarco, S. S. "Stagefright . . . and How to Beat It." *Toastmaster* 42(12), pp. 5–7.

Olivier, Laurence. *On Acting.* New York: Simon and Schuster, 1986, pp. 180–186.

Wiles, T. J. *The Theatre Event: Modern Theories of Performance.* Chicago and London: University of Chicago Press, 1980.

---

12. Laurence Olivier, *On Acting* (New York: Simon and Schuster, 1986), p. 180.
13. Richard Mansfield, "The Story of a Production," *Harper's Weekly,* May 24, 1890, p. 408.

CHAPTER NINE

Auditioning and Preparing a Role

The Audition Process

No matter how trained an actor may feel and how ready that actor is to play the role that is clearly "the role I was born to play," one important step stands between the actor and the fulfillment of that dream—the *audition* or *tryout*. Let us look at some practical matters tied to the audition process, with the aim of making it less frightening and turning it to our advantage.

The audition process itself can vary from one director to another, from one casting director to another, from one company to another, or from play to play. Therefore the following observations will attempt to draw some generalizations about the most frequently encountered situations and available techniques and provide a set of useful guidelines. We shall look at ten important considerations and review each of them.

1. What selection should I read?
2. What does the auditor expect from me?
3. What should I wear?
4. Should I warm up?
5. How should I enter?
6. How do I establish myself?
7. Listen carefully!
8. Maintain eye contact!
9. What if I goof?
10. Do I need a résumé?

1. What selection should I read?

Obviously if you are auditioning for a specific play or a specific part, it is best to familiarize yourself with a sequence from that play which is within the allowable time limit of your audition. Frequently the director will post notices indicating which scenes to read from the play being cast. Know your scene as well as you can, but it is preferable that you *do not memorize* it. Many directors fear an actor who has already learned a scene before the first rehearsal. It might suggest rigidity and a reluctance to change during the rehearsal process. If on the other hand you are auditioning for a company of players, and the casting directors are looking for more than a single character in one play, the choice of the audition piece can vary. Here the memorized piece is preferable. Choose a piece you are comfortable with! As a general piece of advice, do not choose a piece with a major emotional climax. Choose a piece that you feel shows you off in the best light possible. Avoid dialect scenes if you can, as they may mask certain other features the auditor is looking for.

2. What does the auditor expect from me?

Different auditors look for different things, particularly when a specific play is being cast. Such words are probably not very comforting for the auditioner, but here are a few typical observations that will serve you in good stead.

(a) Is the actor prepared? Has he or she walked into this tryout with the determination to earn a role?
(b) Will the actor "grow" and give a first-rate performance when the show opens? Sometimes only the casting director's intuition helps to answer that question.
(c) Is the actor serious about the audition and the work that awaits the company? The attitude the actor displays at the audition can often be a major "tip-off."
(d) Does the actor exude confidence, but not arrogance?

3. What should I wear?

This might seem to be an irrelevant question, but it really isn't. The simplest advice is twofold. First, wear what is comfortable for you to work in and will not inhibit you in any way. Second, wear what fits the play you are trying out for. Don't wear a suit and tie if you are auditioning for the role of a cowboy in a play by Sam Shepard. Don't wear a torn pair of jeans and sweater if you are reading scenes for an English comedy of manners by Noel Coward. When giving a reading for a company, men should wear a pair of neat slacks and an open-necked dress shirt; women should wear a simple dress with few adornments. If you are called back for a second reading at a later time, try to wear the same outfit you wore at the first reading. You want the auditor to remember you, don't you?

4. Should I warm up?

The question seems to answer itself, yet it is surprising how often the implications of the question are overlooked. In other words:

(a) Don't come into the audition giving a cold reading and then have to apologize to the auditor for a "really poor reading."
(b) Get into the emotional color of your scene before you go before an audience of listeners.
(c) Your warm-up does not need to be in a hall somewhere away from the auditorium or audition room, although if you can find some place (or space) for yourself, so much the better. Warm up physically and vocally if you can, and even before you arrive for the audition, go over your material at home.
(d) If you have the opportunity, "walk" the audition space before the audition begins in order to familiarize yourself with the surroundings, and if there is an opportunity, "run" your selection in the audition space. This is not necessarily what we might call a true warm-up, which should take place shortly before you go on, but it is good advice nevertheless.

5. How should I enter?

This is not as amusing a question as it might seem. The most important thing to keep in mind is that the auditors begin forming their opinion of you the moment you walk on stage or walk to the front of the audition space. First impressions are often long-lasting, and they can be very positive or devastating, not only in the theatre but in everyday life. Show yourself to be focused, serious about your work, but also confident. A smile never does any harm, but don't overdo it. Introduce yourself clearly (everyone may not know your name), state the title of the piece/role/play you are auditioning for, and go for it!

6. How do I "establish" myself?

The first step toward making an impression on those who are auditioning you was taken on your entrance. You have begun to establish yourself. Be certain that when delivering your audition piece, it is in a full-sized voice! Most auditions are filled with actors who cannot be heard beyond the first few rows. You usually will have only a few minutes for your audition, so think in terms of true theatre size! If possible, give some indication of your ability to move freely and in a relaxed manner. Remember, if possible, try out your piece before the audition in the theatre or room where the audition will take place. Don't let any distractions, which may come from the listening end of the theatre or room (you may be the fiftieth auditioner in the last two hours and fatigue is showing in the listener), disrupt you. Above all, remain confident, even if you wish the tortures of the damned for those who are auditioning you.

7. Listen carefully to what is said to you!

One aspect of the tryout or audition is something you may not be able to plan, and that is a direction given to you by the person supervising the audition. Perhaps the director wishes to see if you can move, perhaps there is a concern about projection, perhaps you will be asked to do an improvisation to test your imagination, or perhaps you will be asked to give your reading in a different manner. *Be sure you are clear as to what is being asked of you.* Try to follow the directions as precisely as you can, for often the reason for these comments is to determine if you can take direction. And, on a positive note, remember that the reason you are being asked to take these directions in all likelihood indicates that the director is interested in you!

8. Maintain eye contact!

Eye contact does not assume that you should look at the auditor. In fact, that practice is frequently counter-productive because it may make the auditor uncomfortable. Eye contact is the selection of *some point* in the audition room on which to focus. When you are doing an audition piece alone, your material is frequently a selection from a play in which one character is talking to one or more other characters. Select a reference point for the other "character" in your scene, and maintain it. You need not stare at this reference point any more than you would stare if you were talking to an actual person, but it should become a "locale" for the constant return of your focus. If you wish, you might place a chair on the stage and use it as your reference point; this will permit greater freedom of movement on your part and fluency in returning to the point of your eye contact. Should you audition with a partner, the matter of eye contact is self-evident and deserves the type of mutual contact that one would expect during a good rehearsal.

9. *What if I goof?*

Don't be concerned about giving a bad reading, or forgetting a line, or mangling your speech. The people who are conducting the audition, including the director, are invariably sympathetic, want you to succeed, and understand the problems of the audition. Unless you are facing a rigid time limit of about two to three minutes, there is a simple way to deal with an audition that has gone awry. Relax and ask permission if you can start again. In most cases you will find that the listeners are perfectly willing to give you another crack at your audition piece. Remember that they want to see you at your best!

10. *Do I need a résumé?*

The simple answer to this question is "yes." The actor's résumé is a list of the roles he or she has performed, including where the performance took place and under whose direction. It should also include the important information that will help the casting director relate the actor to a potential role. Therefore include:

(a) Name
(b) Height
(c) Weight
(d) Hair color
(e) Eye color
(f) Age range you can play
(g) Telephone number
(h) Special talents such as singing, dancing, juggling, sword swallowing, and so on
(i) A recent 8" × 10" black and white head shot

If you do not have many credits to your name, don't let it concern you. The résumé will become more interesting as you gain experience. Even if there are very few roles that you have performed, a neat résumé, inexpensively reproduced, and a good picture of yourself send a clear message to those doing the casting: "I'm serious about this audition and I will be serious about the rehearsal and performances that are to come!"

> *Whatever success I've had is due to a lot of instinct and a little luck.*
>
> Clint Eastwood

Basic Steps in Developing a Role

Analyzing the Play

Obviously the first step in preparing a role is to read the play. This first reading tells something of the personality of the character to be undertaken and may suggest stage movement and pieces of business that will bring the play to life from the printed page. Even this first reading should put the actor's imagination to work.

The early readings are important. Some actors read through a play hastily, underlining their speeches with a red pencil and never going beyond this superficial examination of the play. Many difficulties encountered later during the rehearsal period could easily have been avoided by a more responsible study of the play during this preliminary stage. Much of the meaning of the play is lost if the actor fails to study it as an integrated whole but skims through it, examining only his or her own lines.

At the first reading of the play one should follow the plot, enjoy the humor or suspense, and let the conflict of the play sustain interest until reaching the climax and final resolution of the story. A play is held together by the action, and it is the story that helps to sustain interest in the characters. After this first reading the actor should read the play again, with greater care, this time examining its organization, its style and mood, and the relation of all the characters to one another and to the play itself. It may be useful to do some preliminary thinking about the following questions during this and subsequent readings:

1. What is the theme of the play? What is the author trying to say?
2. Does the play have a distinctive style?
3. Is the sequence of events clear?
4. Why do the characters react as they do to the various situations developed in the play?
5. What is the function of the character I am going to portray?
6. What is that character's relationship to the other characters in the play?

These and other questions should be discussed with the director and cast members during the early rehearsals. This exchange of ideas will serve to put the character in proper perspective as the actor relates the part (in the literal sense) to the whole. Katharine Cornell has told us that "to understand one's own character thoroughly one must see it in relation not only to itself but to the other characters in the play."[1] Helen Hayes held much the same point of view. Her first conception of a drama is "entirely objective." She is concerned with the structure of the play, and she examines all the parts in order to understand "what they look like, what they are thinking of, what their relationship is to one another, the quality of their personalities."[2] Not until she understood the play "in the language of the theatre" did she begin a detailed examination of her role in terms of its creative challenge.

It is well that few actors in the theatre today follow the example of one popular eighteenth-century actress who had secured a noteworthy reputation as Lady Macbeth. Unfortunately she was so wrapped up in her own performance that she paid little attention to her relation to the play as a whole. When asked one day how her characterization of Lady Macbeth fit into the total fabric of Shakespeare's tragedy, she answered, "I don't know." It seems she had read only those scenes in which she appeared and therefore had only a vague idea as to how the

> *A lot of what acting is, is paying attention.*
>
> Robert Redford

play ended. Just as acting styles have changed during the past hundred years, so too has the actor's responsibility to the play. Extensive rehearsals and attention to detail are important because they help to achieve an integrated production instead of the haphazard productions of the past.

Analyzing the Character

The next step in the preparation of a role requires a thorough examination of the character. This involves a careful scrutiny of the script—a scrutiny to which the actor brings his or her accumulation of experience and observation. This accumulation should continue to be used through the rehearsal period and actual performances. It is used as long as the actor is receptive to new ideas and impressions and does not close off the great potential of the imagination. Precisely on this point, stage and film actor Treat Williams has said that "I always begin with the text. What is he saying, what is he doing, and

---

1. Morton Eustis, *Players at Work: Acting According to the Actors* (New York: Theatre Arts Books, 1937), p. 65.
2. Ibid., p. 15.

Anthony Hopkins and Joan Plowright. National Theatre, London. Photograph by Britain on View Photographic Library.

what is everyone saying about him?" Williams feels it is vital to open up to the full "range of possibilities."[3]

As the actor studies the play it is important to begin to form a solid impression about his or her character. A few simple problems need to be solved in order to provide a preliminary approach to the character. Nazimova, the noted Russian actress, felt it imperative to "study the woman. I look at her under a magnifying glass and say to myself: 'Is she right? Is she logical? Is she true to herself? Can *I* act that woman?' " As an actress she wanted to know "what she is thinking, what her inner response is, her feeling . . . once you know what she *is*, what she does becomes easy to interpret."[4]

Nazimova has left us some valuable advice. Her most significant comment on the preparation of the role is: *"Once you know what she is, what she does becomes easy to interpret."* Clearly, the first step in developing a role is to understand it as thoroughly as possible. It is at this point that the actor may begin to use all available technical and emotional resources to build a believable characterization. "Half the actor's battle is won," said Helen Hayes, "once a clear picture of the character is firmly engraved in the senses."[5]

Once a general picture of the character is formed, the actor begins to build from specific details and ask specific questions about the character. Sidney Poitier works in this manner, and insists that "I must understand what

---

3. Susan Shacter and Don Shewey, *Caught in the Act* (New York: New American Library, 1986), p. 49.

4. Eustis, *Players at Work*, p. 53.

5. Ibid., p. 18.

are the driving forces in the man. In order to understand that, you must find out what are his political, social, economic, religious milieus"[6] in order to understand how they contribute to the full personality of the character. This type of work is essential for all actors.

A useful incident distinctly reinforces this point. When Simon Callow was cast in the role of Mozart in the original production of *Amadeus*, he faced a particularly difficult challenge, not only as the creator of the role, but also having to meet the demands of playwright Peter Shaffer. Shaffer had written a major work about the nature of genius and mediocrity, creative imagination and artistic jealousy, all centralized on the major premise that our view of Mozart the musician incorrectly matched our view of Mozart the man. Indeed Shaffer's title for the play *Amadeus* (Latin for "beloved of God") was a clear statement of Shaffer's attitude about the great paradox. Callow asked for help from director Sir Peter Hall, suggesting perhaps there was a person in real life or an ideal actor, living or dead, who could give Callow some parameters or a point of reference. Hall's suggestion of a young Peter O'Toole before he had his nose fixed was of little help to Callow. Then the actor, having read as much as he could about Mozart, came upon a book he had first rejected, because the title had seemed too daunting—*Mozart: A Documentary Biography*, by Otto Deutsch. Callow's reaction upon beginning to read the book was both immediate and positive.

> Within minutes of flicking through its pages I knew I'd struck gold, . . . There he was, the little bugger . . . portrayed in letters, memoirs and laundry bills by his contemporaries. . . . here was the way people really saw him—partisan, sometimes one-sided, but immediately vivid—a picture of a light, tiny, mercurial, volatile, immature, prodigiously energetic, bird-like creature. . . . making absurd and childish jokes. . . . Much of this is in Peter's play. . . . The moment I saw this Mozart, Shaffer's text fell into place. . . . Once I had found that, the playing style of the piece came easily.[7]

The following analysis chart may be useful in helping to analyze the character.

1. *Social Factors*
   a. Class status: upper, middle, lower
   b. Occupation: What kind of work, attitude toward the job, income, hours at work

---

6. Sidney Poitier, quoted in Lewis Funke and John E. Booth, *Actors Talk about Acting* (New York: Random House, 1961), p. 378.

7. The story of Simon Callow's extraordinary work and performance in *Amadeus* is told in his excellent book *Being an Actor* (New York: St. Martin's Press, 1984), p. 96. Although Callow did not perform the Mozart role in the fine film adaptation of the play, he did appear in the film as Emanuel Schickaneder, Mozart's very close friend who collaborated with Mozart on his final piece for the musical stage, *The Magic Flute*. Schickaneder, incidentally, was also a man of immense talents.

    c. Education: Level of education, schools attended, probable grades, best subjects, worst subjects, etc.

    d. Home: Single, married, divorced, orphan, living with family, living alone, kind of home, etc.

    e. Religion

    f. Community: rural, suburban, city, inner city, place in the community

    g. Race, nationality, ethnic background

    h. Political preferences, activities, interests, etc.

2. *Personal Factors*

    a. Hobbies, amusements, kinds of reading, etc.

    b. Sex life, moral views and attitudes

    c. Ambitions

    d. Attitude to life: Resigned, rebellious, defeatist, etc.

    e. Mental health: complexes, neuroses, obsessions, superstitions, etc.

    f. Personality: introverted, extroverted

    g. Dress habits: neat, sloppy, casual, well-groomed, traditional, non-conformist, etc.

    h. Talents and creativity

One means of helping to realize the character is to establish a general impression about his or her physical and vocal personality. How does the character move and walk on stage: quickly or slowly, with harsh or gentle movements, erect or stooped bearing? Is the character soft-spoken or does he or she speak in a loud voice, rapidly or slowly, in short bursts or in smooth and even phrasing? What kind of pitch, inflectional patterns, and articulation will make the character more meaningful?

Laurence Olivier's key was usually noses. This might seem an odd choice, but it helped Olivier identify a physical characteristic for each particular role. Olivier felt that the visual and physical characteristics of the role are vital. He tells us that ["to] create a character, I first visualize a painting; the manner, movement, gestures, walk all follow."[8] It gave him a sense of the identity of the character toward which he could work. It was merely a starting point, from which he could explore all the other dimensions of a character.

A good starting point for determining these working elements is the script itself. Careful examination of the play will reveal a wealth of detailed information about the character. Five important keys to understanding can be derived from the script:

1. The playwright's description and comments.
2. The character's manner of speech. How the character sees himself or herself.
3. What others in the play say about the character.
4. Suggested business inserted by the playwright.

---

8. See Laurence Olivier, *On Acting* (New York: Simon and Schuster, 1986), p. 153.

5. Distinctive changes in attitude on the part of the character throughout the play.

These considerations and ideas about the role should not be maintained too rigidly. They should serve as a basis for developing a characterization through the rehearsal period, but the actor must be prepared to make adjustments and continue to probe into the subtleties of the characterization. It will be useful here to remind ourselves of the questions the actor should ask in any scene or improvisation, which we called the **W** checklist in Chapter 7.

1. *Who* am I?
2. *Where* am I?
3. *What* do I want?
4. *Why* do I want it?
5. *What* is preventing me from getting it?
6. *What* am I willing to do to get what I want?
7. *Whom* do I want it from?
8. *When* do I need it?

Often, during this early period, such questions as "How does my character walk, move, speak, and so on?" should be resolved only in general terms. Specific solutions will be realized through the use of observation and imagination.

Observation

As Sherlock Holmes often reminded his constant and rather muddleheaded companion, Dr. Watson, to see is not enough. One must learn to use the power of observation. Individuals are differentiated by habits of movement, gesture, posture, and speech patterns. The actor who is sensitive to these differentiations in people will often find much that can be meaningfully transferred to the stage. This process should go on not only as the actor works on a specific role but during everyday activities. It is not necessary to become a walking diary of all that occurs during a day, but sensitive awareness of the environment and those who inhabit it will help solve many difficulties arising out of challenging characterizations. Walter Matthau goes so far as to suggest that it is like being a sponge, in that an observant actor "soaks up everything." Matthau indicates that he enjoys wandering into a cafeteria anonymously and just watching people. "I can look around as much as I like, not that you ever imitate people as such. But you get the feel and smell and the taste of how they behave. . . . Then, when I'm onstage, I use it."[9]

---

9. Walter Matthau in Lillian Ross and Helen Ross, *The Player: A Profile of an Art* (New York: Simon and Schuster, 1962), p. 422.

Probably the most famous impersonation in the history of acting was Charlie Chaplin's immortal tramp. So closely associated is this actor with this role that often we have difficulty in separating the two. We need simply mention the name Charlie Chaplin, and an image of a tramp with baggy pants, oversized shoes, and bowler hat immediately springs to mind. The manner in which this great character was created illustrates how observation can be translated into the creative impulse. In this case it was a chance meeting with a hobo on a street in San Francisco that fanned the spark of Chaplin's imagination. We all meet interesting people every day, but are we aware of the potential such meetings hold for the actor? Let Chaplin describe the meeting in his own words and we can see how his keen observation worked to refine the character of the tramp that he brought to the screen.

> We went into a barroom, he got a drink, and we sat right down then and there to have a bite of lunch. The food and the drink warmed him and brought to the surface the irresponsible joy of life possessed by the nomad and the ne'er-do-well. He told me the story of his life, of long jaunts through the beautiful country, of longer rides on convenient freights, or misfortunes which attend the unfortunate who are found stealing a ride on a "side-door pullman," and of the simplicity of the farmers who lived only a short distance from the city. It was a delight to hear him talk, to gather from it the revelations of his character, to watch his gestures, and his trick of facial expression. *All these elements were carefully watched by me, and noted for future reference.* He was rather surprised when we parted, at my profuse thanks. He had given me a good deal more than I had given him, but he didn't know it. He had obtained a little food and drink and a chance talk from me. From him, I had a brand new idea for a picture.[10] [emphasis added]

Obviously it is not always possible to find one model from which to build a characterization. In many ways Chaplin was lucky, but it is important to remember that he was ready and able to assimilate qualities of the hobo's gestures, facial expression, and attitude toward life into the projected role.

Observation can be useful also in helping to provide a clue to the handling of particularly difficult scenes or problems. One of the legends of the theatre tells of David Garrick while he was working on his role of King Lear and examining the best means of simulating madness. A neighbor, unhappily, provided him with the key. One day the neighbor was holding his two-year-old daughter in his arms as he leaned out of his upper-story window. The child slipped from his grasp and was killed instantly on the stone street below. The unfortunate man lost his mind from shock. Garrick often stopped by his neighbor's home and would see him hold an imaginary child in his arms and then seem to drop it from the same window, breaking off into hor-

---

10. Charlie Chaplin, "How I Made My Success," *Theatre*, September 1915, pp. 120ff.

rible screams and sobs of anguish. From his observation of the distraught father Garrick was able to build his shattering portrayal of the maddened King
Lear, one of the most memorable characterizations in the English theatre.

On such incidents are great roles built. Such occurrences are certainly
rare and not likely to be part of our everyday experience. Yet even the most
seemingly unimportant observation can be of value to the actor. The smallest
gesture, a unique reaction to an incident, a twist of the head, the gait or stoop
of an acquaintance can serve to bring individuality to a characterization. One
needn't go so far as a well-known actor who, upon hearing that a close friend
had been severely injured, stopped momentarily on his way to his friend to
look in the mirror and think to himself, "Oh, that's what someone looks like
who has heard of the death of a dear friend." Perhaps a bit callous, but nevertheless here was the actor always at work—even though the friend did not,
in fact, die.

Laurence Olivier in 1980, after acting for fifty years in the theatre and
film, took time during the shooting of the latest version of *The Jazz Singer* to
wander through the East Side of New York watching elderly Jewish men, in
order to help him prepare his role as the cantor in the film. He never stopped
watching, learning, remembering. When John Lithgow was preparing for the
film *Footloose*, he went to a minister in Provo, Utah, and pretended that he was
in the middle of a deep spiritual crisis so that he could hear someone speak
in earnest about being saved. Lithgow admits that he "felt like a real hypocrite, needless to say, but it was very useful."[11]

Alertness to events in our everyday life is surprisingly useful. Careful
scrutiny of interesting people in a bus, on the street, or in any meeting place
has provided more than one alert actor with the means of building a successful portrait. The important thing to remember is that we must be receptive to the events that take place around us and be ready to make use of them
when the need arises in our role.

Imagination

There will be circumstances in which even the most careful observation or experience will fail to provide the clue needed to develop a character or to play
an especially difficult sequence. Observation is essential, but sometimes we
may find that no file of experience can serve our needs. We may also legiti-
mately argue that there are many emotional situations in the course of a play
for which our stock of experience and observation will be unable to provide
valid information.

Ingrid Bergman amusingly pointed out that when you are playing a

---

11. Shacter and Shewey, *Caught in the Act*, p. 45.

murderer, "you don't go out and murder somebody." The imagination may supply the means of coping with these difficulties. However, we must be careful not to equate imagination simply with sheer invention. Rather, imagination requires creative inspiration and originality firmly based on experience and observation. "Imagination, industry, and intelligence," said Ellen Terry, "are all indispensable to the actress, but of these three the greatest is . . . imagination."[12]

Imagination provides the creative spark that makes meaningful and exciting the most difficult characters and scenes. One of the best examples of the use of imagination involved a particularly difficult scene for the actor Jacob Ben-Ami in Tolstoy's *Redemption*. The character Fedya, on the verge of suicide, is required to place a gun to his temple, but at the fatal moment he must lose his nerve, so that, shattered in spirit, he becomes a broken, ruined shadow of a man for the remainder of the play. Ben-Ami, of course, had never been in a similar situation, nor had he observed anything resembling such an incident. Simply trying to imagine the situation might have been useful, but this too would leave him short of the effect he wished to achieve. His solution was actually quite simple, and the reaction of the audience to his playing of the scene was clear evidence of his success.

Ben-Ami reasoned that a fundamental element in Fedya's loss of courage was his terror of the bullet searing through his brain and the physical pain that would accompany it. Having no accurate experience to serve as a guide, the actor remembered the shock he experienced in the morning stepping into an ice-cold shower. It was this sensation Ben-Ami utilized as he prepared to pull the trigger and was seized by his terrifying hesitation. The actor's imagination had provided the solution that made a highly difficult scene believable.[13]

One distinguished actor has suggested, quite seriously, that when playing a love scene, he often contemplated a delicious plate of spaghetti and meatballs. Perhaps he didn't like his co-star. Donald Pleasance referred to animals and birds for his feelings about a role. Part of his preparation for and portrayal of the old tramp in Pinter's *The Caretaker* was based on his thinking of himself as an alley cat.

When used properly, imagination opens up an entire world of creative potential. It makes feasible the acting of difficult scenes and emotional climaxes that might otherwise be difficult, if not impossible. Imagination may be used as simply as the projection of rage at an adversary by the device of imagining the anger we have felt as we slap furiously at a bothersome mosquito, or it may be used to build a complete character.

---

12. Ellen Terry, *Ellen Terry's Memoirs* (New York: Putnam, 1932), p. 34.
13. This story is known to many actors and directors. Burgess Meredith has spoken of it in his discussion of acting. A detailed retelling of the incident is found in Robert Lewis's *Method—or Madness* (New York: Samuel French, 1958), pp. 12–13.

Two fine actresses also describe this use of imagination quite clearly and practically. When Anne Bancroft first looked at the script of *The Miracle Worker*, she asked herself

> What is the whole thing about? It's about a woman who if she does not teach this child, both she and the child will perish. Of course, I have nothing like that in my own life, so I have to take something else in my life about which I have to say "If I don't do a certain thing, I will perish."[14]

In *The Chapman Report*, Jane Fonda was asked to play a frigid woman and a widow. She did it, she recalled, not by being "like that woman. Instead, I call on what every woman has felt at some time in her life—doubts about herself. This feeling is enough to give me 'insight' into the way that woman feels."[15]

Imagination may not always provide us with the right solution to our difficulties, but it is virtually boundless in its potential. In the trial-and-error process of the early stages of preparing a role, it is better to take a wrong turn than not to make a bold attempt to utilize the actor's creativity.

Celebrated British writer/actor/director Noel Coward was rehearsing a Broadway production with a "movie star" in a leading role. She was a bit slow in memorizing her lines, which was a particular pet peeve of Mr. Coward. One rehearsal was pretty slow as the star hesitated over her lines. She stopped and exclaimed, "I don't understand it, I knew these lines backward last night." To which the usually cool Coward snapped, "And that's the way we're getting them this morning."

Theatrical Anecdote

Learning Lines

The learning of lines is often the most unpleasant task connected with the actor's work in a production. It is recognized as a basic responsibility in the preparation of the role, although little creativeness is involved. Burgess Meredith has called it "turmoil and headsweat," and many actors agree with him. There is no one right way to learn lines. Some actors have the facility to learn lines quickly—they are what we call "quick studies." Others find it laborious and time-consuming.

---

14. Anne Bancroft, quoted in Funke and Booth, *Actors Talk about Acting*, p. 450.
15. Jane Fonda, quoted in Ross and Ross, *The Player*, pp. 99–100.

Three approaches to the learning of lines can be suggested. It is possible, however, that some combination of the three will be most helpful in the memorization of dialogue.

1. *Lines may be learned by constant repetition through silent reading.* This approach is the one most commonly used and involves the age-old drudgery of reading and rereading until the dialogue is firmly fixed in the memory. The dialogue may be studied line by line or phrase by phrase, until constant exposure firmly establishes the lines and cues in the memory. This approach will be most successful for the actor having good visual memory. Often it is helpful to have someone work lines with the actor, to be "on the book," throwing cues and making any corrections when necessary, while the actor gives a reading of his or her lines.

2. *Lines may be learned by examining their emotional and intellectual context.* Rather than memorizing the lines mechanically, some actors find it useful to work for the meaning of the line, striving to find vivid elements or some association of ideas that serve to establish the sense of the line in the memory. This approach has the value of developing comprehension of the role while it frees the actor from the script.

3. *Lines may be learned by relating them to the movement in the play.* We find this device utilized after rehearsals are well under way and the actor is able to *associate* dialogue with movement and principal pieces of business. Often the dialogue is so closely related to the physical characteristics of the production that such association is simple. Long speeches with little movement are clearly the most difficult to memorize in this way. If the movement has already been blocked out, recapitulating the planned movement in private may be helpful in the study of lines.

Most directors prefer that the actor not memorize lines until the play has been blocked out. This prevailing philosophy underscores the belief that the learning of lines should grow out of the meaning and emphasis of the production. If lines need to be learned before rehearsals begin, or if the rehearsal period is somewhat limited (as in summer stock), the first two methods will usually prove necessary.

The learning of lines is an unwelcome chore that more often than not is absolutely necessary before total involvement in a role is possible. During the run of one of their great successes, the team of Lunt and Fontanne encountered a very telling example of the problem. Their biographer recounts the incident.

During one of the San Francisco performances, Fontanne displayed, more remarkably than ever, her thorough absorption in her craft. The Lunts were playing a scene while seated together at a table; suddenly, Lunt realized that Fontanne's silk-jersey costume must have stretched, for her left breast was exposed. He coughed, trying to attract her attention. He tried to indicate with his eyes the source of the problem. Fontanne continued with the scene, taking no notice of Lunt's peculiar behavior. When the curtain descended, he said, "Did you know your left breast was bare to the audience?" An irritated look crossed her face. "Don't bother me with things like that until I know my lines," she said.[16]

The following description of how one actor approaches the learning of lines is not intended to be dogmatic, but it does illustrate a prevalent practice that many actors find successful. Paul Muni's outline of his approach to the learning of lines indicated use of the first two methods, with somewhat greater emphasis on the first.

> This method has been most helpful to me. I have found it best to parrot my lines, to memorize them directly, so that I can speak them without analysis or thought for their meaning. Often I will read a speech over and over, at home, until the phrases come to me automatically and rhythmically.
>
> While parroting my lines, some of the thought behind them is bound to penetrate subconsciously, so that my interpretation is partially set, but not so rigidly that I cannot change it. Once the lines come to me automatically, I discard them completely and think of the thoughts they express . . . until I am confident that the lines are mine and that I need no longer think of them.[17]

Unless a director insists to the contrary, it is wise to learn the lines and cues as soon as possible after blocking rehearsals have started. "Getting rid of the book" is an important step forward, for it permits the actor to concentrate on developing the role without the impediment of the script.

Developing Business

Stage business can be defined as any action, other than the basic movement of the play, that accompanies a situation or a line of dialogue. It may help to tell the story and to impart variety to the production. The insertion of business necessary to propel the story forward is invariably the concern of the director, who will find suggestions for this type of business explicitly indicated in the script or may develop it in relation to the plan of production.

Because business also serves to give an added dimension to the character, the actor must take a major responsibility for developing pieces of business to enhance and enrich the role. Business that grows directly out of the indicated action of the play presents little difficulty in execution once stage technique is mastered. Business that the actor develops personally as an integral part of the character may prove somewhat more difficult to create, in

---

16. Jared Brown, *The Fabulous Lunts* (New York: Atheneum, 1986), p. 246.
17. Paul Muni, "The Actor Plays His Part" in *We Make the Movies*, ed. Nancy Naumberg (New York: Norton, 1937), pp. 131–142.

that it places greater demands on the actor's imagination and creativity. Despite such difficulties, the value of inserting business designed to enhance the character must be clearly recognized.

Business utilized for character embellishment is usually carefully detailed and often quite distinctive from the business that simply advances the plot. Imaginative use of details is a major means of expanding and clarifying a character. The development of even the smallest piece of business may turn a lifeless, cardboard figure into a distinctive personality. The most common pieces of business involve the lighting of cigarettes, the moving of small pieces of furniture, the arrangement of articles of clothing, and the handling of small properties, such as a pencil and pad, a cigarette lighter, a glass, a cup, a book, and the like. Such properties are useful in helping to project particular personality traits. With or without properties, selected pieces of pantomimic action add variety to a performance and may tell us something important about the character. One character may consistently drop cigarette ashes on his coat, another may be addicted to doodling with pad and pencil, another may have the habit of scratching an ear, rubbing his chin, taking off eyeglasses for continual cleaning, and so on.

Clues that may be useful in developing business are often found in the dialogue, either in what the character says or in what others say about him. Sometimes it will grow out of the physical appearance of the character. In his performance as Henry Drummond in *Inherit the Wind*, Paul Muni made skillful use of his colorful suspenders to project a character who was at the same time thoughtful, vigorous, and dynamic. The excellent description by one character of Mrs. Millamant as she is about to make an entrance in Congreve's *The Way of the World*: "Here she comes, i' faith, full sail, with her fan spread and her streamers out, . . ." should provide any intelligent actress with several ideas for business to enliven her portrait of this character.

When Peter Brook directed Alfred Lunt and Lynn Fontanne in Durrenmatt's *The Visit*, he learned what generations of playgoers and directors had learned about the Lunts. English theatre critic J. C. Trewin recounts the incident very precisely.

> . . . Alfred Lunt so endeared himself to Brook by the kind of suggestion only an obsessed actor would make. During the first act, while sitting on a bench, he would take off his shoe, rub his foot, and shake the shoe to empty it before putting it on again. One evening . . . he told Brook that it worried him on shaking the shoe, that nothing fell out; he wondered whether he might not put in two small pebbles, so that the audience could see and hear them drop. Gravely, Brook agreed; but Lunt was not really satisfied yet. He considered the matter again, looking anxiously at the two pebbles in his palm before he spoke. "You don't think," he said, "that it might be better with just one."[18]

---

18. C. Trewin, *Peter Brook: A Biography* (London: Macdonald and Co., 1970), p. 107.

It was because of this acute awareness of business and choices that Montgomery Clift paid Lunt his highest compliment.

> Alfred taught me how to select. . . . Acting is an accumulation of subtle details. And the details of Alfred Lunt's performances were like the observations of a great novelist. . . .[19]

Business may develop constantly throughout the rehearsal period. Some ideas will undoubtedly occur with the first analysis of the character. When rehearsals with actual properties begin, still more business will become obvious and may be integrated into the pattern of the characterization. It is important to remember that the growth of the character, through patience, imagination, and experimentation, continues during each stage of the preparation of the role.

Avoidance of Clichés

A cliché is a conventionalized and stereotyped projection of an emotion or character. It is obvious that few situations and characters in plays are identical; yet the actor is often tempted to fall back on stock tricks and devices because of the failure to develop a role carefully and with perseverance. Such devices may include imitating another performer or using pieces of business that the actor has found successful in previous plays. Although using another actor as a role model is in itself not wrong and has been a device exploited by many fine actors, the danger is that this may become a shortcut that leaves the actor insecure about his own creative imagination.

Even more damaging to creativity is the belief by some actors that all emotional situations can be portrayed by one or another standardized external device. The following descriptions illustrating this type of thinking may seem amusing, but they have been seriously advanced even in recent years as one means of "acting emotional states." We read in one text that to project *contempt* the actor should do as follows: The corner of the mouth twitches up, which exposes a glint on the pointed dog-tooth; the nostril on that side of the face curls, and the eyes narrow. To enact *grief* we are told that the actor should bring the lips together tightly, attempting to control their quivering. The eyes must be veiled slightly by the eyelids, and the brow should be contracted so that the wrinkles lift in the center.[20]

---

19. See the biography of Clift by Patricia Bosworth, *Montgomery Clift* (New York: Harcourt Brace Jovanovich, 1978).

20. This approach is explained in detail in C. C. Mather, A. H. Spaulding, and M. H. Skillen, *Behind the Footlights* (New York: Silver Burdett, 1935).

The question of using external means is not the issue here, for such means are certainly valid and useful for many actors. However, total reliance on such a stock set of reactions and responses is detrimental to creative work. Reliance on stereotyped reactions creates a one-dimensional performance that is unlikely to produce satisfaction for either the audience or the actor. How simple it would be if all villains and heroes could be played in the same manner! Unfortunately we see too many stock performances of this kind caused either by haste or by poor judgment.

The lessons of history and our own observation tell us how erroneous stereotyping may be. Nero stands out clearly as the embodiment of evil and cruelty. When he is enacted on the stage, the actor may be tempted to use all the stock devices to develop a character of consummate evil. Yet it was this man who exclaimed as he signed the routine death sentence of a convicted criminal, "Would to God I had never learned to write!" Clearly there was more to the man than a superficial appraisal would indicate. Furthermore, an intelligent actor coming across this remark uttered by Nero would want to weigh the implications of such a statement. Was Nero making the comment for effect, intended to be overheard by others? Was he really disturbed at signing so many death sentences? Or was Nero tired and anxious to get on to something more interesting? These are all choices the actor can make, choices that lend richness to characterizations.

All stock responses are not to be condemned out of hand. On the contrary, they will occasionally be useful in helping the beginning actor over a particularly difficult hurdle. The continual use, however, of a series of cut-and-dried responses for the purpose of playing certain characters and situations is dangerous, and, if extended over a number of plays, it is likely to limit seriously the development of the actor's resources. There is no substitute for thought and hard work. Good acting requires a good deal of both.

Finding One's Own Approach

"Nothing is more fleeting than any traditional method of impersonation." Henry Irving's remark implies that the actor of the present must not be tied too closely to the past. It is also a plea for *individuality* in the theatre, a point it would be well for all actors to consider.

There is no question that tradition is an important cohesive element in theatre work, binding the present with the best work of the past. However there is frequently a tendency to rely too heavily on the accepted styles and interpretations of successful performers rather than to utilize the well-springs of one's own creative force. Imitation is surely a distinctive type of flattery, and the study of the methods of fine actors such as Alec Guinness, Laurence Olivier, or Hal Holbrook is useful for the beginning actor. Many successful actors who began their professional careers at an early age, watching back-stage and learning from the work of more seasoned performers, openly admit the value of such experience. But they were able to blend these experiences with their own personality and temperament and, instead of becoming carbon copies of their elders, added something refreshing of their own.

In fact many of the finest actors openly acknowledge their debt to other actors and have been candid enough to admit that at some point in their career, either direct or indirect imitation or inspiration may have been very useful. William Hurt has spoken of the inspiration he has received from watching the work of Laurence Olivier, Spencer Tracy, Meryl Streep, and Paul Scofield; Morgan Freeman looked to the work of Gary Cooper, Humphrey Bogart, James Cagney, and Stacy Keach; Peter Weller has talked of the brilliance of two such diverse actors as Cary Grant and particularly Marlon Brando, whom he called "a great inspiration"; Brad Davis has great admiration for John Hurt and also admits to borrowing "from everybody."[21] John Gielgud remembers the admiration he had for his teacher Claude Rains, who later went to Hollywood and carved for himself a brilliant film career, perhaps best remembered as Captain Louis Renault opposite Humphrey Bogart in *Casablanca*. Gielgud has said that he "imitated all the actors I admired when I was young, particularly Claude Rains."[22]

An anonymous wit classically detailed the five stages in a star's life, as seen by a casting director:

1 *Who is Brad Pitt?*
2 *Get me Brad Pitt.*
3 *Get me a Brad Pitt type.*
4 *Get me a young Brad Pitt.*
5 *Who is Brad Pitt?*

Theatrical Anecdote

And Laurence Olivier, perhaps the actor who has had the most influence on actors in this century, "pinched" part of his concept during his preparation for Shylock in *The Merchant of Venice*. "I must admit to having been so impressed by the interpretation of Disraeli by George Arliss in an exceptionally good talkie made in 1929 that, to be honest, I lifted it . . . for my playing of Shylock." But, admitted Olivier: "A few among our critical brethren did, I

---

21. See Shacter and Shewey, *Caught in the Act.*
22. Funke and Booth, *Actors Talk about Acting*, p. 6.

am afraid, being better endowed with memory and observation than I had given them credit for, see through this little ploy."[23]

Olivier candidly admits that his was not the most reliable artistic means of working on a role. On the other hand, Olivier in another of his distinguished performances found a perfect synthesis of using a role model and endowing it with individuality. His performance in *Richard III* is a case in point. In the film version of the play, Olivier read the lines in a choppy but rhythmic cadence that was reportedly suggested by the style used by Henry Irving half a century before. We may be sure that Olivier's performance was no drab imitation of Irving's but one tempered with his own personality and experience. Olivier was not afraid to use the best of the past; indeed, the past had provided a clue, but the actor had held his own mirror up to nature. On the other hand, many young actors who modeled themselves after the distinctive styles and personalities of their favorite actors were more adept at imitating their idols' idiosyncrasies than they were at understanding the creative nature of their work. Reliance on the past is helpful at the outset, but must not be permitted to limit the actor's own style and approach.

It is so easy to fall into the trap of imitation that the actor should be on guard against it at all times. *Hamlet* probably provides the actor with more traditional methods of interpretation than any other play. It would be difficult not to rely on some of the hints offered by other actors who have successfully played the role. Yet the finest American Hamlet of this century, John Barrymore, took no such easy path in his interpretation. His director, Arthur Hopkins, described his approach in unmistakable terms:

> We began with our own conception, and developed it in all parts of the play. I doubt if Hamlet had ever been given a clearer course to sail. . . . We made ourselves completely servants of the play, untempted by any beckoning to leave our personal and peculiar imprint on it.[24]

The same responsibility to individuality applies to every aspect of the creation of a role. It is up to the actor to decide: How much technique should I use? Should I feel my role? What do I know about my character? What can I put meaningfully onstage? What sort of business, movement, and voice can I use for a specific character? The truly creative actor will impress upon each role the stamp of his or her own personality and insight. The major consideration is that the actor approach the role without preconceived notions that might limit the actor's own creative potential. If the actor does this honestly, he or she will be able to maintain individuality as an actor and as an artist.

23. Laurence Olivier, *Confessions of an Actor: An Autobiography* (New York: Simon and Schuster, 1982), p. 283.

24. Gene Fowler, *Good Night, Sweet Prince* (New York: Viking Press, 1944), p. 208.

EXERCISES

1. (a) Each evening try to remember every new person you have met or observed that day.
   (b) Learn to discern at least one distinctive characteristic about each one.
   (c) Make a distinction between the person's manner of speech and his or her movement, whenever possible.
2. Choose an incident that happened the day before you attempt this exercise. Relate the incident in all its details to the group, attempting to recreate your attitude during the incident, and suggest the attitudes of other people connected with the incident by acting out their participation.
3. In order to develop proficiency in the handling of small pieces of business, do the following exercises in pantomime before the class. Have the class evaluate the realism you create. Your observation and imagination will also be called into play in these exercises.
   (a) Sew a button on a coat.
   (b) Mix a cocktail, using various ingredients including ice.
   (c) Try on a new suit (or dress) in a clothing store. Examine it in a full-length mirror.
   (d) Put icing and decorations on a cake.
   (e) Examine a number of books in a library until you find the information you want.
   (f) Try to open a door, discover that none of your keys fits, and proceed to pick the lock.
   (g) Scramble some eggs and serve them to a guest.
   (h) Pack a cardboard box carefully with fragile items, and then tie and label the box.

AMBIGUOUS DIALOGUE

The following exercises deal with purposely ambiguous text. They offer the actor an opportunity to utilize skills using brief and complete units. The actor must deal with all the aspects of text work except that it is not necessary to seek comments by the playwright or look for character qualities in the text. The characters and situations are to be created entirely by the actors, working with the ambiguous dialogue, which provides almost complete freedom for the actor.

In each of the following dialogues there are two characters: A and B. They are engaged in an action that is complete in an even number of speeches from twenty to twenty-six. There are implied objectives and obstacles in each. No references to location, gender, relationship, activity, objects, and so on are given. The scene partners must create the missing information, but it can be from their own experiential level. Then they must rehearse to make the dialogue honest and believable.

These exercises are an effective intermediate step into text study, or they may be used as a supplement to text work.

The focus can be on:

Dealing with lines/words/language.
Reconciling language with character intention and objective.
Making transitions/adjustments to obstacles.
Use of concentration and imagination.

The actor must answer the following questions about the characters in the performance of these very brief "scenes."

Who are they?
Where are they?
What are they doing?
What does each want?
Why do they each want what they want?
What stands in the way of each?
What does each do to get what he or she wants?

Some basic ground rules might include the following. The actor must stay with the written words in the order in which they appear. The actor, however, may create physical business or pauses or change the punctuation. Try to make these dialogues as creative as possible.

Ambiguous Dialogue One

A: Come on in here.
B: Just a minute I'm busy.
A: It will only take a second.
B: I'm right in the middle of something.
A: I only want you to see something . . . just a second.
B: I can't right this minute, tell me about it.
A: I can't tell you about it, if I could tell you about it I wouldn't want you to come and look at it.
B: Do I really have to see it?
A: In a minute it won't make any difference, come on.
B: Okay. *(Enters the space.)* Yeah?
A: Well?
B: What? What am I supposed to see?
A: You know.
B: I wouldn't ask if I knew, would I?
A: It's so easy.
B: But there's a whole lot of stuff to look at.
A: This.
B: This?
A: Yeah. Well?
B: This is what you called me in for?
A: Yeah. Isn't it great?

B: You made me drop what I was doing to look at this?

A: I love it.

B: I can't believe it, I can't believe it.

A: It's great. I love it.

B: I can't believe it.

Ambiguous Dialogue Two

A: Yoohoo, yoohoo . . . hey, somebody . . .

B: What? What's up?

A: I need some help with this.

B: Just a minute.

A: Please hurry, it's slipping.

B: Okay, now what?

A: Hold this.

B: I can't see what you're talking about.

A: Well get out of the light.

B: This?

A: Right. Just hold it tightly, until I . . .

B: Yuck, something's dripping on me.

A: It won't hurt you, just don't let go of that.

B: It's all slimy, yuck.

A: Don't wiggle so much.

B: Watch out with that thing, you might hurt me.

A: I won't hurt you, I've done this a lot of times before.

B: There's always a first time.

A: Just pay attention to what you're supposed to be doing.

B: I am. This is boring. When can I let go and get out of here?

A: Very, very shortly . . . now in fact.

B: Good, I'm glad that's over, oh this slimy stuff stinks.

A: Well go and wash it off.

B: I certainly will.

A: Thanks for the help.

B: Yuck!

Ambiguous Dialogue Three

A: Do you come here often?

B: First time this year.

A: Me too.

B: I try to make it at least three times a year.

A: Yeah. Some people come a lot more.

B: I have a friend who does. Once a month.

A: Once a month! How does he find time?

B: He says that you have to make the time.

A: I guess so. I'm sure you'd get more out of once a month.

B: Lots more. It sure shows on him.

A: Look at that, did you ever see anything like it?

B: Never, it's amazing, isn't it, how they can do that.

A: And it looks so easy, so very easy.

B: I've always wondered. If I took the time and really committed myself, would I be able to do that?

A: I think you would. I think it's just what you said, a matter of commitment. They made an early commitment to what they believed in and look now at the result.

B: Yeah.

A: What do you think?

B: I think you may be right.

A: Darn right I'm right.

B: Well let's move on, ready?

A: Yeah.

B: Next!

Ambiguous Dialogue Four

A: Did you get the other one?

B: I got it.

A: Bring it here. Set it down.

B: I'll start with this.

A: Okay, I'll finish here.

B: Hand me those.

A: What?

B: Those. There.

A: Oh, yeah. You want this too?

B: Huh? Yeah.

A: Where do we keep these things?

B: Under there, right.

A: Now, how can I help.

B: Hold this. Put it in there.

A: That looks good.

B: It's going to be terrific.

A: Is that all?

B: Yeah, take it easy.

A: If you need me . . .

B: Right!

Ambiguous Dialogue Five

A: Oh! Rats!

B: What the devil are you doing?

A: What the devil are you doing?
B: What I'm supposed to be doing.
A: So, what are we going to do about this now?
B: What we're supposed to do about it.
A: Maybe you've got . . .
B: I don't think . . . I don't.
A: You don't?
B: No. Forget it.
A: So what am I supposed to do now? You sure you don't have any?
B: I take care of business. I'm prepared. I do what I'm supposed to do.
A: Well . . . let's see. I guess I've got no choice but to . . .
B: Okay, here.
A: This had better be good. I don't want to go out because it would take too long to change.
B: Oh boy, now I'm going to be . . .
A: Don't worry about it, I won't let you down. You scratch my back . . .
B: Hey, this is my whole life we're talking about.
A: Calm down, for Pete's sake. I'll take care of you in a minute.
B: If you'd just take care of business, this wouldn't happen.
A: Yeah, yeah . . .

Ambiguous Dialogue Six

A: Okay now, just lean back like this . . . and then let all of your body weight go forward, while throwing your arm out . . .
B: Ahhh . . . here goes . . . ahh oooh!
A: Wait, hold it, I think it's caught.
B: You're telling me.
A: Just a sec . . .
B: Ah . . . good grief . . . what do you think I am? . . .
A: You were having fun until now.
B: Do you like this happening to you?
A: It's all part of being . . .
B: Don't give me that stuff.
A: Hey, you're the one who wanted to come.
B: I didn't think that it would be like . . . this . . . it smells.
A: Here goes.
B: Eeeeeeeyyyyooooooooooow!!!!
A: Okay?
B: My arm!!!
A: Come on, let's get started . . .
B: So, how do I do this?
A: Just lean back a little . . .
B: Like this . . . ?

Ambiguous Dialogue Seven

A: Shh. Be quiet.
B: What are you talking about?
A: I asked you to be quiet.
B: I've made less noise than you have.
A: Very well. Just keep your mind on the job.
B: I know what I'm doing.
A: When was the last time you did this?
B: Only last week. Don't you remember?
A: So it was. How is it coming?
B: It's more difficult than I thought.
A: It's much simpler than you're making it out to be.
B: If you think so, why don't you give it a try?
A: I think I will. . . . There, it's almost done.
B: I don't know how you always get it right.
A: Practice, my friend, just practice.
B: You should open a school.
A: That will be the day.
B: Well, what's happening?
A: Good, it's finished. Now we can start.
B: I've been ready for at least an hour. Let's go.

Ambiguous Dialogue Eight

A: Hey! *(pause)* Hey, you out there?
B: What do you want?
A: Come'ere.
B: What?
A: I want you to see something.
B: What for?
A: Just come in here.
B: I'm busy.
A: I want to show you something important.
B: Is it really important?
A: I have to show you.
B: Why don't you just tell me about it?
A: You have to see this.
B: If I don't have a choice in the matter.
A: You coming?
B: Yeah. Okay.
A: Well?
B: What am I supposed to do about it?
A: Isn't it great?
B: What?
A: Have you seen anything like this before?

B: I can't believe it.

A: So?

B: I can't believe you called me in to see that.

A: Well, what do you think now?

B: I'm thirsty.

A: I really like it.

B: That's it for this one, out of here!

Ambiguous Dialogue Nine

A: *(Enters the room carrying something. Puts it on a table and begins to interact with it. Pause.)*

B: *(From off)* Hey!

A: What?

B: Is that you out there?

A: Who did you think it was?

B: Mailman.

A: Mailman comes in and sits down?

B: *(Entering)* I didn't know you came in. I just heard the noise.

A: I certainly don't sound like the mailman.

B: How do you know what the mailman sounds like?

A: I can just imagine.

B: What is that?

A: You can see what it is.

B: Yeah, but what do you need it for?

A: I just . . . I just felt like I needed it, that's all.

B: Don't give me that, you don't need that thing. What am I here for?

A: Sometimes I feel like I'm missing something. Sometimes I don't feel like I'm getting it all.

B: And that thing is supposed to help that?

A: It might.

B: I hope so.

A: Well, I would never have known if I didn't try.

B: I could've told you.

A: What do you know about it?

B: Enough.

Ambiguous Dialogue Ten

A enters and stands, waiting. B enters and stands next to A

A: Excuse me.

B: What?

A: Excuse me, do you have the time?

B: You mean, like what time is it?

A: Yes, of course. What else would that mean?

B: It could mean that you want to know if I have the time to do something for you?

A: No.

B: Sure it could.

A: I mean, no I don't mean that.

B: What?

A: What you said.

B: When?

A: Just now . . . about if you have the time to do something for me.

B: I don't have time to do anything for you.

A: That's fine. All I wanted to know . . . *(B does something unusual)* Hey!

B: *(Stops)* What?

A: Why are you doing that?

B: I just felt like it. I had the time to do it. I did it for myself.

A: That was . . . uh, well, odd, to say the least.

B: Can you do it?

A: Do I want to is a better question.

B: You can't do it.

A: Who couldn't do that?

B: You.

(Pause)

A: What time is it, for God's sake?

B: *(Looks.)* Noon.

The following are ambiguous dialogues for three actors. The characters, including age, lifestyle, gender, and so on; their relationships, intentions, actions, and the like are once again the choices of the actors involved in the exercise. Adding the third actor creates another level of complexity for actors as they concentrate on intention and adjustment on a moment-to-moment basis.

Ambiguous Dialogue Eleven

C enters and goes to a desk. C opens a book and begins to read. A enters, watches C for a moment, and then exits. B enters.

B: *(Calls out a nickname for C.)*!

C: Huh?

B: You seen *(Use A's name here)*?

C: *(A's name)*?

B: Yeah.

C: Nope!

B: You sure?

C: Sure I'm sure.

B: I could swear I saw *(A's name)* coming out of here a minute ago.

C: Then why are you asking me if I saw *(A's name)*, when you just saw *(A's name)*?

B: Just wondered if you'd tell the truth.

C: Why would I lie?

B: You know.

A: *(Entering)* What's going on?

B: Where have you been?

A: Out.

B: What do you mean, out?

A: Just out, I don't need to give you anymore information than that. That's all I owe you.

B: Somebody's getting a little snippy aren't they.

C: So you haven't told me yet.

A: You talking to me?

B: You're talking to me aren't you.

C: Yeah. I want to know why you think I would lie?

A: So I'm out of this?

B: Yeah.

C: Yeah.

A: Then I'm off again. Got a lot to do.

B: What do you have to do now?

A: That's none of your business. Bye y'all. *(A exists.)*

B: Just trying to get my goat. That's all it is.

C: So?

B: Forget it and read whatever it is you're reading. *(B exits and C goes back to the book.)*

Ambiguous Dialogue Twelve

A: Hand me that would you?

B: What?

A: Would you hand me that? There!

B: What do you need that for?

A: It's mine and I don't want it to get mixed in with the rest.

B: It's yours? Since when is it yours?

A: It's not yours, that's all I know.

B: How do you know it's not mine? What gives you that information? When did you become all-knowing?

A: I never saw you with one of these. I'd bet money you don't have one.

C enters the scene and moves to the others.

C: Hey, where'd you find that? I've been looking all over the place for that. I thought I'd lost it for good.

A: What? What're you talking about?

C: I'm talking about this. I'm glad you found it, 'cause I . . .

A: This is mine. It was right here where I dropped it and then I picked it up again. This is nuts. You both claim it? How can you do that?

B: Because I just dropped it myself.

C: I lost it in here the other day.

A: Stand back, stand back. Okay, *(He masks the object from the others.)* Tell me what it looks like and I mean details, give me some details.

C: What details? It's mine I can tell anything you want to know about it.

B: Me too.

C: You saying it's yours too?

B: Yeah, it's mine.

A: All right, all right, what color is it? What colors are on it?

B: Make up your mind. Color or colors?

A: If it was yours you would know.

B: Yeah, but how do I know what you're referring to?

C: It's black (or whatever color it is).

A: *(To B)* Your turn.

B: This is ridiculous, it's got my name on it.

A: Oh, yeah *(looks at object)* no name . . . I don't see any name.

B: Lift that part and look.

A: *(He does)* I never heard anybody call you that.

C: What does it say, Swiss made?

A: Almost. I don't think it belongs to either one of you. I'm keeping it, cause I saw it first. Finders keepers!

SUGGESTIONS FOR FURTHER READING

Funk, Bob. *The Audition Process: A Guide for Actors*. Portsmouth, NH: Heinemann, 1996.

Hunt, Gordon. *How to Audition*, rev. ed. New York: Harper Perennial, 1995.

Huston, Hollis. *The Actor's Instrument: Body, Theory, Stage*. Ann Arbor: University of Michigan Press, 1992.

Itkin, Bella, & Richard Aven. *Acting (Preparation, Practice, Performance)*. New York: HarperCollins, 1994.

Markus, Tom. *An Actor Behaves: From Audition to Performance*. Hollywood, CA: Samuel French, 1992.

Small, Edgar. *From Agent to Actor*. Hollywood, CA: Samuel French, 1991.

Spolin, Viola. *Theater Games for Rehearsal*. Evanston, IL: Northwestern University Press, 1985.

Monologues

1. Monologue from *The Glass Menagerie*, by Tennessee Williams.

   Amanda is speaking to her daughter Laura. She dreams of a fine marriage for her daughter who is, however, crippled and shy. They are poor, but this does not stop Amanda from dreaming, and she has many dreams for her children. In this speech she remembers her own girlhood in the South.

   AMANDA: Possess your soul in patience—you will see! Something I've resurrected from that old trunk! Styles haven't changed so terribly much after all. . . . Now just look at your mother! *(feverishly)* This is the dress in which I led the cotillion. Won the cakewalk twice at Sunset Hill, wore one spring to the Governor's ball in Jackson! See how I sashayed around the ballroom, Laura? *(She raises her skirt and does a mincing step around the room.)* I wore it on Sundays for my gentlemen callers! I had it on the day I met your father—I had malaria fever all that spring. The change of climate from East Tennessee to the Delta—weakened resistance—I had a little temperature all the time—not enough to be serious—just enough to make me restless and giddy!—Invitations poured in—parties all over the Delta!—"Stay in bed," said Mother, "you have fever!"—but I just wouldn't. —I took quinine but kept on going, going!—Evenings, dances!—Afternoons, long, long rides! Picnics—lovely!—So lovely, that country in May.—All lacy with dogwood, literally flooded with jonquils!—That was the spring I had the craze for jonquils. Jonquils became an absolute obsession. Mother said "Honey, there's no more room for jonquils." And still I kept on bringing in more jonquils. Whenever, wherever I saw them, I'd say, "Stop! Stop! I see jonquils!" I made the young men help me gather the jonquils! It was a joke, Amanda and her jonquils! Finally there were no more vases to hold them, every available space was filled with jonquils. No vases to hold them? All right, I'll hold them myself! And then I—met your father!

2. Monologue from *Sweet Bird of Youth*, by Tennessee Williams.

   The play concerns itself with the return of a young man to the Southern city he had left years before, accompanied by a fading actress, "Princess Kosmonopolis." "Princess" is a good deal older than Chance, she is a drug addict, and she lives from pill to pill, with an oxygen tank that she frequently uses when she has an anxiety attack. In this sequence she comes into the gallery of the hotel where they are staying, looking for Chance, who has found that his return to this city has raised a number of old antagonisms. She refers to an argument they had earlier in the day.

PRINCESS: Chance, when I saw you driving under the window with your head held high, with that terrible stiff-necked pride of the defeated which I know so well; I knew that your come-back had been a failure like mine. And I felt something in my heart for you. That's a miracle, Chance. That's the wonderful thing that happened to me. I felt something for someone besides myself. That means my heart's still alive, at least some part of it is, not all of my heart is dead yet. Part's alive still. . . . Chance, please listen to me. I'm ashamed of this morning. I'll never degrade you again, I'll never degrade myself, you and me, again by—I wasn't always this monster. Once I wasn't this monster. And what I felt in my heart when I saw you returning, defeated, to this palm garden, Chance, gave me hope that I could stop being a monster. Chance, you've got to help me stop being the monster that I was this morning, and you can do it, can help me. I won't be ungrateful for it. I almost died this morning, suffocated in a panic. But even through my panic, I saw your kindness. I saw a true kindness in you that you have almost destroyed, but that's still there, a little. . . .

The Sea Gull, by Anton Chekhov. University of Nebraska, Lincoln.

3. Monologue from *The Sea Gull*, by Anton Chekhov, translated by Stark Young.

Nina left home to find success on the stage but found failure instead. She was attracted to a successful playwright, but in this scene she unburdens herself to a young, sensitive writer who still loves her deeply. She has just entered his study, ill and tired.

NINA: Why do you say you kiss the ground I walk on? I ought to be killed. I'm so tired. If I could rest—rest. I'm a sea gull. No, that's not it. I'm an actress. Well, no matter. He didn't believe in the theatre, all my dreams he'd laugh at, and little by little I quit believing in it myself, and lost heart. And there was the strain of love, jealousy, constant anxiety about my little baby. I got to be small and trashy, and played without thinking. I didn't know what to do with my hands, couldn't stand properly on the stage, couldn't control my voice. You can't imagine the feeling when you are acting and know it's dull. I'm a sea gull. No, that's not it. Do you remember, you shot a sea gull? A man comes by chance, sees it, and out of nothing else to do, destroys it. That's not it—*(Puts her hand to her forehead.)* What was I—? I was talking about the stage. Now I'm not like that. I'm a real actress, I act with delight, with rapture, I'm drunk when I'm on the stage, and feel that I am beautiful. And now, ever since I've been here, I've kept walking about, kept walking and thinking, thinking and believing my soul grows stronger every day. Now I know, I understand, Kostya, that in our work—acting or writing—what matters is not fame, not glory, not what I used to dream about, it's how to endure, to bear my cross, and have faith. I have faith and it all doesn't hurt me so much, and when I think of my calling I'm not afraid of life.

4. Monologue from *Death of a Salesman*, by Arthur Miller.

Willy Loman, a broken-down salesman in his mid-sixties, has come to ask his young boss Howard for a job in the home office. Willy is too tired to continue working for commissions on the road. Meeting resistance from Howard, Willy begins to reminisce about how selling has changed since the wonderful days of his youth.

WILLY: Oh, yeah, my father lived many years in Alaska. He was an adventurous man. We've got quite a little streak of self-reliance in our family. I thought I'd go out with my older brother and try to locate him, and maybe settle in the North with the old man. And I was almost decided to go, when I met a salesman in the Parker House. His name was Dave Singleman. And he was eighty-four years old, and he drummed merchandise in thirty-one states. And old Dave, he'd go up to his room, y'understand, put on his green velvet slippers—I'll never forget—and pick up his phone and call the buyers, and without ever leaving his room, at the age of eighty-four, he made his living. And when I saw that, I realized that selling was the greatest career a man could want. 'Cause what could be more satisfying than to be able to go, at the age of eight-four, into twenty or thirty different cities, and pick up a phone, and be remembered and loved and helped by so many different people? Do you know? when he died—and by the way he died the death of a salesman, in his green velvet slippers in the smoker of the New York, New Haven and Hartford, going into Boston—when he died, hundreds of salesmen and buyers were at his funeral. Things were said on a lotta trains for months after that. *(He stands up.* HOWARD *has not looked at him.)* In those days there was personality in it, Howard. There was respect, and comradeship, and gratitude in it. Today, it's all cut and dried, and there's no chance for bringing friendship to bear—or personality. You see what I mean? They don't know me any more.

> *I was doing a scene, I think, from* Death of a Salesman *with another actor and in the middle of it somebody in the back dropped a huge box of dishes. Made a big crash.*
>
> *And afterward Strasberg said, "Well, that was okay. You know somebody dropped a big box of dishes during your scene."*
>
> *I said, "Yes, I know."*
>
> *And he said, "Well you didn't even blink."*
>
> *And I said, "Well yes, I was concentrating."*
>
> *And he said, "You can't do that, that was bad acting. You can't ignore life." And he said, "Everybody in the room jumped and you looked like it didn't happen."*
>
> *And . . . uh . . . that really stuck with me, it was a very valuable lesson particularly when I came to do movies because there's always that element of life interfering. . . . I'm playing a scene with you and a glass gets knocked over and we both go to pick it up and the dialogue suddenly comes alive and it seems . . . real.*
>
> Christopher Walken

5. Monologue from *Death of a Salesman*, by Arthur Miller.

Linda is the hardworking, loyal wife of salesman Willy Loman. She speaks from despair as she explains to her two sons why they must continue to love and respect him. She knows Willy plans suicide and fights the thought in her mind. Her defense of Willy is compassionate but filled with an anger which is directed at her sons.

LINDA: I don't say he's a great man. Willy Loman never made a lot of money. His name was never in the paper. He's not the finest character that ever lived. But he's a human being, and a terrible thing is happening to him. So attention must be paid. He's not to be allowed to fall into his grave like

an old dog. Attention, attention must be finally paid to such a person. . . .
A small man can be just as exhausted as a great man. He works for a company thirty-six years this March, opens up unheard-of territories to their trademark, and now in his old age they take his salary away. . . . When he brought them business, when he was young, they were glad to see him. But now his old friends, the old buyers that loved him so and always found some order to hand him in a pinch—they're all dead, retired. He used to be able to make six, seven calls a day in Boston. Now he takes his valises out of the car and puts them back and takes them out again and he's exhausted. Instead of walking he talks now. He drives seven hundred miles, and when he gets there no one knows him any more, no one welcomes him. And what goes through a man's mind, driving seven hundred miles home without having earned a cent? Why shouldn't he talk to himself? Why? When he has to go to Charley and borrow fifty dollars a week and pretend to me that it's his pay? How long can that go on? How long? You see what I'm sitting here and waiting for? And you tell me he has no character? The man who never worked a day but for your benefit? When does he get the medal for that?

6. Monologue from *Long Day's Journey into Night*, by Eugene O'Neill.

In this very autobiographical play, young Edmund Tyrone is based on the character of Eugene O'Neill. Here Edmund reflects on the days he spent on a variety of ships, a time when he was free in body and in spirit. O'Neill's love of the sea is also reflected in Paddy's speech from *The Hairy Ape*, which has a similar ring of something remembered and something lost.

EDMUND: You've just told me some high spots in your memories. Want to hear mine? They're all connected with the sea. Here's one. When I was on the Squarehead square rigger, bound for Buenos Aires. Full moon in the Trades. The old hooker driving fourteen knots. I lay on the bowsprit, facing astern, with the water foaming into spume under me, the masts with every sail white in the moonlight, towering high above me. I became drunk with the beauty and singing rhythm of it, and for a moment I lost myself—actually lost my life. I was set free! I dissolved in the sea, became white sails and flying spray, became beauty and rhythm, became moonlight and the ship and the high dim-starred sky! I belonged, without past or future, within peace and unity and a wild joy, within something greater than my own life, or the life of Man, to Life itself! To God, if you want to put it that way. Then another time, on the American Line, when I was lookout on the crow's nest in the dawn watch. A calm sea, that time. Only a lazy ground swell and a slow drowsy roll of the ship. The passengers asleep and none of the crew in sight. No sound of man. Black smoke pouring from the funnels behind and beneath me. Dreaming, not keeping lookout, feeling alone, and above, and apart, watching the dawn creep like a painted dream over the sky and sea which slept together. Then the moment of ecstatic freedom came. The peace, the end of the quest, the last harbor, the joy of belonging to a fulfillment beyond men's lousy, pitiful, greedy fears and hopes and dreams! And several other times in my life, when I was swimming far out, or lying alone on a beach, I have had the same experience. Became the sun, the hot sand, green seaweed anchored to a rock, swaying in the tide. Like a saint's vision of beatitude. Like the veil of things as they seem drawn back by an unseen hand. For a second you see—and seeing the secret, are the secret. For a second there is meaning! Then the hand lets the veil fall and you are alone, lost in the fog again, and you stumble on toward nowhere, for no good reason! *(He grins wryly.)* It was a great mistake, my being born a man. I would have been much more successful as a sea gull or a fish. As it is, I will always be a stranger who never feels at home, who does not really want and is not really wanted, who can never belong, who must always be a little in love with death!

7. Monologue from *Long Day's Journey into Night*, by Eugene O'Neill.

The Tyrone family has exhausted itself this day in recriminations, alcoholic abuses, and self-torture. Each character sinks into his or her own escape from the pain of living after their "long journey." Mary, the mother, is a drug addict, and, finding temporary peace, she stares dreamily ahead, her face looking "youthful and innocent." She begins to talk aloud to herself. None of the other members of her family is listening.

MARY: I had a talk with Mother Elizabeth. She is so sweet and good. A saint on earth. I love her dearly. It may be sinful of me but I love her better than my own mother. Because she always understands, even before you say a word. Her kind blue eyes look right into your heart. You can't keep any secrets from her. You couldn't deceive her, even if you were mean enough to want to. *(She gives a little rebellious toss of her head—with girlish pique.)* All the same, I don't think she was so understanding this time. I told her I wanted to be a nun. I explained how sure I was of my vocation, that I had prayed to the Blessed Virgin to make me sure, and to find me worthy. I told Mother I had had a true vision when I was praying in the shrine of Our Lady of Lourdes, on the little island in the lake. I said I knew, as surely as I knew I was kneeling there, that the Blessed Virgin had smiled and blessed me with her consent. But Mother Elizabeth told me I must be more sure than that, even, that I must prove it wasn't simply my imagination. She said, if I was so sure, than I wouldn't mind putting myself to a test by going home after I graduated, and living as other girls lived, going out to parties and dances and enjoying myself; and then if after a year or two I still felt sure, I could come back to see her and we would talk it over again. *(She tosses her head—indignantly.)* I never dreamed Holy Mother would give me such advice! I was really shocked. I said, of course, I would do anything she suggested, but I knew it was simply a waste of time. After I left her, I felt all mixed up, so I went to the shrine and prayed to the Blessed Virgin and found peace again because I knew she heard my prayer and would always love me and see no harm ever came to me so long as I never lost my faith in her. *(She pauses and a look of growing un-*

easiness comes over her face. She passes a hand over her forehead as if brushing cobwebs from her brain—vaguely.) That was in the winter of senior year. Then in the spring something happened to me. Yes, I remember. I fell in love with James Tyrone and was so happy for a time.

8. Monologue from *Georgia Peach*, by Howard Burman.

Ty Cobb, one of the greatest of all baseball players, was also more thoroughly disliked by his fellow ballplayers than any other player who ever donned baseball spikes. At one time he held almost every offensive baseball record possible. When he died, only three players went to his funeral. He maintained an obsession for perfection all his life.

   In this monologue, the seventeen-year-old player is in part talking to the audience and in part talking to his absent parents (particularly his father), who are at home. He is telling them (or us) about his first days in professional baseball, although he is playing for a minor team in a semi-legal league.

TY: I got a clean hit off the meanest delivery in the business yesterday and I was floating a foot off the ground. But today came the lesson. This country kid had his plow cleaned as you used to say. As the runner at first base, I went sprinting to second and slid head-first at the bag. Old Pete was waiting to give me the professional "teach"—which he did by slamming his knee down on the back of my neck, grinding my face untenderly into the dirt. I heard the umpire's well-rounded baritone—"Owwwwtttt!" I walked, or sort of crept, away from there with some skin scraped off. And with Old Pete grinning at me. Next time on I banged into him feet-first, caught him by surprise and knocked him kicking onto the grass, while I slid in safely. He got up, shot a stream of tobacco juice, and looked me over reflectively. "Son, that's how it's done—you've got it," he said. Lesson learned.

9. Monologue from *After the Fall*, by Arthur Miller.

In this play Miller makes use of flashbacks and stream-of-consciousness passages that provide a very fluid means of telling his story. In this speech, Quentin, a man in his forties, addresses the Listener, "who, if he could be seen, would be sitting beyond the edge of the stage itself."

QUENTIN: You know, more and more I think that for many years I looked at life like a case at law, a series of proofs. When you're young you prove how brave you are, or smart; then, what a good lover; then, a good father; finally, how wise, or powerful or what-the-hell-ever. But underlying it all, I see now, there was a presumption. That I was moving on an upward path toward some elevation, where—God knows what—I would be justified, or even condemned—a verdict anyway. I think now that my disaster really began when I looked up one day—and the bench was empty. No judge in sight. And all that remained was the endless argument with oneself—this pointless litigation of existence before an empty bench.

Which, of course, is another way of saying—despair. And, of course, despair can be a way of life; but you have to believe in it, pick it up, take it to heart, and move on again. Instead, I seem to be hung up. *(Slight pause.)* And the days and the months and now the years are draining away. A couple of weeks ago I suddenly became aware of a strange fact. With all this darkness, the truth is that every morning when I awake, I'm full of hope! With everything I know—I open my eyes, I'm like a boy! For an instant there's some—unformed promise in the air. I jump out of bed, I shave. I can't wait to finish breakfast—and then, it seeps in my room, my life and its pointlessness. And I thought—if I could corner that hope, find what it consists of and either kill it for a lie, or really make it mine . . .

10. Monologue from *After the Fall*, by Arthur Miller.

Also see the preceding monologue from this play. In this scene, Quentin tries to create an image of his father in his memory, but the image is mingled with the voice of Quentin's mother, who remembers the father with great affection.

MOTHER: To this day he walks into a room you want to bow! *(Warmly.)* Any restaurant—one look at him and the waiters start moving tables around. *Because*, dear, people know that this is a *man*. Even Doctor Strauss, at my wedding he came over to me, says, "Rose, I can see it looking at him, you've got a wonderful man," and he was always in love with me, Strauss. . . . Oh, sure, but he was only a penniless medical student then, my father wouldn't let him in the house. Who knew he'd end up so big in the gallstones? That poor boy! Used to bring me novels to read, poetry, philosophy, God knows what! One time we even sneaked off to hear Rachmaninoff together. *(She laughs sadly; and with wonder more than bitterness.)* That's why, you see, two weeks after we were married; sit down to dinner and Papa hands me a menu and asks me to read it to him. Couldn't *read*! I got so frightened I nearly ran away! . . . Why? Because your grandmother is such a fine, unselfish woman; two months in school and they put him into the shop! That's what some women are, my dear—and now he goes and buys her a new Packard every year. *(With a strange and deep fear.)* Please, darling, I want you to *draw* the letters, that scribbling is ugly, dear; and your posture, your speech, it can all be beautiful! Ask Miss Fisher, for years they kept my handwriting pinned up on the bulletin board; God, I'll never forget it, valedictorian of the class with a scholarship to Hunter in my hand . . . *(A blackness flows into her soul.)* And I came home, and Grandpa says, "You're getting married!" I was like—like with small wings, just getting ready to fly; I slept all year with the catalogue under my pillow. To learn, to learn everything! Oh darling, the whole thing is such a mystery!

11. Monologue from *The Search for Signs of Intelligent Life in the Universe*, by Jane Wagner.

Lyn, a not quite committed feminist activist, feels the need to consult with a therapist regarding her relationship.

LYN: So, Doctor, we started fighting on the ski lift and Peter let slip he didn't think a woman could make a good President and that the feminist movement was making a monster of me.

It was the worst fight we ever had.
He said Edie was poisoning my mind.
That my CR sessions were making me conscious of everything but his dissatisfaction with the relationship.
And he said . . . and this is what really hurt . . .
he said that I *used* to be so sexy, but now I'd even lost my sex appeal.

I bolted off that ski lift so mad. Halfway down, I slammed smack into a pine stump. I know he saw it, but he skied right past me.

Okay, Doctor, but Gestalt therapy is new to me.
In this chair, I role-play Peter; in this chair, I role-play myself, right?
And in that chair,
you role-play the doctor?

"Peter, I am sick of this suppressive, you-do-as-I-say macho number you have been putting me through."

Now I'm me. No, I'm Peter. "And I'm sick of this suppressive feminist trip you've been dumping on me."

Doctor, who said that? Is this Peter's chair?
"I'd like a *glimpse* of the nurturant female you and your butch/rad/fem friends harp on so much. I want a woman, not a feminist!"

"Ah ha! All it is with you is sex, sex, sex!"

"And all it is with you is sex, sex,
sexual politics! I have *had* it!"

I don't know exactly *what* happened, Doctor,
but I feel like I've just walked out on myself.

12.   Monologue from *The Great Nebula in Orion*, by Lanford Wilson.

In this presentational style piece, the two characters use the audience as a third character and silent confidante. After a number of years the two old school chums met while shopping in Manhattan, and Louise invited Carrie up to her apartment to "bring each other up-to-date." Louise shares by making "aside" comments to the audience.

LOUISE: *(To the audience.)* I'm a year older than Carrie and the year I left Bryn Mawr was the same year Sam came to Haverford which is just a long goodnight walk away. And Carrie had met Sam so they saw each other. They didn't date, God knows. Of course all Sam's friends were older. *(To Carrie suddenly.)* Oh! I've got to tell you. *(Pleased and delighted with this story.)* We were having lunch—a bunch of us girls—no one you

213

know, I don't think. I mean we meet nearly every Friday. We have a table reserved for us. And the conversation never is rough, exactly, but we didn't really notice that we had a new busboy. A very young kid with his hair shaved off—it couldn't have been more than a quarter-inch long and big old ears sticking out from the side of his face—maybe fourteen years old. And the girls were talking while he's passing water and butter around; no one's paying any attention to him and someone asked Berilla what she'd been up to and she said she'd been going to night school. Of course nobody was listening, really. *(Aside to the audience.)* This is an old joke, it's not going to be funny, particularly. *(Back to Carrie.)* But after about half an hour someone turned to Berilla and said whatever are you doing in night school? And the kid's taking off plates by now and Berilla said, "Oh, I'm just taking a course in intercourse, all you have to do is come." And. We laughed, a little. But this kid had never heard it before. I don't imagine he'd ever heard a woman—well, he bit his lip and set the dish back *(Laughing.)* on the table and made a line for the kitchen—his ears—those big old ears just burning. He thought it was the funniest thing he'd—he was so funny and sweet. We just collapsed. He came back flushed and biting his tongue, with tears in his eyes. Such a dear.

13. Monologue from *Two Trains Running*, by August Wilson.

Holloway is an African-American man who all his life has voiced outrage at injustice, with little effect. His belief in the supernatural has enabled him to accept his inability to effect change and continue to pursue life with zest and vigor. Here he reveals that Aunt Ester's advice was the key to the late esteemed Prophet Samuel's evolution from reverend to prophet.

HOLLOWAY: See? There you go talking about being rich. I ain't talking about that. I ain't said nothing about getting rich. I'm talking about getting your luck changed. You go up there with the wrong attitude and come out with worse luck than you had before. That's what the problem is now. Aunt Ester don't buy into that. She don't make people rich. You go up there talking about you wanna get rich and she won't have nothing to do with you. She send you to see Prophet Samuel . . . and you see how far that'll get you. Most people don't know Prophet Samuel went to see Aunt Ester. He wasn't always a prophet. He started out he was a reverend. Had him a truck, and he'd stand on the back of that truck . . . had him a loud-speaker, and he'd go out and preach the word of the gospel and sell barbecue on the side. Everybody knew Reverend Samuel. He even went out where the white folks lived and tried to preach to them. They seen him with that truck and thought he come out there to steal their furniture. Called the police on him. Many a time. He go on and pay his fifty-dollar fine for preaching without a permit and go on back out here.

They had him in big trouble one time. He had all his money going to his church and they arrested him for income-tax evasion. That's when he went to see Aunt Ester. He walked in there a reverend and walked out a prophet. I don't know what she told him. But he went down to see the mayor. Say if they arrested him they had to arrest Mellon too. Say God was gonna send a sign. The next day the stock market fell so fast they had to close it early. Mellon called the mayor and told him to drop the charges. The next day the stock market went right on back up there. Except for Gulf Oil, which Mellon owned. That went higher than it ever went before. Mellon was tickled pink. He sent Prophet Samuel a five-hundred-dollar donation and a brochure advertising his banking services. Had his picture taken with him and everything. That's when Prophet Samuel went big. The police didn't bother him no more. Wouldn't even give him a parking ticket. If he hadn't started walking around in them robes going barefoot and whatnot . . . ain't no telling how big he would have got.

Scenes

Lettice and Lovage, by Peter Shaffer
From Act I, Scene 2

Scene: For two women
Characters: LOTTE (Charlotte Schoen)
FRAMER (Miss Framer, Lotte's assistant)
Setting: Miss Schoen's office at the Preservation Trust, London
Time: Three o'clock in the afternoon
Situation: Lettice Douffet, a tour guide for the Preservation Trust, has been embellishing beyond her prescribed lecture in her description of the historic
events at Fustian Hall. Her supervisor, Lotte Schoen, after Lettice had
gotten to the point of embellishing the facts beyond recognition, looked
in on one of her "performances" and ordered her presence at the Trust of-
fices the next day. However, someone else comes to Lotte first.

*At her desk sits MISS SCHOEN looking darkly through a pile of letters: an official file
lies before her. Three o'clock is heard sounding from Big Ben outside. There is a faint
knocking on the door*
LOTTE: *(Sharply.)* Yes? . . .
(The faint noise continues.)
LOTTE: *(More sharply.)* Yes? . . . Is there anyone there?
(The knock sounds a little louder.)
LOTTE: *Yes! Come in!*
*(The door opens timidly. MISS FRAMER enters: a nervous, anxious Assistant, fright-
ened, breathy, and refined.)*
FRAMER: *(A whisper.)* It's me, Miss Schoen.
LOTTE: What?
FRAMER: *(Just louder.)* It's me, Miss Schoen.
LOTTE: Miss Framer, I do wish you could learn to knock audibly. Not scratch
at the door, or fumble at it like some kind of rodent.
FRAMER: I'm sorry, Miss Schoen.
(LOTTE raps quickly and sharply on the desk, four times.)
LOTTE: That is a knock! Do you understand?
FRAMER: Yes, Miss Schoen.
LOTTE: Then copy it. Alert me to the fact that you wish to enter.
FRAMER: Yes, Miss Schoen.
LOTTE: Now what is it?
FRAMER: *(A whisper.)* Miss Douffet is here to see you.
LOTTE: What?
FRAMER: *(Just louder.)* Miss Douffet is here to see you.

LOTTE: Ah.

FRAMER: I asked her to wait.

LOTTE: That was enterprising of you.

FRAMER: Thank you . . .

LOTTE: How does she seem to be?

FRAMER: Bold, I would say.

LOTTE: Bold?

FRAMER: Her clothes are bold . . . Well, bolder than mine, anyway.

LOTTE: I see . . . Did you have a talk with Mr. Green about her, as I asked you to?

FRAMER: Oh yes, indeed.

LOTTE: He did the original hiring, I understand.

FRAMER: Yes, that's right.

LOTTE: Well? And?

FRAMER: He says when he met her for the first time this Spring he thought she might make a valuable addition to our Staff of Guides. She appeared to be mad on History.

LOTTE: Just mad would seem to be more like it, judging from these letters.

FRAMER: Oh dear . . .

LOTTE: Does he know nothing about her at all?

FRAMER: Nothing whatever, it seems.

LOTTE: Well this file is worse than useless. It just gives her address and nothing else. *(Consulting it.)* Nineteen Rastridge Road, Earls Court . . . Do you know it?

FRAMER: I'm afraid not.

LOTTE: A singularly dreary street. What I would term Victorian Varicose.

FRAMER: *(Laughing sycophantically.)* Oh that's good! That's very good, Miss Schoen. Victorian Varicose! . . . Oh yes, indeed! Most amusing!

LOTTE: *(Ignoring the flattery.)* If she lives in London, what is she doing working in Wiltshire?

FRAMER: I think it was the only position available . . . Apparently Fustian House isn't particularly popular with Guides . . . It was just for the summer.

LOTTE: I see . . . *(Suddenly holding her head.)* Oh God . . .

FRAMER: *(Fussing)* What? What is it?

LOTTE: Nothing.

FRAMER: Is it one of your headaches?

LOTTE: *(Briskly.)* No.

FRAMER: Is there anything at all I can do?

LOTTE: No thank you.

FRAMER: Perhaps an aspirin. Shall I get you an aspirin, Miss Schoen?

LOTTE: Nothing, thank you. Stop fussing! If you want to help, bring me a cup of tea. Strong.

FRAMER: Of course.

LOTTE: And one for that woman out there. She's going to need it.

FRAMER: Yes, Miss Schoen.

LOTTE: Show her in, please.

FRAMER: Yes . . . Yes . . . At once . . . I'm sorry.

(MISS FRAMER goes out.)

The Children's Hour, by Lillian Hellman.
From Act II, Scene 2

Scene: For two females (adolescents)
          MARY, a fourteen-year-old school girl
          ROSALIE, a fourteen-year-old school girl, plump, and wears glasses
Setting: The living room of Mrs. Telford, a dignified woman and Mary's grandmother
Time: An April evening.
Situation: Mary is lying on the floor, playing with a puzzle and chatting with her school chum, Agatha. Mary is a spoiled child, who is attempting to destroy the Wright-Dobie school she attends and the two owners of the school, whom she despises. She has spread a series of lies about Miss Karen Wright and Miss Martha Dobie. Mary's grandmother has told Mary that she need not return to the school and has also called several parents who have removed their children from the school. Some of the girls have not been picked up by their parents and are staying briefly with Mary's grandmother. The scene begins with Agatha just having left the room, when another girl, Rosalie, comes in.

MARY: *(Loudly)* Whooooo! (ROSALIE *jumps up.*) Whooooo! (ROSALIE *frightened, starts hurriedly for door.* MARY *sits up, laughs)* You're a goose.

ROSALIE: *(Comes down to below* L. *end of* L. *love seat. Belligerently)* Oh, so it's you. Well, who likes to hear funny noises at night? You could have been a werewolf.

MARY: What would a werewolf do with you?

ROSALIE: *(Crossing* R. *to armchair)* Just what he'd do with anybody else. (MARY *laughs)* Isn't it funny about school?

MARY: What's funny about it?

ROSALIE: *(Crosses upstage, inspects sideboard)* Don't act like you can come home every night.

MARY: Maybe I can from now on. *(Rolls over on her back luxuriously)* Maybe I'm never going back.

ROSALIE: Am I going back? I don't want to stay home.

MARY: What'll you give to know?

ROSALIE: *(Takes a grape)* Nothing. I'll just ask my mother.

MARY: Will you give me a free T.L. if I tell you?

ROSALIE: *(Comes to behind* R. *of love seat. Thinks for a moment)* All right, Lois Fisher told Helen that you were very smart.

MARY: That's an old one. I won't take it.

ROSALIE: You got to take it.

MARY: Nope.

ROSALIE: *(Laughs)* You don't know, anyway.

MARY: I know what I heard, and I know Grandma phoned your mother in New York five dollars and eighty-five cents to come and get you right away. You're just going to spend the night here. I wish Evelyn could come instead of you.

ROSALIE: *(Comes down to* R. *of* R. *love seat)* But what's happened? Peggy and

Helen and Evelyn and Lois went home tonight, too. Do you think some-body's got secret measles or something?

MARY: No.

ROSALIE: Do *you* know what it is? How'd you find out? (*No answer*) You're al-ways pretending you know everything. You're just faking. (*Flounces away. Sits on the ottoman*) Never mind, don't bother telling me. I think curiosity is very unladylike, anyhow. I have no concern with your silly secrets, none at all. (*She twirls round on ottoman, stops and after long pause*) What did you say?

MARY: I didn't say a thing.

ROSALIE: Oh. (*Twirls around again*)

MARY: (*Laughs. Rises and puts the jigsaw puzzle in a drawer of the highboy*) But now suppose I told you that I just may have said that you were in on it?

ROSALIE: (*Stops twirling*) In on what?

MARY: (*Comes down to* R. *of* R. *love seat*) The secret. Suppose I told you that I *may have* said that you told me about it?

ROSALIE: (*Rises*) Why, Mary Tilford! You can't do a thing like that. I didn't tell you about anything. (MARY *laughs*) Did you tell your grandmother such a thing?

MARY: Maybe.

ROSALIE: (*Crosses to below* R. *love seat, turns to* MARY) Well, I'm going right up to your grandmother and tell her I didn't tell you anything—whatever it is. You're just trying to get me into trouble, like always, and I'm not going to let you. (*Starts for arch*)

MARY: (*Crosses to below armchair*) Wait a minute, I'll come with you.

ROSALIE: (*Stops* U.L. *of armchair*) What for?

MARY: I want to tell her about Helen Burton's bracelet.

ROSALIE: (*Slowly turns to* MARY) What about it?

MARY: Just that you stole it.

ROSALIE: (*Crosses to* MARY) Shut up. I didn't do any such thing.

MARY: Yes, you did.

ROSALIE: (*Tearfully*) You made it up. You're always making things up.

MARY: You can't call me a liar, Rosalie Wells. That's a kind of dare and I won't take a dare. (*She starts for arch.* ROSALIE *blocks her way.*) I guess I'll go tell Grandma, anyway. Then she can call the police and they'll come for you and you'll get tried in court. (*She slowly backs* ROSALIE *to behind* R. *end of* L. *love seat. While she speaks, she pulls* ROSALIE'S *glasses down on her nose and pulls her hair.*) And you'll go to one of those prisons, and you'll get older and older, and when you're good and old they'll let you out, but your mother and father will be dead and you won't have any place to go and you'll beg on the streets—

ROSALIE: (*Crying*) I didn't steal anything. I borrowed the bracelet and I was going to put it back as soon as I'd worn it to the movies. I never meant to keep it.

MARY: Nobody'll believe that, least of all the police. You're just a common, or-dinary thief. Stop that bawling. You'll have the whole house down here in a minute.

ROSALIE: You won't tell? Say you won't tell.

MARY: Am I a liar?

ROSALIE: No.

MARY: Then say: "I apologize on my hands and knees."

ROSALIE: I apologize on my hands and knees. Let's play with the puzzle.

MARY: Wait a minute. Say: "From now on, I, Rosalie Wells—(*Crosses her wrists in front of her*) am the vassal of Mary Tilford and will do and say whatever she tells me under the solemn oath of a knight."

ROSALIE: (*Crosses downstage to below R. end of love seat*) I won't say that. That's the worst oath there is. (MARY *starts down right.*) Mary! Please don't—(*She quickly follows* MARY *and stops her below* R. *love seat*)

MARY: Will you swear it?

ROSALIE: (*Sniffling*) But then you could tell me to do anything.

MARY: (*Starts to move* R.) Say it quick or I'll—

ROSALIE: (*Hurriedly*) From now on—(*Slowly turns and crosses* L. *to* L. *love seat, holding her wrists crossed in front of her*) I, Rosalie Wells, am the vassal of Mary Tilford and will do and say whatever she tells me under the solemn oath of a knight.

MARY: Don't forget that.

Bad Seed, by Maxwell Anderson
From Act I, Scene 4

Scene: For two women

Characters: RHODA PENMARK, an attractive eight-year-old

     CHRISTINE PENMARK, her mother, a gentle, gracious, and pretty woman under thirty

Setting: The apartment of Colonel and Mrs. Penmark in a small Southern town.

Time: A warm afternoon in late spring.

Situation: *Bad Seed* is an adaptation of the novel *The Bad Seed* by William March. The play deals in a chilling manner with the question of inherited evil, in which it is finally revealed that Christine Penmark had been adopted as a child and had been the natural child of a multiple murderess. Christine is unaware of this until the end of the play, but at this point she must deal with the problem of her daughter who may have been lying to her. Rhoda has been unhappy because she did not win the medal for penmanship at school. Her classmate, Claude Daigle, won the medal, but later at a picnic the young man mysteriously drowned and the medal disappeared. Christine has just found the medal hidden in the drawer of Rhoda's table.

RHODA: Did you want me to come in, Mother? When you waved?

CHRISTINE: (*She slaps the medal down on the coffee table.*) So you had the medal, after all. Claude Daigle's medal.

RHODA: (*Warily*) Where did you find it?

CHRISTINE: How did the penmanship medal happen to be hidden under the lining of the drawer of your table, Rhoda? Now I want you to tell me the truth. (RHODA *takes off one of her shoes and examines it. Then smiling a little in a fashion she has always found charming, she asks*)

RHODA: When we move into our new house can we have a scuppernong arbor, Mother? Can we, Mother? It's so shady, and pretty, and I love sitting in it!

CHRISTINE: Answer my question. And remember I'm not as innocent about what went on at the picnic as you think. Miss Fern has told me a great deal. So please don't bother to make up any story for my benefit. (RHODA *is silent, her mind working.*) How did Claude Daigle's medal get in your drawer? It certainly didn't get there by itself. I'm waiting for your answer. (RHODA *is silent.*)

RHODA: I don't know how the medal got there, Mother. How could I?

CHRISTINE: (*Controlling herself*) You know. You know very well how it got there. Did you go on the wharf at any time during the picnic? At any time?

RHODA: (*After a pause*) Yes, Mother. I—I went there once.

CHRISTINE: Was it before or after you were bothering Claude?

RHODA: I wasn't bothering Claude, Mother. What makes you think that?

CHRISTINE: Why *did* you go on the wharf?

RHODA: It was real early. When we first got there.

CHRISTINE: You knew it was forbidden. Why did you do it?

RHODA: One of the big boys said there were little oysters that grew on the pilings. I wanted to see if they did.

CHRISTINE: One of the guards said he saw you coming off the wharf. And he says it was just before lunch time.

RHODA: I don't know why he says that. He's wrong, and I told Miss Fern he was wrong. He hollered at me to come off the wharf and I did. I went back to the lawn and that's where I saw Claude. But I wasn't bothering him.

CHRISTINE: What did you say to Claude?

RHODA: I said if I didn't win the medal, I was glad he did.

CHRISTINE: (*Wearily*) Please, please Rhoda. I know you're an adroit liar. But I must have the *truth*.

RHODA: But it's all true, Mother. Every word.

CHRISTINE: One of the monitors saw you try to snatch the medal off Claude's shirt. Is that all true? Every word?

RHODA: Oh, that big girl was Mary Beth Musgrove. She told everybody she saw me. Even Leroy knows she saw me. (*She opens her eyes wide, and smiles as though resolving on complete candor.*) You see, Claude and I were just playing a game we made up. He said if I could catch him in ten minutes and touch the medal with my hand—it was like prisoner's base—he'd let me wear the medal for an hour. How can Mary Beth say I took the medal? I didn't.

CHRISTINE: She didn't say you took the medal. She said you grabbed at it. And that Claude ran away down the beach. Did you have the medal even then?

RHODA: No, Mommy, not then. (*She runs to her mother and kisses her ardently. This time* CHRISTINE *is the passive one.*)

CHRISTINE: Rhoda, how did you get the medal?

RHODA: Oh, I got it later on.

CHRISTINE: How?

RHODA: Claude went back on his promise and I followed him up the beach. Then he stopped and said I could wear the medal all day if I gave him fifty cents.

CHRISTINE: Is that the truth?

RHODA: (*With slight contempt*) Yes, Mother. I gave him fifty cents and he let me wear the medal.

CHRISTINE: Then why didn't you tell this to Miss Fern when she questioned you?

RHODA: Oh, Mommy, Mommy! (*She whimpers a little*) Miss Fern doesn't like me at all! I was afraid she'd think bad things about me if I told her I had the medal!

CHRISTINE: You knew how much Mrs. Daigle wanted the medal, didn't you?

RHODA: Yes, Mother, I guess I did.

CHRISTINE: Then why didn't you give it to her? (RHODA *says nothing.*) Mrs. Daigle is heart-broken over Claude's death. It's destroyed her. I don't think she'll ever recover from it. (*She disengages herself*) Do you know what I mean?

RHODA: Yes, Mother, I guess so.

CHRISTINE: No! You don't know what I mean.

RHODA: But it was silly to want to bury the medal pinned on Claude's coat. Claude was dead. He wouldn't know whether he had the medal pinned on him or not. (*She senses her mother's sudden feeling of revulsion, and kisses her cheek with hungry kisses.*) I've got the sweetest mother. I tell everybody I've got the sweetest mother in the world!—If she wants a little boy that bad, why doesn't she take one out of the Orphan's Home?

CHRISTINE: Don't touch me! Don't talk to me. We have nothing to say to each other.

RHODA: Well, okay. Okay, Mother. (*She turns away and starts to the den.*)

CHRISTINE: Rhoda! When we lived in Baltimore, there was an old lady, Mrs. Clara Post, who liked you very much.

RHODA: Yes.

CHRISTINE: You used to go up to see her every afternoon. She was very old, and liked to show you all her treasures. The one you admired most was a crystal ball, in which opals floated. The old lady promised this treasure to you when she died. One afternoon when the daughter was shopping at the supermarket, and you were alone with Mrs. Post, she somehow managed to fall down the spiral backstairs and break her neck. You said she heard a kitten mewing outside and went to see about it and somehow missed her footing and fell five flights to the courtyard below.

RHODA: Yes, it's true.

CHRISTINE: Then you asked the daughter for the crystal ball. She gave it to you, and it's still hanging at the head of your bed.

RHODA: Yes, Mother.

CHRISTINE: Rhoda, did you have anything to do, anything at all, no matter how little it was, with Claude getting drowned?

RHODA: What makes you ask that, Mother?

CHRISTINE: Come here, Rhoda. Look me in the eyes and tell me. I must know.

RHODA: No, Mother, I didn't.

CHRISTINE: You're not going back to the Fern School next year. They don't want you any more.

RHODA: Okay. Okay.

CHRISTINE: (*Crosses to telephone.*) I'll call Miss Fern and ask her to come over.

RHODA: She'll think I lied to her.

CHRISTINE: You did lie to her.

RHODA: But not to you, Mother! Not to you!

CHRISTINE: Hello, Fern School. (RHODA *crosses slowly to stool.*) Miss Claudia Fern, please. No. No message. (*She hangs up.*) She's not home yet.

RHODA: What would you tell her, Mother?

CHRISTINE: No! It can't be true. It can't be true. (*She turns and looks at* RHODA, *then embraces her.*)

CURTAIN

Uncommon Women and Others, by Wendy Wasserstein
From Act I, Scene 6

Scene:	For two women
Characters:	LEILAH
	KATE
Setting:	A college for women
Time:	Back and forth between the present and six years earlier
Situation:	An episodic flashback piece about young career women remembering their lives at college and how they prepared for the future. This scene vacillates between philosophy assignments and sex life.

(KATE *lies reading on a bed. She throws down the book she is reading—and takes out another one.*)

KATE: (*Reading.*) "She remembered the way Melissa Blaine with her perfect cameo face had smiled up at Lance. 'Yes,' she said, 'I'm sure you've had most of the desirable women in the city, but I don't want to be among them.' 'Then, I think it's time I changed your mind,' Lance said. Suddenly Lance's hand slid to the back of her gown. With one strong arm he pinned her to his chest so that try as she might, she could not push him away. He deftly unfastened the buttons of her gown, as if he had had long practice in performing such actions. 'What are you doing? I'm not one of your strumpets!' " (LEILAH *knocks at the door. Like* KATE *she is very attractive. But as opposed to* KATE, *who is obviously quite confident,* LEILAH *prefers to walk with her head down.*)

LEILAH: Kate? You're busy.

KATE: I was just reading "The Genealogy of Morals."

LEILAH: How was dinner?

KATE: Leilah, I don't understand why you never come. Even Susie Friend has been asking for you.

LEILAH: I came in to get the Nietzsche assignment.

KATE: Leilah, you don't think I'm a good person do you?

LEILAH: Kate, you're very good.

KATE: Then why don't you ever come in here just to visit instead of always asking for the assignment? Leilah, we roomed together for three years and now I never see you anymore. You're angry about last year in Greece. Aren't you?

LEILAH: That wasn't your fault.

KATE: I felt badly for you when both Iki and Thomas fell in love with me.

Leilah, sometimes I think I should apologize to you and other times I don't know exactly what I should apologize for. I haven't done anything deliberately to hurt you. I want us to stay friends.

LEILAH: I know.

KATE: What are you going to do next year? I don't know what's going to happen if I don't get into law school.

LEILAH: Kate, you're not supposed to hear until April; this is only November.

KATE: Well, I'm Phi Beta Kappa, but I'm worried about my law boards. (*Pause.*) Oh, Leah, pumpkin, don't worry. You'll be Phi Bet by June, in time for graduation. Just think, you could be Muffet, or Samantha, or God forbid, Rita. What are they going to do with their lives? At least you and I aren't limited.

LEILAH: Did I tell you I applied to anthropology graduate school?

KATE: Why aren't you continuing in philosophy?

LEILAH: I really like anthropology. I want to go to small towns in Iraq. Look, I've made a list of Mesopotamia jokes.

KATE: Leilah, things aren't going to be better for you in Iraq. You don't have to make yourself exotic. You're a smart, pretty girl. And anyway, if you can't leave your room in South Hadley, how are you going to get along in Iraq?

LEILAH: Just fine. Kate, what's the Nietzsche assignment? I have more reading to do.

KATE: You always have more reading to do. (LEILAH *begins to move away.*) I'm sorry. Let's talk about something else. Like when we were roommates, okay? Leilah, what do you know about clitoral orgasms?

LEILAH: Well, my gentleman friend, Mr. Peterson, says they're better than others.

KATE: I wonder if I've had any.

LEILAH: Kate, I'm sure you have. It's a fad.

KATE: Well, I never thought I had a problem.

LEILAH: Why don't you ask Rita?

KATE: Rita's f***** up. (*They laugh.*) Leilah, are you leaving philosophy because I'm Phi Bet and you're not? That's stupid. The department likes you as much as me.

LEILAH: Katie, I know you're trying but . . . I don't know. I just want to go away. I don't want to have to think about this place anymore. Kate, do you have the assignment?

KATE: Read the last two chapters in the "Genealogy of Morals." (*Pause.*) Look, Leilah, I'm sorry. I really am. But it's not my fault. You're always predisposed against me.

LEILAH: Kate, are you going to Milk and Crackers? I'll see you later.

KATE: Leilah, did you know Holly used to pick up men on the Yale green when she was a sophomore? She had clitoral orgasms. But that was a long time ago.

LEILAH: Maybe that's why she gets on with Rita. They have that in common.

KATE: Leilah, that's nasty.

LEILAH: (*Strongly.*) We all have hidden potential, Kate. (*Goes to exit.*) Bye Katie.

KATE: I'm going to ask Carter to join us for Milk and Crackers. I think she's very bright. It's been a long time since we've had someone new to talk to in this house, around three years. (*Frustrated, Kate goes back to her book.*) " 'I'm sorry,' Lance said after a moment. 'I suppose I shouldn't have done that. But you were asking for it. You wanted it. And you enjoyed every second of it.' "

Vanities, by Jack Heifner
From Scene 1

Scene: For three women, teenage cheerleaders
Characters: JOANNE
            KATHY
            MARY
Setting: A High School Gymnasium
Time: Fall
Situation: This first scene of three in the lives of three young women as they finish high school and go on, returning to compare notes, at least twice more during the course of the play. They should play this first scene with a regional dialect; a rural Texas dialect was suggested by the author.

JOANNE: Maybe we could sing. You know, teach the kids the words to "Hold That Tiger."

MARY: What words? It's just "Hold That Tiger, Hold That Tiger" over and over.

JOANNE: That's what I mean. (*She sings.*)
Hold That Tiger!
Hold That Tiger!
Hold That Tiger!
Hold That Tiger!

MARY: Well, that's silly. Nobody wants to sing that over and over.

KATHY: They'll get bored. Let's just clap and dance around and for heaven's sake smile! You two act like you lost your best friend. Pep rallies are to raise spirits. Not to make everyone feel bad.

JOANNE: Well, it's hard. Nobody in this school has any spirit. We're out there screaming and crying and nobody cares.

KATHY: That's why we've got to work harder and make them care.

MARY: Remember at last week's game when that guy shouted for us to shut-up? Said he couldn't keep his mind on the game for all we were doing.

KATHY: That's because you started yelling, "Push him back, push him back, way back," when we had the ball. There we all were telling the other team to push ours back.

JOANNE: I've just never been so embarrassed.

MARY: Okay. I was wrong, but you could have told me. I don't know anything about football.

JOANNE: When we have the ball yell something like, "Get that point," or "Do it again, do it again, harder, harder."

KATHY: "Get that point," is when we kick the ball through the two posts. Not for a touchdown.

MARY: Well, when do we do, "Block that kick, block that kick"?

KATHY: Oh, now let me make this clear. When we kick, we yell "Get that point"; and when they kick, we yell "Block that kick." And when they have the ball, we yell "Get that ball."

MARY: What do we yell when we have the ball?

KATHY: You yell . . . well, you yell something encouraging like . . . like "Go! Go!"

JOANNE: Or "Go all the way, all the way!"

MARY: You can't yell "Go all the way" on a football field. What will people think? (MARY *and* JOANNE *laugh.*)

JOANNE: Oh, Mary.

KATHY: Now, we've got to finish this pep rally rundown and go on to other things. So, after "Hail That Tiger."

MARY: (*Correcting* KATHY.) "Hold That Tiger."

KATHY: "Hold That Tiger," then the coach says a few words and we make the victory sign and sing the school song.

MARY: I think we ought to make an announcement that anyone who sits in the card section tonight has got to do his job. Those cards were a mess last week, and if they aren't gonna flip em right then they should sit somewhere else.

JOANNE: I died when they spelled out "Yea Team" and it turned out to be "Yea Meat!"

KATHY: Well, we'll just have to tell people we can trust to get there early and sit in the card section. I don't know what else we can do.

JOANNE: If they spell out "Yea Meat" again tonight, I'll just leave the field. What does the team think when they look to the stands for encouragement and see a huge sign reading "Yea Meat"?

MARY: I don't know, but it makes sense to me. The whole team is good enough to eat.

JOANNE: Now enough of that.

KATHY: Before we go on to anything else, we have to talk about the invocation. Did you get someone to do that?

JOANNE: Me? Our minister did it last week.

KATHY: I know that our minister did it. Now we've got to get someone else. We can't have a Baptist every week. Don't you know anyone?

JOANNE: I guess I could call the Jehovah Witnesses and ask them if they'd be willing to pray at the game if we let them hand out their little books.

KATHY: Well, scrape up somebody for the invocation. And tell em to make it short. Nobody listens anyway.

JOANNE: And I wish somebody would pep-up the National Anthem. We stand there with our hands over our hearts, singing; while most of the people are down at the snack bar getting French fries. Makes me feel stupid.

KATHY: Well, let's just do the best we can.

MARY: Sometimes I think it's all for nothing. Nobody looks at us. They just watch the game.

JOANNE: It's lack of spirit, I tell you. I love that team . . . out there hitting and getting themselves killed for the school. Sometimes I think all those people in the stands just want to have a good time.

MARY: It's the band's fault. They play at the worst times. They never look to see what we're doing. Sometimes they start "The Baby Elephant Walk" right in the middle of our yells.

JOANNE: If they play "Moonriver" again tonight I'll scream. It puts everyone in a down mood. How can you make a touchdown when they're playing "Moonriver"? Everybody goes to sleep.

KATHY: Well, there's nothing we can do about the band. Just ignore them. They're no good anyway.

MARY: They're all creeps. All those girls with glasses and pimples. All those boys with glasses and pimples.

ALL: Creeps!

JOANNE: How many girls in the band have ever been elected to anything in this school?

MARY: Zero.

KATHY: Zilch.

JOANNE: Goose egg.

MARY: The girls in the band are the worst. And those majorettes go to the other extreme. I don't know why becoming a twirler automatically makes a girl easy.

JOANNE: Look at Sarah. I used to like her, but the very minute she became a majorette her reputation went downhill.

MARY: My mother said if she ever caught me going out for a coke in the same car with Sarah, she'd ground me. Said that Sarah was trash and her whole family acted like trash and, if I associated with trash, I'd get what was coming to me.

KATHY: Isn't it funny that I used to like her? I just don't know how some girls can let themselves in for so much talk.

MARY: And what makes me furious is that the boys love her.

JOANNE: Of course, they do. Respect her they don't. Love her they do.

KATHY: Did you see who she had a date with last weekend?

MARY: Sure, I did. Jim and I sat right behind them at the show. If Sarah wants to make-out, I wish she'd just do it in the car. Not in the show.

JOANNE: Sometimes I think she just wants all of us to see her.

MARY: Jim was so hot after watching Sarah, that we barely got to the car before he was all over me.

KATHY: It's hard enough to keep boys down to petting and necking with Sarah putting other ideas in their heads.

MARY: The ideas are already in their heads. Sarah just puts them in their hands.

JOANNE: I just don't understand boys. I'm glad Ted respects me, because I love him; and if he ever tried to go too far, I don't know what I would do.

MARY: He'll try. They all try. Jim loves me, but every night it's a battle. I just turn to him and say, "Jim, keep your pecker in your pants."

JOANNE: I just can't imagine how anyone could lose their self-respect. If I wasn't a virgin, I'd hate myself.

KATHY: Amen!

Buried Child, by Sam Shepard. South Coast Repertory with Raymond J. Barry and Ralph Waite. Photograph by Ron Stone.

Buried Child, by Sam Shepard
From Act II

Scene: For one man, one woman
Characters: VINCE, about 22, the son of Tilden and grandson of Dodge
     SHELLY, Vince's girlfriend, about 19
Setting: Suggests the interior of a house with a porch
Time   Night
Situation: During the course of the first act of this play we are introduced to an ex-tremely dysfunctional family made up of the matriarch, Halie, her hus-band, Dodge, and son Bradley. At the top of the second act their son Tilden, who was in trouble in New Mexico, and his girl friend, Shelly, ar-rive in the middle of the night.

SHELLY: *(laughing, gesturing to house)* This is it? I don't believe this is it!
VINCE: This is it.
SHELLY: This is the house?
VINCE: This is the house.
SHELLY: I don't believe it!
VINCE: How come?
SHELLY: It's like a Norman Rockwell cover or something.
VINCE: What's a' matter with that? It's American.
SHELLY: Where's the milkman and the little dog? What's the little dog's name?
  Spot. Spot and Jane. Dick and Jane and Spot.

VINCE: Knock it off.

SHELLY: Dick and Jane and Spot and Mom and Dad and Junior and Sissy!

(*She laughs. Slaps her knee.*)

VINCE: Come on! It's my heritage. What dya' expect?

(*She laughs more hysterically, out of control.*)

SHELLY: "And Tuffy and Toto and Dooda and Bonzo all went down one day
to the corner grocery store to buy a big bag of licorice for Mr. Marshall's
pussy cat!"

(*She laughs so hard she falls to her knees holding her stomach.* VINCE *stands there looking at her.*)

VINCE: Shelly will you get up!

(*She keeps laughing. Staggers to her feet. Turning in circles holding her stomach.*)

SHELLY: (*continuing her story in kid's voice*) "Mr. Marshall was on vacation. He
had no idea that the four little boys had taken such a liking to his little kitty
cat."

VINCE: Have some respect would ya'!

SHELLY: (*trying to control herself*) I'm sorry.

VINCE: Pull yourself together.

SHELLY: (*salutes him*) Yes sir.

(*She giggles.*)

VINCE: Jesus Christ, Shelly.

SHELLY: (*pause, smiling*) And Mrs. Marshall—

VINCE: Cut it out.

(*She stops. Stands there staring at him. Stifles a giggle.*)

VINCE: (*after pause*) Are you finished?

SHELLY: Oh brother!

VINCE: I don't wanna go in there with you acting like an idiot.

SHELLY: Thanks.

VINCE: Well, I don't.

SHELLY: I won't embarrass you. Don't worry.

VINCE: I'm not worried.

SHELLY: You are too.

VINCE: Shelly look, I just don't wanna go in there with you giggling your head
off. They might think something's wrong with you.

SHELLY: There is.

VINCE: There is not!

SHELLY: Something's definitely wrong with me.

VINCE: There is not!

SHELLY: There's something wrong with you too.

VINCE: There's nothing wrong with me either!

SHELLY: You wanna know what's wrong with you?

VINCE: What?

(SHELLY *laughs.*)

VINCE: (*crosses back left toward screen door*) I'm leaving!

SHELLY: (*stops laughing*) Wait! Stop! Stop! (VINCE *stops*) What's wrong with you
is that you take the situation too seriously.

VINCE: I just don't want to have them think that I've suddenly arrived out of
the middle of nowhere completely deranged.

SHELLY: What do you want them to think then?

VINCE: (*pause*) Nothing. Let's go in.

(*He crosses porch toward stage right interior door.* SHELLY *follows him. The stage right door opens slowly.* VINCE *sticks his head in, doesn't notice* DODGE *sleeping. Calls out toward staircase.*)

VINCE: Grandma!

(SHELLY *breaks into laughter, unseen behind* VINCE. VINCE *pulls his head back outside and pulls door shut. We hear their voices again without seeing them.*)

SHELLY'S VOICE: (*stops laughing*) I'm sorry. I'm sorry Vince. I really am. I really am sorry. I won't do it again. I couldn't help it.

VINCE'S VOICE: It's not all that funny.

SHELLY'S VOICE: I know it's not. I'm sorry.

VINCE'S VOICE: I mean this is a tense situation for me! I haven't seen them for over six years. I don't know what to expect.

SHELLY'S VOICE: I know. I won't do it again.

VINCE'S VOICE: Can't you bite your tongue or something?

SHELLY'S VOICE: Just don't say "Grandma," okay? (*she giggles, stops*) I mean if you say "Grandma" I don't know if I can stop myself.

VINCE'S VOICE: Well try!

SHELLY'S VOICE: Okay. Sorry.

Butterflies Are Free, by Leonard Gershe
From Act I, Scene 1

Scene:	For one man, one woman
Characters:	DON BAKER, twenty years old, lean and good looking. He is blind.
	JILL TANNER, nineteen. His neighbor in the adjoining apartment.
Setting:	Don Baker's apartment on the top floor of an apartment building on the Lower East Side of Manhattan.
Time:	A warm morning in June. The present.
Situation:	Don has been trying to develop an independent life for himself despite his blindness and a somewhat over-protective mother. His neighbor in the adjoining apartment has been playing the TV at a loud volume, and Don has pounded on the walls asking that the sound be lowered. A conversation between Don and Jill begins with the wall serving as a minor barrier. Jill asks if she can have a cup of coffee and then enters Don's apartment through his unlocked door. Don is in the kitchen lighting the burner under the coffee pot as Jill makes her way into his apartment. She is unaware of the fact that he is blind.

JILL: Hi! I'm Jill Tanner.

DON: (*Turning toward her and extending his hand*) Don Baker. (JILL *shakes his hand*)

JILL: I hope you don't mind me inviting myself in. (*Turning her back to him*) Would you do the zipper on my blouse? I can't reach back there. (*There is just a flash of awkwardness as* DON *reaches out for the zipper and zips it up*) Your living room is bigger than mine. How long have you been here?

DON: A month. This isn't the living room. This is the apartment. That's all there is except I have a big bathroom.

JILL: I've got three rooms if you count the kitchen. I just moved in two days ago, but I didn't sign a lease or anything—just by the month. God, you're neat. Everything is so tidy.

DON: It's easy when you haven't got anything.

JILL: (*Looking around*) I haven't got anything, but it manages to wind up all over the place. I'm afraid I'm a slob. I've heard that boys are neater than girls. (*Looking up*) I like your skylight. I don't have that. (*Moves to the bed*) What's this?

DON: What?

JILL: This thing on stilts.

DON: Oh, my bed.

JILL: (*Climbing the ladder*) Your bed? Wow! This is WILD!

DON: Do you like it?

JILL: (*Climbing on the bed*) This is the greatest bed I've ever seen in my life. . . . and I've seen a lot of beds. Did you build it?

DON: No, the guy who lived here before me built it. He was a hippie. He liked to sleep high.

JILL: Suppose you fall out? You could break something.

DON: You could break something falling out of any bed. (*He pours the coffee into the cup, goes to the coffee table and sets it down*) Cream or sugar?

JILL: No, just black.

DON: I could have had your apartment, but I took this one because of the bed.

JILL: I don't blame you. (*Moving to the sofa*) You know, I buy flowers and dumb things like dishtowels and paper napkins, but I keep forgetting to buy coffee. (JILL *settles on the sofa with her feet beneath her. She picks up the coffee and sips it*)

DON: Is it hot enough?

JILL: Great. This'll save my life. I'll pay you back some day.

DON: You don't have to.

JILL: Do you need any dishtowels or paper napkins?

DON: No.

JILL: I've got lots of light bulbs, too—everything but coffee. May I ask you a personal question?

DON: Sure.

JILL: Why don't you want your mother to come here?

DON: How did you know that?

JILL: If you can hear me, I can hear you. I think the sound must go right under that door. What's that door for, anyway?

DON: Your apartment and mine were once one apartment. When they converted it into two, they just locked that door instead of sealing it up. I guess in case they want to make it one again.

JILL: You didn't answer my question.

DON: I forgot what you asked.

JILL: Why don't you want your mother here?

DON: It's a long story. No, it's a short story—it's just been going on a long time. She didn't want me to leave home. She thinks I can't make it on my own. Finally, we agreed to letting me try it for two months. She's to keep away from me for two months. I've got a month to go.

JILL: Why did you tell her you had a party last night?

DON: Boy, you don't miss anything in there, do you?

JILL: Not much.

DON: I always tell her I've had a party . . . or went to one. She wouldn't understand why I'd rather be here alone than keeping her and the cook company. She'll hate this place. She hates it now without even seeing it. She'll walk in and the first thing she'll say is, "I could absolutely cry!"

JILL: Does she cry a lot?

DON: No—she just threatens to.

JILL: If she really wants to cry, send her in to look at my place. At least you're neat. You're old enough to live alone, aren't you? I'm nineteen. How old are you?

DON: As far as my mother's concerned, I'm still eleven—going on ten.

JILL: We must have the same mother. Mine would love me to stay a child all my life—or at least all *her* life. So *she* wont' age. She loves it when people say we look like sisters. If they don't say it, she tells them. Have you got a job?

DON: Not yet . . . but I play the guitar, and I've got a few prospects.

JILL: I heard you last night.

DON: Sorry.

JILL: No, it was good. First I thought it was a record till you kept playing one song over and over.

DON: I can't read music, so I have to learn by ear. I'm trying to put together an act.

JILL: Then what?

DON: Then I'll try to cash in on some of those prospects. I know one thing—I ain't a-goin' back to Scarsdale.

JILL: What is Scarsdale?

DON: You don't know Scarsdale?

JILL: I don't know much about the East. I'm from Los Angeles.

DON: Scarsdale's just outside of New York—about twenty miles.

JILL: Is that where you live?

DON: No, I live here. It's where I used to live.

JILL: Scars-dale. It sounds like a sanitarium where they do plastic surgery. Is there any more coffee?

DON: (*Putting his cigarette out in the ashtray*) Plenty.

JILL: I can get it.

DON: (*Rises and holds out his hand for the cup*) I'm up. (JILL *hands him the cup. He goes to the kitchen to pour her more coffee*) What did you say your name is?

JILL: Jill Tanner. Technically, I guess I'm Mrs. Benson. I was married once . . . when I was sixteen.

DON: Sixteen! Did you have your parents' permission?

JILL: My mother's. I told her I was pregnant, but I wasn't. She cried her eyes out. She hated the thought of becoming a grandmother. I'll bet I know what you're thinking.

DON: What? (DON *returns, sets the cup on the table, and resumes his seat*)

JILL: You're thinking I don't look like a *divorcée.*

DON: No, I wasn't thinking that. What does a divorcée look like?

JILL: Oh, you know. They're usually around thirty-five with tight-fitting dresses and high-heel patent leather shoes and big boobs. I look more like the kid in a custody fight.

DON: How long were you married?

JILL: God, it seemed like weeks! Actually, it was six days. (*She lights a cigarette*) It wasn't Jack's fault. It wasn't anybody's fault. It was just one of those terrible mistakes you make before you can stop yourself, even though you know it's a mistake while you're doing it.

DON: What was he like?

JILL: Jack? Oh . . . (*Uncomfortably*) I really can't talk about him.

DON: Then don't. I'm sorry.

JILL: No, I will talk about him. Once in a while it's good for you to do something you don't want to do. It cleanses the insides. He was terribly sweet and groovy-looking, but kind of adolescent, you know what I mean? Girls mature faster than boys. Boys are neater, but girls mature faster. When we met it was like fireworks and rockets. I don't know if I'm saying it right, but it was a marvelous kind of passion that made every day like the Fourth of July. Anyway, the next thing I knew we were standing in front of a justice of the peace getting married.

DON: How long had you known him?

JILL: Two or three weeks, but I mean there we were getting *married*! I hadn't even finished high school and I had two exams the next day and they were on my mind, too. I heard the justice of the peace saying, "Do you, *Jack*, take Jill to be your lawfully wedded wife?" Can you imagine going through life as Jack and Jill? And then I heard "Till death do you part," and suddenly it wasn't a wedding ceremony. It was a funeral service.

DON: (*Lighting a cigarette*) Jesus!

JILL: You know, that wedding ceremony is very morbid when you think about it. I hate anything morbid and there I was being buried alive . . . under Jack Benson. I wanted to run screaming out into the night!

DON: Did you?

JILL: I couldn't. It was ten o'clock in the morning. I mean you can't go screaming out into ten o'clock in the morning—so I passed out. If only I'd fainted before I said "I do."

DON: As long as you were married, why didn't you try to make it work?

JILL: I did try—believe me. (*She picks up an ashtray and holds it in her hand*) I tried for six days, but I knew it was no good.

DON: Were you in love with him? (DON *flicks an ash from his cigarette onto the table where the ashtray had been before* JILL *moved it.* JILL *reacts to this fleetingly, and shrugs it off*)

JILL: In my way.

DON: What's your way?

JILL: I don't know . . . Well, I think just because you love someone, that doesn't necessarily mean that you want to spend the rest of your life with him. But Jack loved me. I mean he really, really loved me, and I hurt him and that's what I can't stand. I just never want to hurt anybody. I mean marriage is a commitment, isn't it? I just can't be committed or involved. Can you understand?

DON: I understand, but I don't agree. (DON *flicks his ashes onto the table*)

JILL: Then you don't understand really. (JILL *looks at him, oddly*) What is this? Maybe I've got it wrong. Maybe boys mature faster and girls are neater.

DON: What do you mean?

JILL: Or maybe you know something I don't know—like ashes are good for the table? Is that why you keep dropping them there?

DON: Did you move the ashtray?

JILL: (*Holding up the ashtray beside her*) It's right here. Are you blind?

DON: Yes.

JILL: What do you mean *yes*?

DON: I mean yes. I'm blind.

JILL: You're putting me on.

DON: No, I'm blind. I've always been blind.

JILL: Really blind? Not just near-sighted?

DON: The works. I can't see a thing. (JILL *leans over and runs her hands across* DON's *eyes. When he doesn't blink, she realizes he is indeed blind*)

JILL: God! I hope I didn't say anything . . .

DON: Now, don't get self-conscious about it. I'm not.

JILL: Why didn't you tell me?

DON: I just did.

JILL: I mean when I came in.

DON: You didn't ask me.

The Member of the Wedding, by Carson McCullers
From Act I

Scene:	For one girl, one boy
Characters:	FRANKIE, an adolescent girl of twelve
	JOHN HENRY, a bespectacled young man aged seven, Frankie's cousin
Setting:	A Southern backyard and a kitchen.
Time:	An August afternoon, late in the day.
Situation:	Originally conceived as a novel, the work was adapted by the author, Ms. McCullers, for the stage. She called it "an *inward* play" and noted that the conflicts are inward. It is an unconventional kind of play because "the antagonist is not personified, but is a human condition of life." One of these major conflicts is Frankie's awareness of her growing from childhood to womanhood and the changes that are taking place in her life. At this point in the play, Frankie has been left alone after much excitement in the backyard due to the coming marriage of her elder brother, and she calls over to the next house for her cousin, partly to have some companionship, as evening begins to fall.

FRANKIE: John Henry. John Henry.

JOHN HENRY'S VOICE: What do you want, Frankie?

FRANKIE: Come over and spend the night with me.

JOHN HENRY'S VOICE: I can't.

FRANKIE: Why?

JOHN HENRY: Just because.

FRANKIE: Because why? (*John Henry does not answer*) I thought maybe me and you could put up my Indian tepee and sleep out here in the yard. And have a good time. (*There is still no answer*) Sure enough. Why don't you stay and spend the night?

JOHN HENRY: (*quite loudly*). Because, Frankie. I don't want to.

FRANKIE: (*angrily*). Fool! Jackass! Suit yourself! I only asked you because you looked so ugly and so lonesome.

JOHN HENRY: (*skipping toward the arbor*). Why, I'm not a bit lonesome.

FRANKIE: (*looking at the house*). I wonder when that Papa of mine is coming home. He always comes home by dark. I don't want to go into that empty, ugly house all by myself.

JOHN HENRY: Me neither.

FRANKIE: (*standing with outstretched arms, and looking around her*). I think something is wrong. It is too quiet. I have a peculiar warning in my bones. I bet you a hundred dollars it's going to storm.

JOHN HENRY: I don't want to spend the night with you.

FRANKIE: A terrible, terrible dog-day storm. Or maybe even a cyclone.

JOHN HENRY: Huh.

FRANKIE: I bet Jarvis and Janice are now at Winter Hill. I see them just plain as I see you. Plainer. Something is wrong. It is too quiet.

(*A clear horn begins to play a blues tune in the distance.*)

JOHN HENRY: Frankie?

FRANKIE: Hush! It sounds like Honey. (*The horn music becomes jazzy and spangling, then the first blues tune is repeated. Suddenly, while still unfinished, the music stops. Frankie waits tensely.*)

FRANKIE: He has stopped to bang the spit out of his horn. In a second he will finish. (*After a wait*) Please, Honey, go on finish!

JOHN HENRY: (*softly*). He done quit now.

FRANKIE: (*moving restlessly*). I told Berenice that I was leavin' town for good and she did not believe me. Sometimes I honestly think she is the biggest fool that ever drew breath. You try to impress something on a big fool like that, and it's just like talking to a block of cement. I kept on telling and telling and telling her. I told her I had to leave this town for good because it is inevitable. Inevitable. (*Mr. Addams enters the kitchen from the house, calling: "Frankie, Frankie."*)

MR. ADDAMS: (*calling from the kitchen door*). Frankie, Frankie.

FRANKIE: Yes, Papa.

MR. ADDAMS: (*opening the back door*). You had supper?

FRANKIE: I'm not hungry.

MR. ADDAMS: Was a little later than I intended, fixing a timepiece for a railroad man. (*He goes back through the kitchen and into the hall, calling: "Don't leave the yard!"*)

JOHN HENRY: You want me to get the weekend bag?

FRANKIE: Don't bother me, John Henry. I'm thinking.

JOHN HENRY: What you thinking about?

FRANKIE: About the wedding. About my brother and the bride. Everything's been so sudden today. I never believed before about the fact that the earth turns at the rate of about a thousand miles a day. I didn't understand why it was that if you jumped up in the air you wouldn't land in Selma or Fairview or somewhere else instead of the same back yard. But now it seems to me I feel the world going around very fast. (*Frankie begins turning around in circles with arms outstretched. John Henry copies her. They both turn*) I feel it turning and it makes me dizzy.

JOHN HENRY: I'll stay and spend the night with you.

FRANKIE: (*suddenly stopping her turning*). No. I just now thought of something.

JOHN HENRY: You just a little while ago was begging me.

FRANKIE: I know where I'm going. (*There are sounds of children playing in the distance.*)

JOHN HENRY: Let's go play with the children, Frankie.

FRANKIE: I tell you I know where I'm going. It's like I've known it all my life. Tomorrow I will tell everybody.

JOHN HENRY: Where?

FRANKIE: (*dreamily*). After the wedding I'm going with them to Winter Hill. I'm going off with them after the wedding.

JOHN HENRY: You serious?

FRANKIE: Shush, just now I realized something. The trouble with me is that for a long time I have been just an "I" person. All other people can say "we." When Berenice says "we" she means her lodge and church and colored people. Soldiers can say "we" and mean the army. All people belong to a "we" except me.

JOHN HENRY: What are we going to do?

FRANKIE: Not to belong to a "we" makes you too lonesome. Until this afternoon I didn't have a "we," but now after seeing Janice and Jarvis I suddenly realize something.

JOHN HENRY: What?

FRANKIE: I know that the bride and my brother are the "we" of me. So I'm going with them, and joining with the wedding. This coming Sunday when my brother and the bride leave this town, I'm going with the two of them to Winter Hill. And after that to whatever place that they will ever go. (*There is a pause*) I love the two of them so much and we belong to be together. I love the two of them so much because they are the *we* of me.

THE CURTAIN FALLS

The Diary of Anne Frank, by Frances Goodrich and Albert Hackett
From Act II, Scene 2

Scene:	For one man, one woman
Characters:	ANNE FRANK, a girl of fourteen
	PETER VAN DAAN, a boy of eighteen

Setting: Peter's room in the attic of a storage annex in Amsterdam, Holland (a hiding place for the Frank and Van Daan families).

Time: Holland during World War II. Early 1940s.

Situation: The play is based on the actual diary of young Anne Frank, which she kept during the early 1940s. The play relates the plight of two Jewish families, the Franks and the Van Daans, who are hiding from the Nazis during World War II. In all, eight people (including Dr. Dussel, a dentist) have been living secretly in the attic since Anne was thirteen. In fact, they managed to hide from 1942 to 1944, when they were discovered and sent to concentration camps. All died except Otto Frank, Anne's father, who returned to Amsterdam after the war and was given Anne's diary, which had escaped the eye of the Nazis. The building where they hid is now a permanent shrine to Anne's memory and to those who suffer political and religious persecution everywhere.

In this scene from the play, the families have been hiding for some time and their close confinement has led to irritability and personality clashes. The two youngsters find comradeship with each other and also feel the first blush of love.

ANNE: Aren't they awful? Aren't they impossible? Treating us as if we're still in the nursery. (*She sits on the cot.* PETER *gets a bottle of pop and two glasses.*)

PETER: Don't let it bother you. It doesn't bother me.

ANNE: I suppose you can't really blame them . . . they think back to what *they* were like at our age. They don't realize how much advanced we are . . . when I think what wonderful discussions we've had! . . . Oh, I forgot. I was going to bring you some more pictures.

PETER: Oh, these are fine, thanks.

ANNE: Don't you want some more? Miep just brought me some new ones.

PETER: Maybe later. (*He gives her a glass of pop and, taking some for himself, sits down facing her.*)

ANNE: (*Looking up at one of the photographs*) I remember when I got that . . . I won it. I bet Jopie that I could eat five ice cream cones. We'd all been playing ping-pong . . . we used to have heavenly times . . . we'd finish up with ice cream at the Delphi, or the Oasis, where Jews were allowed . . . there'd always be a lot of boys . . . we'd laugh and joke . . . I'd like to go back to it for a few days or a week. But after that I know I'd be bored to death. I think more seriously about life now. I want to be a journalist . . . or something. I love to write. What do you want to do?

PETER: I thought I might go off some place . . . work on a farm or something . . . some job that doesn't take much brains.

ANNE: You shouldn't talk that way. You've got the most awful inferiority complex.

PETER: I know I'm not smart.

ANNE: That isn't true. You're much better than I am in dozens of things . . . arithmetic and algebra and . . . well, you're a million times better than I am in algebra. (*With sudden directness*) You like Margot, don't you? Right from the start you liked her, liked her much better than me.

PETER: (*Uncomfortably*) Oh, I don't know.

ANNE: It's all right. Everyone feels that way. Margot's so good. She's sweet and bright and beautiful and I'm not.

PETER: I wouldn't say that.

ANNE: Oh, no, I'm not. I know that. I know quite well that I'm not a beauty. I never have been and never shall be.

PETER: I don't agree at all. I think you're pretty.

ANNE: That's not true!

PETER: And another thing. You've changed . . . from at first, I mean.

ANNE: I have?

PETER: I used to think you were awful noisy.

ANNE: And what do you think now, Peter? How have I changed?

PETER: Well . . . er . . . you're . . . quieter.

ANNE: I'm glad you don't just hate me.

PETER: I never said that.

ANNE: I bet when you get out of here you'll never think of me again.

PETER: That's crazy.

ANNE: When you get back with all of your friends, you're going to say . . . now what did I ever see in that Mrs. Quack Quack?

PETER: I haven't got any friends.

ANNE: Oh, Peter, of course you have. Everyone has friends.

PETER: Not me, I don't want any. I get along all right without them.

ANNE: Does that mean you can get along without me? I think of myself as your friend.

PETER: No. If they were all like you, it'd be different. (*He takes the glasses and the bottle and puts them away. There is a second's silence and then* ANNE *speaks, hesitantly, shyly.*)

ANNE: Peter, did you ever kiss a girl?

PETER: Yes. Once.

ANNE: (*to cover her feelings*) That picture's crooked. (PETER *goes over, straightening the photograph*) Was she pretty?

PETER: Huh?

ANNE: The girl that you kissed.

PETER: I don't know. I was blindfolded. It was at a party. One of those kissing games.

ANNE: (*Relieved*) Oh, I don't suppose that really counts, does it?

PETER: It didn't with me.

ANNE: I've been kissed twice. Once a man I'd never seen before kissed me on the cheek when he picked me up off the ice and I was crying. And the other was Mr. Kopphuis, a friend of Father's who kissed my hand. You wouldn't say those counted, would you?

PETER: I wouldn't say so.

ANNE: I know almost for certain that Margot would never kiss anyone unless she was engaged to them. And I'm sure too that Mother never touched a man before Pim. But I don't know . . . things are so different now . . . what do you think? Do you think a girl shouldn't kiss anyone except if she's engaged or something? It's so hard to try to think what to do, when here we are with the whole world falling around our ears and you think . . . well . . . you don't know what's going to happen tomorrow and . . . what do you think?

PETER: I suppose it'd depend on the girl. Some girls, anything they do's wrong. But others . . . well . . . it wouldn't necessarily be wrong with them. I've always thought that when two people—(*The carillon starts to ring nine o'clock*)

ANNE: Nine o'clock. I have to go.

PETER: That's right.

ANNE: (*Without moving*) Good night. (*There is a second's pause. Then* PETER *gets up and moves towards the door.*)

PETER: You won't let them stop you coming?

ANNE: No. (*She rises and starts for the door.*) Sometime I might bring my diary. There are so many things in it that I want to talk over with you. There's a lot about you.

PETER: What kind of things?

ANNE: I wouldn't want you to see some of it. I thought you were a nothing, just the way you thought about me.

PETER: Did you change your mind, the way I changed my mind about you?

ANNE: Well . . . you'll see . . . (*For a second* ANNE *stands looking up at* PETER *longing for him to kiss her. As he makes no move, she turns away. Then suddenly* PETER *grabs her awkwardly in his arms, kissing her on the cheek.* ANNE *walks out, dazed.*)

Zoot Suit, by Luis Valdez
From Act II, Scene 3 The Incorrigible Pachuco

Scene:	For one man, one woman
Characters:	HENRY, about 21; Latino gang leader
	ALICE, young crusading reporter, fighting to help Henry
Setting:	San Quentin Prison
Time:	May 1943
Situation:	This "Brechtian" piece is concerned with the so-called Sleepy Lagoon murder trial of Mexican youths in Los Angeles during World War II. Henry Reyna, who was about to join the navy, has been railroaded into prison at the trial, but there is a movement afoot to appeal the case. Among the leaders of the movement is the Anglo reporter and activist, Alice Bloomfield. She visits Henry in San Quentin prison. The Pachuco has one line in the scene, which may be omitted or delivered by someone off stage, out of the main scene.

HENRY:

May 17, 1943

Dear Miss Bloomfield,

I understand you're coming up to Q this weekend, and I would like to talk to you—in private. Can you arrange it?

(*The batos turn away, taking a hint.*)

ALICE: (*Eagerly.*) Yes, yes, I can. What can I do for you, Henry?

(HENRY *and* ALICE *step forward toward each other.* EL PACHUCO *moves in.*)

HENRY: For me? ¡Ni madre!

ALICE: (*Puzzled*) I don't understand.

HENRY: I wanted you to be the first to know, Alice. I'm dropping out of the appeal.

ALICE: (*Unbelieving.*) You're what?

HENRY: I'm bailing out, esa. Dropping out of the case, see?

ALICE: Henry, you can't!

HENRY: Why can't I?

ALICE: Because you'll destroy our whole case! If we don't present a united front, how can we ask the public to support us?

HENRY: That's your problem. I never asked for their support. Just count me out.

ALICE: (*Getting nervous, anxious.*) Henry, please, think about what you're saying. If you drop out, the rest of the boys will probably go with you. How can you even think of dropping out of the appeal? What about George and all the people that have contributed their time and money in the past few months? You just can't quit on them!

HENRY: Oh no? Just watch me.

ALICE: If you felt this way, why didn't you tell me before?

HENRY: Why didn't you ask me? You think you can just move in and defend anybody you feel like? When did I ever ask you to start a defense committee for me? Or a newspaper? Or a fundraising drive and all that other shit? I don't need defending, esa. I can take care of myself.

ALICE: But what about the trial, the sentence. They gave you life imprisonment?

HENRY: It's my life!

ALICE: Henry, honestly—are you kidding me?

HENRY: You think so?

ALICE: But you've seen me coming and going. Writing you, speaking for you, traveling up and down the state. You must have known I was doing it for you. Nothing has come before my involvement, my attachment, my passion for this case. My boys have been everything to me.

HENRY: My boys? My boys! What the hell are we—your personal property? Well, let me set you straight, lady, I ain't your boy.

ALICE: You know I never meant it that way.

HENRY: You think I haven't seen through your bullshit? Always so concerned. Come on, boys. Speak out, boys. Stand up for your people. Well, you leave my people out of this! Can't you understand that?

ALICE: No, I can't understand that.

HENRY: You're just using Mexicans to play politics.

ALICE: Henry, that's the worst thing anyone has ever said to me.

HENRY: Who are you going to help next—the Colored People?

ALICE: No, as a matter of fact, I've already helped the Colored People. What are you going to do next—go to the gas chamber?

HENRY: What the hell do you care?

ALICE: I don't!

HENRY: Then get the hell out of here!

ALICE: (*Furious.*) You think you're the only one who doesn't want to be bothered? You ought to try working in the Sleepy Lagoon defense office for a few months. All the haggling, the petty arguments, the lack of cooperation. I've wanted to quit a thousand times. What the hell am I doing here? They're coming at me from all sides. You're too sentimental and emotional about this, Alice. You're too cold hearted, Alice. You're collecting money and turning it over to the lawyers, while the families are going hungry. They're saying you can't be trusted because you're a Communist, because you're a Jew. Okay! If that's the way they feel about me, then to hell with them! I hate them too. I hate their language, I hate their enchiladas, and I hate their goddamned mariachi music! (*Pause. They look at each other.* HENRY *smiles, then* ALICE—*feeling foolish—and they both break out laughing.*)

HENRY: All right! Now you sound like you mean it.

ALICE: I do.

HENRY: Okay! Now we're talking straight.

ALICE: I guess I have been sounding like some square paddy chick. But, you haven't exactly been Mister Cool yourself . . . ese.

HENRY: So, let's say we're even Steven.

ALICE: Fair enough. What now?

HENRY: Why don't we bury the hatchet, you know what I mean?

ALICE: Can I tell George you'll go on with the appeal?

HENRY: Yeah. I know there's a lot of people out there who are willing and trying to help us. People who feel that our conviction was an injustice. People like George . . . and you. Well, the next time you see them, tell them Hank Reyna sends his thanks.

ALICE: Why don't you tell them?

HENRY: You getting wise with me again?

ALICE: If you write an article—and I know you can—we'll publish it in the People's World. What do you say?

PACHUCO: Article! Pos who told you, you could write, ese?

HENRY: (*Laughs.*) Chale.

ALICE: I'm serious. Why don't you give it a try?

HENRY: I'll think about it. (*Pause.*) Listen, you think you and I could write each other . . . outside the newsletter?

ALICE: Sure.

HENRY: Then it's a deal. (*They shake hands.*)

ALICE: I'm glad we're going to be communicating. I think we're going to be very good friends. (ALICE *lifts her hands to* HENRY's *shoulder in a gesture of comradeship.* HENRY *follows her hand, putting his on top of hers.*)

HENRY: You think so?

ALICE: I know so.

The Piano Lesson, by August Wilson
From Act II, Scene 2

Scene: For one man, one woman
Characters: BERNIECE, an African American woman
                AVERY, an African American man
Setting: The kitchen of the house where Doaker Charles lives

Time: Evening, in the 1920s–1930s

Situation: Berniece is a widow living with her daughter in her uncle's house. Into the situation comes Avery, an elevator operator and part-time preacher. He's ambitious and wants to become a full-time preacher and proposes marriages to Berniece in order to have a good preacher image.

BERNIECE: Who is it?

AVERY: It's me, Avery.

(BERNIECE *opens the door and lets him in.*)

BERNIECE: Avery, come on in. I was just fixing to take my bath.

AVERY: Where Boy Willie? I see that truck out there almost empty. They done sold almost all them watermelons.

BERNIECE: They was gone when I come home. I don't know where they went off to. Boy Willie around here about to drive me crazy.

AVERY: They sell them watermelons . . . he'll be gone soon.

BERNIECE: What Mr. Cohen says about letting you have the place?

AVERY: He say he'll let me have it for thirty dollars a month. I talked him out of thirty-five and he say he'll let me have it for thirty.

BERNIECE: That's a nice spot next to Benny Diamond's store.

AVERY: Berniece . . . I be at home and I get to thinking you up here an' I'm down there. I get to thinking how that look to have a preacher that ain't married. It makes for a better congregation if the preacher was settled down and married.

BERNIECE: Avery . . . not now. I was fixing to take my bath.

AVERY: You know how I feel about you, Berniece. Now . . . I done got the place from Mr. Cohen. I get the money from the bank and I can fix it up real nice. They give me a ten cents a hour raise down there on the job . . . now Berniece, I ain't got much in the way of comforts. I got a hole in my pockets near about as far as money is concerned. I ain't never found no way through life to a woman I care about like I care about you. I need that. I need somebody on my bond side. I need a woman that fits in my hand.

BERNIECE: Avery, I ain't ready to get married now.

AVERY: You too young a woman to close up, Berniece.

BERNIECE: I ain't said nothing about closing up. I got a lot of woman left in me.

AVERY: Where's it at? When's the last time you looked at it?

BERNIECE: (*Stunned by his remark.*) That's a nasty thing to say. And you call yourself a preacher.

AVERY: Anytime I get anywhere near you . . . you push me away.

BERNIECE: I got enough on my hands with Maretha. I got enough people to love and take care of.

AVERY: Who you got to love you? Can't nobody get close enough to you. Doaker can't half say nothing to you. You jump all over Boy Willie. Who you got to love you, Berniece?

BERNIECE: You trying to tell me a woman can't be nothing without a man. But you alright, huh? You can just walk out of here without me—without a woman—and still be a man. That's alright. Ain't nobody gonna ask you, "Avery, who you got to love you?" That's alright for you. But everybody gonna be worried about Berniece. "How Berniece gonna take care of herself? How she gonna raise that child without a man? Wonder what she do with herself. How she gonna live like that?" Everybody got all kinds of questions for Berniece. Everybody telling me I can't be a woman unless I got a man. Well, you tell me, Avery—you know—how much woman am I?

AVERY: It wasn't me, Berniece. You can't blame me for nobody else. I'll own up to my own shortcomings. But you can't blame me for Crawley or nobody else.

BERNIECE: I ain't blaming nobody for nothing. I'm just stating the facts.

AVERY: How long you gonna carry Crawley with you, Berniece? It's been over three years. At some point you got to let go and go on. Life's got all kinds of twists and turns. That don't mean you stop living. That don't mean you cut yourself off from life. You can't go through life carrying Crawley's ghost with you. Crawley's been dead three years. Three years, Berniece.

BERNIECE: I know how long Crawley's been dead. You ain't got to tell me that. I just ain't ready to get married right now.

CHAPTER TEN

Putting the Role Onstage

Thomas Alva Edison was reputed to have told a young reporter that his inventions were the result of 10 percent inspiration plus 90 percent perspiration. It is not likely that such a formula radically distorts the proportions used by the successful actor in building a role. All the preparation the actor undergoes, both in developing as an actor and in working on a specific role, is pointed to the moment when, on opening night, the house lights dim, the curtain rises, and the actor steps out before an audience. Before that moment arrives, the actor should have carefully evolved the characterization, worked out in detail all the business, learned the lines and movement of the play, and prepared carefully to present a character through hard work, tenacity, and imagination. There remain at this point a few vital considerations that must be taken into account before the actor faces the audience for the first time.

Rehearsal Guidelines

Paul Newman has observed that when he begins to rehearse he usually gets everything wrong. However, after rehearsals start, he finds that slowly but surely he gets rid of the "wrong things bit by bit" until he begins to feel secure and move more comfortably within the part. The rehearsal period is a time of great potential for creativity for the actor. Kevin Kline only asks during rehearsal that "At least let me find my way, find out what I have to say about this character and what this character means to me."[1] Laurence Olivier was never afraid to make a fool of himself during rehearsal, and in fact he ". . . tried things out extravagantly, way over the top . . . grasping the nettle early and making a fool of myself."[2]

> *It is an oft-stated belief that a rough final dress rehearsal means a good opening night.*
>
> Theatrical Superstition

As we know, the rehearsal period lays the groundwork for what the actor puts into the performance. One need not fear the situation reported by Michael Redgrave, who, while visiting Russia, came across an actor who had been rehearsing Hamlet for seven years and never played the role because the director had died *before* the production and rehearsal period were finished. It is admirable to be so dedicated to perfection, but the practical demands of the theatre require creativity, good management, and organization. Therefore some practical considerations are clearly necessary.

Knowing *how* to rehearse and how to get the maximum from the rehearsal process is important for all actors. The following suggestions constitute a minimum standard for the actor during rehearsals, from the standpoint of both attitude and procedure.

1. *Promptness:* The actor should be on time or early for every rehearsal call.
2. *Warming up:* The actor must take responsibility as an individual to be ready to rehearse. You must be prepared mentally and physically for creative work during the rehearsal period.
3. *Homework:* The actor must realize that work must be done also outside rehearsal hours in order to make the rehearsal as meaningful as possible.
   a. *Study your script.* Analyze your character. Understand the problems of your character in relation to other characters, or special problems that you have specifically in relation to the role.

---

1. Kevin Kline, quoted in Susan Shacter and Don Shewey, *Caught in the Act* (New York: New American Library, 1986), p. 31.
2. Laurence Olivier, *On Acting* (New York: Simon and Schuster, 1986), p. 156.

    b. *Review your work.* There should be a daily review of what happened during previous rehearsals. Review the blocking and other pertinent notes you have made during the rehearsal periods.

    c. Learn your lines and movement (blocking) as soon as possible—absolutely no later than the time when the director has called for them.

4. *Actor's Rights:* Respect the rights and privileges of your co-workers, including every member of the cast, the director, and the production staff. Work with discipline and energy. Concentrate. Distractions waste time and affect the work of fellow actors and the director. This lack of concentration during rehearsals will eventually show when the play is performed before an audience.

5. *Experiment:* Do not be afraid to try out new ideas, new bits of business, different ways of walking, talking, moving, reacting to your co-workers.

A Midsummer Night's Dream by William Shakespeare, in Elizabethan dress. National Theatre, London. Paul Scofield as Oberon. Photograph by Britain on View Photographic Library.

Don't always settle for your first choice. Keep working and changing until you and your director are satisfied you have "squeezed the orange dry."

The Three Vs of Good Acting

As the time approaches for the final dress rehearsal and the first performance, the good actor takes stock in order to determine whether his or her approach is fundamentally correct and whether the actor is going to realize the full potential of the role. One means of simplifying this period of self-scrutiny is to codify the most important elements into what we shall call the three Vs of good acting. The three Vs—vitality, variety, and validity—must be part of every performance, and when utilized properly they make for exciting and memorable theatre.

Vitality

Of all the factors generally considered essential to any good performance, vitality is the one most difficult to define precisely in terms of the theatre. Some actors refer to this quality as vivacity or intensity; some equate it with the energy expended during the performance; and others suggest that it is an intangible spark possessed by all good actors.

Two actors may approach a role in fundamentally the same manner, rehearse as intensively, and execute it in the same technical terms, yet one performance may be exciting and memorable and the other lifeless and dull. Vitality is probably the most meaningful word that may be found to describe the factor that makes the difference. Vitality has been defined in the dictionary as "vital power, *the ability to sustain life*" (the words italicized here are especially appropriate), and it would be difficult to find a better analysis of what the actor must do with a role before an audience. For the actor, vitality must mean the infusing of the character with the intensity we expect to find in any living thing. Paul Scofield affirms this most necessary component of good acting.

> Output in the theatre requires greater energy than anything else I know. Doubt of one's energy is the worst of all. One's output in the theatre requires energy of a sort that is never a factor in family life.[3]

---

3. Paul Scofield, quoted in Lillian Ross and Helen Ross, *The Player: A Profile of an Art* (New York: Simon and Schuster, 1962), p. 183.

Sometimes a particular stimulus may serve to make a performance exciting and vital. There is a well-known proverb in the theatre that a bad dress rehearsal means a good show. Unhappily, this is usually wishful thinking on the part of cast and director, serving to boost low morale, but we should not overlook an element of truth in the statement. Often a magic transformation takes place when the lights dim, the curtain rises, and the actor steps out before a live audience. Opening night often provides the catalyst to make an otherwise lackluster production intense and alive. For this reason also, many actors give their best performances on opening night. It is said that they are "up" for the performance. The creative juices and adrenalin are flowing.

The actor will usually feel more energy being used when performing before an opening-night audience than he or she had used during any of the rehearsals. The intelligent actor will channel this energy into the vitalization of the role. If one is conscientious, a high degree of energy should be expended during the rehearsal period as well. This will ease the number of adjustments necessary for the first performance.

This expenditure of energy places severe demands on all actors. A healthy body is a prime requisite for every performance, but frequently the beginning actor miscalculates the extent of these demands. The dissipation of the actor's energies in extraneous and unnecessary activities prior to performance may be unwise. The actor alone is the best judge of how to expend energy offstage and still bring to the role a full measure of vitality. Lynn Fontanne's comment that she slept fifteen hours after the opening of Eugene O'Neill's *Strange Interlude* is testimony to the toll of energy imposed on all conscientious actors.

A word of warning is in order here. Vitality must not be confused with loudness, exaggeration, or overemphasis. Such devices are far from the true meaning of vitality. One may think of vitality as the insatiable urge to communicate to an audience all that one has within oneself. If the actor has properly prepared the role and is then truly eager to share his or her concept of the role with the audience, the actor will have taken a solid step forward toward achieving the mysterious force in the theatre known as fire, spark, intensity, or *vitality*.

Variety

A common failing of beginning actors is repetitiousness. Variety in vocal expressiveness and business and in the handling of the body and movement is necessary in every role.

Shakespeare knew that audiences find it difficult to endure a long play that consists only of tragic events, no matter how brilliantly the play may be written and performed. It was primarily for this reason that he invested his great tragedies with many of his finest comic creations: the Nurse in *Romeo and Juliet*, Polonius and the gravediggers in *Hamlet*, the Porter in *Macbeth*, the Fool in *King Lear*, and so on. The tragic portions of the play are more clearly highlighted because of the moments of relief that the comic elements provide. (It is true that the Greeks utilized little comic relief in their tragedies, but their plays were comparatively short, and music and dance imparted the necessary variety.)

Another illustration may be even clearer. We all have dishes that appeal particularly to our palate. We may even look forward eagerly to the next opportunity to indulge our taste. A constant diet of the food, however, would cloy our appetite until we would probably react by pushing away in disgust the very food that had once so appealed to us.

Variety in acting is as necessary as in diet. Constant repetition of a style of phrasing and a piece of business or movement or the unvaried pacing of dialogue soon calls attention to itself. The brilliant piece of business and the deft reading of a line stand out because they are unique. Repeat the same piece of business, rely on the same inflections and pat reactions, and the performance becomes monotonous and dull.

In addition, memorable performances are made up of a series of little details, all chosen by fine actors to shed a little more light on the character. The choices the actor makes (and the good actor always is aware of the necessity of choice) are not only a matter of validity, as we shall see, but the pointing and mingling of those little details in the performance that give the characterization richness and variety. *Variety* is one of the most important considerations in bringing *balance* to a performance.

Validity

Although validity may simply be called truth or honesty, it most neatly sums up all the diverse responsibilities that the actor faces. Validity requires that the actor work honestly and believe in what he or she is doing with the role. Essentially these two ideas are one. Bruce Dern calls this element "reality, honesty, truth. You're saying real things to each other."[4] William Hurt has recalled the electric moment he felt watching Paul Scofield in a performance of a play by Pirandello. He recalled it as the best performance he had ever seen, due in part to the fact that "it was as if his thoughts came out of his body."[5]

As the actor appraises his or her work, honesty must be the touchstone for measuring accomplishment. The actor who resorts to tricks and old habits designed solely to achieve approval from the audience is guilty of bad acting.

---

4. Bruce Dern, quoted in Joanmarie Kalter, *Actors on Acting* (New York: Sterling, 1979), p. 185.

5. William Hurt, quoted in Shacter and Shewey, *Caught in the Act*, p. 110.

A beginning actor may be tempted to utilize a piece of business which he or she considers excellent even though it is not consistent with the character the actor is playing. When asked the reason for choosing that particular piece of business, the actor may seem shocked that someone would question such a clever idea. Sometimes the actor may resort to a trick as a feat of exhibitionism; sometimes the move is simply a miscalculation. No matter what the cause, any business, inflection, or movement that does not truly grow out of the characterization must be eliminated.

A young university actor, for example, cast in the role of a European nobleman of great charm and cultivation, had many opportunities to insert little pieces of business to help project the character's old-world sophistication. The young man sustained his role quite well until he came to the climactic moment. After a duel in which he had been wounded, he staggered across the stage and reached for a cup of wine on a nearby table. The young man seized the wine, gulped it down so rapidly that it was seen to run down his chin, and then wiped his face roughly on the sleeve of his uniform. It was an intense scene and an interesting piece of business calculated to excite the pity of the audience, but in that moment the illusion the actor had striven so hard to achieve during the entire performance was completely shattered. The action might have suited any number of other characters but could not have been part of the personality the actor had worked so hard to formulate. He had evidently hoped that he was projecting suffering, but instead he had permitted a jarring note to intrude itself upon the validity of his characterization. The scene certainly had vitality and it provided variety, but it lacked the third essential **V**, *validity*, to make it really good acting.

Katharine Cornell has commented directly on this point:

> In your mind, worked out with all the imagination and skill you possess, is the thing you want to do. When the performance comes, you must be intent only on that—on the sincerest, best thing that is in you. . . . Nothing else counts, certainly not whether the audience will like it. To try to please the front of the house is nothing short of ruinous.[6]

A spirit of responsibility to the role and to the production will help to eliminate any falseness from the actor's presentation. Self-awareness of a job done honestly and with integrity is more than enough justification for acting and will allow the actor to bring a spirit of truth to the role. Many famous actors have urged this point on their contemporaries and students. Raymond Massey has stated it bluntly: "Good actors, like good plays, are made of flesh and blood, not bundles of tricks."[7]

---

6. Quoted in Helen Ormsbee, *Backstage with Actors* (New York: Crowell, 1938), p. 237.
7. Raymond Massey, "Acting," in *The Theatre Handbook and Digest of Plays*, ed. Bernard Sobel (New York: Crown Publishers, 1948), p. 27.

> *The name George Spelvin has appeared in hundreds of the-*
> *atre programs across the land and yet there is no actor with*
> *such a name. It became a tradition to use the name in the*
> *program if someone was playing double roles or the name of*
> *whoever was playing the part was unknown at the time that*
> *the program went to press. It's a pseudonym for an unknown*
> *or unnamed actor. In Great Britain Walter Plinge plays the*
> *same role.*
>
> Theatrical Trivia

Concentration

The actor at work is constantly hampered by a number of distractions: the whispering of crew members backstage preparing for their next cue, coughs from the audience, and the stumbling of late-comers trying to find their seats. If the actor is affected by such distractions, his or her performance will suffer; it is necessary to accept them as a normal accompaniment to stage perfor- mance.

Concentration—or, rather, attention to the work at hand—is the most obvious means of dealing with such distractions. But no simple formula for concentration can be evolved that will be meaningful for all people. Everyone has known students who claim that they are able to study without difficulty with the radio, television, or stereo on at high volume and other students who are distracted by the slightest disturbance.

In the theatre, concentration is a much more complicated problem. Ac- tors have dealt with the problem of concentrating in many different ways, some amusing, some difficult, and some ultimately frustrating. Richard Burton struggled desperately to maintain his concentration during a perfor- mance of *Hamlet,* when, coming to Hamlet's famous "To be or not to be" so- liloquy, he heard a voice reciting the lines and saw to his chagrin that Winston Churchill was sitting in the first row reciting the lines along with him. Bur- ton's concentration was stretched to its uttermost. During a performance of *Equus,* Anthony Hopkins, in the very difficult role of the psychiatrist, was forced to stop when a large party of noisy theatregoers entered the theatre five minutes late and found their way to their seats. Hopkins apologized to the audience, indicating that he had lost the thread of his concentration, and started the play over from the beginning. John Hurt learned an odd lesson from Ralph Richardson when they were appearing together in a play. As they performed a scene together, a little dark nose and pink eyes popped out of Richardson's shirt, only to reappear at his cuff and disappear again. Hurt

Much Ado about Nothing by William Shakespeare. **Royal Shakespeare Company. Photograph by Britain on View Photographic Library.**

obviously wanted to know what the great but occasionally eccentric actor was up to. Richardson answered that the mouse forced him to not think about the one thing that he must not think about, himself. It forced him to concentrate on other aspects of the total performance. It is not suggested here that rodents are traditional ways of helping an actor's performance, but it does show us, as with the instances of Burton and Hopkins, how concentration is a vital and troublesome factor for fine actors dedicated to the best they can give to their character and the performance.

What do these interesting theatre experiences tell us? Simply trying to eliminate a distraction by an effort to ignore it is not likely to solve the actor's problem. Concentration for stage work does not mean ignoring undesirable disturbances but rather focusing attention in a different direction. We all have had the experience of laughing at an inopportune moment at some inconsequential remark or action and then trying to force ourselves to stop. The more we try to stop laughing by concentrating on the laughter itself, the more difficult it becomes, and we may continue to giggle for a long time. The best way to eliminate the laughter is to concentrate not on it but on some unrelated idea or object. This principle can be applied by the actor: It is possible to learn to eliminate unwarranted disturbances by attention to the role and to objects and actors on stage.

Attention to the Role.   The actor may concentrate entirely upon the performance, upon the execution of business, the reading of lines, and the maintenance of the character. This is usually helpful for the beginning actor with limited stage experience. The first few ventures on stage will be a novel experience, and it may prove extremely useful to concentrate attention on all the planned details of performance until the actor attains more assurance of his or her powers as an interpreter.

Attention to Objects and Actors.   Distractions may be ignored by concentrating on the other actors, their dialogues, business, and movement, or on some of the significant stage properties. At first such concentration may be difficult to achieve. It can be helpful to focus attention on an object on stage. Fingering a prop, rubbing the hand on the back of a chair or sofa, or feeling a table top may be perfectly consistent with the character and can prove to be a good starting point for concentration on the performance.

Whichever means the actor employs, it is imperative to concentrate at all times while on stage. When the actor's attention is diverted, the continuity of the performance is lost and may never be regained. Missing a beat in the pulse of the play may prove fatal.

Getting into the Role

Most beginning actors, and even many quite experienced ones, ponder the question of how involved they really should be, how much should they be "lost in their role?" A history of the controversy over this question has already been sketched in Chapter 2, and it may be helpful to refer to it again at this time. However, this review may seem rather academic and not directly related to the actor's own needs. It is all very well, one may say, to know that there is disagreement on this point, but what approach should *I* take in my work? Unfortunately no pat answer can be given, but it may be useful to anticipate some of the dangers of excess in either direction.

Excessive Emotionalism

Uncontrolled or uncoordinated emotion may be most harmful to a production. Two obvious dangers confront the actor who relies on the inspiration of the moment to bring forth the emotional fervor of a scene. Undoubtedly startling and thrilling effects may be produced during a performance when the actor is so inspired, but there is no guarantee of being able to rely on this "emotional seizure" night after night. In his study of Mrs. Leslie Carter, a turn-of-the-century actress who utilized this approach, Garff Wilson commented:

> Whenever she was able to throw herself into a state of semi-hysteria, she stirred and titillated her audiences; when the mood escaped her she failed to make an impression. Thus it followed that her early performances in any role were generally her best; the longer she played a part the more mechanical it became because, with each repetition she was less able to lose herself in the appropriate emotions.[8]

The second danger stemming from reliance on spur-of-the-moment emotionalism is the risk of destroying the coordinated work of the other actors in the production. It may be very well to startle and excite an audience by one's fervor, but if the other actors are startled also at a sudden, un-rehearsed outburst of passion, the production can only suffer. When Mrs. Carter was taken by emotional fervor, she would "weep, vociferate, shriek, rant, become hoarse with passion, and finally . . . flop and beat the floor."[9] You need only ask if you would wish to perform on stage with an actress given to such unpredictable outbursts. It is worth remembering how Burgess Meredith put the problem in perspective. Do not ". . . mislocate the center of emotions. [It] is right above the eyes."[10]

Lack of Emotionalism

The other side of the coin also poses some difficulties. Complete reliance on technical devices and artifice may produce a stilted and unexciting performance. Few responsible actors do not at least attempt to understand the nature of the emotion the character is supposed to feel. Even if they do not feel it themselves, they must still be able to make the audience believe that the character is feeling it. Some actors, however, remain so aloof from any penetration into the emotional context of a scene that the audience fails to believe any particle of the performance.

Reliance on technique alone has produced many fine performances, but it is usually a technique that is thoroughly refined. The best technique is one that deceives the viewer into thinking it does not exist. Too often the use of technique simply as a demonstration of the actor's adeptness implies, "Look how clever I am." The wheels are seen going around in the actor's head, and the audience is impressed at how well this person "acts" at acting. Such an

---

8. Garff B. Wilson, "Emotionalism in Acting," *Quarterly Journal of Speech* 42 (February 1955), p. 55.

9. William Winter, *The Wallet of Time* (New York: Moffat, Yard, 1913), vol. 2, p. 327.

10. Burgess Meredith, quoted in Ross and Ross, *The Player*, p. 123.

impression, however, is a condemnation of any performance. Another result of using technique without imagination is the conventional, stereotyped playing of all emotional scenes in the same key, which, as we have already noted, should be avoided. The important thing to remember is that it is not really important whether or not the actor feels the emotion but whether or not the audience *thinks* the actor does, in the guise of the character.

The James-Lange Theory

Before we leave this question of emotionalism in acting, it is important to note a psychological theory that has special implications for the actor. We tend to believe that our emotions trigger our physical responses, or that *passion is a cue for action.* In other words, we become frightened and we run; we become unhappy and we cry; we are happy and we laugh. The *James-Lange theory*[11] would reverse this sequence to imply that we are happy *because* we laugh, we are unhappy *because* we cry, and so on. We may see a wild beast and, because experience has trained us to avoid an encounter, we turn and run. Our fright does not come, according to the theory, before we run but is developed and exaggerated by our flight. The physiological reaction thus *follows* the physical action. James explained that, although this sequence might not be applicable in every case, he believed that emotion did follow "upon the bodily expression, in the coarser emotions."

There is now no general agreement in regard to this theory, although it was strongly supported many years ago. The actor should not miss its implications, however. In relation to acting, the theory suggests that if the actor can simulate laughter, he or she will feel happy; if the actor can tremble, he or she may become excited, and so on.

If this theory is correct, the actor does not need to wait to be "carried away" by inspiration in order to vitalize a performance; if the motor activity associated with an emotion can be reproduced correctly, the emotion itself will come. The imaginative, well-rehearsed actor will then be assured of having some emotional reaction during every performance. It may in part explain why the actor who feels "down" before a performance may still be able to work himself or herself into the role once the performance has started. There are many instances of actors preparing to go on stage and utilizing physical devices to bring on a quality of emotional truth. The English actor William Macready would spend minutes off stage, artificially working himself into a rage, cursing in a muffled voice and violently shaking a ladder leaning against a wall, before playing the storm scene in *King Lear.*

---

11. This theory was developed separately by C. H. Lange in 1885 and by William James (in *Principles of Psychology*) in 1890. The theory has been a matter of interest for many years, and during the 1980s many teachers of acting found uses for this technique.

Reliance on the James-Lange theory can be termed as working from the outside in, as opposed to the Stanislavski system, which strongly advocates working from the inside out.

The questions as to which approach is more useful for the actor's needs can be answered only by the individual. We have attempted to suggest some of the pitfalls that exist in the utilization of either extreme. A happy balance between emotion and technique, often termed the "warm heart and cool head" method, may be the most desirable compromise. Only experience will tell the actor which balance of values is most suitable for his or her personality and temperament.

Judging the Actor's Work

Judging Another Actor's Work

Often the actor's work and training involve the performance of scenes viewed by other actors who are equally involved in their own work. It is useful to watch the work of others in the laboratory and workshop. Watching others perform and evaluating their work has the obvious and immediate value of revealing the same types of problems and problem solving that each actor must also solve for himself or herself. The following guidelines are useful in helping to make a specific judgment of work seen either in a workshop scene or a play. Obviously these are questions that the actor can also apply to his or her own work.

> *One can't engage in conversation with actors without sooner or later hearing them comment on critics. They are caught up in a love/hate situation that can turn into feuds of a sort. A British playwright was overheard making this observation about the relationship, "Asking a working actor what he thinks about critics is like asking a lamp-post how it feels about dogs."*
>
> Theatrical Trivia

Checklist for Scene Work

Evaluating Other Actors' Work in Scenes

1. Did the scene look prepared?
2. Did the actors know *who* they were?
3. Did the actors know what their characters wanted in the scene?

Androcles and the Lion by Aurand Harris, California State University, Long Beach. Directed by Ken Rugg. Photograph by Coleman.

4. Did the actors interact with one another, or were they engrossed in their own work?
5. Did the actors "play off" one another, giving the work a feeling of spontaneity?
6. Did the actors use physical actions to lend credibility to their characters?
7. Were the actors physically "stiff" or did their actions seem natural?
8. Were the actors vocally "tight"?
9. Were the actors "suggesting" or "indicating" emotional states, or did they make the emotion seem real?
10. Was something real happening when the actor did not have any lines? Did the actor listen and react?
11. Did the actors give the scene "theatrical size," or were the actors "playing safe"?
12. Did you believe what you just watched?

Judging One's Own Work

Even more difficult than evaluating the work of another actor is the responsibility to evaluate honestly and objectively one's own work. It is true that such judgment is one of the primary duties of directors or acting coaches, but their comments can serve only as a guide for the actor. It is useful to seek out the advice of others, but not infrequently an actor may receive conflicting advice. The actor who grows and develops is one who is able to evaluate each performance as objectively as possible. Following is a set of standards that can be helpful in this self-analysis. Honest and considered answers to these questions will provide a useful framework for judging a performance, either in a complete play or a scene from a play.

The Total Concept

Action	1. Have I thoroughly analyzed the entire play, understanding the sequence of the action and the relation of each part to the other?
Theme	2. Do I understand what the playwright is trying to say in the play?
Organization	3. Can I relate my role to the total fabric of the play?
Style	4. Is my style of playing consistent with that used by the entire cast?

The Role Itself

Voice	1. Have I chosen the voice, manner of speech, tempo, and so on that are consistent with my character and that illuminate the character for the audience?
Business	2. Have I selected business and little actions that are consistent with my character and that illuminate the character for the audience?
Movement	3. Is my manner of movement consistent with the needs of the role?
Motivation	4. (a) Do I understand my character?
	(b) Do I know what my character *wants* and *why?*
	(c) Do I know what obstacles are in the way of my character's intentions?
	(d) Does my character relate to the other characters in the play (or scene)?
	(e) Am I always involved in the action regardless of how much dialogue my character has?

The Actor's Responsibilities

Imagination	1. Have I made full use of my imagination in formulating the characterization?
Clichés	2. Am I satisfied with superficial tricks and clichés, or have I taken the time to delve into all the subtleties of the role?

Three Vs:

Variety	3. Do I play the role with sufficient diversity to maintain the interest of the audience during an entire performance?
Vitality	4. Will I make every effort to communicate my character to the audience with all the energy necessary?
Validity	5. Is my characterization an honest portrait, consistent with my integrity as an actor?
Individuality	6. Does this characterization grow out of my own creative initiative?

All these questions are important, and any unsatisfactory answer should be the stimulus for more work and investigation.

One more question remains to be answered. It is not only a summation of all the questions the actor should ask but must be considered every day from the first rehearsal to the final performance.

Responsibility	7. At this time, is this the best job I am capable of doing?

If the answer to this last question is in the affirmative, the actor should await with great anticipation that moment when the stage manager announces: "Curtain going up."

Scenes

The Effect of Gamma Rays on Man-in-the-Moon Marigolds, by Paul Zindel
From Act II, Scene 1

Scene:	For two women
Characters:	RUTH, a young student
	TILLIE, a student
Setting:	A living space that was once a vegetable store
Time:	The present
Situation:	Tillie, through the course of events in the first half of the play, has become a finalist at the school Science Fair. She, her older sister Ruth, and her mother are getting ready to go to the final presentation at the school auditorium. In the room is Peter the rabbit in a cage.

TILLIE: Are you going to wear that sweater?

RUTH: (*She crosses* U. *of the card table, to the* R. *of* TILLIE.) Look, don't worry about me. I'm not getting up on any stage and if I did I wouldn't be caught dead with a horrible bow like that. (*She reaches for the bow and* TILLIE *protects it.*)

TILLIE: Mother put it . . . (TILLIE *crosses to* D. *of the card table,* RUTH *follows.*)

RUTH: They're going to laugh you right off that stage again like when you cranked that atom in assembly. (*Pause.*) I didn't mean that. (TILLIE *crosses* D. *of* RUTH, *to the* R. *of the kitchen table.*) The one they're going to laugh at is Mama.

TILLIE: What?

RUTH: I said the one they're going to laugh at is Mama. (*She crosses to the* R. *of* TILLIE.) Oh, let me take that bow off.

TILLIE: It's all right. . . .

RUTH: (*Pushing* TILLIE *into the chair* R. *of the table.*) Look, just sit still. I don't want everybody laughing at you. (*She crosses to* U. *of* TILLIE, *takes the bow out of her hair and puts it on the table. She fixes* TILLIE'S *hair.*)

TILLIE: (*Pause.*) What made you say that about Mama?

RUTH: Oh, I heard them talking in the Science Office yesterday. Mr. Goodman and Miss Hanley. She's getting twelve sixty-three to chaperone the thing tonight.

TILLIE: What were they saying?

RUTH: Miss Hanley was telling Mr. Goodman about Mama . . . when she found out you were one of the top five winners. And he wanted to know if there was something wrong with Mama because she sounded crazy over the phone. And Miss Hanley said she *was* crazy and she always has been crazy and she can't wait to see what she looks like after all these years. Miss Hanley said her nickname used to be Betty the Loon.

TILLIE: (*As* RUTH *brushes her hair, brusquely.*) Ruth, you're hurting me.

RUTH: She was just like you and everybody thought she was a big weirdo. (*She finishes the hair, steps to the* L. *of* TILLIE, *turns* TILLIE'S *head and inspects the job.*) There! You look much better! (*She crosses to* U. *of the card table, to the rabbit.*) If anybody stuck you in a pot of boiling water I'd kill them, do you know that? (*To* TILLIE. TILLIE *sticks a label into each pot.*) What do they call boiling the skin off a cat? I call it murder, that's what I call it. They say it was hit by a car and Janice just scooped it up and before you could say *bingo* it was screaming in a pot of boiling water. (*She crosses to the* R. *of* TILLIE.) Do you know what they're all waiting to see? Mama's feathers! (TILLIE *looks to* RUTH.) That's what Miss Hanley said. She said Mama blabs as though she was the Queen of England and just as proper as can be and that her idea of getting dressed up is to put on all the feathers in the world and go as a bird. (*She crosses to the bottom of the stairs.*) Always trying to get somewhere like a great big bird.

TILLIE: (*Rises.*) Don't tell Mama, please. It doesn't matter.

RUTH: I was up there watching her getting ready and sure enough she's got the feathers out.

TILLIE: (*She crosses to* D. *of the kitchen table.*) You didn't tell her what Miss Hanley said?

RUTH: Are you kidding? I just told her I really didn't like the feathers and I didn't think she should wear any. But I'll bet she doesn't listen to me.

TILLIE: It doesn't matter.

RUTH: It doesn't matter? Do you think I want to be laughed right out of the school tonight with Chris Burns there and all? (*She crosses to the* R. *of the card table.*) Laughed right out of the school with your spaghetti hair and her feathers on that stage, and Miss Hanley just splitting her sides.

TILLIE: (*She crosses to the* L. *of the card table.*) Promise me you won't say anything.

RUTH: On one condition.

TILLIE: What?

RUTH: Give Peter to me.

TILLIE: (*Pause, and then she crosses to the sink, picks up the shopping bag, puts it on the chair* R. *of the kitchen table.*) The taxi will be here any minute and I won't have all this stuff ready. (*She crosses* U. C., *pushes the sofa unit from in front of the small table to match the unit facing the shelves and bins. She looks in the drawer of the small table.*) Did you see my speech?

RUTH: (*She crosses to the* R. *of* TILLIE.) I mean it. Give Peter to me.

TILLIE: He belongs to all of us. (*She crosses* D. R. *to the table* U. *of Nanny's door, looks through books on top of the table.* RUTH *follows after her.*)

RUTH: For me. All for me. What do you care? He doesn't mean anything to you anymore now that you've got all those crazy plants.

TILLIE: (*She crosses to* D. *of the card table.* RUTH *follows and grabs* TILLIE'S *arm.*) Will you stop?

RUTH: If you don't give him to me I'm going to tell Mama that everybody's waiting to laugh at her.

TILLIE: (*Crosses to* U. *of the card table, looks under the colored paper, picks up the cage, looking for her speech.*) Where are those typewritten cards?

RUTH: (*Holding on to the cage with* TILLIE.) I MEAN IT! Give him to me!

TILLIE: Does he mean that much to you?

RUTH: Yes!

TILLIE: All right. . . . (*Releases the cage to* RUTH. TILLIE *picks up the speech which was under the cage, crosses to the* L. *of the card table, and sits.* RUTH *puts the cage on the floor* D. *of the card table, sits* R. *of the table and takes the rabbit out.*)

RUTH: (*She laughs.*) Betty the Loon . . . (*She laughs again.*) That's what they used to call her, you know. Betty the Loon!

TILLIE: I don't think that's very nice.

RUTH: First they had Betty the Loon and now they've got Tillie the Loon. (TILLIE *rises, crosses* U. C. *to the window ledge. To the rabbit.*) You don't have to worry about me turning you in for any old plants. (*Pause.*) How much does a taxi cost from here to the school?

TILLIE: Not much. . . . (*She puts her coat on, crosses to the door, looks through the glass for the taxi.*)

RUTH: (*Rises, crosses* U. *of the card table to* U. *of the chair,* R. *of the kitchen table.*) I wish she'd give me the money it cost for a taxi and all that cardboard and paint and flower pots and stuff. (*She crosses to the sofa units, leans against the back of the* D. *unit, still holding the rabbit.*) The only time she ever made a fuss over me was when she drove me nuts.

TILLIE: (*She crosses to the chair* R. *of the kitchen table, gets the shopping bag, crosses to the front door, and leaves the bag,* L. *of the door.*) Tell her to hurry, please.

RUTH: By the way, I went over to see Janice Vickery's pot that she did you know what in and I started telling her and her mother about the worms in Mr. Alexander Brougham's legs and I got thrown out because it was too near dinnertime. That Mrs. Vickery kills me. She can't stand worms in somebody else's legs but she lets her daughter cook a cat.

Lettice and Lovage, by Peter Shaffer
From Act III

Scene:	For two women
Characters:	LOTTE (Charlotte Schoen)
	LETTICE (Lettice Douffet)
Setting:	Miss Douffet's basement flat, London
Time:	Early evening
Situation:	Lettice and Lotte have, as it were, bonded by sharing secrets and their histories. They then began to enact scenes of historical executions. In all cases Lettice was the one to be executed, and then one particular day Lotte expressed a desire to be Charles I at his execution. In the playing, Lettice was holding the "axe" facsimile and there was an accident involving a pet cat. This was followed by a misunderstanding, which up to this point has been cleared up, almost. In the scene that follows, there is a serious attempt at reconciliation.

LOTTE: (*Sharply.*) Let me in!

LETTICE: No . . .

LOTTE: Do you hear me? Let me in at once! . . . *Open it. Lettice!* . . . (*Shouting.*) *Press the damn thing!*

(LETTICE *presses the button and moves miserably back into the room, collapsing on the gold chair.*

The front door opens above and slams. LOTTE *storms down the stairs in outrage.*

She turns on the light at the bottom, making LETTICE *shrink in its glare.*)

LOTTE: *How dare you?* . . . That's disgusting! . . . Snivelling, feeble, whining rubbish! . . . That's not *you!* . . . *I won't have it! I won't stand for it—do you hear?!* . . . How *can* you? . . . You're *Lettice!*

(LETTICE *turns away, hiding her head from the onslaught.*)

LOTTE: All right—I hated the job! You're right: I admit it! I'm glad to be done with it—all right! That doesn't mean I'm going to spend the rest of my life hiding in the Past! . . . Are you listening?

LETTICE: (*Not looking at her.*) I don't hide.

LOTTE: Of course you do! You're worse than those women in my office! (*"Refined" voice.*) "Oh dear! Oh dear, dear, dear!—this horrid nasty *Present!*" . . . (*Hard.*) The Past was just as nasty as we are! Just as stupid! Just as greedy and brutal!

LETTICE: No!

LOTTE: Worse! For most people it was far worse! Cruel and sordid! Far more painful and far more unjust!

LETTICE: (*Hotly.*) At least it was *beautiful!* You said that yourself! "It gets uglier every minute!" You said!

LOTTE: So it does!

LETTICE: So why *shouldn't* I hide? It's hideous here! Everywhere! . . . Hideous and hateful!

LOTTE: Then do something about it! *Fight it! Attack it!* . . . Show some *spunk,* for God's sake! Don't just stay cringing in a basement, playing stupid games!

LETTICE: (*Desperate.*) Well what can I *do!?* . . . What can *you* do?—or anyone? . . . *Look at us!*

LOTTE: I am looking . . . We are two able, intelligent women. I am an experienced Organizer of Tours. You are . . . (*Reflectively.*) the most original Tour Guide. That must suggest something.

LETTICE: What?

LOTTE: We're a combination! We could work together.

LETTICE: What do you *mean?* How? . . . How?

LOTTE: (*Growing excited.*) I have it! Look—do you remember E.N.D.? The Eyesore Negation Detachment?

(LETTICE *nods.*)

LOTTE: Well, what if we revived it?—in another form! Not bombs—*Tours!* . . . Why don't we start our own Firm—*E.N.D. Tours*—dedicated to showing people *the fifty ugliest new buildings in London!* . . . How about that? . . . I can provide the architectural information—you can speak it in your own inimitable way! . . . You lit up the Past with a blazing torch, people said—well now light up the Present! Reveal the ugliness for what it is!

LETTICE: Oh Lotte!

LOTTE: I could advertise everywhere! Send leaflets into every Travel Agency in Britain—why not? No-one will have seen anything like it! (*Theatrically.*) "E.N.D. Tours Presents Lettice Douffet's Dramatic Guide to Disgusting Buildings! . . . Hear her Devastating Denunciations of Modern Design! Before your very eyes she will show you how Beauty has been murdered—and by whom! Exactly which Architects, Builders, Engineers and City Planners! See her point the finger! Hear her name the names!"

LETTICE: Oh, that's *marvellous!*

LOTTE: It could work!

LETTICE: (*Transported.*) It's tremendous! It's the single most *theatrical* idea I ever heard! (*She rises.*) Let's imagine it—how it could go! . . . We are in some vast, horrible office building, surrounded by a huge group of Tourists—hanging on my every word! . . . Let's see! . . . (*Gleefully she addresses her imaginary audience.*) You are standing now in the Main Hall of . . . Computex House—

LOTTE: Splendid!—"Computex"!

LETTICE: Constructed in nineteen-eighty out of British concrete. Observe the cracks, splits and damp-stains, typical of the period.

(LOTTE *laughs.*)

LETTICE: The obvious intention of this building is to resemble as much as possible a Top Security Prison. Note the thousand metal-framed windows—not one of which can be opened.

LOTTE: Made out of tinted solar glass—that's its name.

LETTICE: Substituting for the ghastly glare of sunshine the glorious glow of fluorescence!

LOTTE: Excellent!

Uncommon Women and Others, by Wendy Wasserstein
From Act II, Scene 3

Scene:	For two women
Characters:	LEILAH
	MUFFET (Muffet Di Nicola)
Setting:	A college for women
Time:	Back and forth between the present and six years earlier
Situation:	An episodic flashback piece about young career women remembering how their lives at college affected their futures.

LEILAH: (MUFFET *is putting on make-up.* LEILAH *enters carrying a chocolate bunny.*) Muffy, this package just came for you.

MUFFET: What is this? "For my Muffet. I can't bluff it. An Easter Bunny for my pixie honey."

LEILAH: Is that from Susie Friend?

MUFFET: Christ no! It's from her father. Look, it's signed—Lovens, E. Courtland "Kippy" Friend. He was behind me in the bunny hop at the Father–Daughter weekend. Leilah, do you think I should plan to marry Kippy Friend? It's two months before graduation and I still don't know what I'm going to do next year. But I am prepared for life. I can fold my napkin with the best of them. Leilah, do you want this? I'll give it to Holly, she'll eat it.

LEILAH: I asked my father not to come up this year. Actually, my freshman year he came to Father–Daughter weekend and kept dancing with Katie and telling me how lucky I was to have such a good friend. Kate told him I was the prettiest and the brightest girl here. Ever since then, I make it a point to be busy doing research every Father–Daughter weekend. (*Throws down books.*) Oh, I can't wait to get out of here. I've booked a flight to Iraq for the day after graduation.

MUFFET: Really, Leilah, that's odd. You're very odd.

LEILAH: I won a fellowship.

MUFFET: Pink Pants is leaving right after graduation also. Lei, if he calls would you tell him I went away for the weekend? We had another fight yesterday.

LEILAH: What happened?

MUFFET: Nothing. He told me that next year he wants to work his way around the world on a freighter. I tried to appear like "sure," "that's fine," "Have a nice trip," "send a postcard." I don't understand why when Samantha meets someone suddenly she's pinned and when I want someone they tell me I'm being clutchy and putting too much pressure on them. I don't want any commitment. I like being alone.

LEILAH: Me too.

MUFFET: Leilah, where do women meet men after college? Does Merrill Lynch have mixers with Time Life staffers at the General Foods Media department?

LEILAH: I don't know who I'll meet in Iraq. I like that. Katie says I'm escaping. I think I just need to be in a less competitive culture.

MUFFET: Why does Katie bother you so much?

LEILAH: Excuse me?

MUFFET: I can't understand why Katie bothers you so much.

LEILAH: She doesn't. I like Katie. She's exceptional.

MUFFET: Katie has no hips.

LEILAH: It could be Social Darwinism. Katie could simply be a superior creature.

MUFFET: Pink Pants says you're prettier than Katie.

LEILAH: Sometimes when I'm in the library studying, I look up and I count the Katies and the Leilahs. They're always together. And they seem a very similar species. But if you observe a while longer the Katies seem kind of magical, and the Leilahs are highly competent. And they're usually such good friends—really the best. But I find myself secretly hoping that when we leave here Katie and I will just naturally stop speaking. There's something . . . (LEILAH *begins to cry.*) It's not Katie's fault! Sometimes I wonder if it's normal for a twenty-year-old woman to be so constantly aware of another woman . . . "Thoughts of a dry brain in a dry season."

MUFFET: (*Suddenly concerned for* LEILAH.) Mrs. Plumm thinks about Ada Grudder often.

LEILAH: If we did stop speaking she wouldn't even notice, or if she did, she'd just think she wasn't a good person for a day. I just want to get out of here so I'm not with people who know me in terms of her.

MUFFET: Leilah, why don't you come out with me tonight? I've always wanted to do this. We can go to a bar, not sleazy but also not a place where two nice girls usually go. And we'll sit alone, just you and I, with our two Brandy Alexanders and we won't need any outside attention. We'll be two uncommon women, mysterious but proud. (MUFFET *puts her arm around* LEILAH.)

LEILAH: All right. I'd like that.

MUFFET: (*Honestly.*) Leilah, I do understand a little. It's debilitating constantly seeing your worth in terms of someone else.

VOICE: Male L.D. for Muffet DiNocola. Muffet DiNocola, Male L.D.

LEILAH: I'll take it for you Muffy.

MUFFET: (*Pauses and then gets her coat.*) No, it's got to be Old Pink Pants. Would you sign an overnight slip for me? See, Leilah, I know myself and as soon as the phone rings, I'm just fine.

(MUFFET *leaves with her coat.* LEILAH *is left alone in the room holding the chocolate bunny.*)

END SCENE

And Miss Reardon Drinks a Little, by Paul Zindel
From Act III

Scene:	For three women
Characters:	CEIL (Ceil Adams)
	ANNA (Anna Reardon)
	CATHERINE (Catherine Reardon)
	(Three middle-aged sisters)
Setting:	The living room and dining area of the comfortable apartment of Catherine and Anna Reardon
Time:	An October evening
Situation:	Seven months after their mother's death, Anna, a teacher who lives with her sister Catherine, has had a nervous breakdown in class. Ceil, the third sister, who works at the Board of Education, has come for a "visit" and to observe Anna. Catherine "drinks a little," and Anna is exhibiting some very eccentric behavior. The spinster sisters have become an embarassment to Ceil, and she has plans to have Anna put in a home.

CEIL: (*Rises.*) Anna, go to your room and lie down.

ANNA: Go to your own room!

CEIL: (*To* CATHERINE.) Tell her to leave us alone.

CATHERINE: Now, sis, it is a bit tardy for disciplinary procedures.

CEIL: Catherine . . .

ANNA: Oh, Ceil . . . can't you remember all the fun when we were just getting started as teachers? How we'd all come running home at three o'clock and Mama'd have the water boiling and some kind of pie made with Flako pie crust mix? and Mama'd be dying to know what happened in school all day and we'd be dying to tell her—and we'd sit around this same table and almost pass out laughing? We'd tell Mama what was going on in the schools

and she wouldn't believe it. She'd say the whole world was going crazy. Remember when I told her about little Gracie Ratinski, that nutty kid with bugs
in her hair at Jefferson who used to come into the cafeteria and sing her
lunch order out at the top of her lungs? (CATHERINE *begins to laugh.*) GIVE ME
A PEANUT BUTTER SANDWICH, TRA LA. GIVE ME A PEANUT BUTTER
SANDWICH, TRA LA. Don't you remember that? Don't you?

CATHERINE: (*Laughing harder, joining* ANNA *at the table.*) I remember. I remember, all right. And remember how much Mama laughed when I told her
about Rose Anadale the principal at P.S. 26 who kept the parakeet in her office . . .

ANNA: She used to talk about it on the P.A. system every morning after the
Star Spangled Banner . . .

CATHERINE: (*Howling with* ANNA.) She'd announce to the whole school, remember—GOOD MORNING, CHILDREN . . . GOOD MORNING, CHIL-
DREN . . . LITTLE POLLY AND I HOPE YOU HAVE A WONDERFUL DAY.

ANNA: (*To* CEIL.) Don't you miss telling Mama those stories? Don't you miss it?

CEIL: (*To Catherine.*) Tell her to leave us alone.

CATHERINE: Look, Ceil, it's late—you probably have to get up early tomorrow
and appoint a committee to study the salient factors of something or other . . .

CEIL: If that's the way you want it. (*She goes for her briefcase.*) I've made arrange-
ments . . .

CATHERINE: (*Starting to clear the table.*) You don't say. They are floral, aren't
they?

CEIL: She's going to a hospital.

CATHERINE: No kidding. Far away? Tudor or Swiss? Mountains and view of
lake?

CEIL: (*Taking legal papers from the briefcase.*) It's only a two hour drive from
here.

CATHERINE: No, don't tell me the best feature. It's state supported.

CEIL: (*Ordering.*) All you have to do is get her packed.

ANNA: She's the one who needs a rest, Catherine.

CEIL: (*Moving in with the papers.*) You're going to have to look at these, Catherine.

CATHERINE: (*Slamming a tray down on the buffet making a deafening noise. Then
calmly:*) Don't tell me what I have to do. (*A long silence. Finally:*)

ANNA: Ceil, didn't you ever love us? Mama? Any of us?

CEIL: Our lives are not around this table anymore. (*She moves away from the
table.*)

ANNA: Oh—I must have forgotten. This is all dead now, isn't it? Silent. The
voices gone. Even the whispering forgotten: "Straighten up . . . careful your
slip isn't showing . . . skirt down . . . knees close together. Be careful if someone sits next to you . . . or across the way . . . beware of your eyes . . . he
mustn't think you're looking at him. Even when you're . . . bleeding . . . he'll
know . . . he'll try to find a way to force you apart . . . he'll want to hurt
you . . . crush you . . . cut into you . . ." (ANNA *rises—goes towards the bedroom
hallway.*) And the sounds—you must have forgotten the sounds in the dark
of our rooms . . . the quieting of the wounds by which we could be tracked.
(ANNA *reaches out to touch* CEIL.)

CEIL: Get your hands off me. (*Getting away from* ANNA *and taking a seat at the table.*)

ANNA: Tell me, Ceil, when you're in bed—what does Edward manage to do? Does he actually get on top of you—mount you—and ride you like some blubbering old nag? (*In the middle of* ANNA'S *verbal assault,* CEIL *reaches for the Fanny Farmer box which falls from her hands. At* ANNA'S *last word she picks up the spilled meat and shoves it into* ANNA'S *face.* ANNA *falls to her knees, senses the meat, and screams. She exits.* CATHERINE *goes after* ANNA.)

CEIL: She can wash herself.

CATHERINE: Get out of my way.

CEIL: How the hell much longer did you think you could go on keeping her here?

CATHERINE: As long as I want, that's how long.

CEIL: Why? So you won't be alone? After all the filth and wisecracks are scraped off is that what's underneath? How pathetic you are!

CATHERINE: (*Ringing buffet bell.*) School's over. Everybody's dismissed. (CEIL *yanks the bell out of* CATHERINE'S *hand.*)

CEIL: Don't you think I need anything?

CATHERINE: I thought you always took everything you needed?

CEIL: Anything I did you made me do from the years of gnawing at me—you and her and Mama. The whole pack of you. For what? What was it you hated so much?

CATHERINE: (*Exploding.*) I'll tell you what and I'll tell you when! You see, there was this big hole in the ground with you on one side of it and me on the other—and we were watching them stick a coffin in the ground. But as it was going down I had to shut my eyes because I'll tell you all I could see: I saw you with a lawyer making sure the few bucks of a croaking old lady was transferred to your name. And I was admiring a casket you picked out that wouldn't waste a second getting her corpse back to ashes. And I remember when that imperfect gasping woman was dying how you made certain you didn't have to touch a penny in your bank account. (*She sits at the desk.*)

CEIL: That's not what you hated me for *all* your life! Anything you didn't like you could have done differently. Anything! You're not going to blame me for that or anything about your sick little life. You didn't have to follow me—let me do everything. I didn't bend anybody's arm. You could have lived your own lives you know. You didn't have to feed on me all the time!

CATHERINE: Get out of here.

CEIL: What is it deep down in your gut you so detest about me? That I haven't gone mad or become an obscene nasty witness? That's what you are, Catherine. (*There is a long pause. Then:*)

CATHERINE: You know, Ceil—the way you said that—I mean, you're louder and crueller—but there's a part of you that's just like Mama. I think that's the part of you I've always despised. (CEIL *gets her coat from the closet and gathers up the papers, the gun and the album.*)

CEIL: I'll call you in the morning.

CATHERINE: (*Pouring a drink.*) Not in the morning, if you don't mind. You see, Miss Reardon drinks a little and she'll be sleeping off a colossal load.

CEIL: (*Throws album, gloves and papers to the floor.*) Here! Here's everything. I'm not going to let you pin the rap on me or Mama or anybody anymore. Now it's up to you. For once in your life you pick up the pieces however the hell you want. But no matter what you do, let me tell you this—you're not going to drag me down. Not at this stage of the game, my sweet sisters. Not at this stage of the game. (CEIL *exits leaving* CATHERINE *sitting at the desk.* ANNA *enters.*)

Boys in the Band, by Mart Crowley
From Act I

Scene:	For two men
Characters:	ALAN
	MICHAEL
Setting:	A smartly appointed New York apartment
Time:	The present
Situation:	A group of gay men are arriving at Michael's apartment in New York to celebrate Harold's birthday when Alan, an old friend of Michael's, arrives in town and wants to see him. Several of the guests arrive, and Michael is concerned that they will expose his lifestyle to his old friend, Alan, who may not handle it well. Alan calls and says he is not coming. Michael is a bit relieved, and then Alan shows up unexpectedly.

ALAN: (*To* MICHAEL.) This is a marvelous apartment.

MICHAEL: It's too expensive. I work to pay rent.

ALAN: What are you doing these days?

MICHAEL: Nothing.

ALAN: Aren't you writing any more?

MICHAEL: I haven't looked at a typewriter since I sold the very very wonderful, very very marvelous *screenplay* which never got produced.

ALAN: (*Crosses to* MICHAEL.) That's right, the last time I saw you, you were on your way to California. Or was it Europe?

MICHAEL: Hollywood. Which is not in Europe nor does it have anything whatsoever to do with California.

ALAN: (*Crosses to pillar.*) I've never been there but I would imagine it's awful. Everyone must be terribly cheap.

MICHAEL: No, not everyone. Alan, I want to try to explain this evening . . .

ALAN: What's there to explain? (*Crosses to chair.*) Sometimes you just can't invite everybody to every party and some people take it personally. But I'm not one of them. I should apologize for inviting myself.

MICHAEL: (*Sits bench.*) That's not exactly what I meant.

ALAN: Your friends all seem like very nice guys. That Hank is really a very attractive fellow.

MICHAEL: . . . Yes. He is.

ALAN: We have a lot in common. What's his roommate's name?

MICHAEL: Larry.

ALAN: . . . What does *he* do?

MICHAEL: He's a commercial artist.

ALAN: I liked Donald too. The only one I didn't care too much for was—what's his name—Emory?

MICHAEL: Yes. Emory.

ALAN: (*Puts drink on Upstage table.*) I just can't stand that kind of talk. It just grates on me.

MICHAEL: What kind of talk, Alan?

ALAN: (*Crosses to* MICHAEL.) Oh, you know. His brand of humor, I guess.

MICHAEL: He can be really quite funny sometimes.

ALAN: I suppose so. If you find that sort of thing amusing. He just seems like such a goddamn little pansy. (*Silence. A pause. He steps away.*) I'm sorry I said that. I didn't mean to say that. That's such an awful thing to say about *any- one.* But you know what I mean, Michael—you have to admit he *is* effemi- nate.

MICHAEL: He is a bit.

ALAN: A bit! He's like a . . . a butterfly in heat! I mean there's no wonder he was trying to teach you all a dance. He *probably* wanted to dance *with* you! (*Crosses to* MICHAEL.) Oh, come on, man, you know me—you know how I feel—your private life is your own affair. (*Sits bed chair.*)

MICHAEL: (*Icy.*) No. I *don't* know that-about-you.

ALAN: I couldn't care less what people do—as long as they don't do it in pub- lic—or—or try to force their ways on the whole damned world.

MICHAEL: Alan, what was it you were crying about on the telephone?

ALAN: Oh, I feel like such a fool about that. I could shoot myself for letting my- self act that way. I'm so embarrassed I could die.

MICHAEL: But Alan, if you were genuinely upset—that's nothing to be embar- rassed about.

ALAN: All I can say is—please accept my apology for making such an ass of myself.

MICHAEL: You must have been upset or you wouldn't have said you were and that you wanted to see me—*had* to see me and had to talk to me.

ALAN: Can you forget it? Just pretend it never happened. I know *I* have. Okay?

MICHAEL: Is something wrong between you and Fran?

ALAN: Listen, I've really got to go. (*Rises and crosses Left of* MICHAEL.)

MICHAEL: (*Rises, counters Right to chair.*) Why are you in New York?

ALAN: I'm dreadfully late for dinner.

MICHAEL: *Whose* dinner? Where are you going?

ALAN: Is this the loo?

MICHAEL: Yes.

ALAN: Excuse me. (*He quickly goes into the bathroom.*)

Beyond Therapy, by Christopher Durang
From Act I, Scene 1

Scene: For one man, one woman
Characters: PRUDENCE
                BRUCE

Setting: A restaurant
Time: The present
Situation: Bruce and Prudence meet at a restaurant in response to personal ads in a
              newspaper.

(*A restaurant.* Bruce *is seated, looking at his watch. He* is 30–34, *fairly pleasant look-ing, probably wearing a blazer. Enter* Prudence, 29–32, *attractive, semi-dressed up in a dress or nice skirt and blouse. After hesitating a moment,* she *crosses to* Bruce)

PRUDENCE: Hello.

BRUCE: Hello.

PRUDENCE: (*Perhaps referring to a newspaper in her hand*—The New York Review of Books?) Are you the white male, 30 to 35, 6'1", blue eyes, who's into rock music, movies, jogging and quiet evenings at home?

BRUCE: Yes, I am.

(*Stands*)

PRUDENCE: Hi, I'm Prudence.

BRUCE: I'm Bruce.

PRUDENCE: Nice to meet you.

BRUCE: Won't you sit down?

PRUDENCE: Thank you. (*Sits*) As I said in my letter, I've never answered one of these ads before.

BRUCE: Me neither. I mean, I haven't put one in before.

PRUDENCE: But this time I figured, why not?

BRUCE: Right. Me too. (*Pause*) I hope I'm not too macho for you.

PRUDENCE: No. So far you seem wonderful.

BRUCE: You have lovely breasts. That's the first thing I notice in a woman.

PRUDENCE: Thank you.

BRUCE: You have beautiful contact lenses.

PRUDENCE: Thank you. I like the timbre of your voice. Soft but firm.

BRUCE: Thanks. I like *your* voice.

PRUDENCE: Thank you. I love the smell of Brut you're wearing.

BRUCE: Thank you. My male lover Bob gave it to me.

PRUDENCE: What?

BRUCE: You remind me of him in a certain light.

PRUDENCE: What?

BRUCE: I swing both ways actually. Do you?

PRUDENCE: I don't know. I always insist on the lights being out.

(*Pause*)

BRUCE: I'm afraid I've upset you now.

PRUDENCE: No, it's nothing really. It's just that I hate gay people.

BRUCE: I'm not gay. I'm bisexual. There's a difference.

PRUDENCE: I don't really know any bisexuals.

BRUCE: Children are all innately bisexual, you know. If you brought a child to Plato's Retreat, he'd be attracted to both sexes.

PRUDENCE: I should imagine he'd be terrified.

BRUCE: Well, he might be, of course. I've never taken a child to Plato's Retreat.

PRUDENCE: I don't think they let you.

BRUCE: I don't really know any children. (*Pause*) You have wonderful eyes. They're so deep.

PRUDENCE: Thank you.

BRUCE: I feel like I want to take care of you.

PRUDENCE: (*Liking this tack better*) I would like that. My favorite song is "Someone to Watch Over Me."

BRUCE: (*Sings softly*) "There's a somebody I'm longing duh duh . . ."

PRUDENCE: Yes. Thank you.

BRUCE: In some ways you're like a little girl. And in some ways you're like a woman.

PRUDENCE: How am I like a woman?

BRUCE: (*Searching, romantically*) You . . . dress like a woman. You wear eye shadow like a woman.

PRUDENCE: You're like a man. You're tall, you have to shave. I feel you could protect me.

BRUCE: I'm deeply emotional. I like to cry.

PRUDENCE: Oh I wouldn't like that.

BRUCE: But I *like* to cry.

PRUDENCE: I don't think men should cry unless something falls on them.

BRUCE: That's a kind of sexism. Men have been programmed not to show feeling.

PRUDENCE: Don't talk to me about sexism. You're the one who talked about my breasts the minute I sat down.

BRUCE: I feel like I'm going to cry now.

PRUDENCE: Why do you want to cry?

BRUCE: I feel you don't like me enough. I think you're making eyes at the waiter.

PRUDENCE: I haven't even seen the waiter.

(BRUCE *cries*)

PRUDENCE: *Please,* people are staring at us. They'll think it's something I said.

BRUCE: (*Stops crying after a bit*) I feel better after that. You have a lovely mouth.

PRUDENCE: Thank you.

BRUCE: I can tell you're very sensitive. I want you to have my children.

PRUDENCE: Thank you.

BRUCE: Do you feel ready to make a commitment?

PRUDENCE: I feel I need to get to know you better.

The Little Foxes, by Lillian Hellman
From Act III

Scene:	For two women
Characters:	REGINA GIDDENS, an avaricious and shrewd woman
	ALEXANDRA, her attractive daughter
	(The one line by ADDIE may be cut)
Setting:	The Giddens's living room. A small town in the deep South.
Time:	The turn of the twentieth century.

Situation: Regina's husband, Horace, has just died of a heart attack, not without a little prodding from Regina. She is anxious to get hold of his securities, which will permit her to leave her provincial surroundings and, if invested properly, to live in the populous and socially attractive North. Regina's daughter, Alexandra, is well aware of her mother's intentions and has become increasingly suspicious of the circumstances that led to the death of her father.

REGINA: (*Sits quietly for a second, stretches, turns to look at* ALEXANDRA) What do you want to talk to me about, Alexandra?

ALEXANDRA: (*Slowly*) I've changed my mind. I don't want to talk. There's nothing to talk about now.

REGINA: You're acting very strange. Not like yourself. You've had a bad shock today. I know that. And you loved Papa, but you must have expected this to come some day. You knew how sick he was.

ALEXANDRA: I knew. We all knew.

REGINA: It will be good for you to get away from here. Good for me, too. Time heals most wounds, Alexandra. You're young, you shall have all the things I wanted. I'll make the world for you the way I wanted it to be for me. (*Uncomfortably*) Don't sit there staring. You've been around Birdie so much you're getting just like her.

ALEXANDRA: (*Nods*) Funny. That's what Aunt Birdie said today.

REGINA: (*Nods*) Be good for you to get away from all this. (ADDIE *enters.*)

ADDIE: Cal is back, Miss Regina. He says Dr. Sloan will be coming in a few minutes.

REGINA: We'll go in a few weeks. A few weeks! That means two or three Saturdays, two or three Sundays. (*Sighs*) Well, I'm very tired. I shall go to bed. I don't want any supper. Put the lights out and lock up. (ADDIE *moves to the piano lamp, turns it out*) You go to your room, Alexandra. Addie will bring you something hot. You look very tired. (*Rises. To* ADDIE) Call me when Dr. Sloan gets here. I don't want to see anybody else. I don't want any condolence calls tonight. The whole town will be over.

ALEXANDRA: Mama, I'm not coming with you. I'm not going to Chicago.

REGINA: (*Turns to her*) You're very upset, Alexandra.

ALEXANDRA: (*Quietly*) I mean what I say. With all my heart.

REGINA: We'll talk about it tomorrow. The morning will make a difference.

ALEXANDRA: It won't make any difference. And there isn't anything to talk about. I am going away from you. Because I want to. Because I know Papa would want me to.

REGINA: (*Puzzled, careful, polite*) You *know* your papa wanted you to go away from me?

ALEXANDRA: Yes.

REGINA: (*Softly*) And if I say no?

ALEXANDRA: (*Looks at her*) Say it Mama, say it. And see what happens.

REGINA: (*Softly, after a pause*) And if I make you stay?

ALEXANDRA: That would be foolish. It wouldn't work in the end.

REGINA: You're very serious about it, aren't you? (*Crosses to stairs*) Well, you'll change your mind in a few days.

ALEXANDRA: You only change your mind when you want to. And I won't want to.

REGINA: (*Going up the steps*) Alexandra, I've come to the end of my rope. Somewhere there has to be what I want, too. Life goes too fast. Do what you want; think what you want; go where you want. I'd like to keep you with me, but I won't make you stay. Too many people used to make me do too many things. No, I won't make you stay.

ALEXANDRA: You couldn't, Mama, because I want to leave here. As I've never wanted anything in my life before. Because now I understand what Papa was trying to tell me. (*Pause*) All in one day: Addie said there were people who ate the earth and other people who stood around and watched them do it. And just now Uncle Ben said the same thing. Really, he said the same thing. (*Tensely*) Well, tell him for me, Mama, I'm not going to stand around and watch you do it. Tell him I'll be fighting as hard as he'll be fighting (*Rises*) some place where people don't just stand around and watch.

REGINA: Well, you have spirit, after all. I used to think you were all sugar water. We don't have to be bad friends. I don't want us to be bad friends, Alexandra. (*Starts, stops, turns to* ALEXANDRA) Would you like to come and talk to me, Alexandra? Would you—would you like to sleep in my room tonight?

ALEXANDRA: (*Takes a step toward her*) Are you afraid, Mama? (REGINA *does not answer. She moves slowly out of sight . . .*)

A Streetcar Named Desire, by Tennessee Williams
From Act II, Scene 2
(Scene 6)

Scene:	For one man, one woman
Characters:	BLANCHE DuBOIS
	HAROLD MITCHELL (MITCH)
Setting:	The living room of the Kowalski apartment in the French Quarter of New Orleans.
Time:	Two o'clock in the morning. The present.
Situation:	Blanche DuBois is visiting her sister Stella, who is married to a virile brawler, Stanley Kowalski. Blanche is both attracted and repelled by Stanley. His coarseness disgusts her, but his unabashed masculinity attracts her. Trying to forget her sordid past, the suicide of her husband and the loss of her job as a schoolteacher for seducing one of her students, Blanche has retreated into a world of fantasy and has invented a story of a coming marriage to a millionaire.

Unaware of Blanche's past, Mitch has taken a fancy to her. No longer a young man, Mitch has spent his life caring for his ailing mother. He thinks of Blanche as a potential wife. Blanche knows that Mitch may be her last means of escape from a sordid and hopeless life.

[BLANCHE *and* MITCH *come in. The utter exhaustion which only a neurasthenic personality can know is evident in* BLANCHE'S *voice and manner.* MITCH *is stolid but depressed. They have probably been out to the amusement park on Lake Pontchartrain, for* MITCH *is bearing, upside down, a plaster statuette of Mae West, the sort of prize won at shooting-galleries and carnival games of chance.*)

BLANCHE: (*stopping lifelessly at the steps*) Well—(MITCH *laughs uneasily.*) Well . . .

MITCH: I guess it must be pretty late—and you're tired.

BLANCHE: Even the hot tamale man has deserted the street, and he hangs on till the end. (MITCH *laughs uneasily again.*) How will you get home?

MITCH: I'll walk over to Bourbon and catch an owl-car.

BLANCHE: (*laughing grimly*) Is that streetcar named Desire still grinding along the tracks at this hour?

MITCH: (*heavily*) I'm afraid you haven't gotten much fun out of this evening, Blanche.

BLANCHE: I spoiled it for *you.*

MITCH: No, you didn't, but I felt all the time that I wasn't giving you much— entertainment.

BLANCHE: I simply couldn't rise to the occasion. That was all. I don't think I've ever tried so hard to be gay and made such a dismal mess of it. I get ten points for trying—I *did* try.

MITCH: Why did you try if you didn't feel like it, Blanche?

BLANCHE: I was just obeying the law of nature.

MITCH: Which law is that?

BLANCHE: The one that says the lady must entertain the gentleman—or no dice! See if you can locate my door-key in this purse. When I'm so tired my fingers are all thumbs!

MITCH: (*rooting in her purse*) This it?

BLANCHE: No, Honey, that's the key to my trunk which I must soon be packing.

MITCH: You mean you are leaving here soon?

BLANCHE: I've outstayed my welcome.

MITCH: This it? (*The music fades away.*)

BLANCHE: Eureka! Honey, you open the door while I take a last look at the sky. (*She leans on the porch rail. He opens the door and stands awkwardly behind her.*) I'm looking for the Pleiades, the Seven Sisters, but these girls are not out tonight. Oh, yes they are, there they are! God bless them! All in a bunch going home from their little bridge party. . . . Y' get the door open? Good boy! I guess you—want to go now . . .

[*He shuffles and coughs a little.*]

MITCH: Can I—uh—kiss you—goodnight?

BLANCHE: Why do you always ask me if you may?

MITCH: I don't know whether you want me to or not.

BLANCHE: Why should you be so doubtful?

MITCH: That night when we parked by the lake and I kissed you, you—

BLANCHE: Honey, it wasn't the kiss I objected to. I liked the kiss very much. It was the other little—familiarity—that I—felt obliged to—discourage. . . . I didn't resent it! Not a bit in the world! In fact, I was somewhat flattered that you—desired me! But, honey, you know as well as I do that a single girl, a girl alone in the world, has got to keep a firm hold on her emotions or she'll be lost!

MITCH: (*solemnly*) Lost?

BLANCHE: I guess you are used to girls that like to be lost. The kind that get lost immediately, on the first date!

MITCH: I like you to be exactly the way that you are, because in all my—experience—I have never known anyone like you.

[BLANCHE *looks at him gravely; then she bursts into laughter and then claps a hand to her mouth.*]

MITCH: Are you laughing at me?

BLANCHE: No, honey. The lord and lady of the house have not yet returned, so come in. We'll have a night-cap. Let's leave the lights off. Shall we?

MITCH: You just—do what you want to.

[BLANCHE *precedes him into the kitchen. The outer wall of the building disappears and the interiors of the two rooms can be dimly seen.*]

BLANCHE: (*remaining in the first room*) The other room's more comfortable—go on in. This crashing around in the dark is my search for some liquor.

MITCH: You want a drink?

BLANCHE: I want *you* to have a drink! You have been so anxious and solemn all evening, and so have I; we have both been anxious and solemn and now for these few last remaining moments of our lives together—I want to create—*joie de vivre!* I'm lighting a candle.

MITCH: That's good.

BLANCHE: We are going to be very Bohemian. We are going to pretend that we are sitting in a little artists' cafe on the Left Bank in Paris! (*She lights a candle stub and puts it in a bottle.*) *Je suis la Dame aux Camellias! Vous êtes—Armand!* Understand French?

MITCH: (*heavily*) Naw. Naw, I—

BLANCHE: *Voulez-vous coucher avec moi ce soir? Vous ne comprenez pas? A, quelle dommage!*—I mean it's a damned good thing. . . . I've found some liquor! Just enough for two shots without any dividends, honey. . . .

MITCH: (*heavily*) That's—good.

[*She enters the bedroom with the drinks and the candle.*]

BLANCHE: Sit down! Why don't you take off your coat and loosen your collar?

MITCH: I better leave it on.

BLANCHE: No. I want you to be comfortable.

MITCH: I am ashamed of the way I perspire. My shirt is sticking to me.

BLANCHE: Perspiration is healthy. If people didn't perspire they would die in five minutes. (*She takes his coat from him.*) This is a nice coat. What kind of material is it?

MITCH: They call that stuff alpaca.

BLANCHE: Oh. Alpaca.

MITCH: It's very lightweight alpaca.

BLANCHE: Oh. Lightweight alpaca.

MITCH: I don't like to wear a wash-coat even in summer because I sweat through it.

BLANCHE: Oh.

MITCH: And it don't look neat on me. A man with a heavy build has got to be careful of what he puts on him so he don't look too clumsy.

BLANCHE: You are not too heavy.

MITCH: You don't think I am?

BLANCHE: You are not the delicate type. You have a massive bone-structure and a very imposing physique.

MITCH: Thank you. Last Christmas I was given a membership to the New Orleans Athletic Club.

BLANCHE: Oh, good.

MITCH: It was the finest present I ever was given. I work out there with the weights and I swim and I keep myself fit. When I started there, I was getting soft in the belly but now my belly is hard. It is so hard now that a man can punch me in the belly and it don't hurt me. Punch me! Go on! See? (*She pokes lightly at him.*)

BLANCHE: Gracious. (*Her hand touches her chest.*)

MITCH: Guess how much I weigh, Blanche?

BLANCHE: Oh, I'd say in the vicinity of—one hundred and eighty?

MITCH: Guess again.

BLANCHE: Not that much?

MITCH: No. More.

BLANCHE: Well, you're a tall man and you can carry a good deal of weight without looking awkward.

MITCH: I weigh two hundred and seven pounds and I'm six feet one and one half inches tall in my bare feet—without shoes on. And that is what I weigh stripped.

BLANCHE: Oh, my goodness, me! It's awe-inspiring.

MITCH: (*embarrassed*) My weight is not a very interesting subject to talk about. (*He hesitates for a moment.*) What's yours.

BLANCHE: My weight?

MITCH: Yes.

BLANCHE: Guess!

MITCH: Let me lift you.

BLANCHE: Samson! Go on, lift me. (*He comes behind her and puts his hands on her waist and raises her lightly off the ground.*) Well?

MITCH: You are light as a feather.

BLANCHE: Ha-ha! (*He lowers her but keeps his hands on her waist.* BLANCHE *speaks with an affectation of demureness.*) You may release me now.

MITCH: Huh?

BLANCHE: (*gaily*) I said unhand me, sir. (*He fumblingly embraces her. Her voice sounds gently reproving.*) Now, Mitch. Just because Stanley and Stella aren't at home is no reason why you shouldn't behave like a gentleman.

MITCH: Just give me a slap whenever I step out of bounds.

BLANCHE: That won't be necessary. You're a natural gentleman, one of the very few that are left in the world. I don't want you to think that I am severe and old maid schoolteacherish or anything like that. It's just—well—

MITCH: Huh?

BLANCHE: I guess it is just that I have—old-fashioned ideals!

Georgia Peach by Howard Burman. California State University, Long Beach.
Photo by Keith Ian Polakoff.

Georgia Peach, by Howard Burman
From Act II, Scene 2

Scene:	For one man, one woman
Characters:	TY COBB, an aspiring baseball player, age seventeen
	CHARLIE (CHARLOTTE), a beautiful sixteen-year-old girl
Setting:	A wooden bench at the edge of a rough baseball diamond in Anniston, Georgia.
Time:	May, 1904. Sunset.
Situation:	Ty and Charlie are having a picnic supper that she has brought to the baseball diamond. Ty Cobb is just beginning his baseball career, and he is determined to prove to his father that he can be a success as an athlete. It is his ambition to be the greatest ballplayer in the world.

CHARLIE: How'd you even find this place?
TY: Well, after it didn't quite work out with the Royston club, a sportswriter
    friend got me a tryout with Anniston. A guy by the name of Grantland Rice.
CHARLIE: Sounds like a real friend.

TY: He is. He's also a great sportswriter.

CHARLIE: I bet they're glad. I mean with you leading the league in hitting and all.

TY: Oh, I know it's only a smoky little mill town and I know it's an outlaw league, but they play good ball and the scouts sometimes come by. One from Detroit was here the other day.

CHARLIE: Oh God, whatever you do, don't go to Detroit.

TY: Well, if they ask me . . .

CHARLIE: It's too far away. Besides, you're a good southern boy.

TY: I guess I could live in the city if I had to.

CHARLIE: I don't think I could.

TY: You don't have to.

CHARLIE: But I want to if you're going.

TY: I'm going to the majors, I know that.

CHARLIE: I know that, too, Tyrus Raymond Cobb. And I know I want to be part of that. I want to help you get your dream because that's my dream. Oh, I guess I should want more for me, but I don't really cause I believe in you.

TY: (*Becoming increasingly embarrassed by this.*) You seem to be the only one.

CHARLIE: Except you.

TY: Certainly not my father.

CHARLIE: He will . . . in time.

TY: He's very critical you know. Very strict.

CHARLIE: Talk to him.

TY: It's hard.

CHARLIE: About something he wants to talk about.

TY: What? His books?

CHARLIE: Why not!

TY: (*Laughing to himself.*) Anything but that!

CHARLIE: He loves his books.

TY: How well I know. Last year when I wanted to leave for Royston I knew I couldn't without a good bat of my own. I mean I had to look like a real ball player if I was going to get a chance didn't I? Well, I didn't dare ask my father to buy it. So, one night I slipped into my father's library, and selected one of his most expensive books, traded it for the most beautiful, hand-turned black bat I'd ever seen and complimented myself for a deal well made. It wasn't stealing the way I see it. The library contained books by the score and I didn't have a bat. The exchange was merited. Anyway, who'd ever notice the book was gone?

CHARLIE: Let me guess.

TY: He led me into the library and shut the door.

CHARLIE: Then what?

TY: I couldn't say in front of a girl.

CHARLIE: Ouch!

TY: When he was done, he made me do chores until I had enough money to buy the book back. Then he made me read it—the whole thing and I had to go to an elocution contest and talk about it.

CHARLIE: What was it?

TY: Victor Hugo's biography.

CHARLIE: Ugh!

TY: I guess there's nothing I can do to please him.

CHARLIE: You'll find something.

TY: I don't know. Nothing I ever do is good enough.

CHARLIE: What did he say when he found out you were playing ball?

TY: (*Pulling a telegram from his pocket.*) He sent me this.

CHARLIE: (*Taking it and reading*) "Don't come home a failure."

Oleanna by David Mamet
From Act II

Scene:	For one man, one woman
Characters:	JOHN, a man in his forties
	CAROL, a woman of twenty
Setting:	John's office
Time:	Office hours
Situation:	Carol has accused John, her professor, of sexual harassment to his tenure committee. He has asked her to come to his office to talk about it.

CAROL: What do you want of me?

JOHN: (*Pause*) I was hurt. When I received the report. Of the tenure committee. I was shocked. And I was hurt. No, I don't mean to subject you to my weak sensibilities. All right. Finally, I didn't understand. Then I thought: is it not always at those points at which we reckon ourselves unassailable that we are most vulnerable and . . . (*Pause*) Yes. All right. You find me pedantic. Yes. I am. By nature, by *birth*, by profession, I don't know . . . I'm always looking for a *paradigm* for . . .

CAROL: I don't know what a paradigm is.

JOHN: It's a model.

CAROL: Then why can't you use that word? (*Pause*)

JOHN: If it is important to you. Yes, all right. I was looking for a model. To continue: I feel that one point . . .

CAROL: I . . .

JOHN: One second . . . upon which I am unassailable is my unflinching concern for my students' dignity. I asked you here to . . . in the spirit of *investigation*, to ask you . . . to ask . . . (*Pause*) What have I done to you? (*Pause*) And, and, I suppose, how I can make amends. Can we not settle this now? It's pointless, really, and I want to know.

CAROL: What you can do to force me to retract?

JOHN: That is not what I meant at all.

CAROL: To bribe me, to convince me . . .

JOHN: . . . No.

CAROL: To retract . . .

JOHN: That is not what I meant at all. I think that you know it is not.

CAROL: That is not what I know. I *wish* I . . .

JOHN: I do not want to . . . you wish what?

CAROL: No, you said what amends can you make. To force me to retract.
JOHN: That is not what I said.
CAROL: I have my notes.
JOHN: Look. Look. The Stoics say . . .
CAROL: The Stoics?
JOHN: The Stoical Philosophers say if you remove the phrase "I have been injured," you have removed the injury. Now: Think: I know that you're upset. Just tell me. Literally. Literally: what wrong have I done you?
CAROL: Whatever you have done to me—to the extent that you've done it to *me*, do you know, rather than to me as a *student*, and, so, to the student body, is contained in my report. To the tenure committee.
JOHN: Well, all right. (*Pause*) Let's see. (*He reads.*) I find that I am sexist. That I am *elitist*. I'm not sure I know what that means, other than it's a derogatory word, meaning "bad." That I . . . That I insist on wasting time, in nonprescribed, in self-aggrandizing and theatrical *diversions* from the prescribed *text* . . . that these have taken both sexist and pornographic forms . . . here we find listed . . . (*Pause*) Here we find listed . . . instances ". . . closeted with a student" . . . "Told a rambling, sexually explicit story, in which the frequency and attitudes of fornication of the poor and rich are, it would seem, the central point . . . moved to *embrace* said student and . . . all part of a pattern . . ." (*Pause*)

(*He reads.*) That I used the phrase "The White Man's Burden" . . . that I told you how I'd asked you to my room because I quote like you. (*Pause*)

(*He reads.*) "He said he 'liked' me. That he 'liked being with me.' He'd let me write my examination paper over, if I could come back oftener to see him in his office." (*Pause*) (*To* CAROL:) It's *ludicrous*. Don't you know that? It's not *necessary*. It's going to *humiliate* you, and it's going to cost me my *house*, and . . .
CAROL: It's "*ludicrous* . . ."?
(JOHN *picks up the report and reads again.*)
JOHN: "He told me he had problems with his wife; and that he wanted to take off the artificial stricture of Teacher and Student. He put his arm around me . . ."
CAROL: Do you deny it? Can you deny it . . . ? Do you see? (*Pause*) Don't you see? You don't see, do you?
JOHN: I don't see . . .
CAROL: You think, you think you can deny that these things happened; or, if they *did*, if they *did*, that they meant what you *said* they meant. Don't you see? You drag me in here, you drag us, to listen to you " go on"; and "go on" about this, or that, or we don't "express" ourselves very well. We don't say what we mean. Don't we? Don't we? We *do* say what we mean. And you say that "I don't understand you . . ." Then *you* . . . (*Points.*)
JOHN: "Consult the Report"?
CAROL: . . . that's right.
JOHN: You see. You see. Can't you . . . You see what I'm saying? Can't you tell me in your own words?
CAROL: Those are my own words.

The Crucible, by Arthur Miller
From Act II, Scene 2

Scene:	For one man, one woman
Characters:	JOHN PROCTOR
	ABIGAIL WILLIAMS
Setting:	A wood outside Salem, Massachusetts.
Time:	An evening in the spring of 1692.
Situation:	The town of Salem has entered the period of the infamous witch trials. One of the accusers is Abigail Williams, a young woman who has served in John Proctor's house as a servant during the illness of his wife. She has accused a number of Salem citizens of practicing witchcraft. John knows that Abigail's charges are false and that she is far from being the innocent girl the court believes her to be. He hopes that she can be made to change her testimony.
	Although Proctor was quiet during the initial development of the trials, an accusation brought against his wife forced him to face the problem. When Abigail was in the Proctor household, she and Proctor were intimate. Proctor believes that Abigail's accusation is an attempt to eliminate his wife Elizabeth as a rival. Abigail still desires Proctor, but he wishes only to be free of her so that he can be reconciled with his wife.

[PROCTOR *appears with lantern. He enters glancing behind him, then halts, holding the lantern raised.* ABIGAIL *appears with a wrap over her nightgown, her hair down. A moment of questioning silence*]

PROCTOR: (*searching*) I must speak with you, Abigail. (*She does not move, staring at him.*) Will you sit?

ABIGAIL: How do you come?

PROCTOR: Friendly.

ABIGAIL: (*glancing about*) I don't like the woods at night. Pray you, stand closer. (*He comes closer to her, but keeps separated in spirit.*) I knew it must be you. When I heard the pebbles on the window, before I opened up my eyes I knew. I thought you would come a good time sooner.

PROCTOR: I had thought to come many times.

ABIGAIL: Why didn't you? I am so alone in the world now.

PROCTOR: (*as a fact. Not bitterly*) Are you? I've heard that people come a hundred mile to see your face these days.

ABIGAIL: Aye, my face. Can you see my face?

PROCTOR: (*holds the lantern to her face*) Then you're troubled?

ABIGAIL: Have you come to mock me?

PROCTOR: (*sets lantern and sits down*) No, no, but I hear only that you go to the tavern every night, and play shovelboard with the Deputy Governor, and they give you cider.

ABIGAIL: (*as though that did not count*) I have once or twice played the shovelboard. But I have no joy in it.

PROCTOR: (*He is probing her.*) This is a surprise, Abby. I'd thought to find you gayer than this. I'm told a troop of boys go step for step with you wherever you walk these days.

ABIGAIL: Aye, they do. But I have only lewd looks from the boys.

PROCTOR: And you like that not?

ABIGAIL: I cannot bear lewd looks no more, John. My spirit's changed entirely. I ought to be given Godly looks when I suffer for them as I do.

PROCTOR: Oh? How do you suffer, Abby?

ABIGAIL: (*pulls up dress*) Why, look at my leg. I'm holes all over from their damned needles and pins. (*touching her stomach*) The jab your wife gave me's not healed yet, y'know.

PROCTOR: (*seeing her madness now*) Oh, it isn't?

ABIGAIL: I think sometimes she pricks it open again while I sleep.

PROCTOR: Ah?

ABIGAIL: And George Jacobs . . . (*sliding up her sleeve*) He comes again and again and raps me with his stick—the same spot every night all this week. Look at the lump I have.

PROCTOR: Abby—George Jacobs is in the jail all this month.

ABIGAIL: Thank God he is, and bless the day he hangs and lets me sleep in peace again! Oh, John, the world's so full of hypocrites. (*astonished, outraged*) They pray in jail! I'm told they all pray in jail!

PROCTOR: They may not pray?

ABIGAIL: And torture me in my bed while sacred words are comin' from their mouths? Oh, it will need God himself to cleanse this town properly!

PROCTOR: Abby—you mean to cry out still others?

ABIGAIL: If I live, if I am not murdered, I surely will, until the last hypocrite is dead.

PROCTOR: Then there is no one good?

ABIGAIL: (*softly*) Aye, there is one. *You* are good.

PROCTOR: Am I? How am I good?

ABIGAIL: Why, you taught me goodness, therefore you are good. It were a fire you walked me through, and all my ignorance was burned away. It were a fire, John, we lay in fire. And from that night no woman dare call me wicked anymore but I knew my answer. I used to weep for my sins when the wind lifted up my skirts; and blushed for shame because some old Rebecca called me loose. And then you burned my ignorance away. As bare as some December tree I saw them all—walking like saints to church, running to feed the sick, and hypocrites in their hearts! And God gave me strength to call them liars, and God made men listen to me, and by God I will scrub the world clean for the love of Him! Oh, John, I will make you such a wife when the world is white again! (*She kisses his hand in high emotion.*) You will be amazed to see me every day, a light of heaven in your house, a . . . (*He rises and backs away, frightened, amazed.*) Why are you cold?

PROCTOR: (*in a business-like way, but with uneasiness, as though before an unearthly thing*) My wife goes to trial in the morning, Abigail.

ABIGAIL: (*distantly*) Your wife?

PROCTOR: Surely you knew of it?

ABIGAIL: (*coming awake to that*) I do remember it now. (*as a duty*) How—how—is she well?

PROCTOR: As well as she may be, thirty-six days in that place.

ABIGAIL: You said you came friendly.

PROCTOR: She will not be condemned, Abby.

ABIGAIL: (*her holy feelings outraged. But she is questioning.*) You brought me from my bed to speak of her?

PROCTOR: I come to tell you, Abby, what I will do tomorrow in the court. I would not take you by surprise, but give you all good time to think on what to do to save yourself.

ABIGAIL: (*incredibly, and with beginning fear*) Save myself!

PROCTOR: If you do not free my wife tomorrow, I am set and bound to ruin you, Abby.

ABIGAIL: (*her voice small—astonished*) How—ruin me?

PROCTOR: I have rocky proof in documents that you knew that poppet* were none of my wife's; and that you yourself bade Mary Warren stab that needle into it.

ABIGAIL: (*A wildness stirs in her; a child is standing here who is unutterably frustrated, denied her wish; but she is still grasping for her wits.*) I bade Mary Warren . . . ?

PROCTOR: You know what you do, you are not so mad!

ABIGAIL: (*She calls upwards.*) Oh, hypocrites! Have you won him, too? (*directly to him*) John, why do you let them send you?

PROCTOR: I warn you, Abby.

ABIGAIL: They send you! They steal your honesty and . . .

PROCTOR: I have found my honesty.

ABIGAIL: No, this is your wife pleading, your sniveling, envious wife! This is Rebecca's voice, Martha Corey's voice. You were no hypocrite!

PROCTOR: (*He grasps her arm and holds her.*) I will prove you for the fraud you are!

ABIGAIL: And if they ask why Abigail would ever do so murderous a deed, what will you tell them?

PROCTOR: (*It is hard even to say it.*) I will tell them why.

ABIGAIL: What will you tell? You will confess to fornication? In the court?

PROCTOR: If you will have it so, so I will tell it! (*She utters a disbelieving laugh.*) I say I will! (*She laughs louder, now with more assurance he will never do it. He shakes her roughly.*) If you can still hear, hear this! Can you hear! (*She is trembling, staring up at him as though he were out of his mind.*) You will tell the court you are blind to spirits; you cannot see them anymore, and you will never cry witchery again, or I will make you famous for the whore you are!

ABIGAIL: (*She grabs him.*) Never in this world! I know you, John—you are this moment singing secret Hallelujahs that your wife will hang!

PROCTOR: (*throws her down*) You mad, you murderous bitch!

ABIGAIL: (*rises*) Oh, how hard it is when pretense falls! But it falls, it falls! (*She wraps herself up as though to go.*) You have done your duty by her. I hope it is your last hypocrisy. I pray you will come again with sweeter news for me. I know you will—now that your duty's done. Good night, John. (*She is backing away, raising her hand in farewell.*) Fear naught. I will save you tomorrow. From yourself I will save you. (*She is gone.*)

[PROCTOR *is left alone, amazed in terror. He takes up his lantern and slowly exits as the curtain falls.*]

---

*A cloth doll.

I Don't Have to Show You No Stinking Badges by Luis Valdez
From Act I, Scene 1

Scene:	For one man, one woman
Characters:	BUDDY VILLA
	CONNIE, his wife
Setting:	The kitchen, an apartment in the greater Los Angeles area
Time:	Early morning, the Reagan years
Situation:	The play takes place in a television studio and is played as if it were a television sitcom played before a live audience. There is a Prologue prior to this scene where the Expressionistic quality of the piece is established. However, this scene is played realistically.

Early morning.

> *At rise: Coffee is perking in the kitchen. We hear the up-beat sounds of a 50's Rock-'n'Roll classic. In the den,* CONNIE VILLA, *an attractive 48-year-old Chicana, is dancing. Dressed in a fluffy pink nightgown, she ambles over to the phone and makes a call, while the music on the stereo tape deck plays. Sitting on a wooden stool at the breakfast bar,* CONNIE *dials carefully, dangling a fluffy pink bedroom slipper from her foot. As the music ends, she is talking into the phone with a laid-back, brassy tone and worldly air.*

CONNIE: (*On phone.*) Hello, Betty? This is Constance D'Ville—Connie Villa! How ya doin' today? . . . Great. Listen, any word on that Jack Nicholson picture? . . . Well, when was I supposed to go back for that interview? I know we talked about it yesterday, but . . . well, I was wondering . . . Did you get a chance to ask the casting director about Buddy? . . . Nothing? Nothing at all? Please, Betty. Without him I'm sunk! Central America's out of the question . . . Yeah . . . yeah. I'll hold, sure. (*The back door, down the hall, opens and closes. The sound of heavy breathing and footsteps.*) Buddy? . . . Is that you, *viejo?*

BUDDY: (*Enters, jogging in place.*) *Viejo* my ass. Look at me—I'm an animal! (BUDDY *is a hefty, well-preserved Chicano, hungover but dressed in a jogging suit and running shoes, with the balding hair and body weight of an aging prizefighter. He jogs up to* CONNIE, *tosses her the morning paper and then picks her up and spins her around while she is still talking to her agent.*)

CONNIE: Wait a minute, Betty. There's an animal in the house! No, it's only Buddy. (BUDDY *drops to the floor and does ten, grunting and counting vociferously.*) What? . . . Oh. What about Buddy? . . . Nothing, huh? A part in what? . . . "The Hairy Ape"?

BUDDY: (*Puffing.*) All right! ¿No *que* no?

CONNIE: No, Betty, I don't think so. We don't do waiver theatre. Screw the exposure. We don't work for free.

BUDDY: Twenty minutes flat, old lady! (CONNIE *makes a face and stands, still on the phone. She wipes his sweat off the floor.* BUDDY *hops on the exercise bike.*)

CONNIE: He's right here, dripping sweat all over my floor . . . Yeah, he was out jogging. Or as we say in Spanish—"hogging." (BUDDY *playfully grunts like a hog, heading for the kitchen.*) Which reminds me: the residuals for the AT&T commercial, when do they start? . . . Well okay, keep me posted. See you at the banquet tonight. Ciao. (*Hangs up.*) Betty says there might be something in a couple of days. (BUDDY *opens the refrigerator door, we hear a beer pop open.*) Beer, *hombre?* It's still morning.

BUDDY: Gotta replace my body fluids. Would you believe I just ran five miles?

CONNIE: No.

BUDDY: Okay. Would you believe three miles?

CONNIE: I believe you ran around the house, slowly.

BUDDY: Honest. *Hice jog hasta la* freeway and back. Ran like an Apache . . . (CONNIE *reaches up to the cabinet for vitamins;* BUDDY *eyes her over.*) What's for breakfast?

CONNIE: What would you like?

BUDDY: How about a little *chorizo con huevos . . .* in bed?

CONNIE: Don't start, *señor.*

BUDDY: (*Sidling up to her.*) Jogging always makes me horny.

CONNIE: Breathing makes you horny.

BUDDY: At my age I hate to let a good erection go to waste.

CONNIE: Down, boy. (*Flicks at his feigned erection.*) How about some butterless toast?

BUDDY: I'll stay on my liquid diet. (*He takes a long swig on his beer, and straddles one of the breakfast stools, noticing a letter on the counter. He picks it up as* CONNIE *pours orange juice and sets out the vitamins for* BUDDY.) What's this?

CONNIE: (*Exchanges* BUDDY'S *beer for a glass of juice.*) It's from Lucy. She says Bob and her are doing just fine. Bob just got tenure in the Economics Department at Arizona State, and she's about to open her own practice in pediatrics in downtown Phoenix, which is why they've decided to wait to have a baby of their own. Go ahead, read it.

BUDDY: What the hell for? You just told me all that's in it.

CONNIE: Pick up your beer cans. (*He tosses the letter back on the counter; then he crosses down into the den, taking his beer, and starts picking up other empty beer cans.*) At least your daughter writes. Sonny, on the other hand, forget it. Not one written word since he got back East. We're lucky if he even calls once a month to ask for money. Do you think he's okay?

BUDDY: Sixteen years old and studying pre-law at Harvard? What could go wrong? A bad case of zits? The kid's a prodigy. He'll own his own law firm by the time he's twenty-five.

CONNIE: God knows, the last thing I want to be is one of those clinging *madrecitas* that won't let their kids grow up or they lose their purpose in life. *Chale,* man, not me, boy. I hung up my uterus a long time ago. I like my freedom, and I'm ready to go places.

The Heidi Chronicles, by Wendy Wasserstein
From Act II, Scene 5

Scene: For one man, one woman
Characters: HEIDI
PETER
Setting: Children's ward in a New York Hospital

Time: Christmas season, 1987

Situation: An episodic piece which "chronicles" the life of Heidi Holland, feminist art teacher at Columbia University, and some of her friends as she moves from the 1960s to the edge of the 1990s. In this scene she comes to visit her friend Peter Patrone, a homosexual pediatrician who has opened a clinic for children born with HIV.

HEIDI: Peter, I came to say goodbye.

PETER: Goodbye.

HEIDI: That's it?

PETER: What do you want me to say?

HEIDI: I don't know. You'll call me.

PETER: I'll call you. Heidi, what do you want me to say? You're a brave and remarkable woman. A proud pioneer. My Antonia driving ever forward through the unknown.

HEIDI: (*Softly.*) Peter, sweetie, what is it?

PETER: (*Moves away.*) Nothing. (*He begins straightening the room, putting toys away.*) So you're going to Northfield, Minnesota to start again. Goodbye, New York. Goodbye, mistakes. Make new friends. Give donations to the old.

HEIDI: I hate it when you're like this.

PETER: Heidi, you arrived at midnight and promptly announced you're leaving tomorrow. I'm just feeling my way through this.

HEIDI: I thought you would be the person who would completely understand.

PETER: (*Quite angry.*) Understand what? Looking back at your life and regretting your choices? Deciding your work, your friends, your history are totally expendable?

HEIDI: You have a life here that works for you. I don't.

PETER: Right. So I am expendable, too.

HEIDI: Peter, stop it!

PETER: (*Very distant.*) I'm not doing anything. I was going to spend a quiet Christmas here with the Hardy Boys.

HEIDI: The Hardy Boys?

PETER: For our last midnight donation, we received my sister-in-law Paula Patrone's complete childhood collection of Nancy Drew, the Bobbsey Twins, the Hardy Boys, Honey Bunch, and *Heidi,* which I actually perused last night in your honor. (*He picks up a book from the floor.*) Did you know that the first section is Heidi's year of travel and learning, and the second is Heidi uses what she knows? (*Softly.*) How will you use what you know, Heidi?

HEIDI: I've been sad for a long time. I don't want to be sad anymore.

PETER: This is hard, Heidi. This is very hard. (*He begins going through her boxes.*) What have we got here? The Mamas and the Papas, Gerry and the Pacemakers, Sam the Sham and the Pharoahs. (*He picks up a record.*) "Theodore Bikel Sings Favorite Worksongs from the Fourth International."

HEIDI: Scoop's. From his red diaper period.

PETER: H. W. Jansen, *A History of Art*; Jakob Rosenberg, *Rembrandt's Life and Work; The Secret Life of Salvador Dali*; Alice Elizabeth Chase, *Famous Paintings—An Introduction for Young People; Mary Cassatt and Philadelphia.* Thank you. We don't have any of these.

HEIDI: (*Smiles.*) I thought not.

PETER: The next time some reporter arrives with a surly photographer, I'll tell them, "never mind the kids' immune system, ask them about the secret life of Salvador Dali."

HEIDI: I think your starting this unit is remarkable.

PETER: Your friend Susan's production company sent us a very nice check. Who would have thought three women in a Houston loft would capture the national imagination? It's odd what people find comforting.

HEIDI: What, sweetie?

PETER: Nothing. I was thinking about what people find comforting. I'm sorry. Generally, I try to stay fairly chipper.

HEIDI: Honey, you don't have to be chipper around me.

PETER: You know what's as unappealing in its own insidious way as my sarcasm?

HEIDI: What?

PETER: Your trying too hard. The high voice, the gratuitous "honey" or "sweetie." I can't tell what the hell you're thinking! (*He throws one of the dolls across the room.*)

HEIDI: Peter, where is all this coming from?

PETER: Truth?

HEIDI: It'd be preferable.

PETER: Okay. Heidi, I'd say about once a month now I gather in some church, meeting house or concert hall with handsome men all my own age, and in the front row is usually a couple my parents' age, the father's in a suit and the mother's tasteful, a pleasant face. And we listen for half an hour to testimonials, memories, amusing anecdotes about a son, a friend, a lover, also handsome, also usually my own age, whom none of us will see again. After the first, the fifth, or the fifteenth of these gatherings, a sadness like yours seems a luxury.

HEIDI: I understand.

PETER: No, you don't. Not really. I left out one other thing. My friend Stanley isn't very well. That was my call when you so adventurously arrived. That's where all this is coming from.

HEIDI: Peter, I . . .

PETER: (*Quietly, with feeling.*) You see, my world gets narrower and narrower. A person only has so many close friends. And in our lives, our friends are our families. I'm actually quite hurt you don't understand that. I'm very sorry you don't find that comforting.

HEIDI: There is no one precious to me in the way you are.

PETER: But obviously I can't help you. And you can't help me. So . . .

HEIDI: So . . .

PETER: My best to Jesse James. (*Pause.*)

HEIDI: Peter, we could try.

PETER: Not if you're off to become someone else.

HEIDI: I could become someone else next year. Postpone it. If that's not a little too understanding.

PETER: A little, but I'm listening.

HEIDI: I promise you won't lose this member of your family.

PETER: Who? The sad one or the one I spotted twenty-five years ago at a Miss Crain's School dance?

HEIDI: Split the difference? (*Pause.*)

PETER: However, if you do stay, I have one specific request.

HEIDI: What?

PETER: That you still plan to donate this very fine collection.

HEIDI: All yours. (*Peter begins going through the records again.*)

PETER: Mitch Ryder and the Detroit Wheels. Gary Puckett and the Union Gap. Nelson and the Rocky Fellers. How did we ever become friends?

HEIDI: I'm a sucker for a man of taste and talent.

Beyond Therapy, by Christopher Durang
From Act I, Scene 3

Scene: For one man, one woman

Characters: CHARLOTTE (Mrs. Charlotte Wallace), psychologist
BRUCE, 30–34 years

Setting: Office of Charlotte Wallace

Time: The present

Situation: Bruce, after a very bad beginning with Prudence, whom he met through an ad in the paper, needs to meet with his therapist, Charlotte Wallace, who has problems of her own.

CHARLOTTE: (*Into intercom*) You may send the next patient in, Marcia. (SHE *arranges herself at her desk, smiles in anticipation. Enter* BRUCE. HE *sits*) Hello.

BRUCE: Hello. (*Pause*) Should I just begin?

CHARLOTTE: Would you like to begin?

BRUCE: I threw a glass of water at someone in a restaurant.

CHARLOTTE: Did you?

BRUCE: Yes.

CHARLOTTE: Did they get all wet?

BRUCE: Yes.

(*Silence*)

CHARLOTTE: Did I show you this drawing?

BRUCE: I don't remember. They all look alike.

CHARLOTTE: It was drawn by an emotionally disturbed three-year-old. His parents beat him every morning after breakfast. Orange juice, Toast, Special K.

BRUCE: Uh-huh.

CHARLOTTE: Do you see the point I'm making?

BRUCE: Yes, I do, sort of. (*Pause*) What point are you making?

CHARLOTTE: The point is that when a porpoise first comes to me, it is often immediately clear . . . Did I say porpoise? What word do I want? Porpoise. Pompous. Pom Pom. Paparazzi, Polyester. Pollywog. Olley olley oxen free. Patient. I'm sorry, I mean patient. Now what was I saying?

BRUCE: Something about when a patient comes to you.

Beyond Therapy by Christopher Durang. South Coast Repertory with Gregory Itzin and Annabella Price. Photograph by Ron Stone.

CHARLOTTE: Give me more of a clue.

BRUCE: Something about the child's drawing and when a patient comes to you?

CHARLOTTE: Yes. No, I need more. Give me more of a hint.

BRUCE: I don't know.

CHARLOTTE: Oh I hate this, when I forget what I'm saying. Oh, damn. Oh, damn damn damn. Well, we'll just have to forge on. You say something for a while, and I'll keep trying to remember what I was saying. (SHE *puts her hands over her eyes and moves her lips*)

BRUCE: (*After a bit*) Do you want me to talk?

CHARLOTTE: Would you like to talk?

BRUCE: I had an answer to the ad I put in.

CHARLOTTE: Ad?

BRUCE: Personal ad.

CHARLOTTE: (*Remembering, happy*) Oh, yes. Personal ad. I told you that was how the first Mr. Wallace and I met. Oh yes. I love personal ads. They're so basic. Did it work out for you?

BRUCE: Well, I liked her, and I tried to be emotionally open with her. I even let myself cry.

CHARLOTTE: Good for you!

BRUCE: But she didn't like me. And then she threw water in my face.

CHARLOTTE: Oh, dear. I'm so sorry. One has to be so brave to be emotionally open and vulnerable. Oh, you poor thing. I'm going to give you a hug. (SHE *hugs him*) What did you do when she threw water in your face?

BRUCE: I threw it back in her face.

CHARLOTTE: Oh good for you! Bravo! (SHE *barks for Snoopy* and bounces him up and down*) Ruff ruff ruff! Oh, I feel you getting so much more emotionally expressive since you've been in therapy. I'm proud of you.

BRUCE: Maybe it was my fault. I probably came on too strong.

CHARLOTTE: Life is so difficult. I know when I met the second Mr. Wallace . . . you know, it's so strange, all my husbands have had the same surname of Wallace, this has been a theme in my own analysis . . . Well, when I met the second Mr. Wallace, I got a filing cabinet caught in my throat . . . I don't mean a filing cabinet. What do I mean? Filing cabinet, frying pan, frog's eggs, faculty wives, frankincense, fornication, follies bregère, falling falling, fork, fish fork, fish bone. I got a fish bone caught in my throat.

(*Smiles. Long silence*)

BRUCE: And did you get it out?

CHARLOTTE: Oh yes. Then we got married, and we had quite a wonderful relationship for a while, but then he started to see this fish wife and we broke up. I don't mean fish wife, I mean waitress. Is that a word, waitress?

BRUCE: Yes. Woman who works in a restaurant.

CHARLOTTE: No, she didn't work in a restaurant, she worked in a department store. Sales . . . lady. That's what she was.

BRUCE: That's too bad.

CHARLOTTE: He was buying a gift for me, and then he ran off with the saleslady. He never even gave me the gift, he just left me a note. And then I was so very alone for a while. (*Cries. Stops crying*) I'm afraid I'm taking up too much of your session. I'll knock a few dollars off the bill. You talk for a while. I'm getting tired anyway.

BRUCE: Well, so I'm sort of afraid to put another ad in the paper since seeing how this one worked out.

CHARLOTTE: Oh, don't be afraid! Never be afraid to risk, to risk! I've told you about *Equus*, haven't I? That doctor, Doctor Dysart, with whom I greatly identify, saw that it was better to risk madness and to blind horses with a metal spike, than to be safe and conventional and dull. Ecc, ecc, equus! Naaaaaaay! (*For Snoopy*) Ruff ruff ruff!

BRUCE: So you think I should put in another ad?

CHARLOTTE: Yes I do.

---

*A stuffed dog.

True West, by Sam Shepard
From Act II, Scene 9

Scene:	For two men, one woman
Characters:	AUSTIN, Early 30's, successful writer.
	LEE, Early 40's, Lee's brother, a bum and a thief.
	MOM, In her 60's, very straight.
Setting:	A kitchen in an older Southern California suburb
Time:	Midday, blazing heat.
Situation:	During the course of the first act of this play we are introduced to brothers who are exact opposites. In the course of the play they go through a nearly life-and-death struggle. The house is in chaos from the physical struggle, there are toasters everywhere that Lee has stolen, and the roles of the brothers have been somewhat reversed. Mom appears. She has been on a trip to Alaska.

LEE: Mom?

(AUSTIN *looks up suddenly from his writing, sees* MOM, *stands quickly, long pause,* MOM *surveys the damage*)

AUSTIN: Mom. What're you doing back?

MOM: I'm back.

LEE: Here, lemme take those for ya. (LEE *sets beer on counter then takes both her bags but doesn't know where to set them down in the sea of junk so he just keeps holding them*)

AUSTIN: I wasn't expecting you back so soon. I thought uh—How was Alaska?

MOM: Fine.

LEE: See any igloos?

MOM: No. Just glaciers.

AUSTIN: Cold huh?

MOM: What?

AUSTIN: It must've been cold up there?

MOM: Not really.

LEE: Musta' been colder than this here. I mean we're havin' a real scorcher here.

MOM: Oh? (*She looks at damage*)

LEE: Yeah. Must be in the hundreds.

AUSTIN: You wanna take your coat off, Mom?

MOM: No. (*Pause, she surveys space*) What happened in here?

AUSTIN: Oh um—Me and Lee were just sort of celebrating and uh . . .

MOM: Celebrating?

AUSTIN: Yeah. Uh—Lee sold a screenplay. A story, I mean.

MOM: Lee did?

AUSTIN: Yeah.

MOM: Not you?

AUSTIN: No. Him.

MOM: (*To* LEE) You sold a screenplay?

LEE: Yeah. That's right. We're just sorta' finishing it up right now. That's what we're doing here.

AUSTIN: Me and Lee are going out to the desert to live.

MOM: You and Lee?

AUSTIN: Yeah. I'm taking off with Lee.

MOM: (*She looks back and forth at each of them, pause*) You gonna go live with your father?

AUSTIN: No. We're going to a different desert Mom.

MOM: I see. Well, you'll probably wind up on the same desert sooner or later. What're all these toasters doing here?

AUSTIN: Well—we had kind of a contest.

MOM: Contest?

LEE: Yeah.

AUSTIN: Lee won.

MOM: Did you win a lot of money, Lee?

LEE: Well not yet. It's comin' in any day now.

MOM: (*To* LEE) What happened to your shirt?

LEE: Oh. I was sweatin' like a pig and I took it off. (AUSTIN *grabs* LEE'S *shirt off the table and tosses it to him,* LEE *sets down suitcases and puts his shirt on*)

MOM: Well it's one hell of a mess in here isn't it?

AUSTIN: Yeah, I'll clean it up for you, Mom. I just didn't know you were coming back so soon.

MOM: I didn't either.

AUSTIN: What happened?

MOM: Nothing. I just started missing all my plants.

(*She notices dead plants*)

AUSTIN: Oh.

MOM: Oh, they're all dead aren't they. (*She crosses toward them, examines them closely*) You didn't get a chance to water I guess.

AUSTIN: I was doing it and then Lee came and . . .

LEE: Yeah I just distracted him a whole lot here, Mom. It's not his fault.

(*Pause, as* MOM *stares at plants*)

MOM: Oh well, one less thing to take care of I guess. (*Turns toward brothers*) Oh, that reminds me—You boys will probably never guess who's in town. Try and guess.

(*Long pause, brothers stare at her*)

AUSTIN: Whadya'mean, Mom?

MOM: Take a guess. Somebody very important has come to town. I read it, coming down on the Greyhound.

LEE: Somebody very important?

MOM: See if you can guess. You'll never guess.

AUSTIN: Mom—we're trying to uh—(*Points to writing pad*)

MOM: Picasso. (*Pause*) Picasso's in town. Isn't that incredible? Right now.

(*Pause*)

AUSTIN: Picasso's dead, Mom.

MOM: No, he's not dead. He's visiting the museum. I read it on the bus. We have to go down there and see him.

AUSTIN: Mom—

MOM: This is the chance of a lifetime. Can you imagine? We could all go down and meet him. All three of us.

LEE: Uh—I don't think I'm really up fer meetin' anybody right now. I'm uh—What's his name?

MOM: Picasso! Picasso! You've never heard of Picasso? Austin, you've heard of Picasso.

AUSTIN: Mom, we're not going to have time.

MOM: It won't take long. We'll just hop in the car and go down there. An opportunity like this doesn't come along every day.

AUSTIN: We're gonna be leavin' here, Mom!

(*Pause*)

MOM: Oh.

LEE: Yeah.

(*Pause*)

MOM: You're both leaving?

LEE: (*Looks at* AUSTIN) Well we were thinkin' about that before but now I—

AUSTIN: No, we are! We're both leaving. We've got it all planned.

MOM: (*To* AUSTIN) Well you can't leave. You have a family.

AUSTIN: I'm leaving. I'm getting out of here.

LEE: (*To* MOM) I don't really think Austin's cut out for the desert do you?

MOM: No. He's not.

AUSTIN: I'm going with you, Lee!

MOM: He's too thin.

LEE: Yeah, he'd just burn up out there.

AUSTIN: (*To* LEE) We just gotta' finish this screenplay and then we're gonna' take off. That's the plan. That's what you said. Come on, let's get back to work, Lee.

LEE: I can't work under these conditions here. It's too hot.

AUSTIN: Then we'll do it on the desert.

LEE: Don't be tellin' me what we're gonna' do!

MOM: Don't shout in the house.

LEE: We're just gonna' have to postpone the whole deal.

AUSTIN: I can't postpone it! It's gone past postponing! I'm doing everything you said. I'm writing down exactly what you tell me.

LEE: Yeah, but you were right all along see. It is a dumb story. "Two lame-brains chasin' each other across Texas." That's what you said, right?

AUSTIN: I never said that.

(LEE *sneers in* AUSTIN'S *face then turns to* MOM)

LEE: I'm gonna' just borrow some a your antiques, Mom. You don't mind do ya'? Just a few plates and things. Silverware.

(LEE *starts going through all the cupboards in kitchen pulling out plates and stacking them on counter as* MOM *and* AUSTIN *watch*)

MOM: You don't have any utensils on the desert?

LEE: Nah, I'm fresh out.

AUSTIN: (*To* LEE) What're you doing?

MOM: Well some of those are very old. Bone China.

LEE: I'm tired of eatin' outa' my bare hands, ya' know. It's not civilized.

AUSTIN: (*To* LEE) What're you doing? We made a deal!

MOM: Couldn't you borrow the plastic ones instead? I have plenty of plastic ones.

LEE: (*As he stacks plates*) It's not the same. Plastic's not the same at all. What I need is somethin' authentic. Somethin' to keep me in touch. It's easy to get outa' touch out there. Don't worry I'll get 'em back to ya'.

A Streetcar Named Desire, by Tennessee Williams
From Act III, Scene 2
(Scene 8)

Scene:	For one man, two women
Characters:	BLANCHE DuBOIS
	STELLA KOWALSKI, her sister
	STANLEY KOWALSKI, Stella's husband
Setting:	The living room of the Kowalski apartment in the French Quarter of New Orleans.
Time:	Early evening. The present.
Situation:	See the scene from *A Streetcar Named Desire* (p. 274), which occurs earlier in the play.

Several weeks have passed since the evening Mitch and Blanche had their date. Since that evening, Stanley has discovered the truth about Blanche's past and has told both Stella and Mitch what he has learned. Although Stanley has not revealed his knowledge to Blanche, she senses that something has happened. It is about three-quarters of an hour after Stanley has told Stella. Despite the strained atmosphere, they have gone through the motions of eating a dismal birthday dinner, "celebrating" Blanche's birthday. There is an empty chair at the table. Mitch has not come. Stella is embarrassed and sad; Blanche sits with a tight, artificial smile on her face. Stanley is watching Blanche sullenly as he gnaws a pork chop and licks his fingers.

BLANCHE: (*suddenly*) Stanley, tell us a joke, tell us a funny story to make us all laugh. I don't know what's the matter, we're all so solemn. Is it because I've been stood up by my beau? (STELLA *laughs feebly.*) It's the first time in my entire experience with men, and I've had a good deal of all sorts, that I've actually been stood up by anybody! Ha-ha! I don't know how to take it. . . . Tell us a funny little story, Stanley! Something to help us out.

STANLEY: I didn't think you liked my stories, Blanche.

BLANCHE: I like them when they're amusing but not indecent.

STANLEY: I don't know any refined enough for your taste.

BLANCHE: Then let me tell one.

STANLEY: Yes, you tell one, Blanche. You used to know lots of good stories.

BLANCHE: Let me see, now. . . . I must run through my repertoire! Oh, yes—I love parrot stories! Do you all like parrot stories? Well, this one's about the old maid and the parrot. This old maid, she had a parrot that cursed a blue streak and knew more vulgar expressions than Mr. Kowalski!

STANLEY: Huh.

BLANCHE: And the only way to hush the parrot up was to put the cover back on its cage so it would think it was night and go back to sleep. Well, one morning the old maid had just uncovered the parrot for the day—when who should she see coming up the front walk but the preacher! Well, she rushed back to the parrot and slipped the cover back on the cage and then she let in the preacher. And the parrot was perfectly still, just as quiet as a mouse, but just as she was asking the preacher how much sugar he wanted in his cof- fee—the parrot broke the silence with a loud—(*She whistles.*)—and said— "God *damn*, but that was a short day!"

[*She throws back her head and laughs.* STELLA *also makes an ineffectual effort to seem amused.* STANLEY *pays no attention to the story but reaches way over the table to spear his fork into the remaining chop which he eats with his fingers.*]

BLANCHE: Apparently Mr. Kowalski was not amused.

STELLA: Mr. Kowalski is too busy making a pig of himself to think of anything else!

STANLEY: That's right, baby.

STELLA: Your face and your fingers are disgustingly greasy. Go and wash up and then help me clear the table.

[*He hurls a plate to the floor.*]

STANLEY: That's how I'll clear the table! (*He seizes her arm.*) Don't ever talk that way to me! "Pig—Polack—disgusting—vulgar—greasy!"—them kind of words have been on your tongue and your sister's too much around here! What do you two think you are? A pair of queens? Remember what Huey Long said—"Every Man Is a King!" And I am the king around here, so don't forget it! (*He hurls a cup and saucer to the floor.*) My place is cleared! You want me to clear your places?

[STELLA *begins to cry weakly.* STANLEY *stalks out on the porch and lights a cigarette. The Negro entertainers around the corner are heard.*]

BLANCHE: What happened while I was bathing? What did he tell you, Stella?

STELLA: Nothing, nothing, nothing!

BLANCHE: I think he told you something about Mitch and me! You know why Mitch didn't come but you won't tell me! (STELLA *shakes her head helplessly.*) I'm going to call him!

STELLA: I wouldn't call him, Blanche.

BLANCHE: I am, I'm going to call him on the phone.

STELLA: (*miserably*) I wish you wouldn't.

BLANCHE: I intend to be given some explanation from someone!

[*She rushes to the phone in the bedroom.* STELLA *goes out on the porch and stares re- proachfully at her husband. He grunts and turns away from her.*]

STELLA: I hope you're pleased with your doings. I never had so much trouble swallowing food in my life, looking at that girl's face and the empty chair! (*She cries quietly.*)

BLANCHE: (*at the phone*) Hello. Mr. Mitchell, please. . . . Oh. . . . I would like to leave a number if I may. Magnolia 9047. And say it's important to call. . . . Yes, very important. . . . Thank you.

[*She remains by the phone with a lost, frightened look.* STANLEY *turns slowly back toward his wife and takes her clumsily in his arms.*]

STANLEY: Stell, it's gonna be all right after she goes and after you've had the baby. It's gonna be all right again between you and me the way that it was. You remember that way that it was? Them nights we had together? God, honey, it's gonna be sweet when we can make noise in the night the way that we used to and get the colored lights going with nobody's sister behind the curtains to hear us! (*Their upstairs neighbors are heard in bellowing laughter at something.* STANLEY *chuckles.*) Steve an' Eunice. . . .

STELLA: Come on back in. (*She returns to the kitchen and starts lighting the candles on the white cake.*) Blanche?

BLANCHE: Yes. (*She returns from the bedroom to the table in the kitchen.*) Oh, those pretty, pretty little candles! Oh, don't burn them, Stella.

STELLA: I certainly will.

[STANLEY *comes back in.*]

BLANCHE: You ought to save them for baby's birthdays. Oh, I hope candles are going to glow in his life and I hope that his eyes are going to be like candles, like two blue candles lighted in a white cake!

STANLEY: (*sitting down*) What poetry!

BLANCHE: (*She pauses reflectively for a moment.*) I shouldn't have called him.

STELLA: There's lots of things could have happened.

BLANCHE: There's no excuse for it, Stella. I don't have to put up with insults. I won't be taken for granted.

STANLEY: Goddamn, it's hot in here with the steam from the bathroom.

BLANCHE: I've said I was sorry three times. . . . I take hot baths for my nerves. Hydro-therapy, they call it. You healthy Polack, without a nerve in your body, of course you don't know what anxiety feels like!

STANLEY: I am not a Polack. People from Poland are Poles, not Polacks. But what I am is a one hundred percent American, born and raised in the greatest country on earth and proud as hell of it, so don't ever call me a Polack.

[*The phone rings.* BLANCHE *rises expectantly.*]

BLANCHE: Oh, that's for me, I'm sure.

STANLEY: *I'm* not sure. Keep your seat. (*He crosses leisurely to phone.*) H'lo. Aw, yeh, hello, Mac.

[*He leans against wall, staring insultingly in at* BLANCHE. *She sinks back in her chair with a frightened look.* STELLA *leans over and touches her shoulder.*]

BLANCHE: Oh, keep your hands off me, Stella. What is the matter with you? Why do you look at me with that pitying look?

STANLEY: (*bawling*) QUIET IN THERE!—We've got a noisy woman on the place.—Go on, Mac. At Riley's? No, I don't wanta bowl at Riley's. I had a little trouble with Riley last week. I'm the team-captain, ain't I? All right, then, we're not gonna bowl at Riley's, we're gonna bowl at the West Side or the Gala! All right, Mac. See you! (*He hangs up and returns to the table.* BLANCHE *fiercely controls herself, drinking quickly from her tumbler of water. He doesn't look at her but reaches in a pocket. Then he speaks slowly and with false amiability.*) Sister Blanche, I've got a little birthday remembrance for you.

BLANCHE: Oh, have you, Stanley? I wasn't expecting any, I—I don't know why
Stella wants to observe my birthday! I'd much rather forget it—when you—
reach twenty-seven! Well—age is a subject that you'd prefer to—ignore!

STANLEY: Twenty-seven?

BLANCHE: (*quickly*) What is it? Is it for *me*?

[*He is holding a little envelope toward her.*]

STANLEY: Yes, I hope you like it!

BLANCHE: Why, why—Why, it's a—

STANLEY: Ticket! Back to Laurel! On the Greyhound Tuesday!

(. . . STELLA *rises abruptly and turns her back.* BLANCHE *tries to smile. Then she tries
to laugh. Then she gives both up and springs from the table and runs into the next
room. She clutches her throat and then runs into the bathroom. Coughing, gagging
sounds are heard.*) Well!

STELLA: You didn't need to do that.

STANLEY: Don't forget all that I took off her.

STELLA: You needn't have been so cruel to someone alone as she is.

STANLEY: Delicate piece she is.

STELLA: She is. She was. You didn't know Blanche as a girl. Nobody, nobody,
was tender and trusting as she was. But people like you abused her, and
forced her to change. (*He crosses into the bedroom, ripping off his shirt, and
changes into a brilliant silk bowling shirt. She follows him.*) Do you think you're
going bowling now?

STANLEY: Sure.

STELLA: You're not going bowling. (*She catches hold of his shirt.*) Why did you
do this to her?

STANLEY: I done nothing to no one. Let go of my shirt. You've torn it.

STELLA: I want to know why. Tell me why.

STANLEY: When we first met, me and you, you thought I was common. How
right you was, baby. I was common as dirt. You showed me the snapshot of
the place with the columns. I pulled you down off them columns and how
you loved it, having them colored lights going! And wasn't we happy together, wasn't it all okay till she showed here? (STELLA *makes a slight movement. Her look goes suddenly inward as if some interior voice had called her name.
She begins a slow, shuffling progress from the bedroom to the kitchen, leaning and
resting on the back of the chair and then on the edge of a table with a blind look and
listening expression.* STANLEY, *finishing with his shirt, is unaware of her reaction.*)
And wasn't we happy together? Wasn't it all okay? Till she showed here.
Hoity-toity, describing me as an ape. (*He suddenly notices the change in*
STELLA.) Hey, what is it, Stel? (*He crosses to her.*)

STELLA: (*quietly*) Take me to the hospital.

[*He is with her now, supporting her with his arm, murmuring indistinguishably as they
go outside.*]

CHAPTER
ELEVEN

Style and Other Problems

We have endeavored in the preceding chapters to familiarize the actor with the fundamentals of acting, which are applicable in most acting situations. Nevertheless, various types of plays and productions create special problems. This chapter will examine a number of the problems that occur in specialized areas of acting.

> *Comedy, dear, is just like blowing powder puffs out of a cannon.*
>
> Dame Edith Evans

Comedy and Farce

Let us immediately clear up a common misconception regarding the playing of comedy as distinct from the so-called "serious" play. Comedy is not easier to play, nor does it require less acting ability than tragedy. The reverse is often true, for good acting in comedy requires an acute sense of timing, the knack of punching a line properly, and the ability to project the incongruities and exaggerations that make up the comic tradition.

No single definition will fit all the varied types of comedy that the actor will encounter. It is easier to know when we are watching a comedy than to define it exactly. Nevertheless, it is clear that a comedy is usually a play that ends happily and aims primarily at amusing the audience.

The best comedy usually grows out of the foibles of the characters involved. This is the essence of the comedy of Ben Jonson, Shakespeare, and Molière. Comedy of character that is vested with scintillating dialogue and wit is usually classified as *high comedy.* When the pretensions of aristocrats or highly sophisticated characters are lampooned, we may be witnessing a *comedy of manners,* which has much in common with high comedy. If our sympathies are aroused as we watch young and virtuous lovers triumph over the obstacles of society or the "wrongdoer," we may be viewing *sentimental comedy.*

Comedy and farce are related, but when we examine them closely we may recognize certain differences. Both may grow out of *character* or *incident and intrigue.* The basic distinction separating comedy and farce is related to the probability of the action. Whereas the characters and incidents of comedy may be well within the realm of reason, farce supposes that we have left the sane world and have embarked on a journey where the impossible has become theatrically feasible. Many critics would go so far as to separate the two forms rather than include farce as a branch of comedy. However, farce can be closely related even to highly literate comedy, as in the case of Oscar Wilde's farce *The Importance of Being Earnest,* which has much in common with the tradition of the English comedy of manners. It is not uncommon to find a farcical character in a play that is otherwise a comedy; the reverse is even more likely to be true. Such difficulties present problems in defining each type satisfactorily. The actor will find much in common between these forms, and for our purposes we shall treat the two areas together.

A number of elements are evident in all good comedies and farces. Let us consider three of the most important: *incongruity, exaggeration,* and the *comic spirit.*

Incongruity

One of the fundamental causes of laughter is *incongruity.* The umbrella-wielding female wading into a husky man, the bullfighter running in fright from the bull, the rich matron being slapped in the face with a custard pie, the fainting of a professional wrestler at the sight of a mouse—these move us to laughter by the incongruity of the action.

In creating the role of Inspector Clouseau in *The Pink Panther* film series, Peter Sellers relied heavily on incongruity in developing his delightful character. Presumably an inspector of police is an intelligent individual, but Clouseau's mangling of the language (English or French?) adds to the mirth. He wonders why one has a "bemp" on the head, and destroys property with the same ease with which he destroys words. Incongruously, his preposterous self-assurance only grows. When jumping into bed on a rare Stradivarius violin he comments: "When you've seen one Stradivarius, you've seen them all." Destroying another fine musical instrument, he responds to the comment that "That's a rare Steinway piano" with an unconcerned shrug: "Not any more," he says.

Any incongruity of values may very well aid the comic spirit. The following sequence, typical of old minstrel humor, may indicate how this principle operates. When asked to define a miracle, one of the end men replied:

> Man, if you see a thistle in de meadow, dat ain't no miracle. If you see a bull grazing in de meadow, dat ain't a miracle, an if you see a lark singin' in dat same meadow, pretty as can be, dat still ain't no miracle. But if you see dat bull, sittin' on dat thistle singin' like a lark,—man dat's a miracle.

This story, if well told, will provide the audience with a mirth-provoking picture of the lyrical bull balancing himself on the thistle. The actor must search out any incongruities and point them up in the playing of comedy.

Exaggeration

Exaggeration of physical characteristics or personality traits is a common source of comic invention. Martha Raye and Joe E. Brown have made effective use of their large mouths for comic effect. Jimmy Durante's famous nose provided a fortune for him throughout his career. Jim Carrey is on the way to making his with an elastic face and body. Don Rickles's excessive and exaggerated assault upon individuals of all social levels consistently moves his audiences to laughter. Foster Brooks and Dean Martin have transformed personal alcoholic excesses beyond pity to comedy. The calculated stinginess of Jack Benny was used in almost every radio and television production in which he appeared for several decades. The sight of someone being forced to put a quarter in a slot in order to start Benny's borrowed lawn mower moves us to laughter both by the *exaggeration* of his stinginess and the very *incongruity* of the action.

Much of the humor of Falstaff stems from his tremendous bulk. Cyrano de Bergerac's comment about his enormous nose "which marches on before me by a quarter of an hour" is an obvious example of exaggeration. The miserliness of Harpagon in *The Miser*, the excessive puritanism of Malvolio in *Twelfth Night*, the snobbishness of Lady Bracknell in *The Importance of Being Earnest* all move us to laughter by their excessiveness.

Within the bounds of good taste and the three **V**s of good acting, exaggeration can be used by the actor to highlight the comic potential of his or her character. In farce, particularly, restraint upon exaggeration is almost entirely removed, and excessive exaggeration is, indeed, one of the hallmarks of farcical acting.

The Comic Spirit

Good acting in comedy and farce requires that the audience know as soon as possible that they are supposed to laugh. They must have a frame of reference for the action they will see and the dialogue they will hear. This frame of reference can be termed the *comic spirit*. Watching a comedian in the movies dangling from a clothesline in a blanket five stories above the pavement is amusing; we laugh in the circus as clowns bash each other over the head with crowbars, mallets, baseball bats, and other assorted weapons (usually made of rubber). We laugh because we know that the characters are in no real danger and everything will be solved satisfactorily. Consider also the continual mayhem in the *Tom and Jerry* and *Roadrunner* cartoons. We know, because the form is a cartoon rather than the illusion of life, that nothing in it is really harmful. The mangling of arms, legs, heads, and entire bodies by every means possible is the primary source of amusement. There is never any question in our mind of real danger.

If, however, we are going about our everyday business and see a man dangling precariously above the street or being attacked by another person with a deadly weapon, we would hardly laugh; we would likely be moved to serious action. The actor, therefore, must *project* to the audience that all is *in fun*, that the comic spirit is prevailing, that the work is a comedy. Comic acting means that the actor must not be hesitant about pointing up the incongruity and exaggeration of *both* situation and character.

Timing

One of the most delicate problems in the handling of the comic situation is timing. Timing is something that cannot truly be taught, but some discussion of its value may be useful. Often a well-timed pause will make a seemingly simple line exceedingly amusing. In *Born Yesterday*, a tough but delightful racketeer, Eddie Brock, comes into a dark room and switches on the lights, revealing the "heroine" and her "teacher" sitting on the sofa. Brock's first line, directed to the pair, is "What's this? Night school?" The line will receive its comic impact if the actor pauses after the first brief phrase, reading it as

"What's this?" (*He looks at Paul and Billie and seems somewhat surprised.*) "Night school?"

A word of caution is in order. If the technique is too evident, or if the actor is trying too obviously for a laugh, it is easy to kill it. Often the harder one tries to make a line funny, the less amusing it becomes. A good rule: *Do not make the technique obvious.*

> Some years ago when Alfred Lunt and Lynne Fontanne opened in a comedy, Lunt told his wife and partner that he was certain he would get a laugh on his line, "I would like a cup of tea." After two weeks of performances, he had not received a laugh on that line. He asked his wife why he wasn't getting the anticipated laugh, and her response is well worth noting. "My dear Alfred," she is reported to have told him, "you are asking for a laugh, not for a cup of tea."
>
> Theatrical Anecdote

Handling laughter can also cause some difficulties. An audience should rarely be prevented from laughing if it is so inclined. Jumping in with a cue as the audience begins to laugh at the preceding line is one sure way to restrict their laughter and cause difficulties in being heard. Nor should the actor wait until the laughter has completely died out. This will make the production too labored and slow the pace of the show. Most laughter begins at a low level, builds to a peak, and then fades away. The cue should be picked up *after* the peak is reached and the laughter has started to fade away. If a cue is picked up, and suddenly the laugh builds after a slow start, the actor should simply stop, wait for the downturn in the laugh, and *begin again*.

It is best to go through the rehearsal period without pauses for laughter. It is impossible to predict exactly how an audience will react to a comedy on any given night. During a run of performances in one production, it is surprising to discover how an audience's reactions will differ from night to night. Although the actor has rehearsed without stopping for anticipated laughter, during a performance it is necessary to be ready to make adjustments to the laughter that says that the purpose is being achieved and the audience is enjoying the actor's comic efforts.

Electra by Sophocles. California State University Theatre, Long Beach.
Directed by Ken Rugg. Photograph by Keith Ian Polakoff.

Tragedy

Although both comedy and tragedy grew out of the religious rites of the ancient Greeks in honor of the god Dionysus, the entire mental and spiritual tone of tragedy differs radically from that of comedy. It is not surprising that tragedy had such early roots, for death and suffering are universal to all human beings as well as being the most enigmatic of experiences. Questions that ask "Why must this be so?" may never be answered satisfactorily, but that does not prevent Oedipus, Antigone, Job, Hamlet, and Willy Loman from asking them; these characters have come to their own terms with the inevitable legacy of all mankind.

The Nature of Tragedy

Much has been written about the nature of tragedy, yet a precise definition upon which all critics may agree has eluded us. In recent years there has been much provocative discussion about Arthur Miller's fine play *Death of a Salesman*. Some critics acclaim it as a tragedy; others find in it fundamental departures from what they believe to be the tragic spirit.

In a tragedy the central figure, or protagonist, suffers a crushing defeat, usually ending in death. The protagonist's downfall, accompanied by suffering and violence, does not stem from any accidental source but is triggered by some flaw in his or her personality or by the enigmatic influence of fate. The tragic figure, when placed under the stress of circumstances, is inevitably destroyed.

The protagonist, essentially a good individual of stature and respectability, is like all fellow men and women in the credo "I am a person with the weaknesses common to humanity." Its universal implication makes tragedy meaningful and harrowing for all audiences. The protagonist, altered in the crucible of suffering, comes to terms with his or her problem and dies, not in despair, but in an awareness of the problem and of his or her place in the universe.

One of the qualities most frequently associated with tragedy is the intensification of dialogue to bring into focus the tragic essence of the work and to couch the ideas of the play in the most expressive language possible. For this reason many of the world's great tragedies are *poetic* dramas as well.

Acting Technique in Tragedy

The actor's responsibility and efforts in tragedy are clearly different from those imposed by comedy. As a general rule tragedy requires less "exterior" technique than comedy. Whereas comedy achieves its effects by the careful timing of visual situations and humorous lines, tragedy makes its greatest demands on the emotional and spiritual resources of the actor. Good tragic acting is often as much a sign of human sensitivity as it is of competent acting. This fact reemphasizes the point made in Chapter 1 that the good actor is one who is conversant with human nature, who has observed and has read widely the story of the human race.

More specifically, the actor working in tragedy must fully utilize the potential of the voice to communicate the grandeur of the play's language, which, as we have already noted, is expressive of the real essence and nature of the tragic state. Failure to project properly to an audience the impact of the language will result in a less than successful performance.

The development of business must be approached in a completely different manner from that assumed in comedy. Nothing should be done to interfere with the emotional bond that exists between the audience and the play. All business inserted by the actor should be keyed to the tests of simplicity and honesty and should be less developed than in comedy. The business should normally be projected in broad strokes, keeping audience attention centered on the characters and dialogue. Any digression caused by the insertion of clever business may be perfectly acceptable in comedy but is often antagonistic to the inevitable and methodical development of good tragedy.

Although technique can never be dismissed entirely from the preparation of any role, tragedy will make the greatest demands on the actor's inner resources of imagination and understanding.

Period Plays in General

Period plays, especially the dramas of Shakespeare, are often frightening for beginning actors who like to cut their teeth on modern "realistic" plays. This attitude certainly is not to be condemned, but it would be unfortunate indeed if the actor were always to refrain from participation in some of the greatest plays ever written. One of the reasons for this hesitancy to act in plays of the past—the drama of the Greeks and Romans, Shakespeare, Molière, the Restoration, and the eighteenth century—has already been suggested: They are not "realistic" in the present-day sense of the term. Time has also erected a barrier that makes it difficult for us to understand the social conventions and restraints that work upon the plays and the characters. We often say we have difficulty in "relating" to these works.

This fact poses two specific problems for the actor who is experienced only in modern realistic plays. First, period plays generally require a higher degree of presentational acting than our contemporary drama. In simplest terms, these plays are often frankly theatrical, making no pretense at being "a slice of life." In their own time they were performed primarily in a presentational, or audience-centered, manner. The actors were constantly aware of the fact that theirs was a stage performance, and their acting was directed *to* the audience. Little attempt was made to disguise the fact that a theatrical performance was in progress. Despite this, it should be noted, the actors still attempted to sustain the *illusion* that their actions were real and consistent, and the audience undoubtedly believed the situations and the emotions of the characters. In producing these plays today there is invariably an attempt to retain something of the presentational style in the production so as to preserve the original flavor and intent of the piece. This does not imply that the actor makes no attempt to persuade the audience members to believe what they are seeing and hearing. To this extent the presentational style is perfectly consistent with the creating of an illusion of life, and it may be termed *presentational-illusionistic*. The actor must be aware, however, that these plays are rarely acted in the *representational-illusionistic* style that is utilized for the modern realistic play.

The second problem, often most disturbing to the beginning actor, is posed by the fact that many of the dramas of an earlier period are written in verse rather than prose. Their authors used the verse form because poetry is a heightening of language, a means by which the author is able to express the play's meaning with greater subtlety and economy than is possible in prose. When Horatio, in *Hamlet*, describes the coming of the dawn with the beautiful sequence

> But look, the morn, in russet mantle clad,
> Walks o'er the dew of yon high eastern hill.

we may be sure that he is creating a vivid image for the audience that a long, detailed description in prose *might* equal. To state simply "Look, the sun is coming up" would miss the point and convey little of the essence of the beauty of the new day.

In the preface to *The Admirable Bashville*, George Bernard Shaw, probably the finest prose dramatist of the twentieth century, explained that he had written this piece in verse because he didn't have enough time to write the play in prose. Shaw was, of course, being somewhat facetious, as was his habit on many occasions, but he had a sound purpose in mind. He pointed up the fact that verse permits greater economy than prose in the expression of images and ideas.

In verse drama it is essential that the actor be aware of the full meaning of the images he or she is attempting to communicate. If the actor does not examine and understand the means by which the playwright has given expression to the play's characters and ideas, it is likely that the audience will not understand them either.

Shakespearean Plays

The plays of Shakespeare are produced in American colleges and universities more often than those of any other playwright. His works have transcended his own age; they are meaningful for our day as well. "He was not of an age, but for all time," wrote Ben Jonson of his friend; Jonson certainly was endowed with the gift of prophecy in this instance. Yet too often the contemporary actor is unable to find a point at which to begin work on these plays. This seems to be true not only for Shakespearean plays but many other fine plays of the past separated from our day by manners, habits, and language that may be alien to us.[1]

Some difficulty may also be traced to our early exposure to works of this type. If we have been bogged down in literary dissections of the "classics"

---

1. Although in this section we shall be examining the problems specific to Shakespearean plays, we should not ascribe the implications of these remarks to those plays alone. Much of what we say here applies also to the great dramas of the Greeks and the Romans, Molière, and the Restoration period. All these plays are truly pieces for the theatre, meant to be *performed* to reveal their complete intent.

and exposed to teaching that treats these dramas as musty relics, we lose sight of their origins and purposes. Shakespeare is the most obvious case in point. If we consider him as nothing but required reading in high-school and college literature courses, we forget the most important consideration of all: Shakespeare was an actor. He wrote for actors. He was the most popular playwright of his day because people were willing to pay to be entertained by his plays. His primary intention was to have his plays performed; only secondary was his concern that they be read. Indeed, half of his plays were not published until *after* his death, and even that publication was due only to two loyal friends, who published his plays as a testimonial to their colleague. The actor must approach the plays not as relics of a bygone age but as exciting dramas with flesh-and-blood characters who have provided us with some of our most moving moments in the theatre.

There are a lot of people in the theater who believe that Macbeth *is a cursed play. Some of this no doubt stems from the subject matter: witchcraft. Superstition holds that when you mess with the forces of evil, even in the arts, evil may decide to take some part. Whatever the reason, there are scores of stories about accidents happening to people involved with production of the play. To ward off evil many actors ceased to refer to the play by its title and began referring to it as "The Scottish Play." However, if it is mentioned, there are things that can be done to exorcise the production of the Scottish play curse:*

1. *Counter hex: quote the line, "Angels and ministers of grace defend us." from* Hamlet *(I,iv).*
2. *The one who spoke the words must immediately exit the room, turn around three times, break wind or spit, knock on the door, and ask permission to reenter.*

Theatrical Superstition

It must be granted that the playing of Shakespeare presents something of a challenge. No doubt a hint from the past will be helpful for the modern actor. Although some questions are clouded by debate among modern scholars, there are enough clues to provide a fairly complete picture of the Elizabethan actor. He was evidently a highly flexible performer, capable of acting in both comedy and tragedy, trained in music and dancing, and able to do full justice to the many scenes of violent action that are so important in Shakespeare's plays: the fencing matches, battle scenes, wrestling bouts, swordplay, and so on. Because the plays were generally performed in outdoor theatres, the actor had to have a well-projected voice, capable not only of being heard but also of expressing the subtleties and nuances of Shakespeare's dialogue. The Elizabethan actor, then, was a well-rounded performer, supple in body, and expressive in the use of the voice. The same should hold true for the modern interpreter of Shakespeare.

In dealing with the plays of Shakespeare the modern actor is concerned with two working areas: *interpretation* and the determination of a *reading style*. Let us examine each of these two elements in turn so that we can formulate an approach to the development of such roles.

Interpretation

Although the work of actors of the past may afford us some help in determining how to develop these roles, we must avoid a too deliberate imitation of earlier interpretations. The wisest approach is to depend as much as possible on the texts of the plays themselves. Even if we knew exactly what Burbage's first Hamlet was like, we would want to steer away from a reca-

Merlin **by Tankard Dorst. California Repertory Theatre Company, Long Beach. Directed by Ronald Lindblom. Photograph by Keith Ian Polakoff.**

309

pitulation of what someone else had done. After all, there is no one *right* way to do Hamlet. If there were, there would be little need ever to produce the play again. Finding one's own approach is the only truly creative work in the theatre.

The clues the actor needs to be able to interpret these characters properly are to be found in the plays themselves. Shakespeare has created full-blooded characters, and the plays are filled with illuminating little details that the observant actor should have no difficulty in translating into an exciting characterization. Such comments about the characters are to be found not in an introduction or in stage directions but from the lips of the characters themselves. A few examples may illustrate the storehouse of information to be derived about Shakespeare's characters from the dialogue of the plays. We find such descriptions as the following:

Pinch, the schoolmaster in *The Comedy of Errors*, is "a hungry lean-faced villain, . . . a fortune teller, a needy, hollow-eyed, sharp-looking wretch, a living dead man." Gratiano, in *The Merchant of Venice*, the talkative friend of Bassanio, is "too wild, too rude, and bold of voice [and] speaks an infinite deal of nothing. . . ." Falstaff, in *Henry IV: Part II*, is "a fool and a jester [who needs] two and twenty yards of satin" [for a suit of clothes]. Hamlet is "the glass of fashion and the mould of form. . . . He was likely, had he been put on, to have proved most royally."

We need look no further than Iago's description of Othello for the perfect clue to the playing of this great role. Iago described the Moor as "of a free and open nature, that thinks men honest that but seem to be so. . . ." The actor taking the cue from Shakespeare should have little difficulty in making us understand why Othello was such easy prey for the evil Iago.

In addition, new facets of the character will undoubtedly continue to be uncovered as the actor works on a role. Even experienced actors who play Shakespeare for the first time are impressed by the great freedom that Shakespeare's plays provide. After Alfred Lunt's first Shakespearean role, as Petruchio in *The Taming of the Shrew*, his enthusiasm was unbounded. He was moved to write:

> You read a speech or do a scene, giving it a certain meaning. Then, all of a sudden, a wholly different implication dawns on you, and you say to yourself, "Of course! *This* is what it really means. Why didn't I see it long ago?" And that keeps happening constantly. There is so much room to turn around in, in Shakespeare. No other dramatist old or new gives you so much . . . In that way, Shakespeare is like the Bible. The Bible has a great deal of room to turn around in, too—that is why there are so many opinions about it. With Shakespeare, I suppose the actor's greatest problem is how to fill up the space he finds himself in.[2]

A challenge indeed!

---

2. Quoted in Helen Ormsbee, *Backstage with Actors* (New York: Crowell, 1938), p. 262.

Reading Style

We have already noted that the verse play is essentially nonrealistic and utilizes imagery with telling effect in the projection of description and ideas. We have also noted that the plays of Shakespeare are not performed in the same manner as the modern realistic play. The reading of dialogue is an integral part of this consideration, for we cannot read verse in the same manner as we read dialogue suggestive of everyday conversation. The actor must not hesitate to give full sway to the rhythm and beauty of the language. The reading and the movement (which is related to the style adopted for the reading) should be full and robust. It must be remembered that the playwright has chosen poetry as the vehicle of expression because it permits an elevation of expression, a nobility, and a grandeur that ordinary prose cannot hope to achieve.

The young actor is often loath to give full meaning to the dynamics and tone coloring of the language. He may be afraid of being called a "ham." One question often heard in reference to this problem is: "Isn't it better to try to get the meaning across rather than project only the rhythm and structure of the poetry?" The answer, of course, is that it is best to strike a happy medium, to achieve a balance between the meaning and the rhythm of the verse. It is well to give an intelligent, carefully detailed reading of the lines, but the beauty of the sound must not be overlooked. The young actor would do well to *start by striving primarily for the meaning*, and, if he or she is an alert reader, *the poetry will begin to take care of itself*. Above all else, it is best to avoid the old sing-song elocutionary method so popular early in this century and rightly called "ham" when used today.

If we keep in mind the third **V** of good acting, validity, we shall agree with the early-twentieth-century critic Percy Fitzgerald, who tried to bring truth back to the playing of Shakespeare in a period that favored a more stilted style of playing. He noted that:

> It is always understood that to present *Hamlet* properly and according to tradition, we must adopt a sort of stilted, pedantic system of elocution and bearing.
>
> We must recite, declaim, growl, or vociferate, and stride about. All such things would disappear if the players could only persuade themselves that they were ordinary men and women concerned in a terrible and momentous tragedy—if they would but put emotion and passion and warmth and nature into all they say and do.[3]

Sound advice, and applicable not only for the playing of Shakespeare but for all presentational verse drama as well.

---

3. Percy Fitzgerald, *Shakespearean Representation* (London: Elliot Stock, 1906), p. 7.

The plays of Shakespeare have appealed to actors of every generation, some of whom have built brilliant reputations through their playing of Shakespeare's characters. Other actors have been less than successful, but all have found Shakespeare to be the playwright who brings most to the actor ready to come to him with an open mind and spirit. Walter Huston, a versatile and creative stage and film actor, had one notable failure during his long career. It was the role of Othello. Yet even in failure his pithy and frank comments provide a perfect summation for any discussion of Shakespeare and the actor.

> But the truth is that I have become ensnared by the magic of the guy's web. It is quite clear to me now why so many of the world's great actors (practically all of them) have grown up to play Shakespeare. His work is a challenge to any actor. His work holds a fascination for the actor such as nothing else in the literature of our theatre does. Having played Shakespeare, even in a production which flopped, was an experience by which my life is immensely enriched. I'm tickled pink to have done it.[4]

> *Leather Lungs—nickname for British singer and actress Elaine Page, who played lead roles in London productions of* Hair, Jesus Christ Superstar, *and* Grease. *She played in* Cats *and in* Chess. *Ms. Page also created the role of* Evita.
>
> Theatrical Trivia

Sustained Speeches

Long speeches or monologues must be approached by the actor with special care. Although the extended monologue is often thought to be a characteristics of plays of the past, especially verse drama, it appears in many modern plays as well. A not uncommon habit actors adopted not long ago was to approach a sustained monologue as a *tour-de-force*, so that the speech might serve the same function as a showpiece aria in an opera. Fortunately, few actors have this attitude today. Yet there is no question that the sustained speech poses a special problem for all actors, regardless of their training and experience.

The good actor not only will lavish care on the development of a role but also will take special pains to probe into the structure and organization of ex-

---

4. Walter Huston, "In and Out of the Bag: Othello Sits Up in Bed the Morning After and Takes Notice," *Stage*, March 1937, pp. 54–57.

tended passages. An extended speech is often one of the highlights of a play, in which the character most thoroughly reveals him- or herself to the audience or in which the playwright sees to it that the theme of the play is enunciated in unmistakable terms. As the actor develops an understanding of the role, it will become possible to place the monologue in its proper perspective, that is, in relation to its function in the play. This is the first step, permitting the emotional or intellectual context of the sequence to be related to the play as a whole. The key to the proper preparation of a monologue is good organization. It may also be termed "scoring." During the preparation of the monologue, it may help the actor to consider four factors: pattern of organization, transitions, emphasis, and climax.

Pattern of organization refers to specific divisions that the playwright may insert in the speech, such as paragraphs, sentences, colons; or any arbitrary division used to set off one portion of the material from another.

Words or phrases may indicate a shifting of mood or interest. Such *transitions* may relate to time (e.g., *then, now,* or *later*) or to contrast (e.g., *but, yet, despite all,* or *also*). They may provide a distinct clue to a change in the character's mood or attitude that the actor must impart to the audience.

In examining the sequence of the material, the actor must determine whether all the dialogue is of equal value or whether one portion of the speech requires greater *emphasis*. Even in speeches of simple exposition it is likely that certain portions will need to be highlighted.

A *climax*, or build, is required in speeches of emotional fervor or those that represent a passionate outburst by a character. Careful pacing is important here so that the monologue logically and steadily builds to its peak. A reexamination of the monologue from *Death of a Salesman* should reveal this kind of accelerated drive to a climax.

The following selection will serve to illustrate how careful examination can reveal ways and means of extracting the full dynamic range of an extended speech. The numbers in brackets point out where a mood shifts or a new idea interrupts a stream of thought. We include here only one possible means of preparing this particular monologue. Any actress might approach this role and monologue in a number of different ways.

We have chosen Nina's speech to Trepleff from the last act of Chekhov's *The Sea Gull*. Nina has returned home after a dismal attempt to find success as an actress and an unhappy affair with the playwright Trigorin. Arriving tired and lonely in Trepleff's study, she unburdens herself to him.

NINA: [1] Why do you say you kiss the ground I walk on? I ought to be killed. [2] I'm so tired. If I could rest—rest. I'm a sea gull. No, that's not it. I'm an actress. Well, no matter. [3] He didn't believe in the theatre, all my dreams he'd laugh at, and little by little I quit believing in it myself, and lost heart. And there was the strain of love, jealousy, constant anxiety about my little baby. [4] I got to be small and trashy, and played without thinking. I didn't know what to do with my hands, couldn't stand properly on the stage, couldn't control my voice. [5] You can't imagine the feeling when you are acting and know it's dull. [6] I'm a sea gull. No, that's not it. [7] Do you remember, you shot a sea gull? A man comes by chance, sees it, and out of nothing else to do, destroys it. [8] That's not it— (*Puts her hand to her forehead.*) What was I—? [9] I was talking about the stage. Now I'm not like that. I'm a real actress, I act with delight, with rapture, I'm drunk when I'm on the stage, and feel that I am beautiful. And now, ever since I've been here, I've kept walking about, kept walking and thinking, thinking and believing my soul grows stronger every day. Now I know, I understand, Kostya, that in our work—acting or writing—what matters is not fame, not glory, not what I used to dream about, it's how to endure, to bear my cross, and have faith. I have faith and it all doesn't hurt me so much, and when I think of my calling I'm not afraid of life.

This speech can first be divided into two distinct portions. The first part (including notations [1] through [8] is morbid and self-pitying; the second (notation [9] to the end) is rapturous and lyric. Yet even within this broad division we can discern little transitions that provide means of projecting subtleties and nuances that tell us much about Nina's state of mind.

Part I: Keyed to Self-Pity and Remorse

1. The mood of remorse is set.
2. A slight transition indicating her emotional and physical fatigue.
3. Nina tries to tell Trepleff of her affair with the playwright, Trigorin.
4. Nina honestly faces up to her failure as an actress.
5. A rapid transition in which she reveals her anguish at her own failure.
6. She wanders off for a moment, symbolically comparing herself to a carefree sea gull.
7. A subtle transition in which she relates the symbolic destruction of the sea gull to her own failure.
8. She has lost the sequence of her thoughts for a moment.

Part II: Complete Shift of Mood

9. Nina recovers herself, and in this last portion as a whole we may note a continued build, rising almost to exaltation, as she dismisses her unfortunate past in a burst of idealistic fervor.

Not all monologues can be handled or "scored" in the same manner, but clearly this type of analysis of the material should be useful. While progressing through the rehearsal period, the actor is likely to discover new shades of meaning in such passages. With effective organization and an intelligent awareness of the great variety that may be imparted to them, the actor can make such sequences truly the high moments of a performance.

The Penthouse Theatre, c. 1940. University of Washington Archives.

Central Staging

Although there has been an increasing interest in it in recent years, central staging is actually the oldest of all theatre forms. The outdoor theatre of the Greeks, the medieval pageant-wagons of the craft guilds, and the Elizabethan playhouses all made use of staging techniques that we recognize as a type of central staging. The increasing contemporary vogue of this theatre form requires that we examine how this style of production affects the work of the actor.

Central staging is a term descriptive of a theatre using a centrally located playing area (in relation to the audience) with spectators sitting around two or more sides of the stage area. The most common type of central staging, in which the audience completely surrounds the playing area, is known as *arena staging* or *arena theatre*. Other names often used to describe types of central staging are *flexible staging, circus staging, thrust*, and *theatre in the round*.

The Mark Taper Forum, Los Angeles. (Photo by Craig Schwartz.)

The playing area may be one of several shapes and sizes—a square, rectangle, circle, or oval (see Figures 11.1 through 11.4).

The fundamental feature that distinguishes central staging from proscenium, or conventional, staging is the absence of the proscenium arch separating stage and audience. The removal of this barrier results in a greater proximity of audience to actor. Of all the qualities of central staging, *intimacy* is the one that will require the greatest adjustment on the actor's part.

Most recently great interest has been shown in *thrust* staging, in which the stage extends well beyond the proscenium arch, much in the fashion of the theatre in Shakespeare's time (see Figure 11.4). Thrust staging provides a great sense of "communion" with the audience yet permits entrances and exits to be made from the stage area itself and not through the audience, as is required in true arena staging.

Because of the intimacy of spectator and actor and the usual elimination of all but the basic pieces of stage setting, the oft-repeated statement that this is an actor's theatre is very true. Under such circumstances the work of the

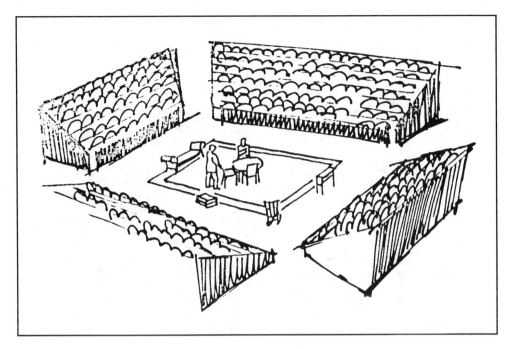

FIGURE 11.1 Central staging: Arena.

actor takes on added dominance over the other aspects of a production, so there is a greater burden on the actor than in conventional staging. The work of both the good and the bad actor is inevitably placed under the magnifying glass of close audience scrutiny.

Adjustments for the Actor

Any competent actor should have little difficulty in making the change from conventional to central staging. The fundamental preparation and development of a role are the same under all production styles. Keeping this in mind, we can examine the few necessary adjustments the actor must make when working in central staging.

Subtlety.   The intimacy provided by central staging will immediately reveal to the spectators any superficiality in the actor's technique and characterization. Especially important in the small arena theatre is the problem of detailed business, which in conventional staging may need to be projected over a dis-

FIGURE 11.2   Central staging: Three-sided or thrust.

tance of perhaps a hundred to two hundred feet. Business must be toned down and performed with almost as much subtlety and simplicity as we would expect to find in an everyday nontheatrical situation.

Body Positions.   The rules relating to body positions and emphatic areas no longer hold true when the audience views the play from more than one direction. An open position to one portion of the audience will seem most awkward and unnatural when viewed from a different section of the house. Rules of body position for conventional staging should be disregarded.

When two actors share a scene, they should rarely face the same direction at the same time. Space between the actors should be sufficient to provide visibility for the members of the audience. Except when one actor is playing with the back to an aisle (in arena staging) actors should *not* face another actor directly. One or both actors should stand slightly sideways in an open position,

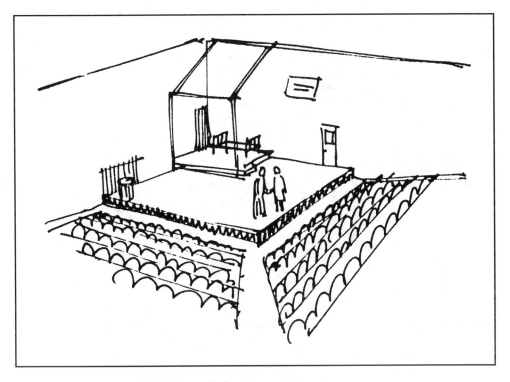

FIGURE 11.3   Central staging: L-shaped.

facing each other in a one-quarter rather than a full-front stance. This is what has been called "twisting the pairs," meaning that part of the audience can see each of the actors over the shoulder of the other. The significant thing to remember is that normally the actors should maintain the same visual relationship as one adopts unconsciously in one's own living room. At home there is no thought of a fourth wall through which the audience is privileged to peep. The same attitude should prevail in the actor's work in a production with central staging.

Concentration.   Because of the proximity of the audience (some actors describe central staging as playing in the laps of the audience), noise made by late-comers, spectators' coughing and jostling, and other distractions are greatly magnified. The actor, playing to an audience assembled just at the edge of the playing area, may find it very difficult to achieve the detachment to which he or she is accustomed in the proscenium theatre. Although the actor can never totally disregard the audience, it is essential to concentrate fully on the play so as not to permit audience distractions to affect the work.

FIGURE 11.4   Proscenium stage

Projection.   The level of projection used by the actor in central staging will depend directly upon the size and shape of the playing area and auditorium. Although the intimacy of central staging may permit the volume level to be dropped, another important principle also operates here. The actor cannot focus all speech in one direction but must be heard by the audience seated on all sides. The actor must be heard as clearly by the spectator seated directly behind as by one in front.

Volume alone is certainly not the solution. We should remember that good projection depends on a number of factors, including volume, clarity, and good articulation. In order to be heard in all parts of the house, the actor must take special care to project effectively, even if the intimacy of the auditorium requires a lowering of the volume level.

Acting in any of the numerous types of central staging provides a very useful experience, especially for actors who have been working exclusively in proscenium theatre. Because of the importance of details, participation in *any* intimate theatre production is helpful in sharpening the acting faculties of the performer. Even if an actor may prefer to work in the conventional stage situation, some exposure to central staging will prove a stimulating experience.

Arena staging: *Landscape of the Body* by John Guare.
University of Washington School of Drama, 1996.
Directed by Robyn Hunt. Photograph by Theodore
Esser.

SUGGESTIONS FOR FURTHER READING

Barton, John. *Playing Shakespeare.* London, Methuen Paperback, 1984/1996.

Blum, Richard A. *American Film Acting: The Stanislavski Heritage.* Studies in Cinema no. 28. Ann Arbor, MI: UMI Research Press, 1984.

Boyle, Walden P. *Central and Flexible Staging.* Berkeley and Los Angeles: University of California Press, 1956.

Callow, Simon. *Acting in Restoration Comedy*, ed. Maria Aitken. New York: Applause Theater Book Publishers, 1988.

Chisman, Isabel, & Hester E. Raven-Hart. *Manners and Movements in Costume Plays.* London: Kenyon-Deane; Boston: Walter H. Baker, n.d.

Joseph, Bertram L. *Elizabethan Acting*, 2nd ed. London: Oxford University Press, 1964.

Miller, Jonathan. *Jonathan Miller on Acting in Opera*, ed. Maria Aitken. The B.B.C. Acting Series. New York: Applause Theater Books, 1988.

Oxenford, Lynn. *Playing Period Plays*. Chicago: Coach House Press, 1974.

Russell, Douglas A. *Period Style for the Theatre*. Boston: Allyn and Bacon, 1980.

Seyler, Athene. *The Craft of Comedy* (correspondence between Athene Seyler and Stephen Haggard). New York: Theatre Arts, 1946.

Sievers, Stiver, & Stanley Kahan. *Directing for the Theatre*, 3rd ed. Dubuque, IA: Brown, 1974.

Scenes

Monologue from The Hairy Ape, by Eugene O'Neill

Paddy is an old Irish sailor, traveling the seas as a stoker in the stokehold of an ocean liner. But he remembers a happier day, when the sea was conquered by the great four-masters with full sail in the breeze.

PADDY: (*Who has been sitting in a blinking, melancholy daze—suddenly cries out in a voice full of old sorrow.*) We belong to this, you're saying? We make the ship to go, you're saying? Yerra then, that Almighty God have pity on us! Oh, to be back in the fine days of my youth, ochone! Oh, there was fine beautiful ships them days—clippers wid tall masts touching the sky—fine strong men in them—men that was sons of the sea as if 'twas the mother that bore them. Oh, the clean skins of them, and the clear eyes, the straight backs and full chests of them! Brave men they was, and bold men surely! We'd be sailing out, bound down round the Horn maybe. We'd be making sail in the dawn, with a fair breeze, singing a chanty song wid no care to it. And astern the land would be sinking low and dying out, but we'd give it no heed but a laugh, and never a look behind. For the day that was, was enough, for we was free men—and I'm thinking 'tis only slaves to be giving heed to the day that's gone or the day to come—until they're old like me. (*with a sort of religious exaltation*) Oh, to be scudding south again wid the power of the Trade Wind driving her on steady through the nights and the days! Full sail on her! Nights and days! Nights when the foam of the wake would be flaming wid fire, when the sky'd be blazing and winking wid stars. Or the full moon maybe. Then you'd see her driving through the gray night, her sails stretching aloft all silver and white, not a sound on the deck, the lot of us dreaming dreams, till you'd believe 'twas no real ship at all you was on but a ghost ship like the *Flying Dutchman* they says does be roaming the seas forevermore widout touching a port. And there was the days, too. A warm sun on the clean decks. Sun warming the blood of you, and wind over the miles of shiny green ocean like strong drink to your lungs. Work—aye, hard work—but who'd mind that at all? Sure, you worked under the sky and 'twas work wid skill and daring to it. And wid the day done, in the dog watch, smoking me pipe at ease, the lookout would be raising land maybe, and we'd see the mountains of South Americy wid the red fire of the setting sun painting their white tops and the clouds floating by them! (*His tone of exaltation ceases. He goes on mournfully.*) Yerra, what's the use of talking? 'Tis a dead man's whisper.

The Rivals, by Richard Brinsley Sheridan
From Act III, Scene 4

Scene:	For two men
Characters:	SIR LUCIUS O'TRIGGER, a middle-aged Irish gentleman
	BOB ACRES, a young country bumpkin
Setting:	Acre's lodgings in Bath, England
Time:	1775
Situation:	In this eighteenth-century comedy of manners Bob Acres has been attempting to carry on a courtship with Lydia Languish, an attractive and wealthy young lady who is in love with Captain Absolute. He has been wooing her disguised as Ensign Beverly. Sir Lucius O'Trigger, on finding that Bob has a "rival," urges him to challenge Beverly to a duel and aids him in writing the letter of challenge.

Enter SIR LUCIUS.

SIR LUCIUS: Mr. Acres, I am delighted to embrace you.

ACRES: My dear Sir Lucius, I kiss your hands.

SIR LUCIUS: Pray, my friend, what has brought you so suddenly to Bath?

ACRES: Faith! I have followed Cupid's Jack-a-Lantern, and find myself in a quagmire at last.—In short, I have been very ill-used, Sir Lucius.—I don't choose to mention names, but look on me as on a very ill-used gentleman.

SIR LUCIUS: Pray what is the case?—I ask no names.

ACRES: Mark me, Sir Lucius, I fall as deep as need be in love with a young lady—her friends take my part—I follow her to Bath—send word of my arrival; and receive answer, that the lady is to be otherwise disposed of.—This, Sir Lucius, I call being ill-used.

SIR LUCIUS: Very ill, upon my conscience.—Pray, can you divine the cause of it?

ACRES: Why, there's the matter: she has another lover, one *Beverley*, who, I am told, is now in Bath.—Odds slanders and lies! he must be at the bottom of it.

SIR LUCIUS: A rival in the case, is there!—and you think he has supplanted you unfairly.

ACRES: Unfairly! to be sure he has.—He never could have done it fairly.

SIR LUCIUS: Then sure you know what is to be done!

ACRES: Not I, upon my soul!

SIR LUCIUS: We wear no swords here, but you understand me?

ACRES: What! fight him!

SIR LUCIUS: Aye, to be sure: what can I mean else?

ACRES: But he has given me no provocation.

SIR LUCIUS: Now, I think he has given you the greatest provocation in the world.—Can a man commit a more heinous offence against another than to fall in love with the same woman? O, by my soul, it is the most unpardonable breach of friendship.

ACRES: Breach of friendship! Aye, aye; but I have no acquaintance with this man. I never saw him in my life.

SIR LUCIUS: That's no argument at all—he has the less right then to take such a liberty.

ACRES: 'Gad that's true—I grow full of anger, Sir Lucius!—I fire apace! Odds hilts and blades; I find a man may have a deal of valour in him, and not know it! But couldn't I contrive to have a little right of my side?

SIR LUCIUS: What the Devil signifies *right*, when your *honour* is concerned? Do you think, *Achilles* or my little *Alexander the Great* ever inquired where the right lay? No, by my soul, they drew their broad-swords, and left the lazy sons of peace to settle the justice of it.

ACRES: Your words are a grenadier's march to my heart! I believe courage must be catching!—I certainly do feel a kind of valour rising as it were—a kind of courage, as I may say—Odds flints, pans, and triggers! I'll challenge him directly.

SIR LUCIUS: Ah, my little friend! if I had *Blunderbuss-Hall* here—I could shew you a range of ancestry, in the O'Trigger line, that would furnish the new room; every one of whom had killed his man!—For though the mansion-house and dirty acres have slipt through my fingers, I thank Heav'n our ho-nour and the family-pictures, are as fresh as ever.

ACRES: O, Sir Lucius! I have had ancestors too!—every man of 'em colonel or captain in the militia!—Odds balls and barrels! say no more—I'm brac'd for it. The thunder of your words has soured the milk of human kindness in my breast!—Zounds! as the man in the play says, "I could do such deeds—"

SIR LUCIUS: Come, come, there must be no passion at all in the case—these things should always be done civilly.

ACRES: I must be in a passion, Sir Lucius—I must be in a rage.—Dear Sir Lu-cius, let me be in a rage, if you love me.—Come, here's pen and paper. [*Sits down to write.*] I would the ink were red!—Indite, I say indite!—How shall I begin? Odds bullets and blades! I'll write a good bold hand, however.

SIR LUCIUS: Pray compose yourself.

ACRES: Come—now, shall I begin with an oath? Do, Sir Lucius let me begin with a damme.

SIR LUCIUS: Pho! pho! do the thing decently, and like a Christian. Begin now—"*Sir*—

ACRES: That's too civil by half.

SIR LUCIUS: "*To prevent the confusion that might arise.*"

ACRES: Well—

SIR LUCIUS: "*From our both addressing the same lady.*"

ACRES: Aye—there's the reason—"*same lady*"—Well—

SIR LUCIUS: "*I shall expect the honour of your company*"—

ACRES: Zounds! I'm not asking him to dinner.

SIR LUCIUS: Pray be easy.

ACRES: Well then, "honour of your company"

SIR LUCIUS: "*To settle our pretensions.*"

ACRES: Well.

SIR LUCIUS: Let me see, aye, *King's Mead-fields* will do—"*in King's Mead-fields.*"

ACRES: So that's done.—Well, I'll fold it up presently; my own crest—a hand and dagger shall be the seal.

SIR LUCIUS: You see now this little explanation will put a stop at once to all confusion or misunderstanding that might arise between you.

ACRES: Aye, we fight to prevent any misunderstanding.

SIR LUCIUS: Now, I'll leave you to fix your own time.—Take my advice, and you'll decide it this evening if you can; then let the worst come of it, 'twill be off your mind to-morrow.

ACRES: Very true.

SIR LUCIUS: So I shall see nothing more of you, unless it be by letter, till the evening.—I would do myself the honour to carry your message; but, to tell you a secret, I believe I shall have just such another affair on my own hands. There is a gay captain here, who put a jest on me lately, at the expence of my country, and I only want to fall in with the gentleman, to call him out.

ACRES: By my valour, I should like to see you fight first! Odds life! I should like to see you kill him, if it was only to get a little lesson.

SIR LUCIUS: I shall be very proud of instructing you.—Well for the present—but remember now, when you meet your antagonist, do everything in a mild and agreeable manner.—Let your courage be as keen, but at the same time as polished as your sword. [*Exeunt severally*]

END OF THE THIRD ACT.

The Miser, by Molière (translated and adapted by Stanley Kahan)
From Act I

Scene:	For two men
Characters:	HARPAGON, a miser
	LA FLÈCHE, a valet to Harpagon's son, Cleante
Setting:	Harpagon's home in Paris.
Time:	Mid-seventeenth century.
Situation:	Harpagon is such a miser that he hides his money in various exotic places, including a particularly large sum in his garden. He lives in continual fear that someone will find his money and rob him. His main passion in life is to pinch pennies and hoard all his money. In this scene, he suspects his son's valet, La Flèche, of spying on him and of finding his hidden money. The scene begins as Harpagon has angrily ordered La Flèche out of the house. The play is filled with sharp satire and delightful comic touches. Harpagon particularly is a sharply drawn comedic character.

HARPAGON: Get out of my house immediately, do you hear? Get out of here, you liar, you cheat, you gallow's meat, and don't answer back!

LA FLÈCHE: (*aside*) I have never seen anyone as nasty as this crusty old man, and if I am not mistaken, the devil has taken possession of him.

HARPAGON: What are you muttering about over there, eh?

LA FLÈCHE: Why do you want me to leave?

HARPAGON: Just the sort of question one would expect from a lout such as you. Get out, and get out now before I kick you out with my own two feet.

LA FLÈCHE: What have I ever done to you?

HARPAGON: You have done more than enough, so get out and get out now!

LA FLÈCHE: But my master, your own son, has ordered me to wait.

HARPAGON: Then go and wait for him out in the street, but do not stay in this house, spying on me, watching everything that is going on, and using it against me. No one is going to spy on me in my own home, particularly a wretch such as you who covets all I own, watches my every little action, and sneaks about to see if he can find something to steal.

LA FLÈCHE: How could anyone even find something to steal from you, when you lock up everything you own and keep guard over it day and night?

HARPAGON: I will lock up anything I want to, and I will guard it as long as it suits me. This is a pretty kettle of fish, when spies lurk around you all the time. (*Quietly, aside*) I tremble if he should even suspect anything about my money. (*Aloud*) So! you are probably just the kind of person who would go around telling everyone about the money hidden in my house.

LA FLÈCHE: You have money hidden in this house?

HARPAGON: No! No! No! I never said that, you rascal. (*To himself*) I am going to explode with rage! (*Aloud*) I simply asked if you would spread the story about because of your bad manners and the ill will you bear me.

LA FLÈCHE: What? What does it matter to anyone if you think you have money or not; the important thing is, do you really have some?

HARPAGON: (*About to strike La Flèche in the face*) Stop arguing with me. I'll slap your nose, and mouth and ears, and then you can think about it. I say again, get out of here.

LA FLÈCHE: Very well, I am leaving!

HARPAGON: Just a moment! You are not taking anything with you, are you?

LA FLÈCHE: And what would I take from you?

HARPAGON: Who knows? I have to look first! Let me see your hands.

LA FLÈCHE: Here they are.

HARPAGON: And the others?

LA FLÈCHE: (*Puzzled*) The other what?

HARPAGON: That's right, the other whats.

LA FLÈCHE: Here, look for yourself. (*Showing him his legs.*)

HARPAGON: (*Pointing to La Flèche's breeches*) You have nothing hidden in there, you lout?

LA FLÈCHE: How would you like to look for yourself?

HARPAGON: (*Feeling La Flèche's pockets*) Those wide breeches of yours are purposely designed to hide things in them. You think you are very clever, don't you?

LA FLÈCHE: (*Aside*) Ah! How a man such as this deserves whatever happens to him—and what a pleasure I would have in robbing him!

HARPAGON: Eh!

LA FLÈCHE: What?

HARPAGON: What did I hear you mutter about robbing me?

LA FLÈCHE: I said if you feel carefully, you can tell if I have robbed you!

HARPAGON: That is just what I intend to do! (*Harpagon sticks his hands in La Flèche's pockets*)

LA FLÈCHE: (*Aside*) May the plague take him and all misers like him.

HARPAGON: What's that? What did you say?

LA FLÈCHE: What did I say?

HARPAGON: Yes, what did you say about misers, eh?

LA FLÈCHE: I said may the plague take all misers and people who act like misers.

HARPAGON: Were you speaking about someone in particular?

LA FLÈCHE: Just about misers.

HARPAGON: And who are these misers you were referring to?

LA FLÈCHE: Moneygrubbers and pennypinchers.

HARPAGON: And who did you have in mind? (*His hands are still in La Flèche's pockets*)

LA FLÈCHE: Why are you so concerned about it?

HARPAGON: I am concerned about what concerns me.

LA FLÈCHE: Did you think I was talking about you?

HARPAGON: I'll think whatever I want to think! I want you to tell me who you were talking about when you said that!

LA FLÈCHE: I am talking to—I am talking to my hat!

HARPAGON: And I am talking to the head beneath that particular hat.

LA FLÈCHE: Do you mean to say I am not permitted to curse pennypinchers?

HARPAGON: No—but not in this house. Stop whimpering and being insulting. Keep your tongue to yourself.

LA FLÈCHE: I didn't mention any names.

HARPAGON: I'll beat you within an inch of your life if you say another word.

LA FLÈCHE: If the shoe fits, one had better wear it.

HARPAGON: Will you keep your tongue in place?

LA FLÈCHE: Yes, but only against my will.

HARPAGON: Ah ha—So—So that's it!

LA FLÈCHE: Look here—(*showing Harpagon a pocket in his doublet*) Here's one you missed! Satisfied?

HARPAGON: Very well—you had better give me what is mine without my having to search you!

LA FLÈCHE: What did you say?

HARPAGON: What have you taken from me?

LA FLÈCHE: I have taken nothing at all from you.

HARPAGON: You swear it?

LA FLÈCHE: Of course!

HARPAGON: Goodbye, then, and you know where you can go!

LA FLÈCHE: (*Aside*) What a delightful and charming way to dismiss someone. (*He starts to leave*)

HARPAGON: (*Calling after him*) I shall leave you to your own conscience, to rob a poor, old, helpless, and generous man such as myself!

The Importance of Being Earnest, by Oscar Wilde
From Act II

Scene: For two women
Characters: GWENDOLYN FAIRFAX, a sophisticated young lady from London in her mid-twenties
       CECILY CARDEW, a charming young girl from the English country, late teens
Setting: The garden of a manor house in the English countryside.
Time: A lovely afternoon in the late 1890s.
Situation: In this delightful scene, two young ladies meet each other and come to the conclusion that they are both in love with the same man, Mr. Ernest Worthing. Actually they are in love with different men, but the machinations of the plot have led to this confusion. They begin to take effective verbal pot shots at each other, while indulging in one of the most hallowed of British institutions, taking tea together.

     The lines of the butler who serves the tea are included in this scene but can be easily cut without affecting the scene.

CECILY: (*advancing to meet her*). Pray let me introduce myself to you. My name is Cecily Cardew.

GWENDOLEN: Cecily Cardew? (*Moving to her and shaking hands*) What a very sweet name! Something tells me that we are going to be great friends. I like you already more than I can say. My first impressions of people are never wrong.

CECILY: How nice of you to like me so much after we have known each other such a comparatively short time. Pray sit down.

GWENDOLEN: (*still standing up*). I may call you Cecily, may I not?

CECILY: With pleasure!

GWENDOLEN: And you will always call me Gwendolen, won't you?

CECILY: If you wish.

GWENDOLEN: Then that is all quite settled, is it not?

CECILY: I hope so. (*A pause. They both sit down together.*)

GWENDOLEN: Perhaps this might be a favorable opportunity for my mentioning who I am. My father is Lord Bracknell. You have never heard of papa, I suppose?

CECILY: I don't think so.

GWENDOLEN: Outside the family circle, papa, I am glad to say, is entirely unknown. I think that is quite as it should be. The home seems to me to be the proper sphere for the man. And certainly once a man begins to neglect his domestic duties he becomes painfully effeminate, does he not? And I don't like that. It makes men so very attractive. Cecily, mamma, whose views on education are remarkably strict, has brought me up to be extremely short-sighted; it is part of her system; so do you mind my looking at you through my glasses?

CECILY: Oh, not at all, Gwendolen. I am very fond of being looked at.

GWENDOLEN: (*After examining* CECILY *carefully through a lorgnette*). You are here on a short visit, I suppose.

CECILY: On, no, I live here.

GWENDOLEN: (*severely*). Really? Your mother, no doubt, or some female relative of advanced years, resides here also?

CECILY: On, no. I have no mother, nor, in fact, any relations.

GWENDOLEN: Indeed?

CECILY: My dear guardian, with the assistance of Miss Prism, has the arduous task of looking after me.

GWENDOLEN: Your guardian?

CECILY: Yes, I am Mr. Worthing's ward.

GWENDOLEN: Oh! It is strange he never mentioned to me that he had a ward. How secretive of him! He grows more interesting hourly. I am not sure, however, that the news inspires me with feelings of unmixed delight. (*Rising and going to her*) I am very fond of you, Cecily; I have liked you ever since I met you. But I am bound to state that now that I know that you are Mr. Worthing's ward, I cannot help expressing a wish you were—well, just a little older than you seem to be—and not quite so very alluring in appearance. In fact, if I may speak candidly—

CECILY: Pray do! I think that whenever one has anything unpleasant to say, one should always be quite candid.

GWENDOLEN: Well, to speak with perfect candour, Cecily, I wish that you were fully forty-two, and more than usually plain for your age. Ernest has a strong upright nature. He is the very soul of truth and honour. Disloyalty would be as impossible to him as deception. But even men of the noblest possible moral character are extremely susceptible to the influence of the physical charms of others. Modern, no less than Ancient History, supplies us with many most painful examples of what I refer to. If it were not so, indeed, History would be quite unreadable.

CECILY: I beg your pardon, Gwendolen, did you say Ernest?

GWENDOLEN: Yes.

CECILY: Oh, but it is not Mr. Ernest Worthing who is my guardian. It is his brother—his elder brother.

GWENDOLEN: (*sitting down again*) Ernest never mentioned to me that he had a brother.

CECILY: I am sorry to say they have not been on good terms for a long time.

GWENDOLEN: Ah! that accounts for it. And now that I think of it I have never heard any man mention his brother. The subject seems distasteful to most men. Cecily, you have lifted a load from my mind. I was growing almost anxious. It would have been terrible if any cloud had come across a friendship like ours, would it not? Of course you are quite, quite sure that it is not Mr. Ernest Worthing who is your guardian?

CECILY: Quite sure. (*A pause*) In fact, I am going to be his.

GWENDOLEN: (*enquiringly*). I beg your pardon?

CECILY: (*rather shy and confidingly*). Dearest Gwendolen, there is no reason why I should make a secret of it to you. Our little county newspaper is sure to chronicle the fact next week. Mr. Ernest Worthing and I are engaged to be married.

GWENDOLEN: (*quite politely, rising*). My darling Cecily, I think there must be some slight error. Mr. Ernest Worthing is engaged to me. The announcement will appear in the *Morning Post* on Saturday at the latest.

CECILY: (*very politely, rising*). I am afraid you must be under some misconception. Ernest proposed to me exactly ten minutes ago. (*Shows diary.*)

GWENDOLEN: (*examines diary through her lorgnette carefully*). It is certainly very curious, for he asked me to be his wife yesterday afternoon at 5:30. If you would care to verify the incident, pray do so. (*Produces diary of her own*) I never travel without my diary. One should always have something sensational to read in the train. I am so sorry, dear Cecily, if it is any disappointment to you, but I am afraid *I* have the prior claim.

CECILY: It would distress me more than I can tell you, dear Gwendolen, if it caused you any mental or physical anguish, but I feel bound to point out that since Ernest proposed to you he clearly has changed his mind.

GWENDOLEN: (*meditatively*). If the poor fellow has been entrapped into any foolish promise I shall consider it my duty to rescue him at once, and with a firm hand.

CECILY: (*thoughtfully and sadly*). Whatever unfortunate entanglement my dear boy may have got into, I will never reproach him with it after we are married.

GWENDOLEN: Do you allude to me, Miss Cardew, as an entanglement? You are presumptuous. On an occasion of this kind it becomes more than a moral duty to speak one's mind. It becomes a pleasure.

CECILY: Do you suggest, Miss Fairfax, that I entrapped Ernest into an engagement? How dare you? This is no time for wearing the shallow mask of manners. When I see a spade I call it a spade.

GWENDOLEN: (*satirically*). I am glad to say that I have never seen a spade. It is obvious that our social spheres have been widely different.

(*Enter* MERRIMAN, *followed by the footman. He carries a salver, tablecloth, and plate-stand.* CECILY *is about to retort. The presence of the servants exercises a restraining influence, under which both girls chafe.*)

MERRIMAN: Shall I lay tea here as usual, miss?

CECILY: (*Sternly, in a calm voice*). Yes, as usual. (MERRIMAN, *begins to clear and lay cloth. A long pause.* CECILY *and* GWENDOLEN *glare at each other.*)

GWENDOLEN: Are there many interesting walks in the vicinity, Miss Cardew?

CECILY: Oh, yes, a great many. From the top of one of the hills quite close one can see five counties.

GWENDOLEN: Five counties! I don't think I should like that. I hate crowds.

CECILY: (*sweetly*). I suppose that is why you live in town? (GWENDOLEN *bites her lip, and beats her foot nervously with her parasol.*)

GWENDOLEN: (*looking around*). Quite a well-kept garden this is, Miss Cardew.

CECILY: So glad you like it, Miss Fairfax.

GWENDOLEN: I had no idea there were any flowers in the country.

CECILY: Oh, flowers are as common here, Miss Fairfax, as people are in London.

GWENDOLEN: Personally I cannot understand how anybody manages to exist in the country, if anybody who is anybody does. The country always bores me to death.

CECILY: Ah! This is what the newspapers call agricultural depression, is it not? I believe the aristocracy are suffering very much from it just at present. It is almost an epidemic amongst them, I have been told. May I offer you some tea, Miss Fairfax?

GWENDOLEN: (*with elaborate politeness*). Thank you. (*Aside*) Detestable girl! But I require tea!

CECILY: (*sweetly*). Sugar?

GWENDOLEN: (*superciliously*). No, thank you. Sugar is not fashionable any more. (CECILY *looks angrily at her, takes up the tongs and puts four lumps of sugar into the cup.*)

CECILY: (*severely*). Cake or bread and butter?

GWENDOLEN: (*in a bored manner*). Bread and butter, please. Cake is rarely seen at the best houses now-a-days.

CECILY: (*cuts a very large slice of cake, and puts it on the tray*). Hand that to Miss Fairfax. (MERRIMAN *does so, and goes out with footman.* GWENDOLEN *drinks the tea and makes a grimace. Puts down cup at once, reaches out her hand to the bread and butter, looks at it, and finds it is cake. Rises in indignation.*)

GWENDOLEN: You have filled my tea with lumps of sugar, and though I asked most distinctly for bread and butter, you have given me cake. I am known for the gentleness of my disposition, and the extraordinary sweetness of my nature, but I warn you, Miss Cardew, you may go too far.

CECILY: (*rising*). To save my poor innocent, trusting boy from the machinations of any other girl there are no lengths to which I would not go.

GWENDOLEN: From the moment I saw you I distrusted you. I felt that you were false and deceitful. I am never deceived in such matters. My first impressions of people are invariably right.

CECILY: It seems to me, Miss Fairfax, that I am trespassing on your valuable time. No doubt you have many other calls of a similar character to make in the neighborhood.

The Doctor in Spite of Himself, by Molière (translated and adapted by Stanley Kahan) From Act I

Scene:	For two men, one woman
Characters:	SGANARELLE, a drunken woodcutter
	MARTINE, his wife
	MONSIEUR ROBERT, a gentleman
Setting:	A forest in France.
Time:	A day during the mid-seventeenth century.
Situation:	This is the opening scene of the play. Sganarelle and Martine are carrying on an argument that they started off-stage. They are low-comedy characters, endowed with little of the "gentility" found among the other characters in the play. Their speech and actions highlight the generally farcical knockabout nature of broad comedic acting.

(*Sganarelle and Martine appear on the stage quarreling*)

SGANARELLE: Absolutely not. I tell you I will do nothing of the kind. It is up to me to decide when to speak, and I will be master here.

MARTINE: And I am telling you that I will live as I wish, and I am not married to you to put up with all of your foolishness.

SGANARELLE: Good grief . . . what a pain in the . . . to have a wife! Aristotle was perfectly right in stating that a woman is worse than the devil.

MARTINE: Look at Mister Smart-Aleck—and his Greek friend Aristotle.

SGANARELLE: That's right. Mister Smart-Aleck. You go and find a better wood chopper who can debate the way I can.—I, who have served a great physician for six years, and who, when only a little boy, knew his grammar by heart!

MARTINE: A plague on this idiot!

SGANARELLE: A plague on this slut of a wife.

MARTINE: Cursed be the hour and the day when I took it in my poor head to say yes to this lout!

SGANARELLE: Cursed be the notary who made me put my mark on that vile contract.

MARTINE: So . . . it is very nice of you to complain about that matter. Shouldn't you rather thank Heaven every second you breathe that you have me for a wife? How did you ever deserve a woman like me?

SGANARELLE: Oh, my sweet, you are much too kind—and I must admit I have had occasions to remember our wedding night with great warmth! Heavens!—Don't make me open my mouth too wide. I might say certain things I shouldn't.

MARTINE: Eh! What? Say? What could you say?

SGANARELLE: Enough of that! Let us drop the matter. It is enough that we know what we know, and that you were very fortunate to meet me at all.

MARTINE: What do you mean—fortunate to meet you. A slob who will send me to a hospital?—a drunken, lying wretch who gobbles up every penny I have?

SGANARELLE: That is a lie: I don't gobble—I drink every penny of it!

MARTINE: A wretch who sells all the furniture in the house?

SGANARELLE: That is called living off one's means.

MARTINE: A fiend who has taken the very bed from under me?

SGANARELLE: That is simply to help you get up earlier in the morning.

MARTINE: An idiot who doesn't leave a stick of furniture in the house.

SGANARELLE: It is just a way of making moving that much easier.

MARTINE: A lout who does nothing from morning till night but gamble and drink.

SGANARELLE: I do that simply to keep from becoming too depressed.

MARTINE: And what am I supposed to do with our family?

SGANARELLE: You can do whatever you like.

MARTINE: I have four poor children on my hands.

SGANARELLE: Then drop them.

MARTINE: They keep asking for a little bread!

SGANARELLE: So then—beat them. When I've had enough to eat and drink, everyone in the house should be satisfied.

MARTINE: Do you mean to tell me, you drunken sot, that things can go on as they have been all this time?

SGANARELLE: My dear wife, let us not get excited, pretty-please?

MARTINE: And that I must bear forever your drunkenness and insults?

SGANARELLE: Let us not get upset, my little pigeon.

MARTINE: And that I don't know how to bring you back to a sense of responsibility?

SGANARELLE: My little canary—you know I am not a patient man—and my arm is beginning to get a little excited!

MARTINE: I give that for your threats. (*snaps her fingers*)

SGANARELLE: My bird, my parrot, my canary—your skin is itching for a good hiding!

MARTINE: You had better observe that I couldn't care less for your threats!

SGANARELLE: My dear little rib—you have set your heart upon a good beating.

MARTINE: Do you think I am frightened of all your talk?

SGANARELLE: Sweet little barbecued chop, I shall belt you in the ears.

MARTINE: Drunken lout!

SGANARELLE: I'll beat you!

MARTINE: Walking wine-cask.

SGANARELLE: I'll pummel you.

MARTINE: Infamous wretch.

SGANARELLE: I'll tan your hide so that you won't forget it.

MARTINE: Lout! villian! scoundrel! drunkard! wretch! dog's meat! horse's tail! liar! deceiver! . . .

SGANARELLE: So you really want it, eh? Very well then. (*He picks up a stick and starts to beat her*)

MARTINE: (*Yelling*) Help! Oh, help! Please help! Help!

SGANARELLE: And this my pet is the best way to shut you up!

M. ROBERT: Hello there! I say, Hello. Good Heavens. What is this? How revolting. The plague take this villian for beating this poor woman so.

MARTINE: (*Her arms crossed, she speaks to M. Robert, forcing him back, and then slaps him across the face*) Maybe I enjoy him beating me. In fact, I do!

M. ROBERT: Really! If that is the case, please continue.

MARTINE: Why are you interfering?

M. ROBERT: I must be wrong.—Pray forgive me.

MARTINE: Is this any of your business?

M. ROBERT: You are absolutely correct!

MARTINE: Look at this fancy peacock, who wants to stop a husband from beating his poor wife.

M. ROBERT: I said I was sorry!

MARTINE: What do you have to say about it—eh?

M. ROBERT: Not another word!

MARTINE: Who asked you to stick your nose in this business?

M. ROBERT: Mum's the word! I won't say anything else!

MARTINE: Mind your own business.

M. ROBERT: I'll be quiet as the grave!

MARTINE: I enjoy being beaten.

M. ROBERT: Good for you.

MARTINE: It doesn't hurt you, does it?

M. ROBERT: You are right. It doesn't.

MARTINE: And you are a first-class ass, who interferes in matters that don't concern you.

M. ROBERT: (*to Sganarelle*) My good friend, I earnestly beg your pardon. Go ahead and beat your wife as much as you wish. As a matter of fact, if you like, I'll lend a hand. Two hands are better than one! (*He moves over to Sganarelle who begins to beat him with the stick he has been using on Martine*)

SGANARELLE: No thank you, I'm quite able to do the job by myself.

M. ROBERT: Ah—Well then, that is quite a different matter.

SGANARELLE: If I feel like beating her, I'll beat her; and if I don't feel like it, I won't.

M. ROBERT: That's wonderful.

SGANARELLE: She happens to be my wife, not yours!

M. ROBERT: I am certainly pleased about that!

SGANARELLE: No one told you to tell me how to deal with my wife.

M. ROBERT: Quite right.

SGANARELLE: I can beat her without your help, understand!

M. ROBERT: Evidently.

SGANARELLE: And it is just your busy-body attitude that makes you meddle in other people's business. Remember what Cicero said: Between the tree and the finger you must not place the bark. (*He beats him and drives him off-stage. He returns to his wife and takes her hand*) Come my dear, let us make up. Let us shake hands.

MARTINE: That's fine now, after you have beaten me!

SGANARELLE: That doesn't bother me. Let's shake hands.

MARTINE: I won't shake hands.

SGANARELLE: What?

MARTINE: No!

SGANARELLE: Come, my little canary.

MARTINE: I won't shake hands.

SGANARELLE: Come, my little porcupine, let's shake hands.

MARTINE: I will do nothing of the kind!

SGANARELLE: Come, now. Come, come on.

MARTINE: I have said no, and I mean it.

SGANARELLE: It's just a trifle. Please do, my little mackerel.

MARTINE: Leave me alone.

SGANARELLE: I said "Shake hands!"

MARTINE: You have treated me too cruelly.

SGANARELLE: All right then! I beg your pardon; put your hand right there.

MARTINE: I forgive you. (*aside, very softly*) I shall see that you pay tenfold for this little escapade.

SGANARELLE: You are silly to take this matter too seriously. These are minor matters that are necessary now and then to show that we love each other. Five or six solid blows only strengthen our bond of affection. There—that's done. Now I'm going into the woods, and I promise that I will return with several full loads today.

The Taming of the Shrew, by William Shakespeare
From Act II, Scene 1

Scene:	For one man, one woman
Characters:	PETRUCHIO, a rich gentleman from Verona
	KATHARINA, an independent young woman, daughter of Baptista
Setting:	A room in Baptista's house in Padua, Italy.
Time:	The sixteenth century.
Situation:	Baptista, an elderly gentleman of Padua, has two daughters of marriage-able age. The older of the two, Katharina, is strong-minded, and no suitor has been able to find favor with her. More than one suitor has felt the sharpness of her tongue and nails. A young gentleman from Verona, Petruchio, has arrived in Padua in order "haply to wive and thrive as best I may." After settling financial arrangements with Baptista, Petruchio sets out to win Katharina for his wife. He finds it no easy task, but he turns out to be a bit more than the young woman bargained for. This is a lusty scene, both verbally *and* physically, as each tries to gain the upper hand.

PETRUCHIO: Good morrow, Kate; for that's your name, I hear.
KATHARINA: Well have you heard, but something hard of hearing: They call me
  Katharine that do talk of me.
PETRUCHIO: You lie, in faith, for you are called plain Kate.
  And bonny Kate, and sometimes Kate the Curst;
  But Kate, the prettiest Kate in Christendom,
  Kate of Kate-Hall, my superdainty Kate,
  For dainties are all Kates—and therefore, Kate,
  Take this of me, Kate of my consolation:
  Hearing thy mildness praised in every town,
  Thy virtues spoke of, and thy beauty sounded,
  Yet not so deeply as to thee belongs,
  Myself am moved to woo thee for my wife.
KATHARINA: Moved! in good time. Let him that moved you hither
  Remove you hence. I knew you at the first
  You were a movable.
PETRUCHIO: Why, what's a movable?
KATHARINA: A joined stool.
PETRUCHIO: Thou hast hit it. Come, sit on me.
KATHARINA: Asses are made to bear, and so are you.
PETRUCHIO: Women are made to bear, and so are you.
KATHARINA: No such jade as you, if me you mean.
PETRUCHIO: Alas, good Kate, I will not burden thee!
  For, knowing thee to be but young and light—
KATHARINA: Too light for such a swain as you to catch,
  And yet as heavy as my weight should be.
PETRUCHIO: Should be! should—buzz!
KATHARINA: Well ta'en, and like a buzzard.
PETRUCHIO: O slow-winged turtle! shall a buzzard take thee?

KATHARINA: Ay, for a turtle, as he takes a buzzard.

PETRUCHIO: Come, come, you wasp. I'faith, you are too angry.

KATHARINA: If I be waspish, best beware my sting.

PETRUCHIO: My remedy is then to pluck it out.

KATHARINA: Aye, if the fool could find it where it lies.

PETRUCHIO: Who knows not where a wasp does wear his sting? In his tail.

KATHARINA: In his tongue.

PETRUCHIO: Whose tongue?

KATHARINA: Yours, if you talk of tails; and so farewell.

PETRUCHIO: What, with my tongue in your tail? nay, come again,
Good Kate, I am a gentleman.

KATHARINA: That I'll try. (*She strikes him.*)

PETRUCHIO: I swear I'll cuff you if you strike again.

KATHARINA: So may you lose your arms.
If you strike me, you are no gentleman,
And if no gentleman, why then no arms.

PETRUCHIO: A herald, Kate? O, put me in thy books!

KATHARINA: What is your crest? a coxcomb?

PETRUCHIO: A combless cock, so Kate will be my hen.

KATHARINA: No cock of mine. You crow too like a craven.

PETRUCHIO: Nay, come, Kate, come. You must not look so sour.

KATHARINA: It is my fashion when I see a crab.

PETRUCHIO: Why here's no crab, and therefore look not sour.

KATHARINA: There is, there is.

PETRUCHIO: Then show it me.

KATHARINA: Had I a glass, I would.

PETRUCHIO: What, you mean my face?

KATHARINA: Well aimed of such a young one.

PETRUCHIO: Now, by Saint George, I am too young for you.

KATHARINA: Yet you are withered.

PETRUCHIO: 'Tis with cares.

KATHARINA: I care not.

PETRUCHIO: Nay, hear you, Kate. In sooth you scape not so.

KATHARINA: I chafe you, if I tarry. Let me go.

PETRUCHIO: No, not a whit. I find you passing gentle.
'Twas told me you were rough and coy and sullen,
And now I find report a very liar;
For thou are pleasant, gamesome, passing courteous,
But slow in speech, yet sweet as springtime flowers.
Thou canst not frown, thou canst not look askance,
Nor bite the lip, as angry wenches will,
Nor hast thou pleasure to be cross in talk,
But thou with mildness entertain'st thy wooers,
With gentle conference, soft and affable.
Why does the world report that Kate doth limp?
O slanderous world! Kate like the hazel twig
Is straight and slender, and as brown in hue
As hazel nuts, and sweeter than the kernels.

O, let me see thee walk. Thou dost not halt.

KATHARINA: Go, fool, and whom thou keep'st command.

PETRUCHIO: Did ever Dian so become a grove

As Kate this chamber with her princely gait?

O, be thou Dian, and let her be Kate,

And then let Kate be chaste and Dian sportful!

KATHARINA: Where did you study all this goodly speech?

PETRUCHIO: It is extempore, from my mother wit.

KATHARINA: A witty mother! Witless else her son.

PETRUCHIO: Am I not wise?

KATHARINA: Yes. Keep you warm.

PETRUCHIO: Marry, so I mean, sweet Katherine, in thy bed.

And therefore, setting all this chat aside,

Thus in plain terms: Your father hath consented

That you shall be my wife, your dowry 'greed on,

And, will you, nill you, I will marry you.

Now Kate, I am a husband for your turn.

For, by this light whereby I see thy beauty,

Thy beauty, that doth make me like thee well,

Thou must be married to no man but me;

For I am he am born to tame you Kate,

And bring you from a wild Kate to a Kate

Conformable as other household Kates.

Here comes your father. Never make denial.

I must and will have Katharine to my wife.

CHAPTER TWELVE

Acting for the Camera

Television and film have become Everyman's theatre. Millions of people who have never seen a professional or amateur stage production are regularly exposed to a great variety of comic and dramatic programs. Television particularly includes soap operas, westerns, detective and spy programs, "sitcoms" (situation comedies), historical dramatization, long-running series extending over several years, mini-series, and one-shot specials. Many of the current stars of television have had equally successful careers in the theatre and film; still others have become famous through television alone.

In the early days of television, a variety of styles evolved for broadcasting television programs. Since the early 1950s, however, film has played the major role in broadcast-television drama. With the development of digital videotape editing and computer enhancement, greater diversity and speed in filming programs have become possible. The new tools have also helped to open a new horizon in creative expression.

> *The relationship between the make-up man and the film actor is that of accomplices in crime.*
>
> Marlene Dietrich

Shooting the Television Drama

Today there are a large number of ways to "film" the television drama. To a great extent, television and cinema have become almost indistinguishable, and we must recognize their great similarity. Some distinctions, however, are worth examining.

Single-Camera Filming.   Traditional movie-filming has utilized one camera, which makes it necessary to start and stop, shoot the drama out of sequence due to the availability of sets, and reshoot a scene several times until it is absolutely right. Much of the critical work in finally putting the program before the audience is the responsibility of the film editor, working long *after* the shooting of the scenes has actually taken place. This type of filming and editing permits attention to little details and the correction of any error, which is not possible in live television. Single-camera filming is also expensive and likely to be used only in a high-budget prestige television production.

Multicamera Filming.   More and more television programs have begun to use multicamera shooting, a technique, incidentally, that was first used in the movies in order to ensure continuity and avoid "mismatches." By having more than one angle on a scene, it was possible to ensure against any later problems of showing the actor using the correct hand when picking up a book, having to show the *precise moment* when the actor put on a coat, or, even more significantly, emotional mismatches, in which the level or intensity of a scene might vary from one shooting sequence to another.

Many television dramas today are shot on videotape, with all the images of each video camera recorded, and the whole tape later edited by the editor and director. Some programs, particularly situation comedies, may be shot twice or three times through, with a multicamera setup before a live audience in a single evening. Often a sequence will be shot from commercial to commercial, or through one entire setting. *Roseanne* and *Seinfeld* used this technique, which permits a high degree of spontaneity on the part of the performers and a freshness not always found in more carefully edited and repeated performances. Other comedies recorded on videotape have been shot without an audience, with up to four cameras each recording a short sequence. Each short sequence is repeated again and again, and the cast and crew do not go on to the next unit until the director is satisfied with the scene.

Sometimes close to fifty hours of videotape will be shot in order to put together a single half-hour show.

Television and the Theatre

When we look at the demands placed on the actor working in the television medium, we should note that certain factors differentiate theatre from television. Most of all we must remember that television is seen and heard in the home, rather than in a theatre together with the members of an audience. Some of these general distinctions between a play in the theatre and a play on the picture tube lead to important considerations for the actor.

The Attention of the Audience Is Easily Diverted. This problem has required sweeping alterations in the structure, character development, and pacing of most television drama. In contrast to his or her behavior in the theatre, the member of the television audience may converse freely with those in the room; attention may be diverted by any number of distractions; and the viewer may change stations if dissatisfied with the play at any point. These circumstances lead to necessarily fast character development, a plot that is developed rapidly, and tension-packed situations that retain audience attention, usually at the expense of the more leisurely exposition found in the theatre.

The Audience Is Broken Down into Small Units or May Consist of One Person. At a play or in a movie theatre, many hundreds of people come together for the joint appreciation of the production. An individual cannot help being affected by the reactions of other people in the audience. Their laughter adds to the enjoyment of the comedy, and their tears will make tragedy more moving than it would have been had the person witnessed the play alone. This well-known psychological concept operates wherever large groups assemble. It ceases to be an important factor, however, in the transmission of drama to the home television audience, which consists of relatively few people, often only one viewer.

In the early 1950s, the *I Love Lucy* sitcom dealt with this difficulty by putting recorded or "canned" laughter on the sound track in order to bring to the home viewer the illusion of being a member of a larger audience. The practice is still carried on today. This device not only permitted the use of comic timing similar to that used in the theatre but gave the home viewer a sense of audience participation. Today, those shows recorded before a live audience are able to deal with the problem of the isolated viewer by incorporating real audience response, although the laugh levels may still be monitored and adjusted by sound engineers for maximum effect.

The Audience Is Greater and More Diverse. Although the audience unit is smaller, the cumulative size of that audience is much greater than any attending a theatre or movie at one particular time. Only a few hundred people may attend the production of a new play, but several million can watch a television show in their homes. In addition, this home audience is not so selective in its tastes as the one that comes together in the theatre. The members of the theatre audience have attended by choice, because there is a specific play that they wish to see. This audience is united by a common interest even before the play begins. In any one home, and from one home to another, the television audience will be composed of individuals of varying ages, interests, and backgrounds. A television audience may include all the members of a family, ranging from the grandparents to the grandchildren, with each member having different program interests. Some may be habitual theatregoers with sophisticated tastes in the theatre, whereas others may never have attended a stage production and have no desire to do so.

Television Drama Is Usually Severely Restricted by Time.   In the theatre, time becomes a crucial factor only when a drama begins to lose the attention of the audience. If a scene may profit from a slow and deliberate pace, the director and actors need not consider whether they will have sufficient time to finish the play. The televised play, however, is usually presented within a prescribed half-hour or hour period. The program must adhere exactly to its allotted time so that the next program, which the audience expects to be broadcast at a specific time, will begin as scheduled. Programs are also broken up into segments of fifteen or twenty minutes or less, separated by announcements and commercials that tend to destroy continuity. With the expansion of cable and other television options, we have begun to see changes in these traditional practices.

The Audience Sees the Actor Differently.   In addition to the general differences just noted, there are unique problems for the actor. In the theatre an audience will view the performance from one fixed position, and the production is planned to make the action and dialogue meaningful for the stationary spectator. In television, the viewer sees the production through the eyes of many cameras, which are mobile. Thus the audience views the actor not only in a variety of positions but also in different sizes—in a long shot, medium shot, or closeup. Furthermore, the camera may move about the playing area during the production, creating differences in composition, balance, and emphasis without any need for the actor to make such changes.

Television Acting

Working before the camera, whether it be a multicamera, multi-tapedeck, or a single camera, requires major mental and physical reorientation by the actor. Warren Beatty recalls his disappointment upon seeing his early films, and comments:

I realized that if I had done the same parts on the stage I would have had the opportunity to come back and do them again, in a better way, trying to find new meanings in them.[1]

The actor's ability to get the most out of the filmed performance, which can never be repeated again, requires an acute awareness of his or her instrument and the way it can most effectively be used in each medium. Nevertheless, the sensitive actor should be able to function successfully in both media. Bruce Dern is quite precise on this point:

People who work in one medium to the exclusion of the other are going to have trouble making the adjustment. But if they're really good actors, they can survive it. The bottom line is that if you're good, you're good.[2]

It will be useful to examine some of the problems unique to television and screen acting, from both the standpoint of multi- and single-camera work.

The Actor as a Unit

During a production the audience views the actor from various distances and angles. Most of this variety is achieved by the movement and refocusing of the television camera, all carefully planned by the director.

The actor is seen within the frame of the television screen. The television director usually works within a range of certain types of shots in relation to the actor's body. The most important of these are:

1. Extreme closeup
2. Closeup
3. Medium closeup
4. Shoulder shot
5. Full figure
6. Two-shot
7. Small group
8. Larger group

These camera shots are illustrated in Figures 12.1 through 12.8.

Additionally, the camera may pan around a group, zoom in and out of a closeup, and constantly change the relationship of the actor to the frame in

---

1. Warren Beatty, quoted in Lillian Ross and Helen Ross, *The Player: A Profile of an Art* (New York: Simon and Schuster, 1962), p. 192.
2. Bruce Dern, quoted in Joanmarie Kalter, *Actors on Acting* (New York: Sterling, 1979), p. 191.

FIGURE 12.1   Camera shots: Extreme closeup.

which the actor is appearing. It is important, therefore, that the actor accept the fact that he or she is one unit in a coordinated production scheme that includes the actor, camera, microphone, and lights, each carefully manipulated by the director according to a preset plan. The intricacy of this coordination will probably be greater than any the actor has experienced in the theatre. Just as each unit must be in a specific place at a certain time, so too the actor must accept stage movement and position as fixed elements in the total design of the composition and organization of a scene.

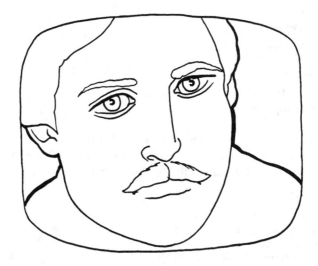

FIGURE 12.2   Camera shots: Closeup.

FIGURE 12.3   Camera shots: Medium closeup.

Hitting the Mark.   In order to preset the location and movement of the actor and equipment, positions are often carefully marked on the floor of the studio. This procedure is almost universally followed during the rehearsal period, when chalk marks are used to define the actor's exact position. It is imperative during rehearsals, and later during performance, particularly if it is a through take (as in multicamera tapings), that although these marks may no longer be visible the actor find the predetermined position. The slightest error off the mark will seriously disturb the planned effect of a scene. Televi-

FIGURE 12.4   Camera shots: Shoulder shot.

FIGURE 12.5   Camera shots: Full figure.

sion lighting is keyed to a certain spot on the studio floor, and if the actor is off the mark, the facial lighting may significantly alter the effect intended by the director and lighting designer. Furthermore, at no time should the audience ever get the impression that the actor is groping for the right position. The actor must work to make these exact movements as naturally as possible.

Extraneous Stage Movement.   The relative freedom of the theatre does not exist in television. Once the actor has hit the mark, it is necessary to remain

FIGURE 12.6   Camera shots: Two shot.

FIGURE 12.7   Camera shots: Four shot (small group).

fixed in the position without making any extraneous movement. This requires a high degree of control and restraint. After the exact position has been taken, any unspecified movement during certain camera shots, as in a closeup, may completely unbalance the prescribed emphasis of the scene, if not actually remove the actor from the picture. Sometimes such demands may call for strangely unorthodox techniques. Hume Cronyn, the versatile stage and film actor, faced just such an experience during his early career when working in a film sequence. He reported:

FIGURE 12.8   Camera shots: Group (larger group).

A move which would be utterly false on stage, which goes directly against every reasonable impulse, may be camera-wise effective and necessary . . . During the meal, I said something upsetting to the character played by Teresa Wright. She turned to me with unexpected violence. I stood up in embarrassment and surprise and automatically took a step backward. However, at the point of the rise, the camera moved in to hold us in a close two-shot, and to accommodate it— that is, to stay in the frame—it became necessary for me to change that instinctive movement so that when I got up from the chair, *I took a step toward the person from whom I was retreating.* . . . I was convinced that the action would look idiotic on the screen, but I was wrong. . . . I had to admit that the occasion passed almost unnoticed even by me.[3]

It is possible that a position assumed by the actor, as when playing in a two-character closeup, may seem uncomfortable and awkward, but the consideration of comfort must be disregarded in these sequences. Awkwardness is relative to the audience's view of the characters, as Hume Cronyn has clearly illustrated. It is the actor's responsibility to avoid any movement during performance, no matter how slight, that has not been previously planned and approved.

Playing Alone

In single-camera shooting, it is not unusual for the actor to be playing a scene alone, although he or she is supposedly speaking to another character. Scenes frequently begin or end with two characters in conversation, but only one character may actually be within the setting, being filmed or taped. The second character may be making a change of costume or moving to or from an adjacent setting. The camera, in closeup, will show only the character speaking, and the audience will naturally assume that the other character is present and listening. Solo work of this kind requires that the actor use a good deal of imagination to make these sequences convincing.

> *Everybody who has ever done one will tell you that those sizzling love scenes in the movies are agonizing to execute. The crew is standing around watching, the lights are hot, and each actor must be constantly vigilant about whether his shadow is falling on the wrong place or if he's looking awkward and ungainly. Actors never know how the director will cut the scene, so a great deal of trust has to be part of the bargain.*
>
> Love scenes in front of the camera

---

3. Hume Cronyn, "Notes on Film Acting," *Theatre Arts,* June 1949, p. 46.

Subtlety and Intimacy

Although acting techniques are generally alike in television and the theatre, the intimacy of television imposes a number of modifications on the actor's projection of a role. Television acting most resembles central-stage acting, in which the same problems of intimacy and multiple focus are brought to the fore. After having worked in productions utilizing central staging, the actor will discover that the "level" of playing is much more similar to that required in television. If the actor's experience has been solely in large proscenium theatres, the necessary alterations will be somewhat more extensive. Bruce Dern reminds us again that in the theatre

> . . . you can be flamboyant, you can take off in different directions, you can hide certain faults, and yet you can't do that in film [and television] because the camera picks up *everything*.[4]

The skills that the actor can transfer to television from experience in a relatively large theatre are proficient memorization of dialogue, imaginative analysis and development of character, and the sustaining of a role physically and vocally throughout a performance. Transposing a stage characterization directly to television, however, without modifications, is likely to make the actor appear inadequate. Such difficulties are usually caused by a misunderstanding of the nature of the medium.

Any observation of the silent films made during the formative years of cinema technique should prove highly instructive. In their early efforts the film pioneers used all the devices of the contemporary theatre. They were unaware that the new medium required a style and technique of its own. If we could watch a succession of films representative of succeeding decades, paying special attention to the acting, we would be aware of a decided change, a definite trend through the years toward naturalism in the performances. This change was fostered not by any notable trends in the theatre but by a growing understanding of the subtlety of the screen. The advent of sound in the late 1920s made further demands for subtlety in film acting. Since the camera and television have much in common, the television industry has learned much from cinema techniques and experimentation. As a result, the development of fundamental techniques has been less prolonged and haphazard than the development of film techniques.

The ensuing comments about the use of the voice and body in television are directly concerned with the demands of subtlety and intimacy inherent in the television medium. One point should be emphasized at once. *The audience sits no more than five to ten feet away from the actor during a performance.* If this fact is kept in mind, much of what we shall discover about television acting will fall logically into place.

---

4. Bruce Dern, quoted in Kalter, *Actors on Acting*, p. 191.

Subtlety in Vocal Acting

One of the common pitfalls that beset the actor in television is overemphasis. On the stage, confronted with the problem of projection over a considerable distance, the actor must be conscious of volume, clarity, and proper body position. Key lines or phrases must be carefully pointed and emphasized so that important information is not lost by the audience, even in the last row of the auditorium. Such delivery in television, magnified even further by the microphone, will seem grotesque and distorted, not at all suited to the intimate nature of the medium. The recognition of this principle has developed, in both film and television, a manner of line reading and projection distinct from that used on the stage.

The most discernible element in this new style of reading dramatic dialogue is the attempt to suggest naturalness of expression. Although television drama is not entirely restricted to the realistic play, this type is prevalent—probably because the medium can best accommodate it. Plays that were conceived in a nonrealistic mode have been conspicuously absent from the television screen, and when they are produced, as in the case of Shakespeare, they are drastically altered in playing style.

One of the most memorable film productions of one of Shakespeare's plays was Laurence Olivier's production of *Hamlet,* in which there was a unique treatment of the great soliloquies. The soliloquy is far removed from the naturalistic concept of drama, but in the film these speeches were super-personalized to the point where Hamlet's lips did not move at all, the words simply being heard on the sound track as the camera seemed to scan the mind of the young prince. The same techniques were used and refined in the BBC series of all of Shakespeare's plays, which aired in the United States in the 1980s.

This is good cinematographic technique but hardly compatible with stage speech. This device has been carried over to television productions as well, and although some may object to it from an aesthetic standpoint, it clearly takes advantage of the great intimacy of the medium. What, indeed, could be *more* intimate than lodging ourselves in the secret compartments of the character's mind and intruding on his or her thoughts? This example is but one illustration of how the intimacy of the television medium has brought about new means of naturalizing standard theatre procedure.

In deciding on the proper means of modifying stage speech for television, two rules should be observed:

1. The low projection level used in radio is appropriate for television acting as well. Although the actor in television is not able to take the optimum microphone position as in radio, members of the studio crew will see to it that the microphone is no more than a few inches away from the actor, in a good pickup position, and out of the view of the television camera.

2. The style of reading will be dictated by the style of the play; thus no one style of reading should be arbitrarily suggested. However, as a general rule, except when working in period plays that require a particular style of expression, the actor should adopt a conversational style of delivery.

Subtlety in Physical Acting

The intimacy of television calls for naturalness in bodily action. Two factors of proximity urge upon the actor important modifications of physical projection associated with the stage. These are the *proximity of the audience* and the *proximity of other actors.*

We have already indicated that the *proximity of the audience* is an essential consideration in all television work. The restraint needed to tone down the projection of physical action is derived from the same conditions of intimacy that bring about the lowered level of vocal projection. When the audience is no longer situated several hundred feet from the actor, the codified system of physical expression normally used on stage must give way to a style that is more intimate and simplified.

The actor in a television production often works only inches away from other actors. Whenever two or more characters are involved in any one scene, the dimensions of the television screen make it essential that they perform in close proximity. Working so closely with other actors prevents the use of expansive gestures and broadly conceived pieces of business. It requires close attention to details and subtle physical shadings to make the same point one would make broadly in the theatre. Lynn Redgrave reminds us:

> You have to have figured out your blocking, of course, you have to know where you're going to sit, where you're going to stand, where the director wants you, where the lighting man needs you to be, your mark, all those technique things.[5]

Leslie Howard once humorously remarked that such closeups in film, in which actors had to watch their positions, attend to details, and avoid casting shadows on other actors, accounted for the apparently alarming number of cross-eyed actors seen on the screen.

It would be erroneous to conclude that proximity forces the actor to be static, expressionless, and wooden. Expressiveness is extremely important and is most effective in television in a form we have not hitherto discussed.

Because the screen is relatively small, television is compelled to make extensive use of the closeup—in fact, even greater use than does the cinema. Such closeups provide the actor with an unusual opportunity to act "from the

---

5. Lynn Redgrave, quoted in Kalter, *Actors on Acting,* p. 82.

neck up." It means that the competent television actor should have a face that is flexible, sensitive, and above all, expressive. Here is the real key to expressiveness in television acting, but, in keeping with the requirements of subtlety and intimacy, facial expression must be handled with finesse. The smallest quivering of a lip in anger, the raising of an eyebrow in surprise, will be as meaningful in television as an expansive and broadly defined gesture or action is on stage. A little facial acting in television is capable of transmitting a great deal. Hume Cronyn has noted:

> In a "close-up" very little becomes much; a whole new range of expression is opened up to the actor . . . a glance, a contraction of a muscle in a manner that would be lost on stage. The camera will often reflect what a man thinks, without the degree of demonstration required in the theatre.[6]

Although facial expression is capable of suggesting essential facets of a characterization when used with taste and restraint, the danger exists that if it is not under perfect control it may seriously distort or hamper the actor's performance. Many of us are guilty of little idiosyncrasies that go almost unnoticed by friends who are accustomed to seeing us daily. We are seldom aware of these habits and often surprised when they are brought to our attention. Such minor habits, exaggerated in a closeup and seemingly part of our characterization, will be detrimental to the performance. All distracting facial mannerisms should be eliminated if the actor hopes to work successfully in television drama. Common habits of this type include biting the lips, frowning, furrowing the forehead, blinking the eyes, tightening the mouth, and so on. Even more subtly, the camera can search out the interior of an actor's consciousness. It can be disconcerting to realize that it is very difficult to "lie" in a closeup. Raul Julia called it a ". . . kind of microscopic search of your soul . . . into what you're doing as a character. It's very interior. It's almost like being in a confessional. . . ."[7]

The power of television to convey even the most subtle emotional responses or "subtext" is so apparent that many politicians, including presidents of the United States, have videotaped their "spontaneous" talks before making the actual live delivery, in order to eliminate unwanted emphases in certain spots or any nervous mannerisms. Self-scrutiny and daily work in front of a mirror by the performer will help to reveal unsuspected habits. Such practice will not only aid in eliminating some of these distracting facial mannerisms but should also help the actor appraise his or her ability to communicate meaningfully by the face alone.

---

6. Hume Cronyn, "Notes on Film Acting," p. 46.
7. Susan Shacter and Don Shewey, *Caught in the Act* (New York: New American Library, 1986), p. 186.

Action and Reaction

An expressive face is nowhere more effective than when it serves to comment on a scene by a series of carefully planned *reactions*. The cinema and television have developed a potent means of heightening the development of a scene by focusing attention on reactions rather than on actions. An effective device often used in a scene between two or more characters is to show not the character who is speaking but to film a closeup of the reactions of the listener or listeners. The following brief scene will illustrate how this principle can make the action of a scene more vivid by focusing on the characters' reactions. Let us take a sequence from a hypothetical mystery drama in which five persons, one of them a detective, are seated around a table. The detective knows that one of the other four in the room is guilty of murder. We shall assume the scene is being shot on videotape with multiple cameras. The scene might be handled in the following manner:

Dialogue	*Camera*
DETECTIVE BARNES: Very well, we're not leaving this room until I discover which one of you turned the trick. You all had a motive and the opportunity, but the question is, which one of you got to him first?	*(A pan shot of entire group, moving finally to Barnes.)*
Was it you, John Flush?—He cheated you out of $50,000, you couldn't forgive him for that, could you?	*(Closeup of Barnes, as he points his finger at each suspect.)*
Or was it you, Hubert Hiebert? He knew a good deal about your illegal gambling operation. He was blackmailing you, wasn't he?	
And you, Claire Voyent, what was your motive? Jealousy? Perhaps his papers will tell the story.	
You needn't look so satisfied, Lord Upjohn, I'm just getting to you. There is a good deal in his diary you would like to get your hands on, isn't there?	
Well, we'll just sit here all night until one of you cracks.	*(Long shot of entire group.)*

Now, this not uncommon scene from any typical crime melodrama might be handled with the camera shots indicated above. They encompass the entire action of the scene and help propel the story forward. Yet this is not the most effective use of the camera in telling the story. Imaginative camera work on reactions would be more to the point and be of greater value in carrying along the action and heightening the suspense. Let us examine the scene again with a different set of camera directions.

Dialogue	Camera
DETECTIVE BARNES: Very well, we're not leaving this room until I discover which one of you turned the trick. You all had a motive and the opportunity, but the question is, which one of you got to him first?	*(A pan shot of entire group, moving finally to closeup of Barnes.)*
Was it you, John Flush?—He cheated you out of $50,000, you couldn't forgive him for that, could you?	*(Closeup of Flush nervously rubbing his chin.)*
Or was it you, Hubert Hiebert? He knew a good deal about your illegal gambling operation. He was blackmailing you, wasn't he?	*(Closeup of Hiebert mopping his perspiring brow.)*
And you, Claire Voyent, what was your motive? Jealousy? Perhaps his papers will tell the story.	*(Closeup of Voyent, coolly manicuring her nails.)*
You needn't look so satisfied, Lord Upjohn, I'm just getting to you. There is a good deal in his diary you would like to get your hands on, isn't there?	*(Closeup of Upjohn, hastily swallowing an aspirin tablet.)*
Well, we'll just sit here all night until one of you cracks.	*(Long shot of entire group.)*

This scene is certainly somewhat exaggerated, but the point should be clear. Reaction to the dialogue by each character is more meaningful than the action of the individual who is speaking. All the characters are acting during the sequence, in the television sense of reacting, as the camera searches out each character in turn.

Critic Dudley Nichols holds strongly to the concept that *reaction* is the key to all successful acting before the camera. His reference in the following comment is to the cinema and specifically to sequences from *In Which We Serve*, directed by Noel Coward and David Lean, but it is also directly applicable to television acting.

> At any emotional crisis of a film, when a character is saying something which profoundly affects another, it is to this second character that the camera instinctively roves, perhaps in close-up . . . If anyone doubts this let him study his own emotions when viewing a good film; . . . I recently did this with some lay friends after a showing of Noël (sic) Coward's *In Which We Serve*, and it was illuminating to find out that they had been most deeply moved by reactions, almost never by actions: the figure of a woman who gets news her husband has been lost at sea, the face of an officer when told his wife had died. . . . In the same film one of the most affecting scenes was the final one where the captain bids good-bye to the remainder of his crew; and while this appears to be action, the

camera shrewdly presented it as reaction: It is the faces of the men, as they file past, that we watch, reaction to the whole experience even in their laconic voices and in the weary figure of the captain.[8]

The foregoing illustrations relating reaction to action are indicative of this most important distinction concerning television acting. The actor experienced only in the theatre correctly holds that although reaction is important, it is the projection of the action that is his or her dominant responsibility on stage. Something of an about-face is required to accept reaction as an equal if not superior means of communicating to a television audience.

Reviewing the Rules

It will be helpful to review the most important modifications imposed upon the actor by television. Although each of these rules may be broken in certain circumstances, they are the important operating principles that should guide the actor when making the transition from theatre to television or screen acting:

1. Accept movement and position as an element to be coordinated with lights, camera, and microphone.
2. Be sure to hit the marked position preset during rehearsals.
3. Avoid all extraneous movement.
4. Do not look at the camera unless ordered to do so by the director.
5. Adopt a conversational level and style for line reading.
6. Keep planned business and movement simple and keyed to the intimate nature of television.
7. Do not overlook the importance of the face in expressing emotions.
8. Reaction to the events of the drama is frequently more important than executing the business or action of the play.

EXERCISES

1. Watch any half-hour program filmed specifically for television. Count the number of closeups used during the program. Watch a telecast of a movie originally produced for showing in a large theatre. Count the number of closeups used during a half-hour segment. Compare your results.

---

8. Dudley Nichols, "The Writer and the Film," in *Twenty Best Film Plays*, eds. John Gassner and Dudley Nichols (New York: Crown Publishers, 1943), pp. xxxiii–xxxiv.

2. Use a videotape recorder. If this is not available, work with a mirror. React facially to each of the following situations for a closeup and for a long shot. Note the differences required for each.

   (a) You *see* the following and then react: (1) a spider crawling up your arm, (2) a building on fire, (3) a new automobile given to you as a gift, (4) an automobile accident, and (5) a gun pointed at you by a madman.

   (b) You *hear* the following and then react: (1) a loud scream in the next room, (2) a long and boring speech, (3) a falling bomb coming nearer and nearer, and (4) someone sneaking up behind you.

   (c) You *touch* the following and then react: (1) a slimy snake, (2) a hot stove, (3) a broken heirloom, and (4) a mink coat.

3. Perform each of the exercises above before the class and ask them to identify each facial expression in turn.

4. Invent three facial reactions of your own for *sight, sound,* and *touch.* Perform them before the class and have the class try to identify them as closely as possible.

5. Choose any of the monologues from Chapter 9. Perform them *seated,* without any movement, as if in a closeup for television. Use the conversational and projection level required for a television closeup. Using a videotape recorder, record the monologue. If one is not available, perform the monologue live before the class. Have the class evaluate your performance in terms of a televised closeup. Compare it to the same selection prepared for a stage production.

6. Choose any three improvisations, including character, locale, and situation, listed in Chapter 7, "Using Improvisation." Adapt them for use in a television production. Explain after each improvisation how you adapted them for television production and how they differ from an improvisation designed to be viewed on stage.

SUGGESTION FOR FURTHER READING

Taylor, Malcolm. *The Actor and the Camera.* London: A. and C. Black, 1994.

A Glossary of Theatre Terms

Above: The general area farther away from the audience. The upstage area is *above* the downstage area.

Action: The progress of the play as made clear to the audience by dialogue, movement, and development of character and character relationships. In Method terminology, action refers to the inner motivation of the character, his or her reason for being on the stage. (In this context, see also **Intention**.)

Ad-Lib: (*ad libitum*—literally, at pleasure) Movement or dialogue inserted in the production that is not specified in the playscript; on occasion inserted during a performance to cover fluffs.

Alignment: Arrangement of the body from head to toe in a straight line.

Antagonist: The character in the play most directly opposed to the main character, or protagonist.

Apron: The portion of the stage nearest to the audience and in front of the proscenium arch or house curtain.

Area: A portion of the stage that has been designated for use during the playing of a scene. The stage is divided into specific *areas*, such as down right, up left, etc.

Aside: A short speech intended only for the ears of the audience, and by convention not heard by other characters on stage. A typical device, for example, of nineteenth-century melodrama, it may be used to impart information or expose the secret thoughts of the speaker. (See also **Soliloquy**.)

Backdrop: Usually a large piece of canvas or other material behind the stage setting, sometimes with a detailed scene painted on it.

Backstage: The area in back or to the sides of the setting not seen by the audience.

Balance: The equalization of attention by bringing actors, properties, set pieces, and other elements into harmony so as to achieve the required physical equilibrium.

Beats: A term employed by Method actors meaning the distance from the beginning to the end of a continuing state of mind or intention of a character, whether or not it be explicitly stated in the dialogue.

Below: A position or area nearer to the audience. The downstage area is *below* the upstage area.

Bit Part: A role with few lines of dialogue.

Blackout: Throwing the playing area into complete darkness by the sudden turning off of all stage lights.

Blocking: The planned movement and stage composition of the production as developed during the early rehearsals.

Border: A curtain hanging behind but parallel to the proscenium to aid in masking lights, the working rigging, and the fly space.

Box Set: Interior setting consisting of three walls and often a ceiling as well. One of the most common of realistic settings.

Build: The increase in energy, tension, or emotional key directed toward a climax, either in a specific scene or through the progress of the play.

Business: Detailed pieces of action developed to enhance characterization, establish mood, and so on. Not the same as the basic stage movement.

Call: The announcement that warns actors when they are to be ready for rehearsals, performances, and individual scenes.

Climax: The high point of interest and/or action in a play, act, scene, or speech. The climax of a play will invariably occur in the second half of the piece.

Close: To turn or adjust the body position so that the actor is turned away from the audience.

Closed Turn: A turn on stage in which the back of the actor is seen by the audience during the turn. (See also **Open Turn.**)

Comedy: (See Chapter 11.)

Company: The persons involved in the production of a play. May also refer to a permanent group involved in a succession of productions, as a "summer stock" company.

Counter: A shifting of position to compensate for the movement of another actor in order to reachieve a balanced and pleasing stage composition.

Cover: To hide from the view of the audience another actor, a property, or a piece of business. Often used deliberately so as not to make obvious the faking of an extremely difficult piece of business, as in a stage fight, stabbing, and so on.

Cross: A movement on stage from one area to another.

Cue: The action or dialogue that signals that the next line is to be spoken or certain business and movement is to take place.

Curtain Call: The receipt of applause by the cast as the curtain is raised at the end of the play.

Cyclorama (also **CYC**):   A backdrop surrounding the setting on three sides. Occasionally used to represent the sky, it is nonspecific in detail.

Dialogue: The words spoken by the actors in the play.

Downstage: The general stage area nearest to the audience.

Dress: (See **Counter.**)

Dress Rehearsal: A rehearsal prior to performance that unites all the elements of the production exactly as they will function during actual performance.

Emotional Memory: One of the most famous aspects of the Stanislavski system. By the development of a technique through arduous training the actor is able to evoke the memory of an emotion similar to the one the character on stage is to feel.

Emphasis: The highlighting or accenting of a particular portion or feature of the production. The actor may give emphasis to a specific action or to a key line and even to one word. (See also **Subordination**.)

Entrance: Coming on stage in view of the audience. Can also refer to the opening in the setting that permits the actor to make his or her way on stage.

Exit: Leaving the playing area of the stage. It can also refer to the doorway or other opening in the setting through which the actor leaves.

Exposition: Material in the play that is included to give the audience the background required in order to understand the development of the story. Often refers to action that has occurred prior to the beginning of the play. Hence the exposition in a play is most likely to occur in the opening scenes.

Extras: Actors who appear in a play with no lines and little or no characterization. They are needed to perform a certain function in the play, as in the case of a member of a crowd scene. Also referred to as *supers*.

Farce: (See Chapter 11.)

Flat: A light wooden frame covered by canvas that constitutes the primary unit used to build such settings as the box set.

Flies: The area immediately over the stage where scenery can be raised by a system of pulleys and counterweights.

Floodlight: A large lighting unit used for illumination of broad portions of the stage, general rather than specific in the area it lights, as it cannot be focused.

Floor Plan: An outline drawing of the setting indicating only the design of the setting as it would be seen from above.

Fluff: A blunder during performance, such as a missed line or one that is garbled in its execution.

Focal Point: The point of greatest interest on stage during the playing of a scene.

Follow Spot: A spotlight that is not permanently focused on one position but can follow the movement of an actor about the playing area.

Footlights: Lights located in the stage floor at the edge of the forestage and permitting general illumination of the stage.

Forestage: (See **Apron**.)

Fourth Wall: The imaginary wall that separates the audience and the playing area. The term is used in reference to the realistic box setting that comprises three walls. The audience, by convention, is permitted to look at the action through the *fourth wall*.

Front: The auditorium and/or lobby, as distinguished from the stage. Used in such terms as *front of house* and *out front*.

Give Stage: To change stage position so as to permit greater emphasis to be focused on another actor.

Given Circumstance: A term utilized in the Stanislavski system referring to any dramatic occurrences that will affect the actor's playing of a scene. These may take place during the play or may have occurred before the beginning of the play. The death of Hamlet's father before the play begins is a *given circumstance.*

Green Room: Traditionally the gathering place for actors in the backstage area, often serving a social function as well.

Grid: (**Gridiron**) A framework of steel beams above the stage that supports the rigging required to fly scenery.

Heads Up!: A warning indicating a piece of scenery or other object is falling or being lowered.

Hold: To stop the action of the play, whether movement or dialogue, usually because of applause or laughter.

House: The part of the theatre in front of the footlights, as opposed to the stage and backstage areas. Usually the auditorium, as in "How's the *house* tonight?" meaning "How many seats are filled?"

Improvisation: The performance of dialogue and/or pantomime without any determined plan from any source other than the actor's own creative spirit, often "on the spur of the moment."

In: Toward the center of the stage.

Intention: A term used in the Stanislavski system that refers to the actor's real reason for being in a scene, regardless of what he may be saying. If a character hates another character, but because of others present is required to speak pleasantly to that person, the proper *intention* of the relationship must still be conveyed by the actor. (See also **Subtext** and **Problems**.)

Kill: To spoil the planned effectiveness of a line, a movement, a piece of business, or a technical effect, usually by a miscalculation in timing.

Lines: Either (1) the speeches of the actors, or (2) the sets of ropes supported by the grid that are used to fly scenery.

Mask: To conceal from the view of the audience any area of the stage not intended to be seen.

Melodrama: A serious play in which the primary emphasis is on spectacle and contrived action rather than logical character development and relationships.

Method, The: An American school of acting that stresses internal development of the actor's resources for the purpose of properly motivating his or her acting. It has grown out of the system devised by the Russian actor-director, Constantin Stanislavski, although it is modified from the original.

Monologue: A long speech by one character without any interspersed dialogue by other characters.

Mood: The dominant atmosphere created by the various elements of the production.

Move On: A movement on the same plane toward the center of the stage, either from stage left or stage right.

Off Stage: The area of the stage not visible to the audience.

On Stage: The playing space of the stage intended to be visible to the audience.

Open: To turn or adjust the body position so that the actor can play more directly to the audience.

Open Turn: A turn on stage in which the front of the actor is seen by the audience during the turn. (See also **Closed Turn**.)

Out: A direction away from the center of the stage.

Overlap: To speak or move before the indicated cue, or before another speech or movement is completed.

Overplay: To give to a scene, dialogue, or action greater exaggeration and emphasis than is required.

Pace: Overall rate of production, including reading of lines, picking up of cues, movement, etc.

Pantomime: The acting out of an incident or story without words.

Parallel Movement: The movement on stage of two or more characters in the same direction at the same time.

Pick Up: A command to increase the pace of the playing, often in reference to the shortening of the interval between the cue and the next line or action.

Places!: A command instructing the company that an act, in rehearsal or performance, is about to begin and each member is to take the proper position.

Plant: To call attention to an object or fact that will have special significance later in the play.

Play Script: The copy of the play including the dialogue and author's stage directions.

Play Up: To emphasize a key line, movement, or piece of business so that it will have greater significance. (Also **Plug**.)

Plot: The story of the play that is developed by the playwright in a logical sequence of events.

Plug: (See **Play Up**.)

Practical: A functioning prop that can actually be *used* by the actor rather than one that is ornamental and cannot be used, in the literal sense. A window that opens, a tap that runs water, are *practical*.

Precast: To choose actors for specific roles before the tryout period is held.

Presentational: (See Chapter 1.)

Problems: In Method terminology, the choice of certain small actions that will best help to project the intention of the character. (See also **Intention**.)

Production: All the various elements that make up the finished play ready to be seen by an audience.

Project: To make dialogue or movement clear to the audience by proper accentuation and intensification.

Prompter: The person who aids a forgetful actor by reading aloud key words or lines (**Prompting**) from off stage, usually from the wings.

Props: (**Properties**) All the furniture, set pieces, and objects that are seen on stage. Large pieces, or props that are not used by the actors, are called *stage props*. Small props used by actors are called *hand props*. Props used only by one character and brought on stage by the actor are termed *personal props*.

Proscenium: The wall and arch that set off the stage area from the audience.

Protagonist: The central figure or hero of the play, from the Greek term meaning the first actor.

Ramp: A sloping platform used to serve the same functions as a step unit.

Rehearsal: The organized periods during which the cast prepares the play for production.

Representational: (See Chapter 1.)

Return: A flat set parallel to the footlights and at the downstage edge of the setting running off into the wings, just above the tormentor.

Routine: A specially rehearsed sequence of actions, as a dance or song number.

Run-Through: A rehearsal in which an entire scene or act is played without any interruptions.

Scene: Either (1) a portion of an act, which by the nature of the action, or some arbitrary division, is a distinct unit by itself; or (2) the locale indicated by the setting, as in: "The *scene* is set in a small living room."

Set: To make permanent the reading of lines or movement and business after a series of rehearsals. (Sometimes used as an abbreviation for **Setting**.)

Setting: The arrangement of the scenery and properties that designate the locale of the action.

Share: To take a position on stage so that equal emphasis is afforded two or more actors.

Sides: A typed script that includes only the speeches of one actor and the relevant cues.

Sight Lines: The visibility of the playing area from the audience, usually from the seats on the extreme right and left sides of the house.

Soliloquy: A monologue spoken by the actor as an extension of his or her thoughts and not directed to, or by convention overheard by, any other actor. It is longer than an aside, and usually the actor delivering the soliloquy is alone on stage.

Spine: (See **Superobjective**.)

Spotlight: A lighting unit used to light only a small section of the stage.

Stage Directions: Instructions in the playscript relative to movement, business, and so on.

Stage Left, Stage Right: To the left and right of the actor when facing the audience.

Static Scene: A scene with little or no movement and often having a slow pace.

Steal: The act of having one actor assume emphasis by drawing attention away from the character to whom it would normally be paid. The term is often used in a derogatory sense.

Step Unit: One group of several steps used in the stage setting.

Stock Company: A permanent group of actors that puts on a number of different plays during a comparatively brief period of time, as in a summer season.

Strong: Having high attention value, as in a strong position or area.

Subordination: To treat any element of the production as of minor or secondary importance so as to focus emphasis elsewhere.

Subtext: A term used in the Stanislavski system that refers to the real meaning underlying the dialogue—the purpose for which the words are spoken or their inner meaning. Hence, the lines are considered the text, the underlying meaning the subtext. (See also **Intention**.)

Superobjective: A term often utilized by Method actors and the Stanislavski system to describe the motivating idea or theme that pervades the entire play. Every major character has his or her own objective deriving from the *spine* or *superobjective* of the play.

Tag Line: The final line of a character when leaving the stage or just prior to the fall of the curtain.

Take Stage: To assume a more prominent body position or move to the most emphatic area so as to receive the focus of attention.

Teaser: A border drapery that masks the fly space and determines the height of the stage opening. It is located behind the house curtain and immediately in front of the tormentors.

Telescope: To have two or more actors overlap the reading of lines or execution of business.

Tempo: The impression that the audience receives of the general rate of the production. Directly dependent upon pace.

Text: In Method terminology, the dialogue without reference to the underlying meaning of the lines. (See also **Intention, Subtext**.)

Throw Away: To underplay deliberately a line or business, often to achieve greater emphasis elsewhere in the scene or play.

Timing: The exact use of time, carefully planned to achieve maximum effectiveness in the reading of a line, execution of business, or movement.

Top: To so emphasize a line or an action that it is more emphatic than the line or action that precedes it.

Tormentors: Two matching flats, usually black in color, located slightly up-stage of the teaser and serving to mask the wings or to vary the size or width of the playing area. Together with the teaser, they effectively serve as a "picture frame" for the stage setting.

Tragedy: (See Chapter 11.)

Trap: An opening in the stage floor that can be used for the ascent or descent of characters or objects. Usually covered by a hinged, removable door.

Tryout: The auditioning of actors for roles in the forthcoming production.

Walk-On: A small role without any lines. (See also **Extras**.)

Warming Up: Exercising the body and/or voice prior to rehearsal or performance.

Weak: Having relatively low attention value, as in a weak position or area.

Wing Setting: Several hinged flats, often in matching pairs, set in sequence at stage right and stage left masking the offstage area. Most frequently used with a backdrop to enclose the playing area.

Wings: The offstage areas to the right and to the left of the playing space.

Continued

Selections from plays are reprinted by permission of the publishers.

Caution: All rights, including professional, amateur, motion picture, recitation, lecturing, public reading, radio broadcasting, and television are strictly reserved. Inquiries on all rights should be directed to the publisher(s).

Index

Page references to scenes are in **bold**.
Page references to photographs are in *italics*.

Actor Prepares, An, 50
Actors, classification of, 9–15
Actors, noted, of the past, 42–46
Actor's Studio, 52, 53
Adler, Luther, 53
Adler, Stella, 52
Admirable Bashville, The, 307
Aesop, 25
African Queen, The, 100–101
After the Fall, **211–212,** *212*
Albee, Edward, 143
Alienation effect, 54
Alignment, 71–72
Allen, Woody, 3
Allyn, Edward, 43
Amadeus, 181
Ambiguous dialogue, 195–204
Analysis:
   character, 179–183
   play, 178–179
Anderson, Maxwell, **220–223**
Anecdote, theatrical, 187, 193, 303
And Miss Reardon Drinks a Little, **266–269**
Androcles and the Lion, 257
Approaches, stage, 128–129
Arena staging (*see* Central staging)
Aristotle, 23
Arliss, George, 193
Arms and legs, 71
Armstrong, Louis, 62
Artaud, Antonin, 56
Articulation, 109–110, 118–119
As You Like It, 32
Audience, television, 341–342
Audition process, 173–178

Bacall, Lauren, 168
Bad Seed, **220–223**
Ball, William, 163
Bancroft, Anne, 187
Barrett, Lawrence, 149
Barry, Raymond J., *228*
Barrymore, John, 5, 6, 7, 18, 60, 194
Barrymore, Lionel, 169, 170
Beatty, Warren, 342–343
Beaux' Stratagem, The, 80–81, *81*
Belasco, David, 18

Belmondo, Jean–Paul, 3
Ben–Ami, Jacob, 186
Benny, Jack, 301
Bergman, Ingrid, 185
Bernhardt, Sarah, 10, 16, 60
Betterton, Thomas, 5, 34–35, 43
Beyond Therapy, **270–272, 289–291,** *290*
Billington, Michael, 55
Body and stage movement, 65–97
Body, how organized, 67–72
Body in action, 75–77
Body positions on stage, 127–137, 318–319
Bogart, Humphrey, 12, 100, 168, 171, 193
Booth, Edwin, 5, 6, 18, 45–46, 149
Born Yesterday, 302–303
Boys in the Band, The, **269–270**
Bracegirdle, Anne, 43
Branagh, Kenneth, 30
Brando, Marlon, 12, 51, 62, 171, 193
Breathing, 102–106
Brecht, Bertolt, 54
Brook, Peter, 57, 190
Brooks, Foster, 301
Brown, Joe E., 301
Brown, John Mason, 14
Building a Character, 50–51
Burbage, Richard, 31, 32, 42–43, 149
Buried Child, *228,* **228–230**
Burman, Howard, **211, 278–280**
Burton, Richard, 16, 171, 251
Business, developing, 189–191
Butterflies Are Free, **230–234**

Cagney, James, 12, 193
Callot, Jacques, 26–27
Callow, Simon, 181
Camera, television, 340–341, 343–347
   single–camera, 340
   multicamera, 340–341
Capitano, 25, 28
Caretaker, The, 186
Carnovsky, Morris, 53
Carrey, Jim, 301
Carter, Mrs. Leslie, 254
Caruso, Enrico, 167–168
Casablanca, 193
Cassius, 4
Central staging, 315–321
Chaplin, Charles, 184
Chapman Report, The, 187

Character acting, 11–14
Chekhov, Anton, 49, **207**, 313
Chest breathing, 104
Children's Hour, The, **218–220**
Churchill, Winston, 251
Cleopatra, 30
Clichés, avoidance of, 191–192
Clift, Montgomery, 53, 191
Climax, 313
Clurman, Harold, 53
Cobb, Lee J., 53
Coghlan, Rose, 101
Colosseum, 25
Columbine, 28
Come Back, Little Sheba, 59
Comedy, 300–303
Comedy of Errors, The, 310
Comic spirit, 302
Commedia dell'arte, 25–29
Concentration, 170, 251–253, 319
Connery, Sean, 9
Converse, Frank, 171
Cooper, Gary, 13, 193
Coquelin, Constant, 39–41, 46
Coriolanus, 31, 55
Cornell, Katherine, 179, 250
Costner, Kevin, 3
Cothurni, 23
Covering, 141, 143, 146
Coward, Noel, 168, 175, 187, 354
Craig, Gordon, 58
Crawford, Cheryl, 53
Creating a Role, 50
Cronyn, Hume, 347–348, 352
Crosby, Bing, 168
Crowley, Mart, **269–270**
Crucible, The, **282–284**
Cruelty, Theatre of, 56
Cruise, Tom, 3
Cumberland, Richard, 36
Cyrano de Bergerac, 76, 145, 301

D'Annunzio, Gabriele, 101
Davis, Brad, 193
Death of a Salesman, **207–208, 208–209,** 305, 313
Delphi, Greek Theatre at, *23*
De Luise, Dom, 6
Dench, Judi, *100*
De Niro, Robert, 3, 51
Depardieu, Gérard, 153
Dern, Bruce, 249, 343, 349
Desdemona, 30
De Vito, Danny, 4, 5

Dialogue, 111–117, 312–314
Diary of Anne Frank, The, **236–239**
Dickens, Charles, 108, 121
Diderot, Denis, 38–39, 40, 41, 49
Dietrich, Marlene, 340
Dionysus, 21
Dionysian festivals, 22
Director and actor, 58–59
Dithyramb, 21, 42
Doctor in Spite of Himself, The, **332–335**
Dolman, John, Jr., 8
Dr. Faustus, 43
Dream Play, A, 55
Dunnock, Mildred, 53
Dürrenmatt, Friedrich, 190
Durang, Christopher, **270–272, 289–291**
Durante, Jimmy, 301
Duse, Eleonora, 1, 60

Eastwood, Clint, 178
Eating on stage, 141–143
Edison, Thomas Alva, 244
Effect of Gamma Rays on Man–in–the–Moon Marigolds, The, **260–262**
Electra, 24, *304*
Elizabethan acting, 29–33, 42
Elizabethan actor, 42
Emotionalism in acting, 38–42, 49, 253–256
Emotional vs. technical acting, 9–11, 38–42
Emotion vs. reason, 38–42
Emphasis in dialogue, 115–117, 313
Epidaurus, Greek Theatre at, *22*
Equus, 171, 251
Evaluating another actor, 256–257
Evaluating oneself, 257–259
Evans, Dame Edith, 299
Ewell, Tom, 53
Exaggeration, 301
External acting, 50

Falling on stage, 146
Falstaff, 4, 301, 310
Farce (*see* Comedy)
Feeling the role, 20
Fielding, Henry, 36–37
Fiennes, Ralph, 8
Fights on stage, 147–148
Finlay, Frank, *50*
Finney, Albert, *13*
First actors, 21
Fitzgerald, Percy H., 311
Flynn, Errol, 3
Fonda, Henry, 13, 18, 149

Fonda, Jane, 187
Fontanne, Lynn, 11, 188–189, 190, 248, 303
Footloose, 185
Ford, Harrison, 3
Forrest, Edwin, 45
Forsythe, John, 53
Franciosa, Anthony, 51
Freeman, Morgan, 193

Garfield, John, 53
Garrick, David, 5, 6, 35–38, *36*, 43–44, 149, 184
Gazzara, Ben, 51
Georgia Peach, **211,** *278,* **278–280**
Gershe, Leonard, **230–234**
Gielgud, John, *4,* 61, 171, 193
Gilbert, W. S., 118–119
Gillette, William, 17–18, 60, 149
Given position, 135–137
Glass Menagerie, The, **205**
Globe, The, 31
Glossary of theatre terms, 357–364
Goodrich, Frances, **236–239**
Good Woman of Setzuan, 55
Gorki, Maxim, 49
Grant, Cary 193
Great Nebula in Orion, The, **213–214**
Greek acting, 21–24
Greek drama, 21–23
Greek theatre, 21–23
Greene, James, *5*
Grotowski, Jerzy, 58
Group Theatre, 53
Guinness, Alec, 12, 13, 192
Guthrie, Tyrone, 7, 14

Hackett, Albert, **236–239**
Hagman, Larry, 15
Hairy Ape, The, **323**
Hall, Peter, 181
Hamlet, 6, 7, 13, 18, 30, 31, 32, 33, 107, 145, 194, 245, 249, 251, 350
Harlequin, 28
Hayes, Helen, 12, 13, 171, 179
Head, part of the body, 69–70
Heidi Chronicles, The, **286–289**
Heifner, Jack, **225–227**
Hellman, Lillian, **218–220, 272–274**
Henry IV, Part 2, 310
Herrmann, Edward, 15
Heston, Charlton, 9, 13, 124
Hitchcock, Alfred, 172
Hitler, The Last Ten Days, 12
Hoffman, Dustin, 3, 7

Holbrook, Hal, 192
Homework (actor's), 245–246
Hope, Bob, 168
Hopkins, Anthony, 57, 171, *180*
Hopkins, Arthur, 58, 100, 194
Howard, Leslie, 351
Hughes, Barnard, 16
Hurt, John, 193, 251
Hurt, William, 249
Huston, Walter, 111, 312
Hypocrite (actor), 23

Ideal actor, 3
I Don't Have to Show You No Stinking Badges, **285–286**
Illusion of the first time, 17–18, 149–150
I Love Lucy, 341
Imagination, 185–187
Importance of Being Earnest, The, 300, 302, **329–332**
Improvisations:
    for larger groups, 153–155
    for one actor, 155–157
    for two or more characters, 157–161
    last line of, 161–162
    purposes of, 152–153
Incongruity, 300–301
Inherit the Wind, 134, 190
Injury, avoiding, 82
Internal acting, 50
In Which We Serve, 354
Iolanthe, 119
Ion, 24
Irving, Henry, 41, 46, 149, 192, 194
Itzin, Gregory, *290*

Jackson, Glenda, 51
James–Lange theory, 255–256
James, William, 255–256
Jazz Singer, The, 185
Jefferson, Joseph, 42, 45
Jones, James Earl, *5*
Jonson, Ben, 307
Judging another actor, 256–257
Judging oneself, 257–259
Julia, Raul, 352
Julius Caesar, 4, 108, 145

Kazan, Elia, 53
Keach, Stacy, 193
Kean, Edmund, 5, 6, 45, 167
Kemble, John Philip, 44
Kempe, Will, 42
Kind Hearts and Coronets, 12
King Lear, 31, 184, 249

King's Men, 30
Kissing on stage, 143–145
Kline, Kevin, 245

Laban, Rudolf, 75
Lady Macbeth, 179
Lahr, Bert, 3
Landscape of the Body, 321
Larynx, 106
Lange, C. H., 255–256
Laughter, 302–303
Lean, David, 354
Learning lines *(see* Memorization)
Le Gallienne, Eva, 168
Lettice and Lovage, **216–217, 262–264**
Lewis, Robert, 53
Lincoln, Abraham, 120
Listening, 148–150
Lithgow, John, 185
Little Foxes, The, **272–274**
Long Day's Journey Into Night, **209–210, 210–211**
Lord Chamberlain's Men, 30
Love scenes, 143–145
    camera, 348
Lunt, Alfred, 11, 188–189, 190, 191, 303, 310

McCullers, Carson, **234–236**
Macbeth, 30, 31, 38, 108, 249, 308
Macklin, Charles, 43
Macready, William, 255
Majority of One, 12
Malden, Karl, 51
Mamet, David, **280–281**
Mansfield, Richard, 172
Marat/Sade, 56, 57
March, Frederic, 171
Mark Taper Forum, The, *316*
Marlowe, Julia, 101, 149
Marowitz, Charles, 58
Martin Chuzzlewit, 108, 121
Martin, Dean, 301
Mason, Edith, 168
Masque of the Red Death, The, 121–122
Massey, Raymond, 10–11, 250
Matthau, Walter, 183
Meaning, 114–117
Meisner, Sanford, 52
Member of the Wedding, The, **234–236**
Memorization, 187–189
Merchant of Venice, The, 167, 193, 310
Meredith, Burgess, 254
Merlin, 309
Method, the, 51–54

Microphones, 350
Midsummer Night's Dream, A, 66, 246
Miller, Arthur, **207–208, 208–209, 211–212, 212, 282–284,** 305
Mimetic instinct, 2
Miracle Worker, The, 187
Miser, The, 302, **326–328**
Mister Roberts, 18
Modjeska, Helena, 8
Molière, 43, **326–328, 332–335**
Monologues, 205–215
Moore, Mary Tyler, 13
Moscow Art Theatre, 49
Movement *(see* Stage movement)
Mozart, Wolfgang Amadeus, 181
Much Ado about Nothing, 252
Muni, Paul, 189, 190
Murder by Death, 12
My Life in Art, 49

Natural acting, 32–33
Nazimova, 180
Nero, 192
Newman, Paul, 53, 245
Nicholas Nickleby, 55, *110*
Nichols, Dudley, 354
Noted actors of the past, 60–62

Observation, 183
Oleanna, **280–281**
Olivier, Sir Laurence, 9, *50,* 55, 61, 148, 167, 171, 182, 185, 192, 193, 194, 245, 350
One Flew over the Cuckoo's Nest, 52
O'Neill, Eugene, **209–210, 210–211,** 248, **323**
Othello, 6, 31, 48, 145, 167, 310, 312
O'Toole, Peter, 181

Pacino, Al, 3, 7, 51
Page, Elaine, 312
Pantalone, 28, *29*
Paradox of Acting, The, 38–39, 41
Parsons, Estelle, 10, 53
Pelvis, 70–71
Penthouse Theatre, The, *315*
Pepys, Samuel, 34
Period plays, 140–141, 306–307
Perrucci, Andrea, 28
Personality acting, 11–14
Petrified Forest, The, 141
Phonation, 106–108, 110–111
Physical standards, 4–7
Piano Lesson, The, **241–243**
Pierrot, 28

Pink Panther, The, 301
Pinter, Harold, 186
Pirates of Penzance, The, 119
Pitch, 112–113
Pitt, Brad, 193
Plato, 24
Plautus, 25
Playfair, Giles, 6
Pleasance, Donald, 11, 186
Plié, 89
Plinge, Walter, 251
Plowright, Joan, *50, 180*
Plutarch, 25
Poe, Edgar Allan, 121–122
Poetic drama, 306–307
Poitier, Sidney, 17
Polus, 24
Poor Theatre, 58
Power, Tyrone, 3
Presentational acting, 14–15, 22, 31, 34, 306–307
Price, Annabella, *290*
Projection, 110–111, 320
Promptness, 245

Quin, James, 35
Quinn, Anthony 18

Rains, Claude, 193
Rashomon, 79
Rate of stage speech, 111–112
Raye, Martha, 301
Reaction (*see* Listening), 150, 353–355
Redemption, 186
Redford, Robert, 179
Redgrave, Lynn, 106, 351
Redgrave, Michael, 245
Rehearsals, 245–247
Relaxation, 73–74, 106–108
Representational acting, 14–15, 31
Resonation, 106–108
Responsibilities of actors, 258–259
Restoration acting, 6
Restoration drama, 33–34
Résumé, 177–178
Ribcage, 70
Riccoboni, Luigi, 28
Richard III, 6, 31, 167, 194
Richardson, Ralph, 61, 251
Rickles, Don, 301
Rights of actors, 246
Rivals, The, 169, **324–326**
Roadrunner, The, 302
Robbins, Jerome, 58

Robinson, Edward G., 12
Role evaluation, 258–259
Roman theatre, 25, 42
Romeo and Juliet, 30, 31, 145, 248
Rooney, Mickey, 7
Roscius, 42
Roseanne, 340
Royal Shakespeare Company, 55

Salvini, Tommaso, 41, 45
Saturday, Sunday, Monday, 50
Scaramouche, 28
School for Scandal, The, 101
Scofield, Paul, 193, 246, 249
Scoring, 313–314
Scottish Play, The, 308
Sea Gull, The, 206, **207**, 313–314
Search for Signs of Intelligent Life in the Universe, The, **212–213**
Seinfeld, 340
Sellers, Peter, 12, 301
Servant of Two Masters, The, 29
Shaffer, Peter, 171, 181, **216–217, 262–264**
Shakespearean drama, 307–309
Shakespeare, William, 4, 29–33, 42, 55, 107, 108, 310, 312, **336–338**, 350
Shared position, 134–135
Shaw, George Bernard, 307
Shepard, Sam, 175, **228–230, 292–295**
Sheridan, Richard Brinsley, **324–326**
Sherwood, Robert E., 141
Shooting on stage, 146
Shoulders, 70
Shylock, 167, 193
Siddons, Sarah, 44
Sitting on stage, 129–131
Skeleton, 67
Skinner, Otis, 6
Smith, Maggie, *81*
Socrates, 24
Sorcerer, The, 118–119
Sothern, E. H., 101
Spelvin, George, 251
Spine and the body, 67–69
Stabbing on stage, 145–146
Stage areas, 125–127
Stage fright, 163–172
Stage movement, 65–97, 124–151
Stage positions and the actor, 127
Stage technique, 124–151
Stamp, Terence, 9
Stanislavski, Constantin, 48–54, 60, 99
Stanislavski system, 49–54

Stapleton, Maureen, 53,167
Star Wars, 12
Stephens, Robert, *81*
Stevenson, Robert Louis, 108
Stewart, James, 13, 59
Stewart, Patrick, *66*
Strange Interlude, 248
Strasberg, Lee, 52
Streetcar Named Desire, A, **274–277, 295–298**
Strindberg, August, 55
Style, 140–141
 reading, 311–312
Subtlety:
 physical, 317–318, 351–352
 vocal, 350–351
Super–marionette, 58
Superstition, theatrical, 165, 166, 169, 170, 172, 245,
 308
Sustained speeches, 312–314
Sweet Bird of Youth, **205–206**

Tale of Two Cities, A, 121
Tales from the Vienna Woods, 142
Talma, François–Joseph, 44–45
Taming of the Shrew, The, 310, **336–338**
Technical acting, 9–11
Television, 340–342
Television acting, 339–356
Ten Nights in a Barroom, 40
Tension, body, 73
Terry, Ellen, 186
Theatre, the (Playhouse), 31
Theatron, 22
Thespis, 21, 42
Timing, 302–303
Timon of Athens, 5
Todd, Mabel Elsworth, 74
To Have and Have Not, 168
Tolstoy, Leo, 186
Tom and Jerry, 302
Tom Jones, 36–37
Tone, Franchot, 53
Tracy, Spencer, 193
Tragedy, 304–306
Trewin, J. C., 190
Trivia, theatrical, 251, 256, 312
True West, **292–295**
Twelfth Night, 302
Two Trains Running, **214–215**
Type-casting, 12

Uncommon Women and Others, **223–225, 264–266**
Upstaging, 132–134

Valdez, Luis, **239–241, 285–286**
Validity in acting, 249–250, 311
Vanities, **225–227**
Variations on Measure for Measure, 57
Variety in acting, 248–249
Verb phrases, 94–96
Verfremdungseffekt (*see* Alienation effect)
Visit, The, 190
Vitality in acting, 247–248
Vocal expressiveness, 114–117
Vocal production, 102–110
Vocal standards, 8, 98–123
Vocal tone, 106–108
Vocal variety, 120–122
Vortex, The, 168

W checklist, 153, 183
Wagner, Jane, **212–213**
Waite, Ralph, *228*
Walken, Christopher, 208
Warming up, 80–83, 245
Warmup, elements of, 175
 shaking, 83–85
 stretching, 91–94
 sustaining, 88–91
 swinging, 85–88
Wasserstein, Wendy, **223–225, 264–266, 286–289**
Wayne, John, 12
Way of the World, The, 100, 190
Weaver, Sigourney, 3
Webster, Daniel, 120–121
Weiss, Peter, 57
Weller, Peter, 193
West Side Story, 145
Who's Afraid of Virginia Woolf?, 143
Wilde, Oscar, 300, **329–332**
Williams, Tennessee, **205, 274–277, 295–298**
Williams, Treat, 179
Wilson, August, **214–215, 241–243**
Wilson, Garff, 254
Wilson, Lanford, **213–214**
Winger, Debra, 3
Winters, Shelley, 51
Woffington, Peg, 44
Wright, Teresa, 348

Young, Sean, 3
Young, Stark, 101

Zindel, Paul, **260–262, 266–269**
Zoot Suit, **239–241**